SHURLEY ENGLISH

HOMESCHOOL MADE EASY

LEVEL 1

Teacher's Edition

By

Brenda Shurley

Shurley Instructional Materials, Inc., Cabot, Arkansas

In Loving Memory of
Gilbert Edwin Strackbein
(Gil)

Dedication

This book is gratefully dedicated to my husband, Billy Shurley, for his love, support, and encouragement during this momentous undertaking.

Acknowledgements

We gratefully thank the following people for their help and support in the preparation of this book:

Ardean Coffman	Stacey See	Rachel Speer
Keith Covington	Billy Ray Shurley, Jr.	Andrea Turkia
Jamie Geneva	Kim Shurley	Jani-Petri Rainer Turkia
Janice Graham	Shurley Method Staff	Bob Wilson, Ph.D

06-02
Homeschool Edition
ISBN 1-58561-048-8 (Level 1 Teacher's Manual)

TABLE OF CONTENTS

TABLE OF CONTENTS

TABLE OF CONTENTS

TABLE OF CONTENTS

Level 1 Homeschool Teacher's Manual

TABLE OF CONTENTS

SHURLEY ENGLISH ABBREVIATIONS FOR LEVEL 1

Abbreviation	Description
N	Noun
SN	Subject Noun
V	Verb
Adv	Adverb
Adj	Adjective
A	Article Adjective
P	Preposition
OP	Object of the Preposition

CHAPTER 1   LESSON 1

Objectives: How to Get Started and Readiness Time (Grouping Skills).

HOW TO GET STARTED

1. The word *students* will be used throughout the text in reference to the child/children you are teaching. The adult teaching this program will be referred to as *teacher*.

2. Stay one lesson ahead of your students. Study the entire lesson thoroughly before you present it. Then, read each lesson like you read a storybook: word-for-word. Your teacher's manual will give you teaching scripts to read out loud to your students. It will also give you teacher's notes, and it will tell you when your students are to participate with you. Do not skip anything, and do not jump ahead. In just a few days, you will be in a comfortable routine that will help your students develop a love of learning.

3. The order of the student book is listed below. (*Note: The sample exercises in the Reference Section of the student's book are keyed to serve as a study guide for the student.*)

Order of Student Book			
1. Jingle Section	pages 1-4	5. Practice Section	pages 27-58
2. Vocabulary Section	pages 5-8	6. Test Section	pages 59-80
3. Synonym & Antonym Section	pages 9-12	7. Activity Section	pages 81-89
4. Reference Section	pages 13-26		

4. The lessons in this book are divided into chapters. Each lesson takes approximately twenty to forty minutes to complete. There are no tests for Chapters 1-6. Chapter 7 begins the testing for Level 1. For best results, you should do one lesson every day.

5. Your *Shurley* kit contains a teacher's manual, a student workbook, and an audio CD which demonstrates the Jingles and the Question and Answer Flows for the Introductory Sentences.

INTRODUCTION TO READINESS TIME

The first four chapters are devoted to readiness skills. The readiness chapters develop classifying skills and are very important in helping students become better learners. In order for students to comprehend and apply new information quickly and easily, it is important that they develop the higher-level thinking skill of classifying. Learning to classify, or group things, makes it easier to compare, analyze, and evaluate new information.

This classifying foundation makes it possible for younger students to look at objects and determine how they are alike and how they are different. It teaches them the relationships of the things they are learning. Facts and new information are easier to remember if they are sequenced and grouped.

Learning to organize information into groups teaches one how things relate to one other. Students learn to analyze when they classify new information into different categories. Then, as learning becomes more abstract, students are better equipped to handle this higher level of learning because they have had plenty of practice in comparing, analyzing, and grouping information. After the grouping technique is learned, it should be applied whenever possible in other learning situations.

CHAPTER 1 LESSON 1 CONTINUED

 READINESS TIME

TEACHER INSTRUCTIONS

Materials needed: A combination of <u>pictures and/or real objects</u> that can be placed in the categories **food, clothing, transportation,** and **furniture / appliance**. Materials for category signs may include cardboard, construction paper, or notebook paper.

For the grouping activities in this chapter, collect pictures from newspapers, brochures, magazines, catalogs, old books, items from around the house, etc.

Teacher's Note: The groups that will be used in this first lesson will be broken down into subgroups in later lessons. To save time, the items that you choose for today's lesson should correspond with the subcategories that will be used in lessons 2-5. *(See the chart below for a list of these subgroups and suggested items for each group.)*

Also, make signs for the four categories and have them ready before you begin this lesson. To make the signs, cut out four strips of cardboard, construction paper, or notebook paper. Write titles on the signs for the **food**, **clothing**, **transportation**, and **furniture / appliance** categories. Use a large black magic marker so the signs can be read easily.

Chapter 1, Groups #1-4		
Group Names	**Subgroup**	**Suggested Items**
1. FOOD	meat & nuts	slice of deli meat, package of sausage, peanuts, pecans, walnuts
	milk & cheese	glass of milk, empty milk carton, slice of cheese
	bread & cereal	loaf of bread, rolls, empty cereal box, oatmeal
	fruits & vegetables	apples, oranges, bananas, potatoes, celery, lettuce, carrots, can of green beans, can of peas
2. CLOTHING	warm weather	shorts, T-shirt, sandals
	cold weather	sweater, coat, sweat pants, mittens/gloves, scarf
	costumes	Halloween costumes, dress-up clothes, dance recital outfits, uniforms
3. TRANSPORTATION	ground	pictures/models of cars, trucks, vans, bicycles, motorcycles
	air	pictures/models of airplanes, hot air balloons, blimps, helicopters
	water	pictures/models of boats, barges, submarines
4. FURNITURE / APPLIANCE	kitchen	pictures of refrigerators, microwaves, stoves/ovens, kitchen sinks, bar stools, tables, hutch, chairs
	bedroom	pictures of beds, dressers, chests, doll-house furniture
	bathroom	pictures of bathroom sinks, toilets, showers/baths, shelf
	living room	pictures of sofas, recliners, televisions, fireplaces, ottoman

CHAPTER 1 LESSON 1 CONTINUED

TEACHING SCRIPT FOR SORTING AND GROUPING ITEMS

Today, we will begin learning how to sort and group items together. These activities will help us understand how things relate to one another. We will study four different groups today. _(Show the four group signs to students and have them repeat the titles with you several times.)_ We will start by identifying items that belong in one of these groups. _(Scatter collected items on the table, floor, or other chosen area in front of the students. Try to include a combination of pictures and real objects for this activity.)_

(Select two different items that belong to the **food group** from the pile.) Can you tell me the name of the group that we would use to identify these two items? _(the **food group**)_ Yes, these items belong to the **food group** because they are both things that we could eat. I will place these items behind the **Food Group** sign. Now, I want you to pick out all the items that you think would belong in the **food group,** and we will place them together in the **Food Group** pile. _(Allow students to pick out all of the **food group** items and place them in the **food group** pile. Once students have finished, direct their attention to the **food group** pile.)_ What is the name of this group? _(the **food group**)_ Let's repeat the name of this group together three times. _(food group, food group, food group)_ Why do all these items belong in the food group? _(They are things that we could eat.)_ Very good!

Now, let's go back to our mixed pile because I would like to show you another group. _(Select two different items from the **clothing group**.)_ Can you tell me the name of the group that we would use to identify these two items? _(the **clothing group**)_ Yes, these items belong to the **clothing group** because they are both things that we could wear. Now, I want you to search through our mixed pile and pick out all the items that you think would belong to the **clothing group** and place them behind the **Clothing Group** sign. _(Allow students to gather all of the **clothing group** items and put them in a **clothing group** pile. Once students have finished, direct their attention to the **clothing group** pile.)_ What is the name of this group? _(the **clothing group**)_ Let's repeat the name of this group together three times. _(clothing group, clothing group, clothing group)_ Why do all these items belong in the clothing group? _(They are all things that we could wear.)_

We must now go back to the mixed pile because there are two more groups that I would like to show you. _(Select four new items from the pile. Two items should be from the **transportation group**, and the other two should be from the **furniture / appliance group**. Hold up the two items from the **transportation group**.)_ What is the name of the group to which these items belong? _(the **transportation group**)_ Right! Both of these items belong in the **transportation group** because we can use them to get from one place to another.

Before I have you find all the **transportation group** items in our mixed pile, I would like to show you one last group. _(Show students the two items you selected from the **furniture / appliance group**.)_ Can you tell me the name of the group that we would use to identify these two items? _(the **furniture / appliance group**)_ Yes, these two items belong to the **furniture / appliance group** because they can be used to furnish rooms in houses.

Now that we have discussed the two new groups, can you name both of them again? _(the **transportation group** and the **furniture / appliance group**)_ Items from both of these groups are still mixed together in one pile. I want you to separate them and place them behind either the **Transportation Group** sign or the **Furniture / Appliance Group** sign.

(Have students sort through the pile of items and place them into two new piles. When they have finished, students should have a total of four piles. Point to each pile and make sure that students are able to properly identify what the items in each pile have in common.)

(End of lesson.)

CHAPTER 1   LESSON 2
Objectives: Readiness Time (Subgrouping Skills), and Activity.

 READINESS TIME

TEACHER INSTRUCTIONS

Materials needed: A combination of <u>pictures and/or real objects</u> that can be placed in the subgroup categories listed in the box below. Materials for subgroup signs may include cardboard, construction paper, or notebook paper.

Chapter 1, Lesson 2, Group #1: Food Group
Subgroups: ① meat & nuts, ② milk & cheese, ③ bread & cereal, ④ fruits & vegetables

Students will learn how larger groups can be broken down into smaller groups, which we call subgroups. They will begin by breaking down the **food group** into smaller subcategories. Again, you will need examples of **food** to illustrate this concept. You will also need to make signs to identify the contents of each subgroup pile. The subgroups that they will learn today are listed above.

Be sure to include several examples of each of the above subgroups in your **food group**. *(You can use pictures or actual objects as your examples. If you cannot find pictures or objects of some of the subgroups listed, you may substitute another appropriate subgroup. Also, make signs to identify the contents of each subgroup pile.) (See page 2 in the teacher's manual for a list of suggested items.)*

TEACHING SCRIPT FOR INTRODUCING SUBGROUPS

*(Scatter only **food group** items in front of the students.)* We learned to identify this group in the last lesson. Can you tell me the name of the group that we would use to identify these items? *(the **food group**)* Yes, all of these items are examples of things that we could eat. That is why we call this group the **food group**.

Today, I want to show you how we can break a large group, like the **food group**, into smaller groups called **subgroups**. A subgroup is a smaller group within a larger group. The smaller **food groups**, or subgroups, have something in common. Each subgroup can be a group by itself, or it can still be part of the larger group, the **food group**, where it was placed originally. Let's repeat the name of the new word *subgroup* together three times. *(subgroup, subgroup, subgroup)*

We have already said that all the items in our pile belong to the **food group**. I want to give you an example of a smaller **food group** or subgroup located within our larger **food group**. *(Choose an item from the first subgroup, **meat & nuts**, and show it to the students. Identify the object/picture.)*

CHAPTER 1 LESSON 2 CONTINUED

This is an example of a subgroup because we can place this **food group** item in a smaller group called the **meat & nut group**. This new subgroup can be a group by itself or it can still be part of the larger **food group**. There are more examples in our **food group** pile that we could sort into this new pile. Can you help me find them? Remember, we are only looking for foods that will fit into the new subgroup called the **meat & nut group**. *(Help students find the other examples of **meats & nuts** and place them into the meat & nut pile.)* We can also make a sign that has the words "Meat & Nut Group" on it. *(Make a sign with the title Meat & Nut Group.)* We will put all the items that belong in this subgroup behind the **<u>Meat & Nut Group</u>** sign.

What is the name of this new group that we have identified? *(the **meat & nut group**)* What two things do all of the items in our new pile have in common? *(All the items are either **meats** or **nuts**, and they are also found in the **food group**.)*

TEACHER INSTRUCTIONS

Introduce each new subgroup, one at a time. **(Additional subgroup examples include *milk & cheese, bread & cereal, fruits & vegetables*.)** Use the method above to identify each group as it is introduced. Then, help students properly sort each subgroup into a new pile until all of the items have been identified and grouped. Once the students have sorted the items into separate piles, have them identify and repeat the name of each subgroup pile.

Then, ask students to make a **food group** pile. To do this, they should combine all the items from the subgroups into a single pile. If you think students need the extra practice, have them sort each item into the proper subgroup pile again.

 ## ACTIVITY / ASSIGNMENT TIME

Have students color, paint, or cut and paste pictures of the different food subgroups on paper plates. Each plate that they create should have one example of each food group. Allow students to design several plates.

Example: hot dog (meat & nut), hot dog bun (bread & cereal), French fries (fruit & vegetables), slice of cheese (milk & cheese)

(End of lesson.)

CHAPTER 1   LESSON 3

Objectives: Readiness Time (Subgrouping Skills), and Activity.

 READINESS TIME

TEACHER INSTRUCTIONS

Materials needed: A combination of <u>pictures and/or real objects</u> that can be placed in the subgroup categories listed in the box below. Materials for subgroup signs may include cardboard, construction paper, or notebook paper.

Chapter 1, Lesson 3, Group #2: Clothing Group

Subgroups: ① warm-weather clothes, ② cold-weather clothes, ③ costumes

---

Students will continue to learn how larger groups can be broken down into smaller subgroups. Today, they will divide the **clothing group** into smaller subcategories. Again, you will need examples of **clothing** to illustrate this concept. The subgroups that they will learn today are listed above.

Make sure to include several examples of each of the subgroups in your **clothing group** items. _(You can use pictures or actual objects as your examples. If you cannot find pictures or objects of some of the subgroups listed, you may substitute another appropriate subgroup. Also, make signs to identify the contents of each subgroup pile.) (See page 2 in the teacher's manual for a list of suggested items.)_

TEACHING SCRIPT FOR PRACTICING SUBGROUPING SKILLS

(Scatter only **clothing group** examples in front of the students.) We have already learned to identify this group in a previous lesson. What is the name of the group that we would use to identify these items? _(the **clothing group**)_ Yes, all of these items are things that we could wear. That is why we call this group the **clothing group**.

Again, I want to show you how we can divide a larger group, like the **clothing group**, into smaller groups called **subgroups**. Remember, a subgroup is a smaller group within a larger group. Now, what is a subgroup? _(a smaller group within a larger group)_ These smaller groups, or subgroups, have something in common. Each subgroup can be a group by itself or it can still be part of the larger group, the **clothing group**, where it was placed originally.

We have already said that all the items in our pile belong to the **clothing group**. But, now I want you to notice that there are also smaller groups located within our larger **clothing group**. _(Choose one example of your first subgroup, **warm-weather clothes**, from the main pile and show it to the students. Identify the object / picture.)_

CHAPTER 1 LESSON 3 CONTINUED

This is an example of a subgroup because we can place this **clothing group** item in a smaller group called the **warm-weather group**. This new subgroup can be a group by itself, or it can still be part of the larger **clothing group**. There are more examples in our **clothing group** pile that we could sort into this new pile. Can you help me find them? Remember, we are only looking for clothing that will fit into the new subgroup pile called **warm-weather group**. *(Help students find the other examples of **warm-weather clothes** and place them into the warm-weather pile.)* We can also make a sign that has the words "Warm-Weather Clothes Group" on it. *(Make a sign with the title Warm-Weather Clothes Group.)* We will put all the items that belong in this subgroup behind the **<u>Warm-Weather Clothes Group</u>** sign.

What is the name of this new group that we have identified? *(the **warm-weather group**)* What two things do all of the items in our new pile have in common? *(All of the items are **warm-weather clothes**, and they are also found in the **clothing group**.)*

TEACHER INSTRUCTIONS

Introduce each new subgroup, one at a time. (**Additional subgroup examples include *cold-weather clothes and costumes*.**) Use the method above to identify each group as it is introduced. Then, help students properly sort each subgroup into a new pile until all of the items have been identified and grouped. Once the students have sorted the items into separate piles, have them identify and repeat the name of each subgroup pile.

Then, ask students to make a **clothing group** pile. To do this, they should combine all of the items from each subgroups into a single pile. If you think the students need the extra practice, have them sort each item into the proper subgroup pile again.

 ## ACTIVITY / ASSIGNMENT TIME

If you used actual objects as your examples, let students play dress-up with clothing from each subgroup after they have properly identified and sorted them into separate piles. Then, combine all three piles into a **clothing group** pile and let students try on silly combinations of warm-weather clothes, cold-weather clothes, and costumes.

(End of lesson.)

CHAPTER 1   LESSON 4

Objectives: Readiness Time (Subgrouping Skills), and Activity.

 READINESS TIME

TEACHER INSTRUCTIONS

Materials needed: A combination of <u>pictures and/or real objects</u> that can be placed in the subgroup categories listed in the boxes below. Materials for subgroup signs may include cardboard, construction paper, or notebook paper.

Chapter 1, Lesson 4, Group #3: Transportation Group
Subgroups: ① ground, ② air, ③ water

Chapter 1, Lesson 4, Group #4: Furniture / Appliance Group
Subgroups: ① kitchen, ② bedroom, ③ bathroom, ④ living room

Students will group the items above into two main groups. *(They studied both groups in an earlier lesson.)* Then, they will properly identify the subgroups that belong in these two groups. The two groups that are used in this lesson are listed above, along with the subgroups for each group. Be sure to include several examples of the subgroups in each main group. *(For this lesson, combine items for the **transportation** and **furniture / appliance** groups into one big pile. Make sure you also have made all the signs for each subgroup and have them ready to use. Then, follow the teaching script below.)*

TEACHING SCRIPT FOR PRACTICING SUBGROUPING SKILLS

*(Mix together and scatter the items from the **transportation group** and the **furniture / appliance group** in front of the students.)* Today, I have mixed together two different groups that we identified in an earlier lesson. I want you to take a moment to look through the items in this pile and see if you can tell me the names of these two groups. *(Let students look through the combined items in the pile.)*

Can you tell me the names of the two groups that we would use to identify the items in our pile? *(the* **transportation group** *and the* **furniture / appliance group***)* Now, I want you to place each item behind the appropriate sign. This sign says <u>**Transportation Group**</u>, and the next sign says <u>**Furniture / Appliance Group**</u>. *(After students have finished placing each item into one of the two piles, have them explain why every item belongs where they placed it.)*

We will now take our two groups, the **transportation group** and the **furniture / appliance group**, and classify them into smaller subgroups. These smaller groups, or subgroups, will all have something in common: all items in our subgroups can either be identified as **transportation** or **furniture / appliance**.

We have already said that all the items in our two piles belong either to the **transportation group** or to the **furniture / appliance group**. But, now, I want you to notice that there are also smaller groups located within our two larger groups. First, let's look at the **transportation group** pile. *(Choose one example of your first subgroup, **ground**, from the **transportation group** pile and show it to the students. Identify the object / picture.)*

CHAPTER 1 LESSON 4 CONTINUED

This is an example of a subgroup because we can place this **transportation group** object into a smaller group called the **ground transportation group**. There are more examples in our **transportation group** pile that we could place into this new pile. Can you help me find them? *(Help students find the other examples of **ground transportation** and place them into a separate pile.)* What is the name of this new group that we have identified? *(the **ground transportation group**)* What two things do all of the items in our new pile have in common? *(All of the items are **ground transportation,** and they are also found in the **transportation group.**)*

TEACHER INSTRUCTIONS

Introduce each new subgroup, one at a time. **(Additional subgroup examples include *air and water transportation*.)** Use the method above to identify each group as it is introduced. Then, help students properly sort each subgroup into a new pile until all of the items have been identified and sorted. Once the students have sorted the items into separate piles, have them identify and repeat the name of each pile.

Then, ask students to make a **transportation group** pile. To do this, they should combine all of the items from each subgroup into a single pile. If you think students need the extra practice, have them sort each item into the proper subgroup piles again.

After students have sorted the **transportation group** into proper subgroups and practiced their grouping skills, follow the same procedure to help students subgroup the **furniture / appliance** pile. **(Subgroup examples include *kitchen, bedroom, bathroom, and living room*.)** If students are demonstrating ease with grouping skills, you may allow independent practice on this second group. However, if students are struggling with this new skill, it is important that you assist them, step-by-step.

 ACTIVITY / ASSIGNMENT TIME

Have students turn to page 82 in the Activity Section of their book and find Chapter 1, Lesson 4, Activity. Go over the directions to make sure they understand what to do. Check and discuss the Activity after students have finished.

Chapter 1, Lesson 4, Activity: Use one sheet of brown construction paper, one sheet of white construction paper, and one sheet of blue construction paper. Follow the directions given below to create different transportation groups.

1. On the brown sheet of paper, draw pictures of roads, trees, and flowers. Then, using newspapers, magazines, catalogs, etc., cut and paste several examples of ground transportation. (Examples: cars, trucks, vans, bicycles, motorcycles, etc.)

2. On the white sheet of paper, draw a sun, clouds, and birds. Then cut and paste several examples of air transportation. (Examples: airplanes, helicopters, blimps, hot-air balloons, etc.)

3. On the blue sheet of paper, draw ocean waves and fish. Then cut and paste several examples of water transportation. (Examples: motor boats, sail boats, cruise ships, jet skis, barges, submarines, etc.)

(End of lesson.)

CHAPTER 1   LESSON 5

Objectives: Readiness Time (Review Grouping and Subgrouping Skills).

 READINESS TIME

TEACHER INSTRUCTIONS FOR REVIEWING GROUPING AND SUBGROUPING SKILLS

You will review all the groups and subgroups that were introduced in this chapter. You should combine all the items that were used in the previous lessons into one large pile. First, have students arrange the signs for the four main groups in an open area (*Food Group, Clothing Group, Transportation Group, and Furniture / Appliance Group*). Second, have students take the items from the big pile and sort them into the four main groups.

Next, have students add the subgroup signs for each main group. Then, have students take the items from each of the four main groups and sort them into the proper subgroups. *(This chapter contains 14 subgroups. Students will need a large working space to complete the second part of this assignment.)* Help students as needed. Discuss what students have learned with this activity. For your convenience, the groups and subgroups from this chapter have been reproduced below.

Chapter 1, Lesson 5, Group #1: Food Group
Subgroups: ① meat & nuts, ② milk & cheese, ③ bread & cereal, ④ fruits & vegetables

Chapter 1, Lesson 5, Group #2: Clothing Group
Subgroups: ① warm-weather clothes, ② cold-weather clothes, ③ costumes

Chapter 1, Lesson 5, Group #3: Transportation Group
Subgroups: ① ground, ② air, ③ water

Chapter 1, Lesson 5, Group #4: Furniture / Appliance Group
Subgroups: ① kitchen, ② bedroom, ③ bathroom, ④ living room

Teacher's Note: For an independent grouping activity, choose two groups for the students to collect items by themselves. If pictures are cut out, label a large envelope or paper bag with the group name on the outside. Have students cut out and insert pictures in the envelope/bag. If household items are collected, have students collect the items in a clothes basket. Set aside a designated time to go over the items collected. Be sure to have the students identify each item in its appropriate group before going to the next item.

(End of lesson.)

CHAPTER 2   LESSON 1

CHAPTER 2   LESSON 1

Objectives: Readiness Time (Grouping Skills).

   READINESS TIME

TEACHER INSTRUCTIONS

Materials needed: A combination of <u>pictures and/or real objects</u> that can be placed in the following categories: *toys, places, animals, and people.* Materials for category signs may include cardboard, construction paper, or notebook paper.

For the grouping activities in this chapter, collect pictures from newspapers, brochures, magazines, catalogs, old books, items from around the house, etc.

Teacher's Note: The groups that will be used in this lesson will be broken down into subgroups in later lessons. To save time, the items that you choose for today's lesson should correspond with the subcategories that will be used in lessons 2-5. *(See the chart below for a list of these subgroups and suggested items for each group.)*

Also, make signs for the four categories and have them ready before you begin this lesson. To make the signs, cut out four strips of cardboard, construction paper, or notebook paper. Write titles on the signs for the **toy**, **place**, **animal**, and **people** categories. Use a large black magic marker so the signs can be read easily.

Chapter 2, Groups #1-4		
Group Names	**Subgroup**	**Suggested Items**
1. TOY	sports equipment	footballs, baseballs, tennis rackets, golf clubs, fishing lures, skis
	dolls/action figures	dolls, action figures, pictures from a toy catalog
	books	several different books from around the house
	video/computer games	video/computer game boxes/cases, game controllers, pictures from advertising circulars or catalogs
	board/card games	several different board games, game pieces, deck of cards
2. PLACE	stores	newspaper advertisements of different kinds of stores (discount, gas stations, clothing, shoe, department)
	castles	pictures of castles from magazines, brochures, or old books
	restaurants	advertisements from a phone book/local newspaper
	cities/towns	cutouts from a map that shows the name of the city/town
3. ANIMAL	farm	pictures of horses, cows, pigs, chickens
	pet	pictures of cats, dogs, gerbils, hamsters, goldfish
	jungle/zoo	pictures of gorillas, snakes, monkeys, giraffes, elephants, hippopotamuses, toucans, camels, flamingos
4. PEOPLE	family	pictures of family members (mom, dad, brother/sister, grandparents)
	community workers	pictures of firefighters, police officers, nurses, doctors, mayor/city officials, librarian, school teachers
	friends	pictures of friends
	presidents	pictures of presidents that students might recognize

CHAPTER 2 LESSON 1 CONTINUED

<u>*TEACHING SCRIPT FOR SORTING AND GROUPING ITEMS*</u>

Today, we will continue learning how to sort and group items together. These activities give you practice in organizing and comprehending new information quickly and easily. We will study four different groups today. *(Show the four group signs to students and have them repeat the titles with you several times.)* We will begin by identifying items that belong in the four new groups. *(Scatter collected items on the table, floor, or other chosen area in front of the students. Try to include a combination of pictures and objects for this activity.)*

*(Select two different items that belong to the **toy group** from the pile.)* Can you tell me the name of the group that we would use to identify these two items? *(the **toy group**)* Yes, these items belong to the **toy group** because they are both things that we could play with. I want you to pick out all of the items that you think would belong in the **toy group** and place them in a pile behind the <u>**Toy Group**</u> sign. *(Allow students to pick out all of the **toy group** items and place them in a **toy group** pile. Once students have finished, direct their attention to the **toy group** pile.)* Can you tell me the name of this group? *(the **toy group**)* Very good!

Now, let's go back to our mixed pile because I would like to show you another group. *(Select two different items from the **place group**.)* Can you tell me the name of the group that we would use to identify these two items? *(the **place group**)* Yes, these items belong to the **place group** because they are both places, or locations, that we could visit. Now, I want you to search through our mixed pile and pick out all the items that you think would belong to the **place group** and put them in a pile behind the <u>**Place Group**</u> sign. *(Allow students to gather all of the **place group** items and put them in a **place group** pile. Once students have finished, direct their attention to the **place group** pile.)* What is the name of this group? *(the **place** group)* Why do all these items belong in the **place group** pile? *(They are places that we could visit.)* What are the two groups that we have identified so far? *(the **toy group** and the **place group**)* *(Make sure all the items have been correctly placed in the two piles.)*

Again, we must go back to the mixed pile because there are two more groups that I would like to show you. *(Select four new objects from the pile. Two objects should be from the **animal group** and the other two should be from the **people group**. Hold up the two objects from the **people group**.)* What is the name of the group to which these items belong? *(the **people group**)* Right! Both of these items belong to the **people group** because they are both examples of a person, or human being.

Before I have you find all of the **people group** items in our mixed pile, I would like to show you one last group. *(Show students the two objects you selected from the **animal group**.)* Can you tell me the name of the group that we would use to identify these two objects? *(the **animal group**)* Yes, these two items belong to the **animal group** because they are both examples of living creatures other than a human being.

Now that we have discussed the two new groups, can you name both of them again? *(the **people group** and the **animal group**)* Items from both of these groups are still mixed together in one pile. I want you to place them in a pile behind the correct sign.

(Have students sort through the pile of items and place them into the two new piles. When they have finished, students should have a total of four piles. Point to each pile and make sure that students are able to properly identify what the items in each pile have in common.)

(End of lesson.)

Level 1 Homeschool Teacher's Manual

CHAPTER 2   LESSON 2

Objectives: Readiness Time (Subgrouping Skills) and Activity.

 READINESS TIME

<u>*TEACHER INSTRUCTIONS*</u>

Materials needed: A combination of <u>pictures and/or real objects</u> that can be placed in the subgroup categories listed in the box below. Materials for subgroup signs may include cardboard, construction paper, or notebook paper.

Chapter 2, Lesson 2, Group #1: Toy Group
Subgroups: ① sports equipment, ② dolls/action figures, ③ books, ④ video/computer games, ⑤ board/card games

Students will continue learning how larger groups can be broken down into smaller groups that we call subgroups. They will begin by breaking down the **toy group** into smaller subcategories. Again, you will need examples of **toys** to illustrate this concept. You will also need to make signs to identify the contents of each subgroup pile. The subgroups that they will learn today are listed above.

Be sure to include several examples of each of the subgroups above in the **toy group**. *(You can use pictures or actual objects as your examples. If you cannot find pictures or objects of some of the subgroups listed, you may substitute another appropriate subgroup.)*

<u>*TEACHING SCRIPT FOR INTRODUCING SUBGROUPS*</u>

*(Scatter only **toy group** items in front of the students.)* We learned to identify this group in the last lesson. Can you tell me the name of the group that we would use to identify these items? *(the **toy group**)* Yes, all these objects are examples of things that we could play with. That is why we call this group the **toy group**.

Today, I want to review how we break a large group, like the **toy group**, into smaller groups called **subgroups**. A subgroup is a smaller group within a larger group. The smaller **toy groups**, or subgroups, have something in common. Each subgroup can be a group by itself, or it can still be part of the larger group, the **toy group**, where it was placed originally. Let's repeat the word *subgroup* together three times. *(subgroup, subgroup, subgroup)*

We have already said that all the items in our pile belong to the **toy group**. I want to give you an example of a smaller **toy group**, or subgroup, located within our larger **toy group**. *(Choose an item from the first subgroup, **sports equipment**, and show it to the students. Identify the object/picture.)*

This is an example of a subgroup because we can place this **toy group** item in a smaller group called the **sports equipment group**. There are more examples in our **toy group** pile that we could place into this new pile. Can you find them? *(Help students find the other examples of **sports equipment** and place them into a separate pile.)*

CHAPTER 2 LESSON 2 CONTINUED

What is the name of this new group that we have identified? *(the **sports equipment group**)* What two things do all the items in our new pile have in common? *(All of the items are **sports equipment**, and they are also found in the **toy group**.)*

TEACHER INSTRUCTIONS

Introduce each new subgroup, one at a time. (**Additional subgroup examples include *dolls and action figures, books, video and computer games, and board and card games*.**) Use the method above to identify each group as it is introduced. Then, help students properly sort each subgroup into a new pile until all of the items have been identified and grouped. Once the students have sorted the items into separate piles, have them identify and repeat the name of each subgroup.

Then, ask students to make a **toy group** pile. To do this, they should combine all the items from the subgroups into a single pile. If you think students need the extra practice, have them sort each item into the proper subgroup piles again.

 ACTIVITY / ASSIGNMENT TIME

Have students turn to page 82 in the Activity Section of their books and find Chapter 2, Lesson 2, Activity. Go over the directions to make sure they understand what to do. Check and discuss the Activity after students have finished.

Chapter 2, Lesson 2, Activity: In the Word Search Puzzle below, find the following words and color each one a different color. The words will appear "down" or "across" in the puzzle.

ANIMALS   PEOPLE   PLACES   TOYS

T	P	L	A	C	E	S
P	Q	A	U	S	K	B
E	W	N	I	D	L	N
O	E	I	O	F	Z	T
P	R	M	P	G	X	O
L	T	A	A	H	C	Y
E	Y	L	B	O	Y	S
S	D	S	F	P	L	E

(End of lesson.)

CHAPTER 2   LESSON 3
Objectives: Readiness Time (Subgrouping Skills), and Activity.

 READINESS TIME

TEACHER INSTRUCTIONS

Materials needed: A combination of <u>pictures and/or real objects</u> that can be placed in the subgroup categories listed in the box below. Materials for subgroup signs may include cardboard, construction paper, or notebook paper.

Chapter 2, Lesson 3, Group #2: Place Group
Subgroups: ① stores, ② castles, ③ restaurants, ④ cities/towns

Students will continue to learn how larger groups are broken down into smaller subgroups. Today, they will divide the **place group** into smaller subcategories. Again, you will need examples of **places** to illustrate this concept. The subgroups that they will learn today are listed above.

Make sure you include several examples of each of the subgroups in your **place group** items. *(You can use pictures or actual objects as your examples. If you cannot find pictures or objects of some of the subgroups listed, you may substitute another appropriate subgroup. Also, make signs to identify the contents of each subgroup pile.) (See page 11 in the teacher's manual for a list of suggested items.)*

TEACHING SCRIPT FOR PRACTICING SUBGROUPING SKILLS

*(Scatter only **place group** examples in front of the students.)* We have already learned to identify this group in a previous lesson. What is the name of the group that we would use to identify these items? *(the **place group**)* Yes, all of these objects are places, or locations, that we could visit. That is why we call this group the **place group**.

Again, I want to show you how we can divide a larger group, like the **place group**, into smaller groups, called **subgroups**. These smaller groups, or subgroups, have something in common. Each subgroup can be a group by itself, or it can still be part of the larger group, the **place group**, where it was placed originally.

We have already said that all the items in our pile belong to the **place group**. I want to give you an example of a smaller place group, or subgroup, located within our larger **place group**. *(Choose an item from the first subgroup, **store**, and show it to the students. Identify the object/picture.)*

CHAPTER 2 LESSON 3 CONTINUED

This is an example of a subgroup because we can put this **place group** item in a smaller group called the **store group**. There are more examples in our **place group** pile that we could put into this new pile. Can you find them? *(Help students find the other examples of **stores** and place them into a separate pile.)*

What is the name of this new group that we have identified? *(the **store group**)* What two things do all of the items in our new pile have in common? *(All of the items are **stores**, and they are also found in the **place group**.)*

TEACHER INSTRUCTIONS

Introduce each new subgroup, one at a time. **(Additional subgroup examples include *castles, restaurants, cities/towns*.)** Use the method above to identify each group as it is introduced. Then, help students properly sort each subgroup into a new pile until all of the items have been identified and grouped. Once the students have sorted the items into separate piles, have them identify and repeat the name of each subgroup pile.

Then, ask students to make a **place group** pile. To do this, they should combine the items from all the subgroups into a single pile. If you think the students need the extra practice, have them sort each object into the proper subgroup pile again.

 ACTIVITY / ASSIGNMENT TIME

Take students on a field trip and point out examples of different places. *(Especially note any of the examples that you used in the lesson.)* You could easily incorporate this into your schedule by making a few extra stops on your way to the grocery store. Students should bring a pencil and a notebook with them to keep track of the places that they see. Also, give students an opportunity to point out and name some of the places that they see while they are traveling.

(End of lesson.)

CHAPTER 2   LESSON 4

Objectives: Readiness Time (Subgrouping Skills), and Activity.

 READINESS TIME

TEACHER INSTRUCTIONS

Materials needed: A combination of <u>pictures and/or real objects</u> that can be placed in the subgroup categories listed in the boxes below. Materials for subgroup signs may include cardboard, construction paper, or notebook paper.

Chapter 2, Lesson 4, Group #3: Animal Group
Subgroups: ① farm animals, ② pets, ③ jungle/zoo animals

Chapter 2, Lesson 4, Group #4: People Group
Subgroups: ① family, ② community workers, ③ friends, ④ presidents

Students will group the items above into two main groups. *(They studied both groups in an earlier lesson.)* Then, they will properly identify the subgroups that belong in these two groups. The two groups that are used in this lesson are listed above, along with the subgroups for each group. Be sure to include several examples of the subgroups in each main group. *(For this lesson, combine items for the **animal** and **people** groups into one big pile. You can use pictures or actual objects as your examples. If you cannot find pictures or objects of some of the subgroups listed, you may substitute another appropriate subgroup. Then, follow the teaching script below. Also, make sure you have made signs that identify the contents of each subgroup pile.)*

TEACHING SCRIPT FOR PRACTICING SUBGROUPING SKILLS

*(Mix together and scatter the items for the **animal group** and the **people group** in front of students.)* Today, I have mixed together two different groups that we identified in an earlier lesson. I want you to take a moment to look through the items in this pile and see if you can tell me the names of these two groups. *(Let students look through the combined items in the pile.)*

Can you tell me the names of the two groups that we would use to identify the items in our pile? *(the **animal group** and the **people group**)* Now, I want you to place each item in the appropriate group. *(Give students time to sort each item into the proper groups. Give them help if they need it. Check to make sure they are grouping the items properly.)*

We will now take our two groups, the **animal group** and the **people group**, and classify them into smaller subgroups. These smaller groups, or subgroups, will all have something in common: All items in our subgroups can either be identified as **animals** or **people**.

CHAPTER 2 LESSON 4 CONTINUED

We have already said that all the items in our two piles belong either to the **animal group** or to the **people group**. But, now I want you to notice that there are also smaller groups located within our two large groups. First, let's look at the **people group** pile. *(Chose one example of your first subgroup, family, from the people group pile and show it to the students. Identify the picture/person.)*

This is an example of a subgroup because we can place this **people group** object in a smaller group called the **family group**. There are more examples in our **people group** pile that we could place into this new pile. Can you help me find them? *(Help students find the other examples of family and place them into a separate pile.)* What is the name of this new group that we have identified? *(the family group)* What two things do all of the items in our new pile have in common? *(All of the items are family, and they are also found in the people group.)*

TEACHER INSTRUCTIONS

Introduce each new subgroup, one at a time. **(Additional subgroup examples include *community workers, friends, and presidents*.)** Use the method above to identify each group as it is introduced. Then, help students properly sort each subgroup into a new pile until all of the items have been identified and sorted. Once the students have sorted the items into separate piles, have them identify and repeat the name of each pile.

Then, ask students to make a **people group** pile. To do this, they should combine all of the items from the subgroups into a single pile. If you think the students need the extra practice, have them sort each item into the proper subgroup piles again.

After students have sorted the **people group** into proper subgroups and practiced their grouping skills, follow the same procedure to help students subgroup the **animal group**. **(Subgroup examples include *farm animals, pets, jungle/zoo animals*.)** If students are demonstrating ease with grouping skills, you may allow independent practice on this second group. However, if students are struggling with this new skill, it is important that you assist them, step-by-step.

 ACTIVITY / ASSIGNMENT TIME

Have students turn to page 83 in the Activity Section of their book and find Chapter 2, Lesson 4, Activity. Go over the directions to make sure they understand what to do. Check and discuss the Activity after students have finished.

Chapter 2, Lesson 4, Activity: Choose four pieces of different-colored construction paper. Follow the directions given below to create different animal groups.

1. On one piece of paper, write the title **Farm Animals**.
2. On the second piece of paper, write the title **Animal Pets**.
3. On the third piece of paper, write the title **Zoo Animals**.
4. On the fourth piece of paper, write the title **Jungle Animals**.
5. Search through old magazines, catalogs, newspapers, and books for examples of animals that would fit under each animal title.
6. Cut out and paste pictures of the animals on the appropriate pieces of construction paper. You might want to draw a few animals of your own.

(End of lesson.)

CHAPTER 2   LESSON 5
Objectives: Readiness Time (Review Grouping and Subgrouping Skills).

 READINESS TIME

TEACHER INSTRUCTIONS FOR REVIEWING GROUPING AND SUBGROUPING SKILLS

You will review all the groups and subgroups that were introduced in this chapter. You should combine all the items that were used in the previous lessons of this chapter into one large pile. First, have students arrange the signs for the four main groups in an open area *(Toy Group, Place Group, Animal Group, and People Group)*. Second, have students take the items from the big pile and sort them into the four main groups.

Next, have students add the subgroup signs for each main group. Then, have students take the items from each of the four main groups and sort them into the proper subgroups. *(This chapter contains 16 subgroups. Students will need a large working space to complete the second part of this assignment.)* Help students as needed. Discuss what students have learned with this activity. For your convenience, the groups and subgroups from this chapter have been reproduced below.

Chapter 2, Lesson 5, Group #1: Toy Group
Subgroups: ① sports equipment, ② dolls/action figures, ③ books, ④ video/computer games, ⑤ board/card games

Chapter 2, Lesson 5, Group #2: Place Group
Subgroups: ① stores, ② castles, ③ restaurants, ④ cities/towns

Chapter 2, Lesson 5, Group #3: Animal Group
Subgroups: ① farm animals, ② pets, ③ jungle/zoo animals

Chapter 2, Lesson 5, Group #4: People Group
Subgroups: ① family, ② community workers, ③ friends, ④ presidents

(End of lesson.)

CHAPTER 3   LESSON 1

Objectives: Readiness Time (Grouping Skills).

 READINESS TIME

TEACHER INSTRUCTIONS

Materials needed: A combination of <u>pictures and/or real objects</u> that can be placed in these categories: **_plants, shapes, musical instruments, physical senses_**. Materials for category signs may include cardboard, construction paper, or notebook paper.

For the grouping activities in this chapter, collect pictures from newspapers, brochures, magazines, catalogs, old books, items from around the house, etc.

Teacher's Note: The groups that will be used in this first lesson will be broken down into subgroups in later lessons. To save time, the objects that you choose for today's lesson should correspond with the subcategories that will be used in lessons 2-5. _(See the chart below for a list of these subgroups and suggested items for each group.)_

Also, make signs for the four categories and have them ready before you begin this lesson. To make the signs, cut out four strips of cardboard, construction paper, or notebook paper. Write titles on the signs for the **_plant, shape, musical instrument,_** and **_physical senses_** categories. Use a large black magic marker so the signs can be read easily.

Chapter 3, Groups #1-4		
Group Names	**Subgroup**	**Suggested Items**
1. PLANT	tree	pictures of different trees (oak, pine, cedar, dogwood, elm, etc.)
	flower	pictures of different flowers, real/artificial flowers
	grass	pictures of grass, a few blades of grass from the yard
2. SHAPE	circle	clock, jar lid, button, construction paper circles, cookies, crackers
	rectangle	rectangular cake pan, piece of notebook paper, construction paper rectangles
	triangle	construction paper triangles, guitar picks, chips, candy corn
	square	construction paper squares, crackers, cookies, Lego toys
3. MUSICAL INSTRUMENT	woodwind	pictures of flutes, clarinets, oboes, etc.
	brass	pictures of trumpets, trombones, tubas, French horns, etc.
	percussion	pictures of drums, xylophones, bells, etc.
	string	pictures of pianos, violins, cellos, etc.
4. PHYSICAL SENSES	hearing	bell, cassette tape/CD, a picture of an ear
	touching	steel wool, cotton balls, sticky tape, picture of a hand
	tasting	items that students can sample (something sweet, sour, spicy), picture of a tongue
	seeing	a pair/picture of eye glasses, picture of eyes, pictures of sunrises, sunsets, scenic view of beaches, waterfalls, mountains, etc.
	smelling	a picture of a nose, perfume/cologne, air freshener, foods with distinct smells (onion, garlic, coffee beans)

CHAPTER 3 LESSON 1 CONTINUED

TEACHING SCRIPT FOR SORTING AND GROUPING ITEMS

Today, we will continue learning how to sort and group items together. These activities give you practice in organizing and comprehending new information quickly and easily. We will begin by identifying items that belong in four new groups. *(Scatter collected items on the table, floor, or other chosen area in front of the students. Try to include a combination of pictures and objects for this activity. You might need to help students with the names of these new groups. Go over the four group names before you begin the activity.)*

*(Select two different items that belong to the **plant group** from the pile.)* Can you tell me the name of the group that we would use to identify these two items? *(the **plant group**)* Yes, these items belong to the **plant group** because they are both things that grow in the soil. I want you to pick out all of the items that you think would belong in the **plant group** and place them in a pile behind the **Plant Group** sign. *(Allow students to pick out all of the **plant group** items and place them in a **plant group** pile. Once students have finished, direct their attention to the new pile.)* Can you tell me the name of this group? *(the **plant group**)*

Now, let's go back to our mixed pile because I would like to show you another group. *(Select two different items from the **shape group**.)* Can you tell me the name of the group that we would use to identify these two items? *(the **shape group**)* Yes, these items belong to the **shape group** because they are both designs. Now, I want you to search through the pile and pick out all the items that you think would belong to the **shape group** and place them in a pile behind the **Shape Group** sign. *(Allow students to gather all of the **shape group** items and put them in a **shape group** pile. Once students have finished, direct their attention to the **shape group** pile.)* What is the name of this group? *(the **shape group**)* Why do all these items belong in the **shape group** pile? *(They are designs.)* What are the two groups that we have identified so far? *(the **plant group** and the **shape group**)* *(Make sure all the items have been correctly placed in the two piles.)*

Now, we must go back to the mixed pile because there are two more groups that I would like to show you. *(Select four new objects from the pile. Two objects should be from the **musical instrument group** and the other two should be from the **physical senses group**. Hold up the two objects from the **musical instrument group**.)* What is the name of the group to which these items belong? *(the **musical instrument group**)* Right! Both of these objects belong to the **musical instrument group** because they are both sources of music.

Before I have you find all of the **musical instrument group** items in our mixed pile, I would like to show you one last group. *(Show students the two objects you selected from the **physical senses group**.)* Can you tell me the name of the group that we would use to identify these two objects? *(the **physical senses group**)* Yes, these two items belong to the **physical senses group** because they are both examples of how we experience our world.

Now that we have discussed the two new groups, can you name both of them again? *(the **musical instrument group** and the **physical senses group**)* Items from both of these groups are still mixed together in one pile. I want you to sort them into their correct groups, the **musical instrument group** or the **physical senses group**. *(Have students sort through the pile of items and place them into the two new piles. When they have finished, students should have a total of four piles. Point to each pile and make sure that students are able to properly identify what the items in each pile have in common.)*

(End of lesson.)

CHAPTER 3   LESSON 2

Objectives: Readiness Time (Subgrouping Skills), and Activity.

 READINESS TIME

TEACHER INSTRUCTIONS

Materials needed: A combination of <u>pictures and/or real objects</u> that can be placed in the subgroup category listed in the box below. Materials for subgroup signs may include cardboard, construction paper, or notebook paper.

Chapter 3, Lesson 2, Group #1: Plant Group
Subgroups: ① trees, ② flowers, ③ grass/weeds

Students will continue learning how larger groups can be broken down into smaller groups that we call subgroups. They will begin by breaking down the **plant group** into smaller subcategories. Again, you will need examples of **plants** to illustrate this concept. The subgroups that they will learn today are listed above.

Be sure to include several examples of each of the subgroups above in your **plant group**. *(You can use pictures or actual objects as your examples. If you cannot find pictures or objects of some of the subgroups listed, you may substitute another appropriate subgroup. Make signs that properly identify each subgroup pile.)*

TEACHING SCRIPT FOR INTRODUCING SUBGROUPS

*(Scatter only **plant group** examples in front of the students.)* We learned to identify this group in the last lesson. Can you tell me what the name of the group that we would use to identify these objects? *(the **plant group**)* Yes, all these objects are examples of things that grow in the soil. That is why we call this group the **plant group**.

Today, I want to review how we break a large group, like the **plant group**, into smaller groups, called **subgroups**. A subgroup is a smaller group within a larger group. The smaller **plant groups**, or subgroups, have something in common. Each subgroup can be a group by itself, or it can still be part of the larger group, the **plant group**, where it was placed originally.

We have already said that all the items in our pile belong to the **plant group**. I want to give you an example of a smaller plant group, or subgroup, located within our larger **plant group**. *(Choose an item from the first subgroup, **trees**, and show it to the students. Identify the object/picture.)*

This is an example of a subgroup because we can place this **plant group** item into a smaller group called the **tree group**. There are more examples in our **plant group** pile that we could place into this new pile. Can you find them? *(Help students find the other examples of **trees** and place them into a separate pile.)*

CHAPTER 3 LESSON 2 CONTINUED

What is the name of this new group that we have identified? *(the **tree group**)* What two things do all the items in our new pile have in common? *(All of the items are **trees**, and they are also found in the **plant group**.)*

TEACHER INSTRUCTIONS

Introduce each new subgroup, one at a time. **(Additional subgroup examples include *flowers* and *grass*.)** Use the method above to identify each group as it is introduced. Then, help students properly sort each subgroup into a new pile until all of the items have been identified and grouped. Once the students have sorted the items into separate piles, have them identify and repeat the name of each subgroup pile.

Then, ask students to make a **plant group** pile. To do this, they should combine all the items from the subgroups into a single pile. If you think students need the extra practice, have them return each item to the proper subgroup piles.

 ACTIVITY / ASSIGNMENT TIME

Take students on a nature hike around the neighborhood, through the park, or in your own yard. Point out examples of trees, flowers, and grass. Give students an opportunity to name each tree, flower, and type of grass. If no one knows the names, look them up in plant books or on the internet.

After students return from their nature hike, give students a large sheet of construction paper or butcher paper. Have students draw and color a picture of trees, flowers, and grass they saw on their nature hike. Encourage students to add other things like a house, animals, the sun, a fence, etc. Have students show their picture to other family members.

(End of lesson.)

CHAPTER 3   LESSON 3
Objectives: Readiness Time (Subgrouping Skills), Activity 1, and Activity 2.

 READINESS TIME

TEACHER INSTRUCTIONS

Materials needed: A combination of <u>pictures and/or real objects</u> that can be placed in the subgroup category listed in the box below. Materials for subgroup signs may include cardboard, construction paper, or notebook paper.

Chapter 3, Lesson 3, Group #2: Shape Group
Subgroups: ① circle, ② rectangle, ③ triangle, ④ square

Students will continue to learn how larger groups are broken down into smaller subgroups. Today, they will divide the **shape group** into smaller subcategories. Again, you will need examples of **shapes** to illustrate this concept. The subgroups that they will learn today are listed above.

Make sure you include several examples of each of the subgroups in your **shape group** pile. *(You can use pictures or actual objects as your examples. If you cannot find pictures or objects of some of the subgroups listed, you may substitute another appropriate subgroup. Also, make signs that properly identify each subgroup.)* *(See page 20 in the teacher's manual for a list of suggested items.)*

TEACHING SCRIPT FOR PRACTICING SUBGROUPING SKILLS

*(Scatter only **shape group** examples in front of the students.)* We have already learned to identify this group in a previous lesson. What is the name of the group that we would use to identify these items? *(the **shape group**)* Yes, all of these objects are designs. That is why we call this group the **shape group**.

Again, I want to show you how we can divide a large group, like the **shape group**, into smaller groups, called **subgroups**. These smaller **shape groups**, or subgroups, have something in common. Each subgroup can be a group by itself, or it can still be part of the larger group, the **shape group**, where it was placed originally.

We have already said that all the items in our pile belong to the **shape group**. I want to give you an example of a smaller **shape group**, or subgroup, located within our larger **shape group**. *(Choose an item from the first subgroup, a **circle**, and show it to the students. Identify the object/picture.)*

CHAPTER 3 LESSON 3 CONTINUED

This is an example of a subgroup because we can put this **shape group** item in a smaller group called the **circle group**. There are more examples in our **shape group** pile that we could put into this new pile. Can you find them? *(Help students find the other examples of **circles** and place them into a separate pile.)*

What is the name of this new group that we have identified? *(the **circle group**)* What two things do all of the items in our new pile have in common? *(All of the items are **circles**, and they are also found in the **shape group**.)*

TEACHER INSTRUCTIONS

Introduce each new subgroup one at a time. **(Additional subgroup examples include *rectangles*, *triangles*, and *squares*.)** Use the method above to identify each group as it is introduced. Then, help students properly sort each subgroup into a new pile until all of the items have been identified and grouped. Once the students have sorted the items into separate piles, have them identify and repeat the name of each subgroup pile.

Then, ask students to make a **shape group** pile. To do this, students should combine the items from all the subgroups into a single pile. If you think the students need the extra practice, have them sort each object back into the proper subgroup pile.

 ACTIVITY / ASSIGNMENT TIME

Activity 1:

Take students on an identification tour through every room in your house. Point out different objects, and have students name each object and tell you the subgroup to which that object belongs.
(Example: clock - **circle group**)

After students have finished their object tour, give students a large sheet of construction paper or butcher paper. Have students draw a picture using only the four shapes in this lesson. (circles, rectangles, triangles, and squares) Have students color the picture and show it to other family members and friends.

(Possible examples of objects: square house, rectangular doors and windows, triangular roof, tree with rectangular trunk and circle top, etc.)

Activity 2:

Have a platter of fruit, crackers, and other food items that can be identified as a circle, square, rectangle, and triangle. Have students select one item at a time, name the shape, and eat the item.

(End of lesson.)

CHAPTER 3   LESSON 4

Objectives: Readiness Time (Subgrouping Skills), Activity 1, and Activity 2.

 READINESS TIME

TEACHER INSTRUCTIONS

Materials needed: A combination of <u>pictures and/or real objects</u> that can be placed in the subgroup category listed in the boxes below. Materials for subgroup signs may include cardboard, construction paper, or notebook paper.

Chapter 3, Lesson 4, Group #3: Musical Instrument Group
Subgroups: ① woodwind, ② brass, ③ percussion, ④ string

Chapter 3, Lesson 4, Group #4: Physical Senses Group
Subgroups: ① hearing, ② touching, ③ tasting, ④ seeing, ⑤ smelling

Students will group the items above into two main groups. *(They studied both groups in an earlier lesson.)* Then, they will properly identify the subgroups that belong in these two groups. The two groups that are used in this lesson are listed above, along with the subgroups for each group. Be sure to include several examples of the subgroups in each main group. *(For this lesson, combine items for the **musical instrument** and **physical senses** groups into one big pile. You can use pictures or actual objects as your examples. If you cannot find pictures or objects of some of the subgroups listed, you may substitute another appropriate subgroup. Then, follow the teaching script below. Also, make sure you have made signs that properly identify the contents of each subgroup pile.)*

TEACHING SCRIPT FOR PRACTICING SUBGROUPING SKILLS

*(Mix together and scatter the items for the **musical instruments group** and the **physical senses group** in front of students.)* Today, I have mixed together two different groups that we identified in an earlier lesson. I want you to take a moment to look through the items in this pile and see if you can tell me the names of these two groups. *(Let students look through the combined items in the pile.)*

Can you tell me the names of the two groups that we would use to identify the items in our pile? *(the **musical instrument group** and the **physical senses group**)* Now, I want you to place each item in the appropriate group. *(Give students time to sort each item into the proper groups. Give them help if they need it. Check to make sure they are grouping the items properly.)*

We will now take our two groups, the **musical instrument group** and the **physical senses group**, and classify them into smaller subgroups. These smaller groups, or subgroups, will all have something in common: all the items in our subgroups can either be identified as **musical instruments** or **physical senses**.

Level 1 Homeschool Teacher's Manual

CHAPTER 3 LESSON 4 CONTINUED

We have already said that all the objects in our two piles belong either to the **musical instruments group** or to the **physical senses group**. But, now, I want you to notice that there are also smaller groups located within our larger groups. First, let's look at the **musical instruments group**. *(Chose one example of your first subgroup, **woodwinds**, from the **musical instruments group** pile and show it to the students. Identify the picture / instrument.)*

Teacher's Note: Before you begin the **musical instruments group**, discuss the names of the subgroups (woodwind, brass, percussion, string) and the types of instruments in each group. Use the information from the Chapter 3 Suggestion Chart on page 20.

This is an example of a subgroup because we can place this **musical instruments group** object into a smaller group called the **woodwind group**. There are more examples in our **musical instruments group** pile that we could place into this new pile. Can you help me find them? *(Help students find the other examples of **woodwinds** and place them into a separate pile.)* What is the name of this new group that we have identified? *(the **woodwind group**)* What two things do all of the items in our new pile have in common? *(All of the items are **woodwinds**, and they are also found in the **musical instruments group**.)*

TEACHER INSTRUCTIONS

Introduce each new subgroup one at a time. **(Additional subgroup examples include *brass*, *percussion*, and *string*.)** Use the method above to identify each group as it is introduced. Then, help students properly sort each subgroup into a new pile until all of the items have been identified and sorted. Once the students have sorted the objects into separate piles, have them identify and repeat the name of each pile.

Then, ask students to make a **musical instruments group** pile. To do this, they should combine all of the items into a single pile. If you think the students need the extra practice, have them sort each item back into the proper subgroup piles.

After students have sorted the **musical instrument group** into proper subgroups and practiced their grouping skills, follow the same procedure to help students subgroup the **physical senses group**. **(Subgroup examples include *hearing*, *touching*, *tasting*, *seeing*, and *smelling*.)** If students are demonstrating ease with grouping skills, you may allow independent practice on this second group. However, if students are struggling with this new skill, it is important that you assist them, step-by-step.

CHAPTER 3 LESSON 4 CONTINUED

ACTIVITY / ASSIGNMENT TIME

Activity 1:

The activities below should help reinforce students' understanding of the five senses. Have students close their eyes (or blindfold them) for these activities.

1. FOR TOUCH: Let students feel objects with different textures and temperatures. Be sure to include something hard (rock), soft (pillow or stuffed animal), rough (sandpaper), smooth (window pane or mirror), flat (table top), round (ball), warm (warm faucet water), and cold (ice cube).

2. FOR SMELL: Let students identify the following smells: perfume/cologne, vanilla extract, an apple, a lemon, a dryer sheet, and peanut butter.

3. FOR HEARING: Let students identify different sounds around the house. These sounds may include running water, tearing paper, bouncing ball, different power tools, blender, can opener, TV or radio, different songs or music, alarm clock, electric shaver, etc.

4. FOR TASTE: Provide small samples of items for students to taste, and see if they can identify the following tastes: sweet (a pinch of brown sugar, honey, or fruit), sour (a taste of lemon, lime, persimmon), and spicy (a pinch of cinnamon or garlic).

5. FOR SIGHT: For the last part of this activity, have students open their eyes or remove their blindfold. Have them go outside and name things that are green, blue, brown, black, and white. Have them describe where they live. Then, list two activities that use the sense of sight, and one that uses one of the other senses. See if students can identify an activity that does not use the sense of sight. (Sample activities: watching television, reading a book, singing, etc.)

Activity 2:

Have students turn to page 83 in the Activity Section of their books and find Chapter 3, Lesson 4, Activity. Go over the directions to make sure they understand what to do. Check and discuss the Activity after students have finished.

Chapter 3, Lesson 4, Activity 2: In the Word Search Puzzle below, find the following words and color each one a different color. The words will appear "down" or "across" in the puzzle.

HEAR   SIGHT   SMELL   TASTE   TOUCH

S	M	E	L	L	A	S
U	E	Q	I	E	E	T
S	L	T	G	H	H	O
I	L	A	H	E	M	U
G	T	S	C	A	B	C
H	O	T	K	R	G	H
T	W	E	S	T	E	K

(End of lesson.)

CHAPTER 3   LESSON 5

Objectives: Readiness Time (Review Grouping and Subgrouping Skills).

 READINESS TIME

TEACHER INSTRUCTIONS

You will review all the groups and subgroups that were introduced in this chapter. You should combine all the items that were used in the previous lessons into one large pile. First, have students arrange the signs for the four main groups in an open area _(**Plant Group**, **Shape Group**, **Musical Instruments Group**, and **Physical Senses Group**)_. Second, have students take the items from the big pile and sort them into the four main groups.

Next, have students add the subgroup signs for each main group. Then, have students take the items from each of the four main groups and sort them into the proper subgroups. _(This chapter contains 16 subgroups. Students will need a large working space to complete the second part of this assignment.)_ Help students as needed. Discuss what students have learned with this activity. For your convenience, the groups and subgroups from this chapter have been reproduced below.

Chapter 3, Lesson 5, Group #1: Plant Group
Subgroups: ① tree, ② flower, ③ grass

Chapter 3, Lesson 5, Group #2: Shape Group
Subgroups: ① circle, ② rectangle, ③ triangle, ④ square

Chapter 3, Lesson 5, Group #3: Musical Instrument Group
Subgroups: ① woodwinds, ② brass, ③ percussion, ④ string

Chapter 3, Lesson 5, Group #4: Physical Senses Group
Subgroups: ① hearing, ② touching, ③ tasting, ④ seeing, ⑤ smelling

(End of lesson.)

CHAPTER 4   LESSON 1
Objectives: Readiness Time (Winter Collage).

 READINESS TIME

TEACHER INSTRUCTIONS

Materials needed for Chapter 4: Four pieces of poster board and a combination of <u>pictures and/or real objects</u> that can be placed in the following categories: ***winter, spring, summer, autumn/fall***.

Chapter 4, Subgroup #1		
Group	Subgroup	Suggested items for students to include in their collage:
SEASONS	winter	Pictures that demonstrate the weather and temperature. Pictures that demonstrate the foliage. Pictures that demonstrate the traditional games played in winter. Pictures that demonstrate winter clothing. Pictures/items from any holidays within the subgroup.

The **seasons group** and its four subgroups (***winter, spring, summer, autumn/fall***) will be the focus of Chapter 4. The grouping activities that students will be doing in this chapter will be different from the activities that they did in the previous chapters. In this chapter, the students will collect pictures from newspapers, travel brochures, magazines, catalogs, old books, and items from around the house to make a collage for each of the four seasons.

TEACHING SCRIPT FOR MAKING A WINTER COLLAGE

Today, we will continue practicing how to recognize smaller subgroups within a larger group. We will start by identifying items that belong in larger groups. Did you know that winter, spring, summer, and autumn/fall can be classified into a single group? Do you know what the name of this group is? (*the seasons group*) That is correct. **Winter, spring, summer, and autumn/fall** all name different **seasons** of the year.

We begin the **seasons group** by learning about its first subgroup, **winter**. Winter has several unique characteristics that make it different from any of the other seasons. (*Discuss with your students some of the characteristics that make **winter** unique. Be sure to mention the weather, temperature, appearance of foliage, traditional games or sports that are common for that season, winter clothing, and any holidays that you would normally celebrate within that period, including important birthdays.*)

We will do a fun project today to celebrate our first seasonal subgroup, **winter**. In a moment, I will give you a large poster board and some cutting materials. But, first, I want to make sure you understand the definition of a collage. A **collage** is an artistic collection made of various materials glued on a surface. We are going to collect pictures and objects that remind us of winter and paste them onto our poster board. Be sure to include items that illustrate the weather, temperature, appearance of foliage, traditional games, winter clothing, and special holidays. (*Give students their first piece of poster board, several old magazines, travel brochures, catalogs, scissors, and glue. They should label their poster board with the name of the season before they begin to paste items on it.*)

CHAPTER 4   LESSON 2

Objectives: Readiness Time (Spring Collage).

  READINESS TIME

TEACHER INSTRUCTIONS

Chapter 4, Subgroup #2		
Group	**Subgroup**	**Suggested items for students to include in their collage:**
SEASONS	spring	Pictures that demonstrate the weather and temperature. Pictures that demonstrate the foliage. Pictures that demonstrate the traditional games played in spring. Pictures that demonstrate spring clothing. Pictures/items from any holidays within the subgroup.

Students will continue studying the **seasons group** as they start on their second seasonal collage today.

TEACHING SCRIPT FOR MAKING A SPRING COLLAGE

In the last lesson, we learned that **winter**, **spring**, **summer**, and **autumn/fall** can be classified into a single group. Do you remember the name of that group? (*the **seasons group***) Yes, we learned that **winter**, **spring**, **summer**, and **autumn/fall** are all subgroups that name different **seasons** of the year.

When we studied the first seasonal subgroup, **winter**, we celebrated by making a *winter collage*. In our collage, we included pictures and objects that reminded us of *winter*. What are some of the objects that we included in our *winter collage*? *(Have students name a few of the items that they pasted on their winter collage poster board and explain why they chose these objects.)* Today, we are going to discuss a second seasonal subgroup, **spring**.

Spring has several unique characteristics that make it different from any of the other seasons. *(Discuss with your students some of the characteristics that make **spring** unique. Be sure to mention the weather, temperature, appearance of foliage, games or sports that are common for that season, spring clothing, and any holidays that you would normally celebrate within that period, including important birthdays.)*

Now that we have learned about the characteristics of **spring**, we are going to make a collage of objects and materials that remind us of **spring**. In a moment, I will give you a large poster board and some cutting materials. But, first, I want to make sure you remember the meaning of the word *collage*. A **collage** is an artistic collection made of various materials glued on a surface. We are going to collect pictures and objects that remind us of **spring** and paste them on our poster board. Be sure to include items that illustrate the weather, temperature, appearance of foliage, traditional games, spring clothing, and special holidays. *(Give students their second piece of poster board, several old magazines, travel brochures, catalogs, scissors, and glue. They should label their poster board with the name of the season before they begin to paste items on it.)*

(End of lesson.)

CHAPTER 4   LESSON 3

Objectives: Readiness Time (Summer Collage).

 READINESS TIME

TEACHER INSTRUCTIONS

Chapter 4, Subgroup #3		
Group	**Subgroup**	**Suggested items for students to include in their collage:**
SEASONS	summer	Pictures that demonstrate the weather and temperature. Pictures that demonstrate the foliage. Pictures that demonstrate the traditional games played in summer. Pictures that demonstrate summer clothing. Pictures/items from any holidays within the subgroup.

Students will continue studying the **seasons group** as they start on their third seasonal collage today.

TEACHING SCRIPT FOR MAKING A SUMMER COLLAGE

We have already learned that **winter, spring, summer, and autumn/fall** can be classified into a single group. Do you remember what the name of this group is? (*the seasons group*) Yes. **Winter**, **spring**, **summer**, and **autumn/fall** all name different seasons of the year.

We have already studied the first two seasonal subgroups, **winter** and **spring**. After we discussed the characteristics that make these two seasons unique, we made a collage for each season. In our *winter* collage, we included pictures and objects that reminded us of *winter* and in our *spring* collage, we included pictures and objects that reminded us of *spring*. What are some of the objects that we included in our *winter* collage? (*Have students name a few of the items that they pasted on their winter collage poster board and explain why they chose these objects.*) What are some of the objects that we included in our *spring* collage? (*Have students name a few of the items that they pasted on their spring collage poster board and explain why they chose these objects.*) Today, we are going to discuss a third seasonal subgroup: **summer**.

Summer has several unique characteristics that make it different from any of the other seasons. (*Discuss with your students some of the characteristics that make **summer** unique. Be sure to mention the weather, temperature, appearance of foliage, traditional games or sports that are common for that season, summer clothing, and any holidays that you would normally celebrate within that period, including important birthdays.*)

Now that we have learned about the characteristics of **summer**, we are going to make a collage of objects and materials that remind us of **summer**. In a moment, I will give you a large poster board and some cutting materials. We are going to collect pictures and objects that remind us of **summer** and paste them on our poster board. Be sure to include items that illustrate the weather, temperature, appearance of foliage, traditional games, summer clothing, and special holidays. (*Give students their third piece of poster board, several old magazines, travel brochures, catalogs, scissors, and glue. They should label their poster board with the name of the season before they begin to paste items on it.*)

(End of lesson.)

CHAPTER 4   LESSON 4
Objectives: Readiness Time (Autumn/Fall Collage).

 READINESS TIME

TEACHER INSTRUCTIONS

Chapter 4, Subgroup #4		
Group	**Subgroup**	**Suggested items for students to include in their collage:**
SEASONS	autumn/fall	Pictures that demonstrate the weather and temperature. Pictures that demonstrate the foliage. Pictures that demonstrate the traditional games played in autumn/fall. Pictures that demonstrate autumn/fall clothing. Pictures/items from any holidays within the subgroup.

TEACHING SCRIPT FOR MAKING AN AUTUMN/FALL COLLAGE

(Students will continue studying the seasons group as they start on their fourth seasonal collage today.) We have already learned that **winter, spring, summer, and autumn/fall** can be classified into a single group. Do you remember what the name of that group? *(the **seasons group**)* Yes, **winter, spring, summer, and autumn/fall** all name different seasons of the year.

We have already studied the first three seasonal subgroups. Can you tell me the names of these subgroups? *(**winter**, **spring**, and **summer**)* Each time we introduced a new season, we discussed the characteristics that made each season unique, and we made a collage for that season. Our collages included pictures and objects that reminded us of each season. What are some of the objects that we included in our *winter* collage? *(Have students name a few of the items that they pasted on their winter collage poster board and explain why they chose these objects.)* What are some of the objects that we included in our *spring* collage? *(Have students name a few of the items that they pasted on their spring collage poster board and explain why they chose these objects.)* What are some of the objects that we included in our *summer* collage? *(Have students name a few of the items that they pasted on their summer collage poster board and explain why they chose these objects.)* Today, we are going to discuss our fourth and final seasonal subgroup: **autumn/fall**.

Autumn/Fall has several unique characteristics that make it different from any of the other seasons. *(Discuss with your students some of the characteristics that make **autumn/fall** unique. Be sure to mention the weather, temperatures, appearance of foliage, traditional games or sports that are common for that season, autumn/fall clothing, and any holidays that you would normally celebrate within that period, including important birthdays.)*

Now that we have learned about the characteristics of **autumn/fall**, we are going to make a collage of objects and materials that remind us of **autumn/fall**. In a moment, I will give you a large poster board and some cutting materials. We are going to collect pictures and objects that remind us of **autumn/fall** and paste them on our poster board. Be sure to include items that illustrate the weather, temperature, appearance of foliage, autumn/fall clothing, games played in the fall, and special holidays. *(Give students their fourth piece of poster board, several old magazines, travel brochures, catalogs, scissors, and glue. They should label their poster board with the name of the season before they begin to paste items on it.)*

(End of lesson.)

CHAPTER 4 LESSON 5

Objectives: Readiness Time (Reviewing the Four Seasons, Oral Presentation) and Activity.

 READINESS TIME

TEACHING SCRIPT FOR REVIEWING THE FOUR SEASONS

This week, we studied the subgroups of the **seasons group**. Can you tell me the names of these subgroups? *(winter, spring, summer, autumn/fall)* Yes, **winter, spring, summer, and autumn/fall** are all subgroups, or smaller categories, that are part of the **seasons group**.

In each lesson, we discussed a new season and the characteristics of that season. *(Have students name some of the characteristics of winter, spring, summer, and autumn/fall. If they have trouble remembering any, have them use their seasonal collages as a reference.)* We also made a collage for each season.

Today, you are going to use your collages for an oral presentation. During your presentation, be sure to discuss the weather, appearance of the leaves, temperature, clothing, games, and special holidays that occur in each season.

You will share your presentation with family members or friends. Your collages will be your visual aid. As you discuss each season, make sure you point out examples in your collage. Tell your family members and friends why you have chosen to include certain objects as examples in your collage.

 ACTIVITY / ASSIGNMENT TIME

Have students turn to page 83 in the Activity Section of their book and find Chapter 4, Lesson 5, Activity. Go over the directions to make sure they understand what to do. Check and discuss the Activity after students have finished. *(The correct order is given in the key below.)*

Chapter 4, Lesson 5, Activity: Write the correct numbers in the blanks to match the seasons with their activities. On writing paper, write a story about one of the seasons below.

(End of lesson.)

CHAPTER 5   LESSON 1
Objectives: Readiness Time (Grouping, Classifying), and Jingles (Noun, Verb).

 READINESS TIME

TEACHING SCRIPT FOR GROUPING AND CLASSIFYING

There's a reason we have spent so much time learning how to group things. When things are grouped, it helps us to see how all the little parts fit into the big picture. This helps us to understand how things are connected. When we group things, we call it classifying.

Let's say this new word three times. ***Classifying, classifying, classifying.*** Let's say it one more time for good luck: ***Classifying!*** What do we do when we classify? We group things. What do we do when we group things? We classify things.

Now, I want you to define *classifying* with me three times so you will always know what *classifying* means.
1. What do we do when we classify? We group things. What do we do when we group things? We classify things.
2. What do we do when we classify? We group things. What do we do when we group things? We classify things.
3. What do we do when we classify? We group things. What do we do when we group things? We classify things.

Things are classified into groups so they will make sense to us. In this chapter, we will begin to classify groups of words by putting them in a certain order. We will learn how to group written words into sentences. You will be writing sentences soon, and you need to know how to group written words into the sentences you want to write.

We will learn how to classify words a few at a time. It will be fun. Classifying words is like putting a puzzle together. It is done piece by piece. We will start by learning the noun and verb jingles today. When we are ready to use the information in the noun and verb jingles, you will already know about nouns and verbs. *(Read the Jingle Guidelines on the next page before you begin Jingle Time with your students.)*

CHAPTER 5 LESSON 1 CONTINUED

 **JINGLE TIME**

Read the five *Jingle Guidelines* below before you teach jingles to your students. These guidelines will give you ideas and help you establish procedures for the recitation of jingles.

Jingle Guidelines

1. **Jingles are used** to learn English definitions. Knowing English definitions makes learning English concepts easier because children can use the definitions to remember how to classify words used in sentences.

2. **Approach Jingle Time** as a learning time. Most of the jingles are presented as choral chants with enough rhythm to make them easy to remember, but you can also sing, rap, or just read them. Learning definitions in jingle form makes this necessary practice more fun. *(Listen to the CD for an example.)*

3. **Jingles are more fun** if you make up motions for each jingle. Motions use the kinesthetic learning style of students and help them learn faster. Motions should be incorporated for several of the jingles. Relax and have fun. Have your children help make up motions they enjoy.

4. **You only need** to spend a short time on jingles (*five to ten minutes daily*) because you will be working with the jingles every day. Jingle Time should be fun as well as educational.

5. **Demonstrate each new jingle** for your students; then, lead them in reciting the jingles. Let your students lead the jingles as soon as they are ready.

Have students turn to page 2 in the Jingle Section in their books. The teacher will lead the students in reciting the new jingles (*Noun and Verb*) below. Practice the new jingles several times until students can recite them smoothly. Emphasize reciting with a rhythm. Students and teacher should be together! (*Do not try to explain the new jingles at this time. Just have fun reciting them. Add motions for more fun and laughter*.)

Jingle 1: Noun Jingle
This little noun Floating around Names a person, place, or thing. With a knick knack, paddy wack, These are English rules. Isn't language fun and cool?

Jingle 2: Verb Jingle		
A verb shows action, There's no doubt! It tells what the subject does, Like sing and shout.	Action verbs are fun to do. Now, it's time to name a few. So, clap your hands And join our rhyme; Say those verbs in record time!	Wiggle, jiggle, turn around; Raise your arms And stomp the ground. Shake your finger and wink your eye; Wave those action verbs good-bye.

(End of lesson.)

CHAPTER 5 LESSON 2

Objectives: Jingles, Grammar (Sentence, "The Little Words' Great Sentence Adventure"), and Jingle (Sentence).

 **JINGLE TIME**

Have students turn to the Jingle Section of their books. The teacher will lead the students in reciting the previously-taught jingles.

 GRAMMAR TIME

TEACHING SCRIPT FOR A SENTENCE

In the last lesson, we talked about things being classified into groups that make sense to us. Today, we will learn how words are grouped together. When we think, speak, and write, we are organizing groups of words into a big group called sentences.

A **sentence** is a place for words to be organized. We use words in sentences every day as we think, speak, or write. The more we know about how all the words fit together correctly in sentences, the more confident we will become in our ability to handle language. We will learn how important it is to know and understand how words are used in sentences.

Now, I will read a story to you about words and sentences. After the story, you will learn the Sentence Jingle. I will read the story to you the first time for enjoyment. Then, I will read the story again in the next lesson and ask you some questions about it.

The Little WORDS' Great SENTENCE Adventure

The WORDS all lived in WORD VILLAGE. It was the dream of every little WORD to make the trip to the SENTENCE KINGDOM to become a SENTENCE. WORDS by the thousands came to the SENTENCE KINGDOM to see if they could become a SENTENCE. But, the SENTENCE COUNCIL had very strict rules for WORDS to follow before they could be accepted. When WORDS followed the rules and passed all three tests, they were given the highest honor a WORD could have. They were crowned a SENTENCE and invited to join the other SENTENCES in the SENTENCE KINGDOM.

When WORDS did not follow the rules, they could not be called a SENTENCE. Thousands of WORDS tried everyday to become SENTENCES. Some WORDS were successful as they made the long, difficult journey to the SENTENCE KINGDOM. But, alas! Hundreds of WORDS failed. Some WORDS never tried to become a SENTENCE again, but some WORDS kept coming back, trying and trying and trying until they made it! This is a story of one such group of WORDS.

CHAPTER 5 LESSON 2 CONTINUED

Everyone in WORD VILLAGE would catch their breath and gaze in awe whenever they met a SENTENCE from the SENTENCE KINGDOM. All the Mother WORDS wanted their Baby WORDS to grow up to be SENTENCES. WORDS were trained from childhood to eventually take the SENTENCE test.

The SENTENCE KINGDOM was located on top of SENTENCE MOUNTAIN. It was the highest mountain around. SENTENCE KINGDOM was the most important kingdom in the whole wide world. The PARAGRAPH KINGDOM and the ESSAY KINGDOM depended entirely on the SENTENCE KINGDOM for their survival. It took weeks for anyone to get to the huge castle of the SENTENCE COUNCIL, but everyone was welcome. On the huge double doors was nailed a sign for everyone to read. It said, in big bold letters:

Here are the three rules WORDS must follow in order to become a SENTENCE in the SENTENCE KINGDOM.

Three Rules of a SENTENCE
1. The WORDS should tell who or what the SENTENCE is about.
2. The WORDS should tell what something does.
3. The WORDS should make complete sense.

The WORDS **pretty, the, bird,** and **yellow** wanted to be a SENTENCE. They made the long journey to SENTENCE MOUNTAIN and made an appointment to see the SENTENCE COUNCIL. They were very nervous as they came before the powerful SENTENCE COUNCIL. They said in scared little voices, "We want to be a SENTENCE!"

The SENTENCE COUNCIL looked at the scared little WORDS. They asked gently, "Are you ready to take the test?"

The WORDS gulped and shook their heads yes. They were too scared to even speak again. The SENTENCE COUNCIL nodded their wise heads in agreement. Then, the SENTENCE COUNCIL said to the WORDS, "Prepare yourselves!"

The WORDS tried hard to appear confident as they struggled to organize themselves into a SENTENCE. It was so embarrassing. They fell all over each other. They bumped into furniture. They stumbled more than once. Finally, they nodded that they were ready.

The SENTENCE COUNCIL held up their hands to start the check. Their voices boomed through the enormous room and down the long hallways as they read the order of the WORDS so that all could hear. "Let it be known that the SENTENCE COUNCIL will check the WORDS in this order: **pretty, the, bird, yellow.**" And the check began.

CHAPTER 5 LESSON 2 CONTINUED

1. **First rule:** Do these WORDS tell what the sentence is about? (*No, they do not tell what the sentence is about.*) The SENTENCE COUNCIL gave the WORDS a thumbs down. They did not follow the first rule.

2. **Second rule:** Do these WORDS tell what something does? (*No, they do not tell what something does.*) The SENTENCE COUNCIL gave the WORDS a thumbs down. They did not follow the second rule.

3. **Third rule:** Do these WORDS make complete sense? (*No, they do not have enough information to make complete sense.*) The SENTENCE COUNCIL gave the WORDS a thumbs down. They did not follow the third rule.

The SENTENCE COUNCIL made the dreaded announcement as the WORDS hung their heads, "The WORDS have failed the SENTENCE test. They are still fragments!"

Since the WORDS did not pass any of the three rules to become a SENTENCE, they could not join the SENTENCE KINGDOM. When WORDS did not follow the three rules of a SENTENCE, they were called fragments. As the poor little WORDS dragged themselves back down the mountain, the trees seemed to shout, "**Fragment, fragment, fragment, fragment, fragment. If WORDS are not a SENTENCE, they are a fragment, fragment, fragment!**" The little WORDS broke into a run. They were so ashamed.

After a few weeks, the WORDS **pretty, the, bird,** and **yellow**, still wanted to be a SENTENCE. They wanted to be a SENTENCE more than anything else. They finally realized that they had not been ready. They were embarrassed for weeks, but it helped make them more determined than ever to try again. They knew now that they did not make sense.

After thinking and thinking, planning and planning, they decided they needed help. They would go to NOUN TOWN to get help. The WORDS in NOUN TOWN were wise and helped the WORDS put themselves in another order to make more sense. The wise WORDS in NOUN TOWN showed the WORDS how to organize themselves to show what they were about. The WORDS decided to put themselves in this order: **The pretty yellow bird**.

Now, they were ready for another trip to the SENTENCE KINGDOM. Off they went with high hopes. They made another appointment and appeared before the SENTENCE COUNCIL again. This time, their knees did not shake quite so badly, and they were able to speak above a squeak. Finally, they nodded that they were ready.

The SENTENCE COUNCIL again held up their hands to start the check. Their voices boomed through the enormous room and down the long hallways as they read the order of the WORDS so that all could hear. "Let it be known that the SENTENCE COUNCIL will check the WORDS in this order: **The pretty yellow bird.**" And the check began.

CHAPTER 5 LESSON 2 CONTINUED

1. **First rule:** Do these WORDS tell what the sentence is about? (*Yes, they tell that the sentence is about a bird.*) The SENTENCE COUNCIL gave the WORDS a thumbs up. They followed the first rule.

2. **Second rule:** Do these WORDS tell what something does? (*No, they do not tell what the bird does.*) The SENTENCE COUNCIL gave the WORDS a thumbs down. They did not follow the second rule.

3. **Third rule:** Do these WORDS make complete sense? (*No, they do not have enough information to make complete sense.*) The SENTENCE COUNCIL gave the WORDS a thumbs down. They did not follow the third rule.

Since the WORDS did not follow all three rules to become a SENTENCE, they still could not join the SENTENCE KINGDOM. The WORDS were very, very sad. They were still fragments because they did not have what it took to become a SENTENCE. They dreaded the trip back down the mountain because they knew what the trees would say. But this time the trees did not shout; they whispered, **"Fragment, fragment, fragment, fragment, fragment. If WORDS are not a SENTENCE, they are a fragment, fragment, fragment!"** The little WORDS were still embarrassed, but, this time, they did not run.

A few weeks went by and the WORDS still wanted to be a SENTENCE more than ever. They decided they must get more help. After thinking and thinking, and planning and planning, they went to VERBVILLE to get more help. Some of the adventuresome WORDS in VERBVILLE joined the WORDS in their quest for the SENTENCE KINGDOM. The WORDS in VERBVILLE showed the WORDS how to organize themselves to show what the bird does. They decided to put themselves in this order: **The pretty yellow bird flew away.**

Now, they were ready for another trip to the SENTENCE KINGDOM. They were very confident this time. They had planned and prepared and worked very hard for a long time. So, off they went with high hopes. They made another appointment and appeared before the SENTENCE COUNCIL again. This time, their knees did not shake at all, and they were able to speak in a normal voice. Finally, they nodded that they were ready.

The SENTENCE COUNCIL again held up their hands to start the check. Their voices boomed through the enormous room and down the long hallways as they read the order of the WORDS so that all could hear. "Let it be known that the SENTENCE COUNCIL will check the WORDS in this order: **The pretty yellow bird flew away.**" And the check began.

1. **First rule:** Do these WORDS tell what the sentence is about? (*Yes, they tell that the sentence is about a bird.*) The SENTENCE COUNCIL gave the WORDS a thumbs up. They followed the first rule.

2. **Second rule:** Do these WORDS tell what something does? (*Yes, they tell that the bird flew.*) The SENTENCE COUNCIL gave the WORDS a thumbs up. They followed the second rule.

3. **Third rule:** Do these WORDS make complete sense? (*Yes, they have enough information to make complete sense.*) The SENTENCE COUNCIL gave the WORDS a thumbs up. They followed the third rule.

CHAPTER 5 LESSON 2 CONTINUED

For one second, the whole castle was filled with respected silence. Then, the celebration began. The trumpets sounded victory across the SENTENCE KINGDOM. SENTENCES from all over the kingdom came running. The SENTENCE COUNCIL beamed proudly as they congratulated the WORDS on becoming a SENTENCE and immediately ordered the royal chefs to begin preparing the celebration feast! In minutes, the whole SENTENCE KINGDOM had gathered within hearing distance!

The happy WORDS were still stunned by all the activity. All they could do was stand around, smiling and saying, "Thank you! Thank you!" as other SENTENCES came up to congratulate them on receiving the highest honor a WORD could ever have.

Then, the big moment came. The SENTENCE COUNCIL, dressed in flowing robes and carrying their royal scepters, led the SENTENCE procession to the royal banquet hall for the crowning ceremonies. The WORDS knew that they would never be called fragments again. They would live happily ever after in the SENTENCE KINGDOM with all the other SENTENCES.

As the celebration continued, the trees smiled knowingly and gently swayed to a different beat as they sang joyfully, "Little WORDS, little WORDS, we are so proud of you. May you always be good SENTENCES and live your lives honest and true!"

 **JINGLE TIME**

Now, we will recite the Sentence Jingle together. Turn to the Jingle Section of your book. I will lead you as we recite the Sentence Jingle together. (*Practice the new jingle several times until students can recite it smoothly. Emphasize reciting with a rhythm. Add motions for more fun and laughter.*)

Jingle 3: Sentence Jingle	
A sentence, sentence, sentence Is complete, complete, complete When 5 simple rules It meets, meets, meets.	Add a capital letter, letter And an end mark, mark. Now, we're finished, and aren't we smart! Now, our sentence has all its parts!
It has a subject, subject, subject And a verb, verb, verb. It makes sense, sense, sense With every word, word, word.	REMEMBER Subject, Verb, Com-plete sense, Capital letter, and an end mark, too. That's what a sentence is all about!

(End of lesson.)

CHAPTER 5   LESSON 3

Objectives: Jingles, Grammar (Review "The Little Words' Great Sentence Adventure"), and Activity.

 **JINGLE TIME**

Have students turn to the Jingle Section of their books. The teacher will lead the students in reciting the previously-taught jingles.

 GRAMMAR TIME

TEACHING SCRIPT FOR THE SENTENCE STORY

In the last lesson, we learned how to use the three rules of a sentence to see if a group of words is a sentence or a fragment by listening to a story. Most people listen to stories for enjoyment the first time. When they hear something or see something *(story, movie, cartoons, etc.)* for the second time, they see things they missed the first time. That is true of the story you heard in the previous lesson. Today, we will listen to the Sentence story again to see if you learn anything new that you didn't learn the first time it was read. *(Read "The Little WORDS' Great SENTENCE Adventure" to your students again.)*

The Little WORDS' Great SENTENCE Adventure

The WORDS all lived in WORD VILLAGE. It was the dream of every little WORD to make the trip to the SENTENCE KINGDOM to become a SENTENCE. WORDS by the thousands came to the SENTENCE KINGDOM to see if they could become a SENTENCE. But, the SENTENCE COUNCIL had very strict rules for WORDS to follow before they could be accepted. When WORDS followed the rules and passed all three tests, they were given the highest honor a WORD could have. They were crowned a SENTENCE and invited to join the other SENTENCES in the SENTENCE KINGDOM.

When WORDS did not follow the rules, they could not be called a SENTENCE. Thousands of WORDS tried everyday to become SENTENCES. Some WORDS were successful as they made the long, difficult journey to the SENTENCE KINGDOM. But, alas! Hundreds of WORDS failed. Some WORDS never tried to become a SENTENCE again, but some WORDS kept coming back, trying and trying and trying until they made it! This is a story of one such group of WORDS.

Everyone in WORD VILLAGE would catch their breath and gaze in awe whenever they met a SENTENCE from the SENTENCE KINGDOM. All the Mother WORDS wanted their Baby WORDS to grow up to be SENTENCES. WORDS were trained from childhood to eventually take the SENTENCE test.

CHAPTER 5 LESSON 3 CONTINUED

The SENTENCE KINGDOM was located on top of SENTENCE MOUNTAIN. It was the highest mountain around. SENTENCE KINGDOM was the most important kingdom in the whole wide world. The PARAGRAPH KINGDOM and the ESSAY KINGDOM depended entirely on the SENTENCE KINGDOM for their survival. It took weeks for anyone to get to the huge castle of the SENTENCE COUNCIL, but everyone was welcome. On the huge double doors was nailed a sign for everyone to read. It said, in big bold letters:

Here are the **three** rules WORDS must follow in order to become a SENTENCE in the SENTENCE KINGDOM.

Three Rules of a SENTENCE
1. The WORDS should tell who or what the SENTENCE is about.
2. The WORDS should tell what something does.
3. The WORDS should make complete sense.

The WORDS **pretty, the, bird,** and **yellow** wanted to be a SENTENCE. They made the long journey to SENTENCE MOUNTAIN and made an appointment to see the SENTENCE COUNCIL. They were very nervous as they came before the powerful SENTENCE COUNCIL. They said in scared little voices, "We want to be a SENTENCE!"

The SENTENCE COUNCIL looked at the scared little WORDS. They asked gently, "Are you ready to take the test?"

The WORDS gulped and shook their heads yes. They were too scared to even speak again. The SENTENCE COUNCIL nodded their wise heads in agreement. Then, the SENTENCE COUNCIL said to the WORDS, "Prepare yourselves!"

The WORDS tried hard to appear confident as they struggled to organize themselves into a SENTENCE. It was so embarrassing. They fell all over each other. They bumped into furniture. They stumbled more than once. Finally, they nodded that they were ready.

The SENTENCE COUNCIL held up their hands to start the check. Their voices boomed through the enormous room and down the long hallways as they read the order of the WORDS so that all could hear. "Let it be known that the SENTENCE COUNCIL will check the WORDS in this order: **pretty, the, bird, yellow.**" And the check began.

CHAPTER 5 LESSON 3 CONTINUED

1. **First rule:** Do these WORDS tell what the sentence is about? (*No, they do not tell what the sentence is about.*) The SENTENCE COUNCIL gave the WORDS a thumbs down. They did not follow the first rule.

2. **Second rule:** Do these WORDS tell what something does? (*No, they do not tell what something does.*) The SENTENCE COUNCIL gave the WORDS a thumbs down. They did not follow the second rule.

3. **Third rule:** Do these WORDS make complete sense? (*No, they do not have enough information to make complete sense.*) The SENTENCE COUNCIL gave the WORDS a thumbs down. They did not follow the third rule.

The SENTENCE COUNCIL made the dreaded announcement as the WORDS hung their heads, "The WORDS have failed the SENTENCE test. They are still fragments!"

Since the WORDS did not pass any of the three rules to become a SENTENCE, they could not join the SENTENCE KINGDOM. When WORDS did not follow the three rules of a SENTENCE, they were called fragments. As the poor little WORDS dragged themselves back down the mountain, the trees seemed to shout, "**Fragment, fragment, fragment, fragment, fragment. If WORDS are not a SENTENCE, they are a fragment, fragment, fragment!**" The little WORDS broke into a run. They were so ashamed.

After a few weeks, the WORDS **pretty, the, bird,** and **yellow,** still wanted to be a SENTENCE. They wanted to be a SENTENCE more than anything else. They finally realized that they had not been ready. They were embarrassed for weeks, but it helped make them more determined than ever to try again. They knew now that they did not make sense.

After thinking and thinking, planning and planning, they decided they needed help. They would go to NOUN TOWN to get help. The WORDS in NOUN TOWN were wise and helped the WORDS put themselves in another order to make more sense. The wise WORDS in NOUN TOWN showed the WORDS how to organize themselves to show what they were about. The WORDS decided to put themselves in this order: **The pretty yellow bird.**

Now, they were ready for another trip to the SENTENCE KINGDOM. Off they went with high hopes. They made another appointment and appeared before the SENTENCE COUNCIL again. This time, their knees did not shake quite so badly, and they were able to speak above a squeak. Finally, they nodded that they were ready.

The SENTENCE COUNCIL again held up their hands to start the check. Their voices boomed through the enormous room and down the long hallways as they read the order of the WORDS so that all could hear, "Let it be known that the SENTENCE COUNCIL will check the WORDS in this order: **The pretty yellow bird.**" And the check began.

CHAPTER 5 LESSON 3 CONTINUED

1. **First rule:** Do these WORDS tell what the sentence is about? (*Yes, they tell that the sentence is about a bird.*) The SENTENCE COUNCIL gave the WORDS a thumbs up. They followed the first rule.

2. **Second rule:** Do these WORDS tell what something does? (*No, they do not tell what the bird does.*) The SENTENCE COUNCIL gave the WORDS a thumbs down. They did not follow the second rule.

3. **Third rule:** Do these WORDS make complete sense? (*No, they do not have enough information to make complete sense.*) The SENTENCE COUNCIL gave the WORDS a thumbs down. They did not follow the third rule.

Since the WORDS did not follow all three rules to become a SENTENCE, they still could not join the SENTENCE KINGDOM. The WORDS were very, very sad. They were still fragments because they did not have what it took to become a SENTENCE. They dreaded the trip back down the mountain because they knew what the trees would say. But this time the trees did not shout; they whispered, **"Fragment, fragment, fragment, fragment, fragment. If WORDS are not a SENTENCE, they are a fragment, fragment, fragment!"** The little WORDS were still embarrassed, but, this time, they did not run.

A few weeks went by and the WORDS still wanted to be a SENTENCE more than ever. They decided they must get more help. After thinking and thinking, and planning and planning, they went to VERBVILLE to get more help. Some of the adventuresome WORDS in VERBVILLE joined the WORDS in their quest for the SENTENCE KINGDOM. The WORDS in VERBVILLE showed the WORDS how to organize themselves to tell what the bird does. They decided to put themselves in this order: **The pretty yellow bird flew away**.

Now, they were ready for another trip to the SENTENCE KINGDOM. They were very confident this time. They had planned and prepared and worked very hard for a long time. So, off they went with high hopes. They made another appointment and appeared before the SENTENCE COUNCIL again. This time, their knees did not shake at all, and they were able to speak in a normal voice. Finally, they nodded that they were ready.

The SENTENCE COUNCIL again held up their hands to start the check. Their voices boomed through the enormous room and down the long hallways as they read the order of the WORDS so that all could hear. "Let it be known that the SENTENCE COUNCIL will check the WORDS in this order: **The pretty yellow bird flew away.**" And the check began.

1. **First rule:** Do these WORDS tell what the sentence is about? (*Yes, they tell that the sentence is about a bird.*) The SENTENCE COUNCIL gave the WORDS a thumbs up. They followed the first rule.

2. **Second rule:** Do these WORDS tell what something does? (*Yes, they tell that the bird flew.*) The SENTENCE COUNCIL gave the WORDS a thumbs up. They followed the second rule.

3. **Third rule:** Do these WORDS make complete sense? (*Yes, they have enough information to make complete sense.*) The SENTENCE COUNCIL gave the WORDS a thumbs up. They followed the third rule.

CHAPTER 5 LESSON 3 CONTINUED

For one second, the whole castle was filled with respected silence. Then, the celebration began. The trumpets sounded victory across the SENTENCE KINGDOM. SENTENCES from all over the kingdom came running. The SENTENCE COUNCIL beamed proudly as they congratulated the WORDS on becoming a SENTENCE and immediately ordered the royal chefs to begin preparing the celebration feast! In minutes, the whole SENTENCE KINGDOM gathered within hearing distance!

The happy WORDS were still stunned by all the activity. All they could do was stand around, smiling and saying, "Thank you! Thank you!" as other SENTENCES came up to congratulate them on receiving the highest honor a WORD could ever have.

Then, the big moment came. The SENTENCE COUNCIL, dressed in flowing robes and carrying their royal scepters, led the SENTENCE procession to the royal banquet hall for the crowning ceremonies. The WORDS knew that they would never be called fragments again. They would live happily ever after in the SENTENCE KINGDOM with all the other SENTENCES.

As the celebration continued, the trees smiled knowingly and gently swayed to a different beat as they sang joyfully, "Little WORDS, little WORDS, we are so proud of you. May you always be good SENTENCES and live your lives honest and true!"

TEACHER INSTRUCTIONS

Ask students the following comprehension questions about the story.

1. What did the little Words want more than anything else? (*to be a sentence*)
2. How many rules did the little Words need to follow to become a Sentence? (*three*)
3. Where would the Words live if they became a Sentence? (*in the Sentence Kingdom*)
4. How many rules did the Words follow the first time? (*none*)
5. What did the trees say? (*fragment, fragment, fragment*)
6. How many rules did the Words follow the second time? (*one*)
7. Where did the Words go for help after they failed the second time? (*to the verbs in Verbville*)
8. What happened when the Words went to the Sentence Council the third time? (*They passed and became a sentence.*)
9. How do you think the Words felt after they became a Sentence? (*Answers will vary.*)

 ACTIVITY / ASSIGNMENT TIME

Materials Needed: glitter, sequins, and ric rac; king's crown pattern duplicated on large-size yellow construction paper

Give students a crown pattern duplicated on a large-size yellow construction paper. Have students cut out the crown and decorate it with glitter, sequins, and ric rac. Staple the crown for students to wear.

(End of lesson.)

CHAPTER 5   LESSON 4

Objectives: Jingles, Grammar (Sentences, Fragments), and Activity.

 **JINGLE TIME**

Have students turn to the Jingle Section of their books. The teacher will lead the students in reciting the previously-taught jingles.

 GRAMMAR TIME

TEACHING SCRIPT FOR SENTENCES AND FRAGMENTS

In the last lesson, we learned how to use the three rules of a sentence to see if a group of words was a sentence or a fragment by listening to a story. Today, we will pretend we are the Sentence Council and check a group of words. But first, you must know the three rules of a sentence. Turn to page 14 in the Reference Section of your book and look at Reference 1. We will use this reference as members of the Sentence Council. Now, let's review what we learned in the story:

1. A group of words must follow the three rules of a sentence before it can become a sentence.
2. The first rule says that words in a sentence tell who or what the sentence is about.
3. The second rule says that words in a sentence tell what something does.
4. The third rule says that words in a sentence should make complete sense.
5. If a group of words follows all three rules, it is a sentence.
6. If a group of words is not a sentence, it is a fragment.

Reference 1: Three Rules of a SENTENCE
1. The WORDS tell who or what the SENTENCE is about.   2. The WORDS tell what something does.   3. The WORDS should make complete sense.

We will check a group of words to see if it is a sentence or a fragment. I want you to say, "**The strong tiger**," aloud. (_Give them time to say the words aloud several times._)

Now, we will go through the rules of a sentence to see if this group of words is a sentence or a fragment. I want you to put your thumbs up every time this group of words follows one of the three sentence rules. Put your thumbs down every time this group of words does not follow one of the three sentence rules.

1. **First rule:** Do the words tell what the sentence is about? (_Yes, they tell that the sentence is about a strong tiger._) Sentence Council, put your thumbs up or put your thumbs down. (_Thumbs up._) Yes, it follows the first rule.

CHAPTER 5 LESSON 4 CONTINUED

2. **Second rule:** Do the words tell what something does? (*No, they do not tell what the tiger does.*) Sentence Council, put your thumbs up or put your thumbs down. (*Thumbs down.*) No, it does not follow the second rule.

3. **Third rule:** Do the words make complete sense? (*No, they do not give enough information to make complete sense.*) Sentence Council, put your thumbs up or put your thumbs down. (*Thumbs down.*) No, it does not follow the third rule.

Since the words did not follow all three rules to be a sentence, they cannot be called a sentence. What do we call a group of words that is not a sentence? (*fragment, fragment, fragment.*)

We will check this sentence again after improvements have been made to see if it is a sentence or if it is still a fragment. I want you to say, "**The strong tiger roared loudly**," several times. (*Give students time to say the words several times.*) Now, we will go through the rules of a sentence to see if this new group of words is a sentence or a fragment.

1. **First rule:** Do these Words tell what the sentence is about? (*Yes, they tell that the sentence is about a strong tiger.*) Sentence Council, put your thumbs up or put your thumbs down. (*Thumbs up.*) Yes, it follows the first rule.

2. **Second rule:** Do these Words tell what something does? (*Yes, they tell that the tiger roared.*) Sentence Council, put your thumbs up or put your thumbs down. (*Thumbs up.*) Yes, it follows the second rule.

3. **Third rule:** Do these Words make complete sense? (*Yes, they have given enough information to make complete sense.*) Sentence Council, put your thumbs up or put your thumbs down. (*Thumbs up.*) Yes, it follows the third rule.

Sentence Council, are these words a sentence? Since the words "**The strong tiger roared loudly**" follows all three rules to become a sentence, they may be called a sentence. Let the celebration begin! (*Begin clapping for the sentence.*)

 ACTIVITY / ASSIGNMENT TIME

Materials Needed: length of yarn, Cheerios, plastic straws cut into small sections

To celebrate correct sentence structure, have each student make a Celebration Necklace. Give each child a length of yarn on which to string Cheerios and small sections of plastic straws as "beads." Put the Cheerios and pre-cut sections of plastic straws in bowls for students to use. Let students decide on the "bead" pattern they want to use. (*Put masking tape on ends of the yarn to form a point and use it as a needle.*) After stringing the first "bead," loop the yarn around it and tie it to the end of the yarn so that the other "beads" will not fall off.

(End of lesson.)

Level 1 Homeschool Teacher's Manual

CHAPTER 5   LESSON 5

Objectives: Jingles, Grammar (Review Nouns and Verbs), Verb Activity, Noun Activity 1, and Noun Activity 2.

JINGLE TIME

Have students turn to the Jingle Section of their books. The teacher will lead the students in reciting the previously-taught jingles.

GRAMMAR TIME

TEACHING SCRIPT FOR A REVIEW OF NOUNS AND VERBS

First, I want to review **nouns**. A noun is a naming word. What does a noun name? (_A noun names a person, place, or thing._) Can you name a noun that names a person? (_Grandmother, boy, girl, aunt, etc._) Can you name a noun that names a place? (_ocean, Texas, Miami, home, store, etc._) Can you name a noun that names a thing? (_horse, bird, plate, flag, cupcakes, baseball, etc._)

Next, we will review **verbs**. A verb is an action word that tells what a person or thing can do. I will name an animal, and you give me several verbs that tell what the animal can do. The animal is a dog. (_Answers will vary._) As you can see, verbs work with nouns to help sentences make sense.

ACTIVITY / ASSIGNMENT TIME

Verb Activity:

Tell students you are going to read them a verb story, and they will help you. Their job will be to demonstrate the action of the verbs used in the story by acting out what each action verb does. (_Read the story below and have students act out the action of the verbs printed in bold type._)

The Adventuresome Little Rabbits

Once upon a time, three little rabbits lived with their family in the forest. The rabbits were tired of hanging around home. They wanted adventure and excitement! They asked their mother if they could go to the river and look around. Their mother said they could, but they must be back before dark.

So, off the little rabbits hurried. They **hopped, hopped, hopped** to the river. It was a long way; so, they kept hopping. **Hop, hop, hop. Hop, hop, hop**. Finally, they saw the river. They were almost there. **Hop, hop, hop. Hop, hop, hop**.

They were so excited. They had made it all the way to the river by themselves. Then, they heard a strange sound. They stood very still and listened. The ground started shaking. The rabbits hopped for cover! **Hop! Hop! Hop! Hop! Hop! Hop! Hide**, rabbits, **hide!**

CHAPTER 5 LESSON 5 CONTINUED

They could hear something big coming to the river. It was a herd of elephants! They walked slowly. (*Walk with a heavy lumbering walk around the room.*) **Boom, Boom, Boom. Boom, Boom, Boom.** They went to the river for a drink of water. **Drink, drink, drink**! Then, the elephants left. **Boom, Boom, Boom. Boom, Boom, Boom.**

The elephants were gone. The little rabbits came out of hiding. Suddenly, they heard another sound. Quickly, they scampered for cover again. **Hide**, rabbits, **hide!** As they looked out from their hiding place, they saw eagles! They were flying toward the river to get a drink of water. (*Flap arms and then spread arms to soar.*) **Flap, flap, flap. Soar, soar, soar**. The little rabbits did not move. They knew what eagles could do to little rabbits! Finally, the eagles left. **Flap, flap, flap. Soar, soar, soar.**

As soon as the eagles left, the little rabbits quickly hopped back home. **Hop, hop, hop. Hop, hop, hop.** They were out of breath, but they kept hopping. **Hop, hop, hop. Hop, hop, hop.** At last, they were home. They did not want to go out again for a while! They were very tired! (*Lay head on arms and close eyes.*) **Rest, rest, rest. Rest. Rest. Rest.**

Noun Activity 1:

Take the students on a NOUN HUNT in the house. Give students three plastic or paper bags in which to gather their nouns. Help students label each bag with one of these labels: person, place, thing. Tell students they can hunt for four of each kind of noun. (*They can use pictures for some of the items.*) Have them bend low like they are hunting. Have them do a hunting chant. (*We're hunting, hunting, hunting. We're hunting, hunting, hunting. We're hunting for nouns!*) After students have collected four nouns in each bag, have them share what they selected and tell why they chose the nouns that they collected. Then, ask students to put the nouns back where they got them.

Noun Activity 2:

(*Have a big pot with a long wooden spoon in the middle of the floor or study table.*) I am going to make noun soup. I want you to help me gather the things I need. I will stir the soup with my long wooden spoon while you are gathering the nouns. The nouns must be small enough to fit in my pot, and the nouns must represent persons, places, or things. (*They can use pictures for some of the items.*) We will discuss your choices after the pot is full. You can also help me sing the Noun-Soup Chant. It is located on page 84 in the Activity Section of your book under Chapter 5, Lesson 5, Activity 2. Let's recite it together before we begin.

Chapter 5, Lesson 5, Activity 2: Help sing the Noun Soup Chant listed below.
Mmmm, hot, delicious noun soup. I am making noun soup. I need nouns for my soup. Won't you add a noun to my soup? This is hot, delicious noun soup. Please add a noun to my soup. Ahhh, yummy, yummy noun soup. It makes the tummy, tummy glad for noun soup. Mmmm, hot, delicious noun soup.
Thank you for helping with my noun soup. We are having fun making hot, delicious noun soup. Look at the nouns, swirling around, in our noun soup! Ahhh, noun soup, hot delicious noun soup.

(*Before each student adds a noun to the soup, he/she must tell what type of noun he/she is adding: person, place, or thing. Students may use pictures or toys to represent persons, places, or things. Repeat the chant after each noun has been added to the pot. After several nouns have been added, you may end the activity. This activity can also be played with friends and other family members.*)

(End of lesson.)

CHAPTER 6   LESSON 1

Objectives: Jingles, Vocabulary #1, and Grammar (Sentence Structure, Question and Answer Flow, Review Noun and Verb).

 **JINGLE TIME**

Have students turn to the Jingle Section of their books. The teacher will lead the students in reciting the previously-taught jingles.

 VOCABULARY TIME

Words are very important to you. As you learn more words, you will be able to read other people's ideas as they write them on paper, and you will be able to write down your own ideas. Learning words will also help you do your work in homeschool. Learning new words is called building your **vocabulary**. Vocabulary is just another name for the words that you will learn and use.

Since you will be learning new words almost every day, we will call this time **Vocabulary Time**. During Vocabulary Time, you will learn what the new words look like and how to pronounce them. Then, you will hear and use the words in the sentences that you classify during Grammar Time. Your new vocabulary words are listed on page 6 in the Vocabulary Section of your workbook. *(Have students turn to page 6 and show them how to locate a set of vocabulary words for any given lesson. First, they should look at the chapter number. Next, they should look at the number listed for that box. They will look for #1 because this represents the first set of vocabulary words in Chapter 6. The second set in Chapter six will be written as #2, etc.)*

Chapter 6, Vocabulary Words #1
cats, boys, bears, sat, ran

Teacher's Notes: You should follow the Six-Step Vocabulary Plan in the box below to present all the new vocabulary words to your students.

Six-Step Vocabulary Plan

1. Have students point to the word.

2. Pronounce the word for your students.

3. Lead students as they pronounce the word three times in a rhythmic chant.

4. Give the meanings for any words that your students might not know. (*Even though the vocabulary words are used in the sentences that students classify, you may need to make up other sentences to help define new words your students do not understand. You might also have students make up sentences of their own in order to show their understanding.*)

5. After you have introduced the new words in the vocabulary list, have students pronounce the words independently to make sure they know them.

6. Students will be given a new word list for each lesson during Vocabulary Time.

CHAPTER 6 LESSON 1 CONTINUED

 GRAMMAR TIME

TEACHING SCRIPT FOR SENTENCE STRUCTURE AND THE QUESTION & ANSWER FLOW

When you look at a sentence and know all the parts that make up the sentence, you understand sentence structure. Everyone repeat the words **sentence structure**. (*Sentence structure*) Sentence structure is how a sentence is put together. What is sentence structure? (*Sentence structure is how a sentence is put together.*) Sentence structure is like a puzzle. Once you know how all the parts of a puzzle fit together, it is easier to put the puzzle together again, right? (*Right*) Learning about sentence structure will make it easier to write good sentences.

Before we begin learning the parts of a sentence, we will learn another vocabulary term that we will use often in our study of sentences. This term is **Question and Answer Flow**. You will soon learn to ask certain questions in order to find the answers about different parts of a sentence. These questions and answers are called the **Question and Answer Flow**. Repeat the words *Question and Answer Flow* with me three times. (*Question and Answer Flow, Question and Answer Flow, Question and Answer Flow.*)

In a Question and Answer Flow, you ask questions to get answers. What do you do in a Question and Answer Flow? (*You ask questions to get answers.*) (*Do not worry if students do not totally understand what you are talking about. You are just exposing them to the vocabulary terms that you will be using. It will be reinforced as they move through the program.*) This vocabulary term is easy to remember because it tells you exactly what it is. When you "question," you will ask a question. When you "answer," you will get an answer. You will be using Question and Answer Flows in the next lesson. You may need to say this term several times today in order to remember it easily.

TEACHING SCRIPT TO REVIEW THE NOUN

We have already learned a lot about nouns. Now, we will review several things about them. The Noun Jingle says a **noun** names a person, place, or thing. The noun is also known as a naming word. We will use the letter **N** to identify a noun when we do not spell it out. Look around the room and name three nouns that you see.

(*Give students time to identify three nouns in the room. For extra practice, have students identify the nouns found in several different rooms of your house. You could also have them cut out several "N" letters and place them on the nouns identified. Examples: books, curtains, bed, pictures, sink, stove, toys, etc.*)

TEACHING SCRIPT TO REVIEW THE VERB

We have already learned several things about verbs. Today, we will review several things about them. A **verb** tells what a person or thing does. We will use the letter **V** to identify a verb when we do not spell it out. Think about what a dog does. Now, name four verbs that tell what a dog does.

(*Examples: A dog runs, jumps, eats, sleeps, barks, growls, etc. For extra practice, have students act out four things that a dog can do.*)

(End of lesson.)

Level 1 Homeschool Teacher's Manual

CHAPTER 6   LESSON 2

Objectives: Jingles, Vocabulary #1 (Review), Grammar (Introductory Sentences, Classifying and Labeling, Two Main Parts of a Sentence), and Activity.

 **JINGLE TIME**

Have students turn to the Jingle Section of their books. The teacher will lead the students in reciting the previously-taught jingles.

 VOCABULARY TIME

Have students turn to page 6 in the Vocabulary Section of their books. Review the vocabulary words listed in the vocabulary box below by reciting them together with your students. *(Normally, you can expect Vocabulary Time to be presented in Lessons 2-5 of each chapter, just before Grammar Time. This will give you an opportunity to go over the new vocabulary words that will be used during Grammar Time as students classify the new sentences.)*

Chapter 6, Vocabulary Words #1
cats, boys, bears, sat, ran

 GRAMMAR TIME

Put the introductory sentences from the box below on the board. Use these sentences as you go through the new concepts covered in your teaching scripts. For the greatest benefit, students must participate orally with the teacher. *(You might put the introductory sentences on notebook paper if you are doing one-on-one instruction with your students.)*

Chapter 6, Introductory Sentences for Lesson 2
1. Cats sat.
2. Boys sat.
3. Bears ran.

TEACHING SCRIPT FOR CLASSIFYING AND LABELING

We learned earlier that when things are grouped, it helps us to see how all the little parts fit into the big picture. This helps us to understand how things are connected. When we group things, we call it classifying. We will learn to group words in a certain order to make a sentence.

CHAPTER 6 LESSON 2 CONTINUED

When you learn how to name the parts of a sentence, we say you are **classifying** a sentence. When you **classify** a sentence, you name the parts of the sentence. What do you do when you name the parts of a sentence? (*You classify a sentence.*) After you name, or classify, different words in a sentence, you will write some letters above the words to show that you can name them. This is called **labeling** because you label the words by writing letters above them.

Don't worry about the words *classifying* and *labeling*. We will learn more about classifying and labeling as we continue the lesson. (*Do not worry if students do not totally understand what you are talking about. You are just exposing them to the vocabulary terms that you will be using. It will be reinforced as they move through the program.*)

TEACHING SCRIPT FOR THE TWO MAIN PARTS OF A SENTENCE: THE SUBJECT AND VERB

Today, we will begin our study of sentence parts and how to put them together. First, we will learn the two main parts of a sentence. The two main parts of a sentence are called the *subject* and the *verb*. We will learn how to use nouns for the subject, and we will classify these nouns as **subject nouns**. The **subject noun** tells *who* the sentence is about or *what* the sentence is about.

The subject questions are **who** or **what**. Ask *who* **if the sentence is about people**. Ask *what* **if the sentence is about animals or things**.

First, I will show you how to ask the right questions to find the **subject noun** in a sentence. Then, I will show you how to ask the questions to find the **verb**. Remember, this is called a Question and Answer Flow. Listen carefully as I demonstrate how to use the Question and Answer Flow to classify the first sentence. (*Follow the script. Always read the sentence before you start classifying it.*)

Look at Sentence 1: Cats sat.

What sat? cats - subject noun (*Write SN above cats.*)

Since cats are animals, we asked the subject question "*what.*" The subject noun *cats* tells *what* the sentence is about. Notice that I wrote the **SN** label above *cats* to identify, or name, the noun acting as the subject of the sentence.

Now, we will identify the **verb**. The verb normally shows action. The verb tells what the subject is doing. To find the verb, ask this verb question, "*what is being said about*" the subject. Since this verb question is hard to remember at first, we will recite it five times. Begin. (*Have your students recite "what is being said about" in unison at least five times. This will help them remember this important verb question.*)

 "What is being said about? What is being said about? What is being said about? What is being said about? What is being said about?"

Level 1 Homeschool Teacher's Manual

CHAPTER 6 LESSON 2 CONTINUED

Now, I will demonstrate how to use the Question and Answer Flow to classify, or name, the verb in the first sentence.

What is being said about cats? cats sat - verb (*Write V above sat.*)

I asked the verb question, *what is being said about*, to find the verb. Then, I wrote the **V** label above *sat* to identify, or name, the word acting as the verb of the sentence.

I will classify Sentence 1 again, but this time you will classify the sentence with me. Remember, classifying is grouping. We are finding the sentence parts. We will work on reciting them smoothly so we can see how all the parts of a sentence work together.

After we finish Sentence 1, we will practice classifying two more sentences. (*This should be a lot of fun for your students. There is no pressure, and the format will be repeated over and over. It is not necessary to give students worksheets at this time.*)

Teacher's Note: Make sure students say the Question and Answer Flows correctly.

Question and Answer Flow for Sentence 1: Cats sat.
1. What sat? cats - subject noun (Write SN above *cats*.)
   (Since *cats* are animals, we begin the subject question with *what*.
   The subject noun *cats* tells *what* the sentence is about.)
2. What is being said about cats? cats sat - verb (Write V above *sat*.)

Classified Sentence:
    SN   V
    Cats sat.

Question and Answer Flow for Sentence 2: Boys sat.
1. Who sat? boys - subject noun (Write SN above *boys*.)
   (Since *boys* are people, we begin the subject question with *who*.
   The subject noun *boys* tells *who* the sentence is about.)
2. What is being said about boys? boys sat - verb (Write V above *sat*.)

Classified Sentence:
    SN   V
    Boys sat.

Question and Answer Flow for Sentence 3: Bears ran.
1. What ran? bears - subject noun (Write SN above *bears*.)
   (Since *bears* are animals, we begin the subject question with *what*.
   The subject noun *bears* tells *what* the sentence is about.)
2. What is being said about bears? bears ran - verb (Write V above *ran*.)

Classified Sentence:
    SN   V
    Bears ran.

CHAPTER 6 LESSON 2 CONTINUED

TEACHER INSTRUCTIONS

Have students recite the Question and Answer Flows for the first <u>two</u> sentences with you again. This time, they should trace the labels on their desks with the first three fingers of their writing hand as they classify. This is excellent practice to develop dexterity and to learn at a faster pace.

Next, have students write the <u>third</u> sentence on a sheet of paper. Have them recite the Question and Answer Flow for the third sentence with you again, but this time they should write the labels above the words on their paper. This will give them practice writing the labels before they are tested.

The key to success is to keep students constantly saying the Question and Answer Flows until they know them automatically. Follow the suggestions below for your students to get the greatest benefits from the grammar lessons.

1. Be sure to have the students read each sentence with you, in unison, before classifying it.
2. Make sure students are saying the **questions** and the **answers** with you as each Question and Answer Flow is recited.

 ACTIVITY / ASSIGNMENT TIME

This is a great listening and recitation exercise for students. Go through the chants below with your students. The first column provides students with the subject and verb of each sentence classified earlier, but in a fun, chanting rhythm. The second column gives students an opportunity to hear the two main parts of a sentence, the subject and verb, spoken together.

I Say, You Say Chants	
1. I say **cats**; you say **sat**.	Cats sat.
2. I say **boys**; you say **sat**.	Boys sat.
3. I say **bears**; you say **ran**.	Bears ran.

(End of lesson.)

Level 1 Homeschool Teacher's Manual

CHAPTER 6   LESSON 3

Objectives: Jingles, Vocabulary #2, Grammar (Practice Sentences), and Activity.

 **JINGLE TIME**

Have students turn to the Jingle Section of their books. The teacher will lead the students in reciting the previously-taught jingles.

 VOCABULARY TIME

Have students turn to page 6 in the Vocabulary Section of their books. Introduce the vocabulary words listed in the vocabulary box below by reciting them together with your students.

Chapter 6, Vocabulary Words #2
girls, dogs, played

 GRAMMAR TIME

Put the Practice Sentences from the box below on the board or on notebook paper. Use these sentences as you practice the concepts that have been taught. For the greatest benefit, students must participate orally with the teacher.

Chapter 6, Practice Sentences for Lesson 3
1. Girls played.
2. Dogs ran.
3. Boys played.

TEACHING SCRIPT FOR PRACTICE SENTENCES

We will classify these three sentences to practice the subjects and verbs in the Question and Answer Flows. We will classify the sentences together. Begin.

CHAPTER 6 LESSON 3 CONTINUED

Question and Answer Flow for Sentence 1: Girls played.

1. Who played? girls - subject noun (Write SN above *girls*.)
   (Since *girls* are people, we use the subject question *who*.
   The subject noun *girls* tells *who* the sentence is about.)
2. What is being said about girls? girls played - verb (Write V above *played*.)

Classified Sentence: SN   V
                                Girls   played.

Question and Answer Flow for Sentence 2: Dogs ran.

1. What ran? dogs - subject noun (Write SN above *dogs*.)
   (Since *dogs* are animals, we use the subject question *what*.
   The subject noun *dogs* tells *what* the sentence is about.)
2. What is being said about dogs? dogs ran - verb (Write V above *ran*.)

Classified Sentence: SN   V
                                Dogs   ran.

Question and Answer Flow for Sentence 3: Boys played.

1. Who played? boys - subject noun (Write SN above *boys*.)
   (Since *boys* are people, we use the subject question *who*.
   The subject noun *boys* tells *who* the sentence is about.)
2. What is being said about boys? boys played - verb (Write V above *played*.)

Classified Sentence: SN   V
                                Boys   played.

TEACHER INSTRUCTIONS

Have students recite the Question and Answer Flows for the first <u>two</u> sentences with you again. This time, they should trace the labels on their desks with the first three fingers of their writing hand as they classify. This is excellent practice to develop dexterity and to learn at a faster pace.

Next, have students write the <u>third</u> sentence on a sheet of paper. Have them recite the Question and Answer Flow for the third sentence with you again, but this time they should write the labels above the words on their paper. This will give them practice writing the labels before they are tested.

CHAPTER 6 LESSON 3 CONTINUED

 ACTIVITY / ASSIGNMENT TIME

These are great listening and recitation exercises for students. Go through the chants below with your students. The first column provides students with the subject and verb of each sentence classified earlier, but in a fun, chanting rhythm. The second column gives students an opportunity to hear the two main parts of a sentence, the subject and verb, spoken together.

I Say, You Say Chants	
1. I say **girls**; you say **played**.	Girls played.
2. I say **dogs**; you say **ran**.	Dogs ran.
3. I say **boys**; you say **played**.	Boys played.

I Say, You Say Chants (Review)	
4. I say **cats**; you say **sat**.	Cats sat.
5. I say **boys**; you say **sat**.	Boys sat.
6. I say **bears**; you say **ran**.	Bears ran.

Have students turn to page 84 in the Activity Section of their books and find Chapter 6, Lesson 3, Activity. Go over the directions to make sure they understand what to do. Check and discuss the Activity after students have finished. *(The five noun boxes that are shaded should be colored yellow.)*

Chapter 6, Lesson 3, Activity: Find all the nouns in the boxes below. Then, color each noun box yellow.		
girls	ran	cats
sat	bears	walked
boys	played	dogs

(End of lesson.)

CHAPTER 6   LESSON 4

Objectives: Jingles, Vocabulary #3, Grammar (Practice Sentences), and Activity.

 **JINGLE TIME**

Have students turn to the Jingle Section of their books. The teacher will lead the students in reciting the previously-taught jingles.

 VOCABULARY TIME

Have students turn to page 6 in the Vocabulary Section of their books. Introduce the vocabulary words listed in the vocabulary box below by reciting them together with your students.

Chapter 6, Vocabulary Words #3
walked, airplanes, flew

 GRAMMAR TIME

Put the Practice Sentences from the box below on the board or on notebook paper. Use these sentences as you practice the concepts that have been taught. For the greatest benefit, students must participate orally with the teacher.

Chapter 6, Practice Sentences for Lesson 4
1. Girls walked.
2. Cats ran.
3. Airplanes flew.

TEACHING SCRIPT FOR PRACTICE SENTENCES

We will classify these three sentences to practice the subjects and verbs in the Question and Answer Flows. We will classify the sentences together. Begin.

CHAPTER 6 LESSON 4 CONTINUED

Question and Answer Flow for Sentence 1: Girls walked.

1. Who walked? girls - subject noun (Write SN above *girls*.)
   (Since *girls* are people, we use the subject question *who*.
   The subject noun *girls* tells *who* the sentence is about.)

2. What is being said about girls? girls walked - verb (Write V above *walked*.)

Classified Sentence: SN   V
                       Girls   walked.

Question and Answer Flow for Sentence 2: Cats ran.

1. What ran? cats - subject noun (Write SN above *cats*.)
   (Since *cats* are animals, we use the subject question *what*.
   The subject noun *cats* tells *what* the sentence is about.)

2. What is being said about cats? cats ran - verb (Write V above *ran*.)

Classified Sentence: SN   V
                       Cats   ran.

Question and Answer Flow for Sentence 3: Airplanes flew.

1. What flew? airplanes - subject noun (Write SN above *airplanes*.)
   (Since *airplanes* are things, we use the subject question *what*.
   The subject noun *airplanes* tells *what* the sentence is about.)

2. What is being said about airplanes? airplanes flew - verb (Write V above *flew*.)

Classified Sentence: SN   V
                    Airplanes   flew.

TEACHER INSTRUCTIONS

Have students recite the Question and Answer Flows for the first <u>two</u> sentences with you again. This time, they should trace the labels on their desks with the first three fingers of their writing hand as they classify. This is excellent practice to develop dexterity and to learn at a faster pace.

Next, have students write the <u>third</u> sentence on a sheet of paper. Have them recite the Question and Answer Flow for the third sentence with you again, but this time they should write the labels above the words on their paper. This will give them practice writing the labels before they are tested.

CHAPTER 6 LESSON 4 CONTINUED

ACTIVITY / ASSIGNMENT TIME

These are great listening and recitation exercises for students. Go through the chants below with your students. The first column provides students with the subject and verb of each sentence classified earlier, but in a fun, chanting rhythm. The second column gives students an opportunity to hear the two main parts of a sentence, the subject and verb, spoken together.

I Say, You Say Chants	
1. I say **girls**; you say **walked**.	Girls walked.
2. I say **cats**; you say **ran**.	Cats ran.
3. I say **airplanes**; you say **flew**.	Airplanes flew.

I Say, You Say Chants (Review)	
4. I say **girls**; you say **played**.	Girls played.
5. I say **dogs**; you say **ran**.	Dogs ran.
6. I say **boys**; you say **played**.	Boys played.

I Say, You Say Chants (Review)	
7. I say **cats**; you say **sat**.	Cats sat.
8. I say **boys**; you say **sat**.	Boys sat.
9. I say **bears**; you say **ran**.	Bears ran.

Have students turn to page 84 in the Activity Section of their books and find Chapter 6, Lesson 4, Activity. Go over the directions to make sure they understand what to do. Check and discuss the Activity after students have finished. *(The five verb boxes that are shaded should be colored red.)*

Chapter 6, Lesson 4, Activity: Find all the verbs in the boxes below. Then, color each verb box red.		
walked	played	cats
girls	ran	sat
boys	airplane	flew

(End of lesson.)

Level 1 Homeschool Teacher's Manual

CHAPTER 6   LESSON 5

Objectives: Jingles, Vocabulary #4, Grammar (Practice Sentences), and Writing (Journal).

 **JINGLE TIME**

Have students turn to the Jingle Section of their books. The teacher will lead the students in reciting the previously-taught jingles.

 VOCABULARY TIME

Have students turn to page 6 in the Vocabulary Section of their books. Introduce the vocabulary words listed in the vocabulary box below by reciting them together with your students.

Chapter 6, Vocabulary Words #4
ducks, barked, kittens

 GRAMMAR TIME

Put the Practice Sentences from the box below on the board or on notebook paper. Use these sentences as you practice the concepts that have been taught. For the greatest benefit, students must participate orally with the teacher.

Chapter 6, Practice Sentences for Lesson 5
1. Ducks walked.
2. Dogs barked.
3. Kittens played.

TEACHING SCRIPT FOR PRACTICE SENTENCES

We will classify these three sentences to practice the subjects and verbs in the Question and Answer Flows. We will classify the sentences together. Begin.

© SHURLEY INSTRUCTIONAL MATERIALS, INC.

CHAPTER 6 LESSON 5 CONTINUED

Question and Answer Flow for Sentence 1: Ducks walked.

  1. What walked? ducks - subject noun (Write SN above *ducks*.)
  2. What is being said about ducks? ducks walked - verb (Write V above *walked*.)

Classified Sentence: SN   V
                                   Ducks   walked.

Question and Answer Flow for Sentence 2: Dogs barked.

  1. What barked? dogs - subject noun (Write SN above *dogs*.)
  2. What is being said about dogs? dogs barked - verb (Write V above *barked*.)

Classified Sentence: SN   V
                                   Dogs   barked.

Question and Answer Flow for Sentence 3: Kittens played.

  1. What played? kittens - subject noun (Write SN above *kittens*.)
  2. What is being said about kittens? kittens played - verb (Write V above *played*.)

Classified Sentence: SN   V
                                   Kittens   played.

TEACHER INSTRUCTIONS

Have students recite the Question and Answer Flows for the first <u>two</u> sentences with you again. This time, they should trace the labels on their desks with the first three fingers of their writing hand as they classify. This is excellent practice to develop dexterity and to learn at a faster pace.

Next, have students write the <u>third</u> sentence on a sheet of paper. Have them recite the Question and Answer Flow for the third sentence with you again, but this time they should write the labels above the words on their paper. This will give them practice writing the labels before they are tested.

CHAPTER 6 LESSON 5 CONTINUED

 **WRITING TIME**

TEACHING SCRIPT FOR JOURNAL WRITING

Now, turn to the Reference Section and look at Reference 2 on page 14. You will begin journal writing today, but, before you begin, I want to share some important information about this type of writing. (*Read the information in the reference box below.*)

Reference 2: What is Journal Writing?

Journal Writing is a written record of your personal thoughts and feelings about things or people that are important to you. You can record your dreams, memories, feelings, and experiences. You can ask questions and answer some of them. It is fun to go back later and read what you have written because it shows how you have changed in different areas of your life. Writing in a journal is an easy and enjoyable way to practice your writing skills without worrying about a writing grade.

What do I write about?

Journals are personal, but sometimes it helps to have ideas to get you started. Remember, in a journal, you do not have to stick to one topic. Write about someone or something you like. Write about what you did last weekend or on vacation. Write about what you hope to do this week or on your next vacation. Write about home, school, friends, hobbies, special talents (yours or someone else's), or the hopes and fears you have about things now and in the future. If something bothers you, record it in your journal. If something interests you, record it. After all, it is your journal!

How do I get started writing in my personal journal?

You need to put the day's date on the title line of your paper: **Month, Day, Year.** Skip the next line and begin your entry. You might write one or two sentences, a paragraph, a whole page, or several pages. Except for the journal date, no particular organizational style is required for journal writing. You decide how best to organize and express your thoughts. Feel free to include pictures or lists if they will help you remember your thoughts about different things. You will also need a spiral notebook, a pen, a quiet place, and at least 5-10 minutes of uninterrupted writing time.

Note: Any drawings you might include do not have to be masterpieces — stick figures will do nicely.

TEACHER INSTRUCTIONS

Have students write the title *My Personal Journal for the Year* ____, indicating the current year on the front covers of their journal notebooks or folders. Students should use their journal notebooks for their journal-writing assignments.

Writing Assignment: Have students make the first entry in their journals at this time.

Teacher's Note: Journal writing helps students express themselves in written form, helps students feel comfortable with writing, and gives students an opportunity to practice what they are learning. Check to make sure students are making their entries. Make it a writing routine to have a five-to-ten minute journal-writing time whenever journal writing is assigned. Keeping a journal should develop into a life-long habit.

(End of lesson.)

CHAPTER 7   LESSON 1
Objectives: Jingle (Adverb), Synonyms, Antonyms, and Activity.

JINGLE TIME

Have students turn to the Jingle Section in their books and recite the previously-taught jingles. Then, lead students in reciting the new jingle (Adverb) below. Practice the new jingle several times until students can recite it smoothly. Emphasize reciting with a rhythm. (*Do not try to explain the new jingle at this time. Just have fun reciting it. Add motions for more fun and laughter.*)

Jingle 4: Adverb Jingle
An adverb modifies a verb.   An adverb asks *How? When? Where?*   To find an adverb: **Go, Ask, Get**.   Where do I **go**? To a verb.   What do I **ask**? How? When? Where?   What do I **get**? An ADVERB! (Clap) (Clap) That's what!

SYNONYM AND ANTONYM TIME

TEACHING SCRIPT FOR SYNONYMS AND ANTONYMS

Knowing different vocabulary words can help you express exactly what is on your mind, and it will also help others to understand your thoughts and ideas. What you say is more effective when you do not use the same words over and over again. That is why it is necessary to learn new vocabulary words.

Today, we will learn about synonyms and antonyms and how to mark them. Look at Reference 3 on page 14 in your student book. (*Reference 3 is reproduced on the next page.*) Follow along as I read the definition for synonyms. **Synonyms are words that have similar, or almost the same, meanings**. Listen to these examples of synonyms: big, large / mad, angry / night, evening / happy, glad. (*Discuss the meanings of each set of words and why their meanings are similar, or almost the same.*)

Now, listen to the definition for antonyms. **Antonyms are words that have opposite, or different, meanings**. Listen to these examples of antonyms: big, small / stop, go / night, day / happy, sad. (*Discuss the meanings of each set of words and why their meanings are opposite, or different.*)

Look at the Reference box again. The directions for identifying synonyms and antonyms are located below the definitions. Put your finger on the word directions. Follow along as I read the directions for the sample exercise on synonyms and antonyms. **Identify each pair of words as synonyms or antonyms by drawing a line under the *syn* or *ant*.** We will go through each example to make sure you understand what to do. (*Follow the teaching script on the next page to teach synonyms and antonyms.*)

CHAPTER 7 LESSON 1 CONTINUED

Reference 3: Synonyms and Antonyms

Definitions: Synonyms are words that have similar, or almost the same, meanings.
Antonyms are words that have opposite, or different, meanings.

Directions: Identify each pair of words as synonyms or antonyms by drawing a line under the **syn** or **ant**.

1. small, tiny	**syn** ant	2. up, down	syn **ant**	3. happy, cheerful	**syn** ant

Look at the words **small** and **tiny** beside number 1. <u>First</u>, you should pronounce the two words. (*Have students pronounce the words small and tiny.*) <u>Second</u>, you should think about what the two words mean. (*Discuss the meaning of small and the meaning of tiny.*) <u>Third</u>, you must decide if the meanings are almost the same or if the meanings are opposite. If they mean the same thing, they are synonyms. If they mean the opposite, they are antonyms. Do the words **small** and **tiny** mean almost the same thing, or do they mean the opposite? (*the same thing*) (*Discuss the meanings of the two words to show students how the two meanings are similar.*)

Since **small** and **tiny** mean the same thing, are they synonyms or antonyms? (*synonyms*) How do we indicate that they are synonyms? (*by drawing a line under the syn abbreviation*) (*For number 1, have students point to the line drawn under the syn in their practice box.*)

We will go through number 2 and number 3 in the same way. Look at the words **up** and **down** beside number 2. <u>First</u>, you should pronounce the two words. (*Have students pronounce the words up and down.*) <u>Second</u>, you should think about what the two words mean. (*Discuss the meaning of up and the meaning of down.*) <u>Third</u>, you must decide if the meanings are almost the same or if the meanings are opposite. If they mean the same, they are synonyms. If they mean the opposite, they are antonyms. Do the words **up** and **down** mean almost the same thing, or do they mean the opposite? (*the opposite*) (*Discuss the meanings of the two words to show students how the two meanings are opposite.*)

Since **up** and **down** mean the opposite, are they synonyms or antonyms? (*antonyms*) How do we indicate that they are antonyms? (*by drawing a line under the ant abbreviation*) (*For number 2, have students point to the line drawn under the ant in their practice box.*)

Look at the words **happy** and **cheerful** beside number 3. <u>First</u>, you should pronounce the two words. (*Have students pronounce the words happy and cheerful.*) <u>Second</u>, you should think about what the two words mean. (*Discuss the meaning of happy and the meaning of cheerful.*) <u>Third</u>, you must decide if the meanings are almost the same or if the meanings are opposite. If they mean the same thing, they are synonyms. If they mean the opposite, they are antonyms. Do the words **happy** and **cheerful** mean almost the same thing, or do they mean the opposite? (*the same thing*) (*Discuss the meanings of the two words to show students how the two meanings are similar.*)

Since **happy** and **cheerful** mean the same thing, are they synonyms or antonyms? (*synonyms*) How do we indicate that they are synonyms? (*by drawing a line under the syn abbreviation*) (*For number 3, have students point to the line drawn under the syn in their practice box.*)

CHAPTER 7 LESSON 1 CONTINUED

Teacher's Note: The exercises in the Reference section of the students' books are keyed in order to serve as a reference guide that students may study or refer to later. Make sure you go over each exercise thoroughly. You may put the examples on the board for a visual demonstration as you teach and discuss new concepts.

TEACHING SCRIPT FOR A NEW SET OF SYNONYMS AND ANTONYMS

Now that we know about synonyms and antonyms, we will learn a new set each week. Remember the three steps we use to identify the new synonyms and antonyms: <u>First</u>, you should pronounce the two words. <u>Second</u>, you should think about what the two words mean. <u>Third</u>, if the meanings are the same, or almost the same, you will underline the **syn** label, indicating that the two words are synonyms. If the meanings are opposite, you will underline the **ant** label, indicating that the two words are antonyms.

(In the teacher's manual, each new set of synonyms and antonyms is provided in Lesson 1 in a box under Synonym and Antonym Time. Have students turn to page 10 in the Synonym and Antonym Section of their books. Introduce the new words listed for Chapter 7 in the box below. Make sure students know the meanings of the new synonyms and antonyms. Then, have students underline the correct answer in their books. They should study these words again before their test. If it is hard for students to understand any set of synonyms and antonyms, go over the synonyms and antonyms again in the next several lessons. Make sure students know the synonyms and antonyms before they are tested on Day 5.)

Chapter 7: Underline the **syn** if the words are synonyms. Underline the **ant** if the words are antonyms.

1. in, out	syn **ant**	2. right, wrong	syn **ant**	3. quit, stop	**syn** ant

 ### ACTIVITY / ASSIGNMENT TIME

This activity gives students an opportunity to improve their listening skills and their synonym/antonym skills. Say each word aloud and have students name and point out the objects around the house that are antonyms or synonyms for these words. (*Answers may vary.*)

Name an antonym for each of the following words.		Name a synonym for each of the following words.	
Words	**Antonyms**	**Words**	**Synonyms**
1. ceiling	**floor**	4. blinds	**curtains**
2. salt	**pepper**	5. toilet	**commode**
3. washer	**dryer**	6. sofa	**couch**

(End of lesson.)

CHAPTER 7   LESSON 2

Objectives: Jingles, Vocabulary #1, and Grammar (Introductory Sentences, Adverb).

 **JINGLE TIME**

Have students turn to the Jingle Section of their books. The teacher will lead the students in reciting the previously-taught jingles.

 VOCABULARY TIME

Have students turn to page 6 in the Vocabulary Section of their books. Introduce the vocabulary words listed in the vocabulary box below by reciting them together with your students.

Chapter 7, Vocabulary Words #1
quietly, today, fast

 GRAMMAR TIME

Put the introductory sentences from the box below on the board. Use these sentences as you go through the new concepts covered in your teaching scripts. For the greatest benefit, students must participate orally with the teacher. (*You might put the introductory sentences on notebook paper if you are doing one-on-one instruction with your students.*)

Chapter 7, Introductory Sentences for Lesson 2
1. Cats sat quietly today.
2. Boys sat quietly today.
3. Bears ran fast.

TEACHING SCRIPT FOR THE ADVERB

You are learning that jingles give you a lot of information quickly and easily. I will review several things that the Adverb Jingle tells us about the adverb. Listen carefully. **The Adverb Definition:** An adverb modifies a verb. **The Adverb Questions:** How? When? Where?

Teacher's Notes: In Level 2, your child will learn that an adverb also modifies an adjective and another adverb. You are concentrating on modifiers of the verb in Level 1.

CHAPTER 7 LESSON 2 CONTINUED

The adverb definition uses the word *modifies*. The word **modify** means to describe. When the adverb definition says that an adverb modifies a verb, it means that an adverb describes a verb. The abbreviation you will use for an adverb is **Adv**.

You will now learn how to use the adverb definition and the Question and Answer Flow to find the adverbs in sentences. But, first, we will classify the main parts of a sentence, the subject and verb, before we find the adverbs.

Classify Sentence 1: Cats sat quietly today.
What sat quietly today? cats - subject noun (*Write SN above **cats**.*)
What is being said about cats? cats sat - verb (*Write V above **sat**.*)

The Adverb Jingle tells you the adverb definition and the adverb questions. Look at the Adverb Jingle in the Jingle Section on page 3 and repeat the Adverb Jingle with me. (*Repeat the Adverb Jingle with your students again.*) I am going to ask you some questions that will show you how to use the Adverb Jingle to find adverbs. You may look at the Adverb Jingle in your book so you can answer my questions about adverbs.

1. Where do you go to find an adverb? (*to the verb*)

2. What is the verb in Sentence 1? (*sat*)

3. What do you ask after you go to the verb *sat*?

    (*one of the adverb questions: how? when? where?*)

4. How do you know which adverb question to ask?

    (*Look at the words around the verb: quietly, today. These words will guide you.*)

5. Which adverb question would you use to find the first adverb in this sentence? (*how?*)

This is how you would ask an adverb question and give an adverb answer in the Question and Answer Flow: **Sat how? quietly - adverb** (*Write **Adv** above the word **quietly**.*)

Look at the sentence again. As you can see, there is another word that needs to be classified. In order to classify this word, you must again ask the questions that you have learned. You will continue this question-and-answer procedure until all words in the sentence have been identified. That is why we call it the Question and Answer Flow.

Let's go back to the verb and do the Question and Answer Flow for another adverb:
Sat when? today - adverb (*Write **Adv** above the word **today**.*)

I will classify Sentence 1 again, but this time you will classify it with me. I will lead you as we follow the series of questions and answers that I have just demonstrated. Then, we will classify Sentences 2-3.

CHAPTER 7 LESSON 2 CONTINUED

Question and Answer Flow for Sentence 1: Cats sat quietly today.

1. What sat quietly today? cats - subject noun (Trace over the SN above *cats*.)
2. What is being said about cats? cats sat - verb (Trace over the V above *sat*.)
3. Sat how? quietly - adverb (Trace over the Adv above *quietly*.)
4. Sat when? today - adverb (Trace over the Adv above *today*.)

Classified Sentence:

	SN	V	Adv	Adv
	Cats	sat	quietly	today.

Question and Answer Flow for Sentence 2: Boys sat quietly today.

1. Who sat quietly today? boys - subject noun (Write SN above *boys*.)
2. What is being said about boys? boys sat - verb (Write V above *sat*.)
3. Sat how? quietly - adverb (Write Adv above *quietly*.)
4. Sat when? today - adverb (Write over the Adv above *today*.)

Classified Sentence:

	SN	V	Adv	Adv
	Boys	sat	quietly	today.

Question and Answer Flow for Sentence 3: Bears ran fast.

1. What ran fast? bears - subject noun (Write the SN above *bears*.)
2. What is being said about bears? bears ran - verb (Write V above *ran*.)
3. Ran how? fast - adverb (Write Adv above *fast*.)

Classified Sentence:

	SN	V	Adv
	Bears	ran	fast.

TEACHER INSTRUCTIONS

Have students recite the Question and Answer Flows for the first <u>two</u> sentences with you again. This time, they should trace the labels on their desks with the first three fingers of their writing hand as they classify. Next, have students write the <u>third</u> sentence on a sheet of paper. Have them recite the Question and Answer Flow for the third sentence with you again, but this time they should write the labels above the words on their paper. This will give them practice writing the labels before they are tested.

(End of lesson.)

CHAPTER 7   LESSON 3

Objectives: Jingles, Vocabulary #2, Grammar (Practice Sentences), and Activity.

 **JINGLE TIME**

Have students turn to the Jingle Section of their books. The teacher will lead the students in reciting the previously-taught jingles.

 VOCABULARY TIME

Have students turn to page 6 in the Vocabulary Section of their books. Introduce the vocabulary words listed in the vocabulary box below by reciting them together with your students.

Chapter 7, Vocabulary Words #2
quickly, loudly, slowly

 GRAMMAR TIME

Put the Practice Sentences from the box below on the board or on notebook paper. Use these sentences as you practice the concepts that have been taught. For the greatest benefit, students must participate orally with the teacher.

Chapter 7, Practice Sentences for Lesson 3
1. Girls walked quickly.
2. Dogs barked loudly.
3. Bears ran slowly today.

TEACHING SCRIPT FOR PRACTICE SENTENCES

We will classify these three sentences to practice adverbs as we add them to the Question and Answer Flows. We will classify the sentences together. Begin. (_You might have students write the labels above the sentences at this time._)

CHAPTER 7 LESSON 3 CONTINUED

Question and Answer Flow for Sentence 1: Girls walked quickly.

1. Who walked quickly? girls - subject noun (Write SN above *girls*.)
2. What is being said about girls? girls walked - verb (Write V above *walked*.)
3. Walked how? quickly - adverb (Write Adv above *quickly*.)

Classified Sentence: SN   V   Adv
                                    Girls   walked   quickly.

Question and Answer Flow for Sentence 2: Dogs barked loudly.

1. What barked loudly? dogs - subject noun (Write SN above *dogs*.)
2. What is being said about dogs? dogs barked - verb (Write V above *barked*.)
3. Barked how? loudly - adverb (Write Adv above *loudly*.)

Classified Sentence: SN   V   Adv
                                    Dogs   barked   loudly.

Question and Answer Flow for Sentence 3: Bears ran slowly today.

1. What ran slowly today? bears - subject noun (Write SN above *bears*.)
2. What is being said about bears? bears ran - verb (Write V above *ran*.)
3. Ran how? slowly - adverb (Write Adv above *slowly*.)
4. Ran when? today - adverb (Write Adv above *today*.)

Classified Sentence: SN   V   Adv   Adv
                                    Bears   ran   slowly   today.

ACTIVITY / ASSIGNMENT TIME

Have students turn to page 84 in the Activity Section of their books and find Chapter 7, Lesson 3, Activity. Go over the directions to make sure they understand what to do. Check and discuss the Activity after students have finished. (*The four boxes with synonyms in them are shaded and should be colored orange. The rest of the boxes have antonyms in them and should be colored green.*)

Chapter 7, Lesson 3, Activity: Find all the synonyms words in the boxes below and color them orange. Then, find the antonym words and color them green.

sit, stand	lost, found	leap, jump
boat, ship	start, begin	empty, full
easy, hard	small, little	sad, happy

(End of lesson.)

CHAPTER 7   LESSON 4

Objectives: Jingles, Vocabulary #3, Grammar (Practice Sentences), and Writing (Journal).

 **JINGLE TIME**

Have students turn to the Jingle Section of their books. The teacher will lead the students in reciting the previously-taught jingles.

 VOCABULARY TIME

Have students turn to page 6 in the Vocabulary Section of their books. Introduce the vocabulary words listed in the vocabulary box below by reciting them together with your students.

Chapter 7, Vocabulary Words #3
swiftly, yesterday, low

 GRAMMAR TIME

Put the Practice Sentences from the box below on the board or on notebook paper. Use these sentences as you practice the concepts that have been taught. For the greatest benefit, students must participate orally with the teacher.

Chapter 7, Practice Sentences for Lesson 4
1. Boys ran swiftly yesterday.
2. Kittens ran quickly.
3. Airplanes flew low today.

TEACHING SCRIPT FOR PRACTICE SENTENCES

We will classify these three sentences to practice the new parts in the Question and Answer Flows. We will classify the sentences together. Begin.

CHAPTER 7 LESSON 4 CONTINUED

Question and Answer Flow for Sentence 1: Boys ran swiftly yesterday.

1. Who ran swiftly yesterday? boys - subject noun (Write SN above *boys*.)
2. What is being said about boys? boys ran - verb (Write V above *ran*.)
3. Ran how? swiftly - adverb (Write Adv above *swiftly*.)
4. Ran when? yesterday - adverb (Write Adv above *yesterday*.)

Classified Sentence:
SN	V	Adv	Adv
Boys	ran	swiftly	yesterday.

Question and Answer Flow for Sentence 2: Kittens ran quickly.

1. What ran quickly? kittens - subject noun (Write SN above *kittens*.)
2. What is being said about kittens? kittens ran - verb (Write V above *ran*.)
3. Ran how? quickly - adverb (Write Adv above *quickly*.)

Classified Sentence:
SN	V	Adv
Kittens	ran	quickly.

Question and Answer Flow for Sentence 3: Airplanes flew low today.

1. What flew low today? airplanes - subject noun (Write SN above *airplanes*.)
2. What is being said about airplanes? airplanes flew - verb (Write V above *flew*.)
3. Flew how? low - adverb (Write Adv above *low*.)
4. Flew when? today - adverb (Write Adv above *today*.)

Classified Sentence:
SN	V	Adv	Adv
Airplanes	flew	low	today.

TEACHER INSTRUCTIONS

Have students recite the Question and Answer Flows for the first <u>two</u> sentences with you again. This time, they should trace the labels on their desks with the first three fingers of their writing hand as they classify. Next, have students write the <u>third</u> sentence on a sheet of paper. Have them recite the Question and Answer Flow for the third sentence with you again, but this time they should write the labels above the words on their paper. This will give them practice writing the labels before they are tested.

 WRITING TIME

Have students make an entry in their journals.

(End of lesson.)

CHAPTER 7   LESSON 5
Objectives: Jingles, Vocabulary #4, Grammar (Practice Sentences), Test, Check, Writing (Journal), and Activity.

 **JINGLE TIME**

Have students turn to the Jingle Section of their books. The teacher will lead the students in reciting the previously-taught jingles.

 VOCABULARY TIME

Have students turn to page 6 in the Vocabulary Section of their books. Introduce the vocabulary words listed in the vocabulary box below by reciting them together with your students.

Chapter 7, Vocabulary Words #4
away, jumped, puppies

 GRAMMAR TIME

Put the Practice Sentences from the box below on the board or on notebook paper. Use these sentences as you practice the concepts that have been taught. For the greatest benefit, students must participate orally with the teacher.

Chapter 7, Practice Sentences for Lesson 5
1. Ducks walked slowly away.
2. Cats jumped quickly.
3. Puppies played quietly yesterday.

TEACHING SCRIPT FOR PRACTICE SENTENCES

We will classify these three sentences to practice the new parts in the Question and Answer Flows. We will classify the sentences together. Begin.

CHAPTER 7 LESSON 5 CONTINUED

Question and Answer Flow for Sentence 1: Ducks walked slowly away.

1. What walked slowly away? ducks - subject noun (Write SN above *ducks*.)
2. What is being said about ducks? ducks walked - verb (Write V above *walked*.)
3. Walked how? slowly - adverb (Write Adv above *slowly*.)
4. Walked where? away - adverb (Write Adv above *away*.)

Classified Sentence: SN   V   Adv   Adv
                           Ducks walked slowly away.

Question and Answer Flow for Sentence 2: Cats jumped quickly.

1. What jumped quickly? cats - subject noun (Write SN above *cats*.)
2. What is being said about cats? cats jumped - verb (Write V above *jumped*.)
3. Jumped how? quickly - adverb (Write Adv above *quickly*.)

Classified Sentence: SN   V   Adv
                           Cats jumped quickly.

Question and Answer Flow for Sentence 3: Puppies played quietly yesterday.

1. What played quietly yesterday? puppies - subject noun (Write SN above *puppies*.)
2. What is being said about puppies? puppies played - verb (Write V above *played*.)
3. Played how? quietly - adverb (Write Adv above *quietly*.)
4. Played when? yesterday - adverb (Write Adv above *yesterday*.)

Classified Sentence: SN   V   Adv   Adv
                         Puppies played quietly yesterday.

 TEST TIME

Have students turn to page 60 in the Test Section of their books and find Chapter 7 Test. Go over the directions to make sure they understand what to do. (*Chapter 7 Test key is on the next page*.)

Chapter 7 Test
(Student Page 60)

Exercise 1: Classify each sentence. Use **SN** for subject noun, **V** for verb, and **Adv** for adverb.

	SN	V	Adv
1.	Cats	jumped	quickly.

	SN	V	Adv	Adv
2.	Puppies	played	quietly	yesterday.

Exercise 2: Underline the <u>**syn**</u> if the words are synonyms. Underline the <u>**ant**</u> if the words are antonyms.

1. in, out	syn **ant**	2. quit, stop	**syn** ant	3. right, wrong	syn **ant**

Exercise 3: In your journal, write a paragraph summarizing what you have learned this week.

CHECK TIME

After students have finished, check and discuss their test papers. Make sure they understand why their answers are right or wrong. Use the Question and Answer Flows on page 77 in this chapter to check the sentences on the Chapter 7 Test. (*For total points, count each required answer as a point.*)

Teacher's Note: There are no tests for Chapters 1-6. Chapter 7 begins the Testing Section for Level 1.

ACTIVITY / ASSIGNMENT TIME

Have students turn to page 85 in the Activity Section of their books and find Chapter 7, Lesson 5, Activity. Go over the directions to make sure they understand what to do. Check and discuss the Activity after students have finished.

Chapter 7, Lesson 5, Activity: In the Word Search Puzzle below, find the following words and color each one a different color. The words will appear "down" or "across" in the puzzle.

ADVERB   ANTONYM   NOUN   SYNONYM   VERB

S	Y	N	O	N	Y	M
A	V	S	A	C	Q	W
A	N	T	O	N	Y	M
N	T	H	K	O	P	N
R	V	E	R	B	S	O
F	G	H	J	L	K	U
A	D	V	E	R	B	N

(End of lesson.)

CHAPTER 8 LESSON 1

Objectives: Jingle (Adjective), Synonyms, and Antonyms.

 **JINGLE TIME**

Have students turn to the Jingle Section of their books and recite the previously-taught jingles. Then, lead students in reciting the new jingle (*Adjective*) below. Practice the new jingle several times until students can recite it smoothly. Emphasize reciting with a rhythm. (*Do not try to explain the new jingle at this time. Just have fun reciting it. Add motions for more fun and laughter.*)

Jingle 5: Adjective Jingle
An adjective modifies a noun. An adjective asks *What kind? Which one? How many?* To find an adjective: **Go, Ask, Get**. Where do I **go**? To a noun. What do I **ask**? What kind? Which one? How many? What do I **get**? An ADJECTIVE! (Clap) (Clap) That's what!

 SYNONYM AND ANTONYM TIME

Have students turn to the Synonym and Antonym Section of their books. Introduce the new words listed for Chapter 8 in the box below. Make sure students know the meanings of the new synonyms and antonyms. Then, have students underline the correct answers in their books. They should study these words again before their test.

Chapter 8: Underline the **syn** if the words are synonyms. Underline the **ant** if the words are antonyms.
1. over, under syn **ant**   2. warm, cold syn **ant**   3. stone, rock **syn** ant

(End of lesson.)

CHAPTER 8   LESSON 2

Objectives: Jingles, Vocabulary #1, and Grammar (Introductory Sentences, Adjective).

 **JINGLE TIME**

Have students turn to the Jingle Section of their books. The teacher will lead the students in reciting the previously-taught jingles.

 VOCABULARY TIME

Have students turn to page 6 in the Vocabulary Section of their books. Introduce the vocabulary words listed in the vocabulary box below by reciting them together with your students.

Chapter 8, Vocabulary Words #1
two, black, big, brown

 GRAMMAR TIME

Put the introductory sentences from the box below on the board. Use these sentences as you go through the new concepts covered in your teaching scripts. For the greatest benefit, students must participate orally with the teacher. (*You might put the introductory sentences on notebook paper if you are doing one-on-one instruction with your students.*)

Chapter 8, Introductory Sentences for Lesson 2
1. Two black cats sat quietly today.
2. Two big airplanes flew swiftly away.
3. Big brown bears ran fast.

TEACHING SCRIPT FOR THE ADJECTIVE

Remember, jingles give you a lot of information quickly and easily. I will review several things that the Adjective Jingle tells us about the adjective. **The Adjective Definition:** An adjective modifies a noun **The Adjective Questions:** What kind? Which one? How many?

Teacher's Notes: In Level 2, your child will learn that an adjective also modifies a pronoun. You are concentrating on <u>modifiers of the noun</u> in Level 1.

CHAPTER 8 LESSON 2 CONTINUED

The adjective definition also uses the word *modifies*. Remember, the word **modify** means to describe. When the adjective definition says that an adjective modifies a noun, it means that an adjective describes a noun. The abbreviation you will use for an adjective is **Adj**.

You will now learn how to use the adjective definition and the Question and Answer Flow to find the adjectives in sentences. But first, we will classify the subject, verb, and adverb before we find the adjectives.

Classify Sentence 1: Two black cats sat quietly today.
What sat quietly today? cats - subject noun (*Write SN above the word* **cats**.)
What is being said about cats? cats sat - verb (*Write V above the word* **sat**.)
Sat how? quietly - adverb (*Write Adv above the word* **quietly**.)
Sat when? today - adverb (*Write Adv above the word* **today**.)

We will use this same procedure to find the adjectives. The Adjective Jingle tells you the adjective definition and the adjective questions. Look at the Adjective Jingle in the Jingle Section on page 3 and repeat the Adjective Jingle with me. (*Repeat the Adjective Jingle with your students again.*) I am going to ask you some questions that will show you how to use the Adjective Jingle to find adjectives. You may look at the Adjective Jingle in your book so you can answer my questions about adjectives.

1. Where do you go to find an adjective? (*to a noun*)
2. What is the subject noun in Sentence 1? (*cats*)
3. What do you ask after you go to the subject noun *cats*?
   (*one of the adjective questions: what kind? which one? how many?*)
4. How do you know which adjective question to ask?
   (*Look at the word or words around the noun: two, black. These words will guide you.*)
5. Which adjective questions would you use to find an adjective in this sentence?
   (*What kind?* and *How many?*)

This is how you would ask an adjective question and give the adjective answer in the Question and Answer Flow: **What kind of cats? black - adjective** (*Write Adj above the word* **black**.)

Look at the sentence again. As you can see, there is another word that needs to be classified. In order to classify this word, you must again ask one of the questions that you have learned. You will continue this question-and-answer procedure until all words in the sentence have been identified. That is why we call it the Question and Answer Flow.

Let's go back to the noun and do the Question and Answer Flow for another adjective:
How many cats? two - adjective (*Write Adj above the word* **two**.)

I will classify Sentence 1 again, but this time you will classify it with me. I will lead you as we follow the series of questions and answers that I have just demonstrated. Then, we will classify Sentences 2-3.

CHAPTER 8 LESSON 2 CONTINUED

Question and Answer Flow for Sentence 1: Two black cats sat quietly today.

1. What sat quietly today? cats - subject noun (Trace over the SN above *cats*.)
2. What is being said about cats? cats sat - verb (Trace over the V above *sat*.)
3. Sat how? quietly - adverb (Trace over the Adv above *quietly*.)
4. Sat when? today - adverb (Trace over the Adv above *today*.)
5. What kind of cats? black - adjective (Trace over the Adj above *black*.)
6. How many cats? two - adjective (Trace over the Adj above *two*.)

Classified Sentence:

Adj	Adj	SN	V	Adv	Adv
Two	black	cats	sat	quietly	today.

Question and Answer Flow for Sentence 2: Two big airplanes flew swiftly away.

1. What flew swiftly away? airplanes - subject noun (Write SN above *airplanes*.)
2. What is being said about airplanes? airplanes flew - verb (Write V above *flew*.)
3. Flew how? swiftly - adverb (Write Adv above *swiftly*.)
4. Flew where? away - adverb (Write Adv above *away*.)
5. What kind of airplanes? big - adjective (Write Adj above *big*.)
6. How many airplanes? two - adjective (Write Adj above *two*.)

Classified Sentence:

Adj	Adj	SN	V	Adv	Adv
Two	big	airplanes	flew	swiftly	away.

Question and Answer Flow for Sentence 3: Big brown bears ran fast.

1. What ran fast? bears - subject noun (Write the SN above *bears*.)
2. What is being said about bears? bears ran - verb (Write V above *ran*.)
3. Ran how? fast - adverb (Write Adv above *fast*.)
4. What kind of bears? brown - adjective (Write Adj above *brown*.)
5. What kind of bears? big - adjective (Write Adj above *big*.)

Classified Sentence:

Adj	Adj	SN	V	Adv
Big	brown	bears	ran	fast.

TEACHER INSTRUCTIONS

Have students recite the Question and Answer Flows for the first two sentences with you again. This time, they should trace the labels on their desks with the first three fingers of their writing hand as they classify. Next, have students write the third sentence on a sheet of paper. Have them recite the Question and Answer Flow for the third sentence with you again, but this time they should write the labels above the words on their paper. This will give them practice writing the labels before they are tested.

(End of lesson.)

CHAPTER 8   LESSON 3

Objectives: Jingles, Vocabulary #2, Grammar (Practice Sentences), and Activity.

 **JINGLE TIME**

Have students turn to the Jingle Section in their books. The teacher will lead the students in reciting the previously-taught jingles.

 VOCABULARY TIME

Have students turn to page 6 in the Vocabulary Section of their books. Introduce the vocabulary words listed in the vocabulary box below by reciting them together with your students.

Chapter 8, Vocabulary Words #2
three, laughed, squirmy

 GRAMMAR TIME

Put the Practice Sentences from the box below on the board or on notebook paper. Use these sentences as you practice the concepts that have been taught. For the greatest benefit, students must participate orally with the teacher.

Chapter 8, Practice Sentences for Lesson 3
1. Three boys laughed loudly.
2. Three squirmy puppies barked loudly today.
3. Two brown ducks sat quietly yesterday.

TEACHING SCRIPT FOR PRACTICE SENTENCES

We will classify these three sentences to practice adjectives as we add them to the Question and Answer Flows. We will classify the sentences together. Begin. (*You might have students write the labels above the sentences at this time.*)

CHAPTER 8 LESSON 3 CONTINUED

Question and Answer Flow for Sentence 1: Three boys laughed loudly.

1. Who laughed loudly? boys - subject noun (Write SN above *boys*.)
2. What is being said about boys? boys laughed - verb (Write V above *laughed*.)
3. Laughed how? loudly - adverb (Write Adv above *loudly*.)
4. How many boys? three - adjective (Write Adj above *three*.)

Classified Sentence:

Adj	SN	V	Adv
Three	boys	laughed	loudly.

Question and Answer Flow for Sentence 2: Three squirmy puppies barked loudly today.

1. What barked loudly today? puppies - subject noun (Write SN above *puppies*.)
2. What is being said about puppies? puppies barked - verb (Write V above *barked*.)
3. Barked how? loudly - adverb (Write Adv above *loudly*.)
4. Barked when? today - adverb (Write Adv above *today*.)
5. What kind of puppies? squirmy - adjective (Write Adj above *squirmy*.)
6. How many puppies? three - adjective (Write Adj above *three*.)

Classified Sentence:

Adj	Adj	SN	V	Adv	Adv
Three	squirmy	puppies	barked	loudly	today.

Question and Answer Flow for Sentence 3: Two brown ducks sat quietly yesterday.

1. What sat quietly yesterday? ducks - subject noun (Write SN above *ducks*.)
2. What is being said about ducks? ducks sat - verb (Write V above *sat*.)
3. Sat how? quietly - adverb (Write Adv above *quietly*.)
4. Sat when? yesterday - adverb (Write Adv above *yesterday*.)
5. What kind of ducks? brown - adjective (Write Adj above *brown*.)
6. How many ducks? two - adjective (Write Adj above *two*.)

Classified Sentence:

Adj	Adj	SN	V	Adv	Adv
Two	brown	ducks	sat	quietly	yesterday.

TEACHER INSTRUCTIONS

Have students recite the Question and Answer Flows for the first two sentences with you again. This time, they should trace the labels on their desks with the first three fingers of their writing hand as they classify. Next, have students write the third sentence on a sheet of paper. Have them recite the Question and Answer Flow for the third sentence with you again, but this time they should write the labels above the words on their paper. This will give them practice writing the labels before they are tested.

 ACTIVITY / ASSIGNMENT TIME

Time students for one minute as they name nouns that can be described by the color red.

(End of lesson.)

CHAPTER 8   LESSON 4

Objectives: Jingles, Vocabulary #3, Grammar (Practice Sentences), and Writing (Journal).

 **JINGLE TIME**

Have students turn to the Jingle Section in their books. The teacher will lead the students in reciting the previously-taught jingles.

 VOCABULARY TIME

Have students turn to page 6 in the Vocabulary Section of their books. Introduce the vocabulary words listed in the vocabulary box below by reciting them together with your students.

Chapter 8, Vocabulary Words #3
several, little, happily, four

 GRAMMAR TIME

Put the Practice Sentences from the box below on the board or on notebook paper. Use these sentences as you practice the concepts that have been taught. For the greatest benefit, students must participate orally with the teacher.

Chapter 8, Practice Sentences for Lesson 4
1. Several little girls laughed happily.
2. Little kittens ran swiftly yesterday.
3. Four big airplanes flew fast today.

TEACHING SCRIPT FOR PRACTICE SENTENCES

We will classify these three sentences to practice the new parts in the Question and Answer Flows. We will classify the sentences together. Begin.

CHAPTER 8 LESSON 4 CONTINUED

Question and Answer Flow for Sentence 1: Several little girls laughed happily.

1. Who laughed happily? girls - subject noun (Write SN above *girls*.)
2. What is being said about girls? girls laughed - verb (Write V above *laughed*.)
3. Laughed how? happily - adverb (Write Adv above *happily*.)
4. What kind of girls? little - adjective (Write Adj above *little*.)
5. How many girls? several - adjective (Write Adj above *several*.)

Classified Sentence: Adj   Adj   SN   V   Adv

                           Several   little   girls   laughed   happily.

Question and Answer Flow for Sentence 2: Little kittens ran swiftly yesterday.

1. What ran swiftly yesterday? kittens - subject noun (Write SN above *kittens*.)
2. What is being said about kittens? kittens ran - verb (Write V above *ran*.)
3. Ran how? swiftly - adverb (Write Adv above *swiftly*.)
4. Ran when? yesterday - adverb (Write Adv above *yesterday*.)
5. What kind of kittens? little - adjective (Write Adj above *little*.)

Classified Sentence: Adj   SN   V   Adv   Adv

                           Little   kittens   ran   swiftly   yesterday.

Question and Answer Flow for Sentence 3: Four big airplanes flew fast today.

1. What flew fast today? airplanes - subject noun (Write SN above *airplanes*.)
2. What is being said about airplanes? airplanes flew - verb (Write V above *flew*.)
3. Flew how? fast - adverb (Write Adv above *fast*.)
4. Flew when? today - adverb (Write Adv above *today*.)
5. What kind of airplanes? big - adjective (Write Adj above *big*.)
6. How many airplanes? four - adjective (Write Adj above *four*.)

Classified Sentence: Adj   Adj   SN   V   Adv   Adv

                           Four   big   airplanes   flew   fast   today.

TEACHER INSTRUCTIONS

Have students recite the Question and Answer Flows for the first <u>two</u> sentences with you again. This time, they should trace the labels on their desks with the first three fingers of their writing hand as they classify. Next, have students write the <u>third</u> sentence on a sheet of paper. Have them recite the Question and Answer Flow for the third sentence with you again, but this time they should write the labels above the words on their paper. This will give them practice writing the labels before they are tested.

 WRITING TIME

Have students make an entry in their journals.

(End of lesson.)

CHAPTER 8   LESSON 5

Objectives: Jingles, Vocabulary #4, Grammar (Practice Sentences), Test, Check, Writing (Journal), and Activity.

 **JINGLE TIME**

Have students turn to the Jingle Section in their books. The teacher will lead the students in reciting the previously-taught jingles.

 VOCABULARY TIME

Have students turn to page 6 in the Vocabulary Section of their books. Introduce the vocabulary words listed in the vocabulary box below by reciting them together with your students.

Chapter 8, Vocabulary Words #4
yellow, waddled, children

 GRAMMAR TIME

Put the Practice Sentences from the box below on the board or on notebook paper. Use these sentences as you practice the concepts that have been taught. For the greatest benefit, students must participate orally with the teacher.

Chapter 8, Practice Sentences for Lesson 5
1. Several little yellow ducks waddled away.
2. Four little kittens jumped quickly.
3. Several children played quietly today.

TEACHING SCRIPT FOR PRACTICE SENTENCES

We will classify these three sentences to practice the new parts in the Question and Answer Flows. We will classify the sentences together. Begin.

CHAPTER 8 LESSON 5 CONTINUED

Question and Answer Flow for Sentence 1: Several little yellow ducks waddled away.

1. What waddled away? ducks - subject noun (Write SN above *ducks*.)
2. What is being said about ducks? ducks waddled - verb (Write V above *waddled*.)
3. Waddled where? away - adverb (Write Adv above *away*.)
4. What kind of ducks? yellow - adjective (Write Adj above *yellow*.)
5. What kind of ducks? little - adjective (Write Adj above *little*.)
6. How many ducks? several - adjective (Write Adj above *several*.)

Classified Sentence:	Adj	Adj	Adj	SN	V	Adv
	Several	little	yellow	ducks	waddled	away.

Question and Answer Flow for Sentence 2: Four little kittens jumped quickly.

1. What jumped quickly? kittens - subject noun (Write SN above *kittens*.)
2. What is being said about kittens? kittens jumped - verb (Write V above *jumped*.)
3. Jumped how? quickly - adverb (Write Adv above *quickly*.)
4. What kind of kittens? little - adjective (Write Adj above *little*.)
5. How many kittens? four - adjective (Write Adj above *four*.)

Classified Sentence:	Adj	Adj	SN	V	Adv
	Four	little	kittens	jumped	quickly.

Question and Answer Flow for Sentence 3: Several children played quietly today.

1. Who played quietly today? children - subject noun (Write SN above *children*.)
2. What is being said about children? children played - verb (Write V above *played*.)
3. Played how? quietly - adverb (Write Adv above *quietly*.)
4. Played when? today - adverb (Write Adv above *today*.)
5. How many children? several - adjective (Write Adj above *several*.)

Classified Sentence:	Adj	SN	V	Adv	Adv
	Several	children	played	quietly	today.

TEST TIME

Have students turn to page 61 in the Test Section of their books and find Chapter 8 Test. Go over the directions to make sure they understand what to do. (*Chapter 8 Test key is on the next page.*)

Level 1 Homeschool Teacher's Manual

Chapter 8 Test
(Student Page 61)

Exercise 1: Classify each sentence. Use **SN** for subject noun, **V** for verb, **Adv** for adverb, and **Adj** for adjective.

	Adj	Adj	SN	V	Adv	Adv
1.	Three	squirmy	puppies	barked	loudly	today.

	Adj	Adj	SN	V	Adv	Adv
2.	Two	brown	ducks	sat	quietly	yesterday.

Exercise 2: Underline the <u>syn</u> if the words are synonyms. Underline the <u>ant</u> if the words are antonyms.

1. stone, rock	**syn** ant	2. warm, cold	syn **ant**	3. over, under	syn **ant**

Exercise 3: In your journal, write a paragraph summarizing what you have learned this week.

 **CHECK TIME**

After students have finished, check and discuss their test papers. Make sure they understand why their answers are right or wrong. Use the Question and Answer Flows on page 84 in this chapter to check the sentences on the Chapter 8 Test. (*For total points, count each required answer as a point.*)

 ACTIVITY / ASSIGNMENT TIME

Tell students that they will make shakers today. They can use the shakers during Jingle Time or during break time. Shakers are popular instruments in many places. Have students decorate a cardboard paper-towel roll. Fill the roll with beads, rice, or dried beans. Seal both ends with cellophane or wax paper, held tight by rubber bands. For a different shaker, have students decorate two paper cups or two paper plates. Add dry beans, then tape the two cups or the two paper plates together. Ribbon or crepe paper streamers can be added to the shakers for more variety. This will give students a chance to have fun during Jingle Time or while they stretch during break time.

(End of lesson.)

CHAPTER 9   LESSON 1

Objectives: Jingle (Article Adjective), Synonyms, and Antonyms.

 **JINGLE TIME**

Have students turn to the Jingle Section in their books and recite the previously-taught jingles. Then, lead students in reciting the new jingle (*Article Adjective*) below. Practice the new jingle several times until students can recite it smoothly. Emphasize reciting with a rhythm. (*Do not try to explain the new jingle at this time. Just have fun reciting it. Add motions for more fun and laughter.*)

Jingle 6: Article Adjective Jingle

We are the article adjectives,
Teeny, tiny adjectives:
A, AN, THE - A, AN, THE.

We are called article adjectives and noun markers;
We are memorized and used every day.
So, if you spot us, you can mark us
With the label A.

We are the article adjectives,
Teeny, tiny adjectives:
A, AN, THE - A, AN, THE.

 SYNONYM AND ANTONYM TIME

Have students turn to the Synonym and Antonym Section of their books. Introduce the new words listed for Chapter 9 in the box below. Make sure students know the meanings of the new synonyms and antonyms. Then, have students underline the correct answers in their books. They should study these words again before their test.

Chapter 9: Underline the **syn** if the words are synonyms. Underline the **ant** if the words are antonyms.

1. up, down	syn **ant**	2. push, pull	syn **ant**	3. start, begin	**syn** ant

---

(End of lesson.)

CHAPTER 9   LESSON 2

Objectives: Jingles, Vocabulary #1, and Grammar (Introductory Sentences, Article Adjective).

 **JINGLE TIME**

Have students turn to the Jingle Section of their books. The teacher will lead the students in reciting the previously-taught jingles.

 VOCABULARY TIME

Have students turn to page 6 in the Vocabulary Section of their books. Introduce the vocabulary words listed in the vocabulary box below by reciting them together with your students.

Chapter 9, Vocabulary Words #1
yawned, horse, raced

 GRAMMAR TIME

Put the introductory sentences from the box below on the board. Use these sentences as you go through the new concepts covered in your teaching scripts. For the greatest benefit, students must participate orally with the teacher. (*You might put the introductory sentences on notebook paper if you are doing one-on-one instruction with your students.*)

Chapter 9, Introductory Sentences for Lesson 2
1. The three yellow cats walked quietly today.
2. Four squirmy puppies yawned loudly yesterday.
3. A brown horse raced quickly away.

TEACHING SCRIPT FOR THE ARTICLE ADJECTIVE

Today, we have another adjective to identify. This new adjective is known as the article adjective. There are only three article adjectives. Let's recite the Article Adjective Jingle again to learn more about the article adjectives. (*Recite the Article Adjective Jingle with your students.*)

CHAPTER 9 LESSON 2 CONTINUED

Article Adjectives are the three most commonly-used adjectives. The three article adjectives are *a, an,* and *the.* Everyone repeat the words *article adjective* three times. (*article adjective, article adjective, article adjective*) Article adjectives are sometimes called noun markers because they tell that a noun is close by.

The article adjectives must be <u>memorized</u> because there are no questions in the Question and Answer Flow to find the article adjectives. Article adjectives are labeled with an **A**. This is how you would identify an article adjective in the Question and Answer Flow: **The – article adjective** (*Write **A** above the word **The**.*) Now, we will classify a set of sentences together to practice the new concepts. Begin.

Question and Answer Flow for Sentence 1: The three yellow cats walked quietly today.

1. What walked quietly today? cats - SN (subject noun)
2. What is being said about cats? cats walked - V (verb)
3. Walked how? quietly - Adv (adverb)
4. Walked when? today - Adv (adverb)
5. What kind of cats? yellow - Adj (adjective)
6. How many cats? three - Adj (adjective)
7. The - A (*Say: article adjective.*)

Classified Sentence:

A	Adj	Adj	SN	V	Adv	Adv
The	three	yellow	cats	walked	quietly	today.

Question and Answer Flow for Sentence 2: Four squirmy puppies yawned loudly yesterday.

1. What yawned loudly yesterday? puppies - SN (subject noun)
2. What is being said about puppies? puppies yawned - V (verb)
3. Yawned how? loudly - Adv (adverb)
4. Yawned when? yesterday - Adv (adverb)
5. What kind of puppies? squirmy - Adj (adjective)
6. How many puppies? four - Adj (adjective)

Classified Sentence:

Adj	Adj	SN	V	Adv	Adv
Four	squirmy	puppies	yawned	loudly	yesterday.

Question and Answer Flow for Sentence 3: A brown horse raced quickly away.

1. What raced quickly away? horse - SN (subject noun)
2. What is being said about horse? horse raced - V (verb)
3. Raced how? quickly - Adv (adverb)
4. Raced where? away - Adv (adverb)
5. What kind of horse? brown - Adj (adjective)
6. A - A (*Say: article adjective.*)

Classified Sentence:

A	Adj	SN	V	Adv	Adv
A	brown	horse	raced	quickly	away.

TEACHER INSTRUCTIONS

Have students recite the Question and Answer Flows for the first <u>two</u> sentences with you again. This time, they should trace the labels on their desks with the first three fingers of their writing hand as they classify. Next, have students write the <u>third</u> sentence on a sheet of paper. Have them recite the Question and Answer Flow for the third sentence with you again, but this time they should write the labels above the words on their paper. This will give them practice writing the labels before they are tested.

(End of lesson.)

CHAPTER 9   LESSON 3

Objectives: Jingles, Vocabulary #2, Grammar (Practice Sentences, Parts of Speech), and Activity.

 **JINGLE TIME**

Have students turn to the Jingle Section of their books. The teacher will lead the students in reciting the previously-taught jingles.

 VOCABULARY TIME

Have students turn to page 6 in the Vocabulary Section of their books. Introduce the vocabulary words listed in the vocabulary box below by reciting them together with your students.

Chapter 9, Vocabulary Words #2
excited, shouted, tired

 GRAMMAR TIME

Put the Practice Sentences from the box below on the board or on notebook paper. Use these sentences as you practice the concepts that have been taught. For the greatest benefit, students must participate orally with the teacher.

Chapter 9, Practice Sentences for Lesson 3
1. An excited boy shouted loudly.
2. The three tired kittens yawned quietly today.
3. The four black horses raced swiftly.

TEACHING SCRIPT FOR PRACTICE SENTENCES

We will classify these three sentences to practice article adjectives as we add them to the Question and Answer Flows. We will classify the sentences together. Begin. (*You might have students write the labels above the sentences at this time.*)

Question and Answer Flow for Sentence 1: An excited boy shouted loudly.

1. Who shouted loudly? boy - SN (subject noun)
2. What is being said about boy? boy shouted - V (verb)
3. Shouted how? loudly - Adv (adverb)

4. What kind of boy? excited - Adj (adjective)
5. An - A (*Say: article adjective.*)

Classified Sentence:

A	Adj	SN	V	Adv
An	excited	boy	shouted	loudly.

CHAPTER 9 LESSON 3 CONTINUED

Question and Answer Flow for Sentence 2: The three tired kittens yawned quietly today.

1. What yawned quietly today? kittens - SN (subject noun)
2. What is being said about kittens?
   kittens yawned - V (verb)
3. Yawned how? quietly - Adv (adverb)
4. Yawned when? today - Adv (adverb)
5. What kind of kittens? tired - Adj (adjective)
6. How many kittens? three - Adj (adjective)
7. The - A (*Say: article adjective*)

Classified Sentence:	A	Adj	Adj	SN	V	Adv	Adv
	The	three	tired	kittens	yawned	quietly	today.

Question and Answer Flow for Sentence 3: The four black horses raced swiftly.

1. What raced swiftly? horses - SN (subject noun)
2. What is being said about horses? horses raced - V (verb)
3. Raced how? swiftly - Adv (adverb)
4. What kind of horses? black - Adj (adjective)
5. How many horses? four - Adj (adjective)
6. The - A (*Say: article adjective*)

Classified Sentence:	A	Adj	Adj	SN	V	Adv
	The	four	black	horses	raced	swiftly.

TEACHING SCRIPT FOR THE PARTS OF SPEECH

What are the parts of a sentence that we have learned during the Question and Answer Flows so far? *(nouns, verbs, adverbs, adjectives, and article adjectives)* These parts of a sentence that you have just named are known as **parts of speech.** Any time we talk about the parts of a sentence, I will say the words *parts of speech.* We will identify the article adjective as an adjective when we talk about parts of speech. So, how many parts of speech have we studied? *(Four: nouns, verbs, adverbs, and adjectives)*

ACTIVITY / ASSIGNMENT TIME

Have students turn to page 85 in the Activity Section of their books and find Chapter 9, Lesson 3, Activity. Go over the directions to make sure they understand what to do. Check and discuss the Activity after students have finished.

Chapter 9, Lesson 3, Activity: Follow the directions below to make a noun box.

Cover a shoe box and the lid of the shoe box with white paper. You can use glue or tape to make the white paper fit the box neatly. This is your noun box. Divide the inside of the shoe box into three sections with two cardboard pieces. Identify each section as **person, place,** or **thing**. Using items around the house *(magazines, catalogs, books, travel brochures, etc.)*, cut out pictures of nouns and place them in their appropriate section.

Each night, have a member of the family draw a noun from the box. The family member must use the noun in a sentence that he/she writes on a strip of paper. After you read their sentence, color the sentence strip and glue it on the noun box. Friends and other relatives may also participate in decorating the noun box with sentence strips. They should sign their names on the sentence strips they have written. Later, another game can be played to guess who wrote the sentences using the nouns from the noun box. Everyone can guess who wrote the most sentences.

(End of lesson.)

CHAPTER 9   LESSON 4

Objectives: Jingles, Vocabulary #3, Grammar (Practice Sentences), and Writing (Journal).

 **JINGLE TIME**

Have students turn to the Jingle Section of their books. The teacher will lead the students in reciting the previously-taught jingles.

 VOCABULARY TIME

Have students turn to page 6 in the Vocabulary Section of their books. Introduce the vocabulary words listed in the vocabulary box below by reciting them together with your students.

Chapter 9, Vocabulary Words #3
large, ships, sailed, rapidly

 GRAMMAR TIME

Put the Practice Sentences from the box below on the board or on notebook paper. Use these sentences as you practice the concepts that have been taught. For the greatest benefit, students must participate orally with the teacher.

Chapter 9, Practice Sentences for Lesson 4
1. Four large ducks waddled slowly.
2. A large horse jumped quickly.
3. Several large ships sailed rapidly away.

TEACHING SCRIPT FOR PRACTICE SENTENCES

We will classify these three sentences to practice the new parts in the Question and Answer Flows. We will classify the sentences together. Begin.

CHAPTER 9 LESSON 4 CONTINUED

Question and Answer Flow for Sentence 1: Four large ducks waddled slowly.

1. What waddled slowly? ducks - SN (subject noun)
2. What is being said about ducks?
   ducks waddled - V (verb)
3. Waddled how? slowly - Adv (adverb)
4. What kind of ducks? large - Adj (adjective)
5. How many ducks? four - Adj (adjective)

Classified Sentence:

Adj	Adj	SN	V	Adv
Four	large	ducks	waddled	slowly.

Question and Answer Flow for Sentence 2: A large horse jumped quickly.

1. What jumped quickly? horse - SN (subject noun)
2. What is being said about horse? horse jumped - V (verb)
3. Jumped how? quickly - Adv (adverb)
4. What kind of horse? large - Adj (adjective)
5. A - A (*article adjective*)

Classified Sentence:

A	Adj	SN	V	Adv
A	large	horse	jumped	quickly.

Question and Answer Flow for Sentence 3: Several large ships sailed rapidly away.

1. What sailed rapidly away? ships - SN (subject noun)
2. What is being said about ships? ships sailed - V (verb)
3. Sailed how? rapidly - Adv (adverb)
4. Sailed where? away - Adv (adverb)
5. What kind of ships? large - Adj (adjective)
6. How many ships? several - Adj (adjective)

Classified Sentence:

Adj	Adj	SN	V	Adv	Adv
Several	large	ships	sailed	rapidly	away.

TEACHER INSTRUCTIONS

Have students recite the Question and Answer Flows for the first two sentences with you again. This time, they should trace the labels on their desks with the first three fingers of their writing hand as they classify. Next, have students write the third sentence on a sheet of paper. Have them recite the Question and Answer Flow for the third sentence with you again, but this time they should write the labels above the words on their paper. This will give them practice writing the labels before they are tested.

 **WRITING TIME**

Have students make an entry in their journals.

(End of lesson.)

CHAPTER 9   LESSON 5

Objectives: Jingles, Vocabulary #4, Grammar (Practice Sentences), Test, Check, and Writing (Journal).

 **JINGLE TIME**

Have students turn to the Jingle Section of their books. The teacher will lead the students in reciting the previously-taught jingles.

 VOCABULARY TIME

Have students turn to page 6 in the Vocabulary Section of their books. Introduce the vocabulary words listed in the vocabulary box below by reciting them together with your students.

Chapter 9, Vocabulary Words #4
busy, beavers, worked

 GRAMMAR TIME

Put the Practice Sentences from the box below on the board or on notebook paper. Use these sentences as you practice the concepts that have been taught. For the greatest benefit, students must participate orally with the teacher.

Chapter 9, Practice Sentences for Lesson 5
1. The busy beavers worked yesterday.
2. A little squirmy puppy yawned happily.
3. Two large ships sailed away yesterday.

TEACHING SCRIPT FOR PRACTICE SENTENCES

We will classify these three sentences to practice the new parts in the Question and Answer Flows. We will classify the sentences together. Begin.

CHAPTER 9 LESSON 5 CONTINUED

Question and Answer Flow for Sentence 1: The busy beavers worked yesterday.

1. What worked yesterday? beavers - SN (subject noun)
2. What is being said about beavers?
   beavers worked - V (verb)
3. Worked when? yesterday - Adv (adverb)
4. What kind of beavers? busy - Adj (adjective)
5. The - A (*article adjective*)

Classified Sentence:	A	Adj	SN	V	Adv
	The	busy	beavers	worked	yesterday.

Question and Answer Flow for Sentence 2: A little squirmy puppy yawned happily.

1. What yawned happily? puppy - SN (subject noun)
2. What is being said about puppy?
   puppy yawned - V (verb)
3. Yawned how? happily - Adv (adverb)
4. What kind of puppy? squirmy - Adj (adjective)
5. What kind of puppy? little - Adj (adjective)
6. A - A (*article adjective*)

Classified Sentence:	A	Adj	Adj	SN	V	Adv
	A	little	squirmy	puppy	yawned	happily.

Question and Answer Flow for Sentence 3: Two large ships sailed away yesterday.

1. What sailed away yesterday?
   ships - SN (subject noun)
2. What is being said about ships?
   ships sailed - V (verb)
3. Sailed where? away - Adv (adverb)
4. Sailed when? yesterday - Adv (adverb)
5. What kind of ships? large - Adj (adjective)
6. How many ships? two - Adj (adjective)

Classified Sentence:	Adj	Adj	SN	V	Adv	Adv
	Two	large	ships	sailed	away	yesterday.

 **TEST TIME**

Have students turn to page 62 in the Test Section of their books and find Chapter 9 Test. Go over the directions to make sure they understand what to do. (*Chapter 9 Test key is on the next page.*)

Chapter 9 Test
(Student Page 62)

Exercise 1: Classify each sentence. Use **SN** for subject noun, **V** for verb, **Adv** for adverb, **Adj** for adjective, and **A** for article adjective.

	A	Adj	Adj	SN	V	Adv	Adv
1.	The	three	yellow	cats	walked	quietly	today.

	A	Adj	SN	V	Adv	Adv
2.	A	brown	horse	raced	quickly	away.

Exercise 2: Underline the <u>syn</u> if the words are synonyms. Underline the <u>ant</u> if the words are antonyms.

| 1. start, begin | <u>syn</u> ant | 2. up, down | syn <u>ant</u> | 3. push, pull | syn <u>ant</u> |

Exercise 3: Name the four parts of speech that you have studied. (*You may use abbreviations.*)
(The order of the answers may vary.)

1. **noun (N)**   2. **verb (V)**   3. **adjective (Adj)**   4. **adverb (Adv)**

Exercise 4: In your journal, write a paragraph summarizing what you have learned this week.

CHECK TIME

After students have finished, check and discuss their test papers. Make sure they understand why their answers are right or wrong. Use the Question and Answer Flows on page 92 in this chapter to check the sentences on the Chapter 9 Test. (*For total points, count each required answer as a point.*)

(End of lesson.)

CHAPTER 10   LESSON 1

Objectives: Jingles, Synonyms, Antonyms, Skill (Complete Subject and Complete Predicate), and Practice Exercise.

 **JINGLE TIME**

Have students turn to the Jingle Section in their books. The teacher will lead the students in reciting the previously-taught jingles.

 SYNONYM AND ANTONYM TIME

Have students turn to the Synonym and Antonym Section of their books. Introduce the new words listed for Chapter 10 in the box below. Make sure students know the meanings of the new synonyms and antonyms. Then, have students underline the correct answers in their books. They should study these words again before their test.

Chapter 10: Underline the <u>**syn**</u> if the words are synonyms. Underline the <u>**ant**</u> if the words are antonyms.		
1. giant, huge <u>**syn**</u> ant	2. front, back syn <u>**ant**</u>	3. rough, smooth syn <u>**ant**</u>

 SKILL TIME

TEACHING SCRIPT FOR COMPLETE SUBJECT AND COMPLETE PREDICATE

You are learning new vocabulary words that will help you understand English terms. Today, you will learn about the **complete subject** and the **complete predicate**. Look at Reference 4 on page 15 in your Reference Section. (*Reference 4 is located on the next page.*)

Before we begin, I want you to say the words **complete subject** three times. (*Repeat the words **complete subject** three times with your students.*)

Look at number 1 in your reference box. Follow along as I read the definition to you. **"The complete subject is the subject and all the words that describe the subject."** The complete subject usually starts at the beginning of the sentence and includes every word up to the verb of the sentence. In other words, the complete subject has the subject noun plus all the words that tell about the subject.

CHAPTER 10 LESSON 1 CONTINUED

Reference 4: Definitions for Complete Subject, Complete Predicate
1. The **complete subject** is the subject and all the words that describe the subject.
2. The **complete predicate** is the verb and all the words that describe the verb.
Sample Sentence: <u>The little brown pony</u> <u><u>galloped swiftly yesterday</u></u>.

Let's find the complete subject in the sample sentence in Reference 4. What is the complete subject? (*The little brown pony*) Notice that the complete subject has been underlined one time to identify all the subject parts. (*The little brown pony*) Remember, you should never include the verb in the complete subject.

Now, we will learn about the complete predicate. Since the first part of the sentence is the complete subject, it will be easy for you to find the complete predicate. But, first, I want you to say the words **complete predicate** three times. (*Repeat the words **complete predicate** three times with your students.*)

Look at number 2 in your reference box. Follow along as I read the definition to you. "**The complete predicate is the verb and all the words that describe the verb.**" The complete predicate usually starts with the verb and includes every word after the verb. In other words, the complete predicate has the verb plus all the words that tell about the verb.

Let's find the complete predicate in the sample sentence. What is the complete predicate? (*galloped swiftly yesterday*) Notice that the complete predicate has been underlined two times to identify all the predicate parts. (*galloped swiftly yesterday*) Remember, you should start with the verb and go to the end of the sentence for the complete predicate.

 PRACTICE TIME

Have students turn to page 28 in the Practice Section of their book and find Chapter 10, Lesson 1, Practice. Go over the directions to make sure they understand what to do. Check and discuss the Practice after students have finished. (*Chapter 10, Lesson 1, Practice key is given below.*)

Chapter 10, Lesson 1, Practice: Classify the sentence below. Use **SN** for subject noun, **V** for verb, **Adv** for adverb, **Adj** for adjective, and **A** for article adjective. Underline the complete subject <u>one</u> time and the complete predicate <u>two</u> times.
A   Adj   Adj   SN   V   Adv   Adv <u>The   seven   white   rabbits</u>   <u><u>hopped   quickly   away</u></u>.

(End of lesson.)

CHAPTER 10   LESSON 2

Objectives: Jingles, Vocabulary #1, Grammar (Practice Sentences), and Practice Exercise.

 **JINGLE TIME**

Have students turn to the Jingle Section of their books. The teacher will lead the students in reciting the previously-taught jingles.

 VOCABULARY TIME

Have students turn to page 6 in the Vocabulary Section of their books. Introduce the vocabulary words listed in the vocabulary box below by reciting them together with your students.

Chapter 10, Vocabulary Words #1
stopped, suddenly, clowns

 GRAMMAR TIME

Put the Practice Sentences from the box below on the board or on notebook paper. Use these sentences as you practice the concepts that have been taught. For the greatest benefit, students must participate orally with the teacher.

Chapter 10, Practice Sentences for Lesson 2
1. Three large beavers walked slowly.
2. The excited boys stopped suddenly.
3. Four big clowns laughed loudly.

TEACHING SCRIPT FOR PRACTICE SENTENCES

We will classify these three sentences to practice what we have learned. We will classify the sentences together. Begin.

CHAPTER 10 LESSON 2 CONTINUED

Question and Answer Flow for Sentence 1: Three large beavers walked slowly.

1. What walked slowly? beavers - SN (subject noun)
2. What is being said about beavers? beavers walked - V (verb)
3. Walked how? slowly - Adv (adverb)

4. What kind of beavers? large - Adj (adjective)
5. How many beavers? three - Adj (adjective)

Classified Sentence:

Adj	Adj	SN	V	Adv
Three	large	beavers	walked	slowly.

Question and Answer Flow for Sentence 2: The excited boys stopped suddenly.

1. Who stopped suddenly? boys - SN (subject noun)
2. What is being said about boys? boys stopped - V (verb)
3. Stopped how? suddenly - Adv (adverb)

4. What kind of boys? excited - Adj (adjective)
5. The - A (*article adjective*)

Classified Sentence:

A	Adj	SN	V	Adv
The	excited	boys	stopped	suddenly.

Question and Answer Flow for Sentence 3: Four big clowns laughed loudly.

1. Who laughed loudly? clowns - SN (subject noun)
2. What is being said about clowns? clowns laughed - V (verb)
3. Laughed how? loudly - Adv (adverb)

4. What kind of clowns? big - Adj (adjective)
5. How many clowns? four - Adj (adjective)

Classified Sentence:

Adj	Adj	SN	V	Adv
Four	big	clowns	laughed	loudly.

 PRACTICE TIME

Have students turn to page 28 in the Practice Section of their book and find Chapter 10, Lesson 2, Practice. Go over the directions to make sure they understand what to do. Check and discuss the Practice after students have finished. (*Chapter 10, Lesson 2, Practice key is given below.*)

Chapter 10, Lesson 2, Practice: Classify the sentence below. Use **SN** for subject noun, **V** for verb, **Adv** for adverb, **Adj** for adjective, and **A** for article adjective. Underline the complete subject <u>one</u> time and the complete predicate <u>two</u> times.

A	Adj	Adj	SN	V	Adv
The	three	young	actors	bowed	gracefully.

(End of lesson.)

CHAPTER 10   LESSON 3

Objectives: Jingles, Vocabulary #2, Grammar (Practice Sentences), and Practice Exercise.

 **JINGLE TIME**

Have students turn to the Jingle Section of their books. The teacher will lead the students in reciting the previously-taught jingles.

 VOCABULARY TIME

Have students turn to page 6 in the Vocabulary Section of their books. Introduce the vocabulary words listed in the vocabulary box below by reciting them together with your students.

Chapter 10, Vocabulary Words #2
five, home, cute, baby

 GRAMMAR TIME

Put the Practice Sentences from the box below on the board or on notebook paper. Use these sentences as you practice the concepts that have been taught. For the greatest benefit, students must participate orally with the teacher.

Chapter 10, Practice Sentences for Lesson 3
1. The five big ships sailed home yesterday.
2. An excited dog barked loudly today.
3. A cute little baby played happily.

TEACHING SCRIPT FOR PRACTICE SENTENCES

We will classify these three sentences to practice what we have learned. We will classify the sentences together. Begin.

CHAPTER 10 LESSON 3 CONTINUED

Question and Answer Flow for Sentence 1: The five big ships sailed home yesterday.

1. What sailed home yesterday? ships - SN (subject noun)
2. What is being said about ships? ships sailed - V (verb)
3. Sailed where? home - Adv (adverb)
4. Sailed when? yesterday - Adv (adverb)

5. What kind of ships? big - Adj (Adjective)
6. How many ships? five - Adj (adjective)
7. The - A (*article adjective*)

Classified Sentence:

A	Adj	Adj	SN	V	Adv	Adv
The	five	big	ships	sailed	home	yesterday.

Question and Answer Flow for Sentence 2: An excited dog barked loudly today.

1. What barked loudly today? dog - SN (subject noun)
2. What is being said about dog? dog barked - V (verb)
3. Barked how? loudly - Adv (adverb)

4. Barked when? today - Adv (adverb)
5. What kind of dog? excited - Adj (adjective)
6. An - A (*article adjective*)

Classified Sentence:

A	Adj	SN	V	Adv	Adv
An	excited	dog	barked	loudly	today.

Question and Answer Flow for Sentence 3: A cute little baby played happily.

1. Who played happily? baby - SN (subject noun)
2. What is being said about baby? baby played - V (verb)
3. Played how? happily - Adv (adverb)

4. What kind of baby? little - Adj (adjective)
5. What kind of baby? cute - Adj (adjective)
6. A - A (*article adjective*)

Classified Sentence:

A	Adj	Adj	SN	V	Adv
A	cute	little	baby	played	happily.

 PRACTICE TIME

Have students turn to page 28 in the Practice Section of their book and find Chapter 10, Lesson 3, Practice. Go over the directions to make sure they understand what to do. Check and discuss the Practice after students have finished. (*Chapter 10, Lesson 3, Practice key is given below.*)

Chapter 10, Lesson 3, Practice: Classify the sentence below. Use **SN** for subject noun, **V** for verb, **Adv** for adverb, **Adj** for adjective, and **A** for article adjective. Underline the complete subject <u>one</u> time and the complete predicate <u>two</u> times.

A	Adj	Adj	SN	V	Adv	Adv
The	two	busy	children	played	happily	today.

(End of lesson.)

CHAPTER 10   LESSON 4

Objectives: Jingles, Vocabulary #3, Grammar (Practice Sentences), Activity, and Writing (Journal).

JINGLE TIME

Have students turn to the Jingle Section of their books. The teacher will lead the students in reciting the previously-taught jingles.

VOCABULARY TIME

Have students turn to page 6 in the Vocabulary Section of their books. Introduce the vocabulary words listed in the vocabulary box below by reciting them together with your students.

Chapter 10, Vocabulary Words #3
unhappy, cried, happy, six

GRAMMAR TIME

Put the Practice Sentences from the box below on the board or on notebook paper. Use these sentences as you practice the concepts that have been taught. For the greatest benefit, students must participate orally with the teacher.

Chapter 10, Practice Sentences for Lesson 4
1. The unhappy baby cried loudly today.
2. The happy puppies barked loudly.
3. Six black bears walked slowly away.

TEACHING SCRIPT FOR PRACTICE SENTENCES

We will classify these three sentences to practice what we have learned. We will classify the sentences together. Begin.

Question and Answer Flow for Sentence 1: The unhappy baby cried loudly today.

1. Who cried loudly today? baby - SN (subject noun)
2. What is being said about baby? baby cried - V (verb)
3. Cried how? loudly - Adv (adverb)
4. Cried when? today - Adv (adverb)
5. What kind of baby? unhappy - Adj (adjective)
6. The - A (*article adjective*)

Classified Sentence:

A	Adj	SN	V	Adv	Adv
The	unhappy	baby	cried	loudly	today.

Level 1 Homeschool Teacher's Manual

CHAPTER 10 LESSON 4 CONTINUED

Question and Answer Flow for Sentence 2: The happy puppies barked loudly.

1. What barked loudly? puppies - SN (subject noun)
2. What is being said about puppies?
   puppies barked - V (verb)

3. Barked how? loudly - Adv (adverb)
4. What kind of puppies? happy - Adj (adjective)
5. The - A (*article adjective*)

Classified Sentence:

A	Adj	SN	V	Adv
The	happy	puppies	barked	loudly.

Question and Answer Flow for Sentence 3: Six black bears walked slowly away.

1. What walked slowly away? bears - SN (subject noun)
2. What is being said about bears?
   bears walked - V (verb)
3. Walked how? slowly - Adv (adverb)

4. Walked where? away - Adv (adverb)
5. What kind of bears? black - Adj (adjective)
6. How many bears? six - Adj (adjective)

Classified Sentence:

Adj	Adj	SN	V	Adv	Adv
Six	black	bears	walked	slowly	away.

ACTIVITY / ASSIGNMENT TIME

Have students turn to page 85 in the Activity Section of their books and find Chapter 10, Lesson 4, Activity. Go over the directions to make sure they understand what to do. Check and discuss the Activity after students have finished.

Chapter 10, Lesson 4, Activity: Use the code in the box below to find grammar words. Using the code numbers, write the correct letters for each blank. Then, make up your own code for several words.

Code			Words
1. n	6. o	11. t	<u>n</u> <u>o</u> <u>u</u> <u>n</u> <u>a</u> <u>d</u> <u>v</u> <u>e</u> <u>r</u> <u>b</u>
2. d	7. j	12. i	1 6 5 1 3 2 4 9 8 10
3. a	8. r	13. c	<u>v</u> <u>e</u> <u>r</u> <u>b</u> <u>a</u> <u>d</u> <u>j</u> <u>e</u> <u>c</u> <u>t</u> <u>i</u> <u>v</u> <u>e</u>
4. v	9. e		4 9 8 10 3 2 7 9 13 11 12 4 9
5. u	10. b		

WRITING TIME

Have students make an entry in their journals.

(End of lesson.)

CHAPTER 10   LESSON 5

Objectives: Jingles, Vocabulary #4, Grammar (Practice Sentences), Test, Check, and Writing (Journal).

 **JINGLE TIME**

Have students turn to the Jingle Section of their books. The teacher will lead the students in reciting the previously-taught jingles.

 VOCABULARY TIME

Have students turn to page 6 in the Vocabulary Section of their books. Introduce the vocabulary words listed in the vocabulary box below by reciting them together with your students.

Chapter 10, Vocabulary Words #4
hungry, birds, monkeys

 GRAMMAR TIME

Put the Practice Sentences from the box below on the board or on notebook paper. Use these sentences as you practice the concepts that have been taught. For the greatest benefit, students must participate orally with the teacher.

Chapter 10, Practice Sentences for Lesson 5
1. The hungry birds flew away quickly.
2. The little brown monkeys played happily.
3. Five tired boys sat quietly.

TEACHING SCRIPT FOR PRACTICE SENTENCES

We will classify these three sentences to practice what we have learned. We will classify the sentences together. Begin.

CHAPTER 10 LESSON 5 CONTINUED

Question and Answer Flow for Sentence 1: The hungry birds flew away quickly.

1. What flew away quickly? birds - SN (subject noun)
2. What is being said about birds?
   birds flew - V (verb)
3. Flew where? away - Adv (adverb)
4. Flew how? quickly - Adv (adverb)
5. What kind of birds? hungry - Adj (adjective)
6. The - A (*article adjective*)

Classified Sentence:
       A   Adj   SN   V   Adv   Adv
       The hungry birds flew away quickly.

Question and Answer Flow for Sentence 2: The little brown monkeys played happily.

1. What played happily? monkeys - SN (subject noun)
2. What is being said about monkeys?
   monkeys played - V (verb)
3. Played how? happily - Adv (adverb)
4. What kind of monkeys? brown - Adj (adjective)
5. What kind of monkeys? little - Adj (adjective)
6. The - A (*article adjective*)

Classified Sentence:
       A   Adj   Adj   SN   V   Adv
       The little brown monkeys played happily.

Question and Answer Flow for Sentence 3: Five tired boys sat quietly.

1. Who sat quietly? boys - SN (subject noun)
2. What is being said about boys? boys sat - V (verb)
3. Sat how? quietly - Adv (adverb)
4. What kind of boys? tired - Adj (adjective)
5. How many boys? five - Adj (adjective)

Classified Sentence:
       Adj Adj SN V Adv
       Five tired boys sat quietly.

TEST TIME

Have students turn to page 63 in the Test Section of their books and find Chapter 10 Test. Go over the directions to make sure they understand what to do. (*Chapter 10 Test key is on the next page.*)

Chapter 10 Test
(Student Page 63)

Exercise 1: Classify each sentence. Use **SN** for subject noun, **V** for verb, **Adv** for adverb, **Adj** for adjective, and **A** for article adjective. For Sentence 1, underline the complete subject <u>one</u> time and the complete predicate <u>two</u> times.

```
      A     Adj   Adj    SN      V       Adv       Adv
1.   The   five   big   ships   sailed   home    yesterday.
```

```
      A     Adj    SN      V      Adv     Adv
2.   An   excited  dog   barked  loudly  today.
```

Exercise 2: Underline the <u>**syn**</u> if the words are synonyms. Underline the <u>**ant**</u> if the words are antonyms.

1. front, back	syn **ant**	2. rough, smooth	syn **ant**	3. giant, huge	**syn** ant

Exercise 3: Name the four parts of speech that you have studied. (*You may use abbreviations.*)
(The order of the answers may vary.)

1. **noun (N)**   2. **verb (V)**   3. **adjective (Adj)**   4. **adverb (Adv)**

Exercise 4: In your journal, write a paragraph summarizing what you have learned this week.

 **CHECK TIME**

After students have finished, check and discuss their test papers. Make sure they understand why their answers are right or wrong. Use the Question and Answer Flows on page 105 in this chapter to check the sentences on the Chapter 10 Test. (*For total points, count each required answer as a point.*)

(End of lesson.)

CHAPTER 11   LESSON 1

Objectives: Jingles, Synonyms, Antonyms, Skills (Five Parts of a Complete Sentence, Two Kinds of Sentences, Using Labels and Parts-of-Speech Word Bank), and Practice Exercise.

 **JINGLE TIME**

Have students turn to the Jingle Section in their books. The teacher will lead the students in reciting the previously-taught jingles.

 SYNONYM AND ANTONYM TIME

Have students turn to the Synonym and Antonym Section of their books. Introduce the new words listed for Chapter 11 in the box below. Make sure students know the meanings of the new synonyms and antonyms. Then, have students underline the correct answers in their books. They should study these words again before their test.

Chapter 11: Underline the **syn** if the words are synonyms. Underline the **ant** if the words are antonyms.		
1. form, shape **syn** ant	2. inside, outside syn **ant**	3. end, finish **syn** ant

 SKILL TIME

TEACHING SCRIPT FOR THE FIVE PARTS THAT MAKE A COMPLETE SENTENCE

You have been reciting the five parts that make a complete sentence every time you chant your Sentence Jingle. Listen carefully while I give you the definition for a complete sentence. A **complete sentence** is a group of words that has a subject, a verb, and makes sense *(which means that it must state a complete idea).* A complete sentence should also begin with a capital letter and end with an end mark.

Did you hear the five parts that make a complete sentence when we recited the Sentence Jingle? Of course, you did. Most people know that a complete sentence is a group of words that has a subject and a verb and makes sense. But we should also add that a complete sentence begins with a capital letter and ends with an end mark in order to be correct in our writing. You are learning these five parts of a sentence the easy way, by reciting the Sentence Jingle. Now, listen for the five parts of a sentence as you recite the Sentence Jingle one more time. *(Recite the Sentence Jingle one more time.)*

CHAPTER 11 LESSON 1 CONTINUED

Teacher's Note: The Sentence Jingle is also known as the Editing Jingle. For example, if your child brings a sentence to you that does not have an end mark, tell your child that he/she has one of the five parts missing. Have your child recite the last verse of the Sentence Jingle (the verse after *Remember*), find the mistake, correct it, show you the correction, and explain why he/she made the correction. This is a wonderful way to have your child learn basic editing skills very early in the program.

TEACHING SCRIPT FOR TWO KINDS OF SENTENCES

You have just learned that to be written correctly, a complete sentence should have a subject and verb, make sense, and have a capital letter and an end mark. We are now going to learn two kinds of sentences. These two kinds of sentences are the statement and the question. A sentence that <u>tells something</u> is called a **statement**. A sentence that <u>asks something</u> is called a **question**. What kind of sentence tells something? *(statement)* What kind of sentence asks something? *(question)* Look at Reference 5 on page 15 in your student book. Follow along as I read everything in the reference box. *(Read and discuss the information in the reference box below with your students.)*

Reference 5: Two Kinds of Sentences	
1. A **statement** is a sentence that <u>tells</u> something. A statement starts with a capital letter and ends with a <u>period</u>. Example: **T**he big bear walked away**.**	2. A **question** is a sentence that <u>asks</u> something. A question starts with a capital letter and ends with a <u>question mark</u>. Example: **D**o the boys work here**?**

What are the five parts of a complete sentence? *(subject, verb, complete sense, capital letter, and an end mark)* What are the names of the two kinds of sentences that we just learned about? *(statement and question)* There are three things that I want you to remember about each kind of sentence. The statement tells something, starts with a capital letter, and ends with a period. The question asks something, starts with a capital letter, and ends with a question mark.

TEACHING SCRIPT FOR USING SENTENCE LABELS AND PARTS-OF-SPEECH WORD BANK

Now that you know about sentences, we will learn how to build new sentences. We will use the labels that we write above each sentence part to help us write new sentences.

Look at the Reference 6 on page 15. The words in this reference box are a collection of nouns, verbs, adjectives, adverbs, and article adjectives that have been put together for you to use in building a sentence. We are going to call this collection of words a **Word Bank**. Your Word Bank will make it easy for you to build a sentence.

(Put the example given on the next page on the board. Use the reference example to demonstrate how to build a sentence using the Word Bank. Do not allow your students to write during this demonstration. Make sure you go over the written directions given in the reference box so that your students will understand what to do when they see it again on a test. Use the teaching script on the next page to walk students through writing a sentence using parts of speech from a Word Bank.)

CHAPTER 11 LESSON 1 CONTINUED

Reference 6: Parts-of-Speech Word Bank

On notebook paper, write a sentence using the words in the Word Bank. Put the words you select in the same order as the Sentence Labels listed below. Write the correct label above each word in your sentence.

Nouns	Verbs	Adjectives	Adverbs
puppies kittens duck	barked, quacked, yawned, climbed, played, waddled, ran	a, an, the, two, black, yellow, brown, excited, sleepy, hungry, unhappy, cute, little	loudly, excitedly, fast, happily, rapidly, noisily, quietly, today

Sentence Labels: A Adj SN V Adv   or   A Adj Adj SN V Adv Adv

Sentence Examples:
1. The sleepy puppies yawned noisily.
2. The two excited puppies barked loudly today.

Sentence Checklist:
1. Did you follow the labels?
2. Did you use the words in the Word Bank?
3. Did you check for the five sentence parts?
4. Did you write neatly?

This activity is fun because we can easily make completely different sentences by simply choosing different parts of speech from our Word Bank. These steps will show us how to build sentences using words from the Parts-of-Speech Word Bank. Listen carefully. (*Read the steps to your students.*)

1. Go to the subject noun label (**SN**). You are looking for a word that tells who or what the sentence is about. Since the subject noun is a noun word, you must go to the noun Word Bank and choose a noun that you want to use for the subject noun. Remember, this noun tells who or what the sentence is about. After you have chosen a noun for the subject, put it *below* the label **SN**.

2. Next, go to the verb label (**V**). You are looking for a word that tells what the subject does. You must go to the verb Word Bank and choose a verb that tells what your subject does. Remember, the subject and verb must make sense and work together. After you have chosen a verb, put it *below* the label **V**.

3. After you have selected a verb, go to the adverb label (**Adv**). Since an adverb modifies the verb, you must go to the verb and ask an adverb question in order to select an adverb from the adverb Word Bank. Remember, the adverb questions are *how, when, or where*. After you have chosen an adverb, put it *below* the label **Adv**.

4. Now, we are ready to find adjectives. Since an adjective modifies a noun, you must go to a noun and ask an adjective question in order to select an adjective from the adjective Word Bank. Remember, the adjective questions are *what kind, which one, or how many*. After you have chosen an adjective, put it *below* the label **Adj**.

5. Our last label is for an article adjective. There are three article adjectives: *a, an*, and *the*. Remember, there are no questions for an article adjective, but you must make sure that the article adjective you choose makes sense in the sentence. Article adjectives are found in the adjective Word Bank because they are adjectives. After you have chosen an article adjective, put it *below* the label **A**.

6. The last step is to go through a Sentence Checklist. Look at the bottom part of your reference box. (*Read and discuss the four things listed under the Sentence Checklist.*) What are the five sentence parts? (*Subject, verb, makes sense, starts with a capital letter, and ends with an end mark.*) The best way to check for sentence sense is to read your sentence out loud. As you read your sentence, listen very carefully to what you have written.

CHAPTER 11 LESSON 1 CONTINUED

 PRACTICE TIME

Have students turn to pages 28 and 29 in the Practice Section of their books and find Chapter 11, Lesson 1, Practice *(1-2)*. Go over the directions to make sure they understand what to do. Check and discuss the Practices after students have finished. *(Chapter 11, Lesson 1, Practice keys are given below.)*

Chapter 11, Lesson 1, Practice 1: On notebook paper, write each sentence correctly. Capitalize the first word of each sentence and put a (**.**) or a (**?**) at the end.

1.	did the car lights dim suddenly	**D**id the car lights dim suddenly**?**
2.	the chocolate cake baked slowly	**T**he chocolate cake baked slowly**.**
3.	the hungry baby cried softly	**T**he hungry baby cried softly**.**
4.	the school telephone rang loudly	**T**he school telephone rang loudly**.**

Chapter 11, Lesson 1, Practice 2: On notebook paper, write a sentence using the words in the Word Bank. Put the words you select in the same order as the Sentence Labels listed below. Write the correct label above each word in your sentence.

WORD BANK			
Nouns	**Verbs**	**Adjectives**	**Adverbs**
babies puppies toddlers	whined, cried, yawned, played, smiled, crawled, napped	a, an, the, two, tiny, upset, hungry, excited, three, pretty, unhappy, sleepy	swiftly, softly, loudly, quietly, happily, noisily, yesterday

Sentence Labels: A   Adj   SN   V   Adv   (Bonus)   A   Adj   Adj   SN   V   Adv   Adv

Teacher's Note: Beginning with this lesson, students will have no new concepts introduced in this chapter. This will give them time to practice what they have learned. You will classify the new sentences with your students if they need it and then give them a test to fine-tune their skills.

(End of lesson.)

CHAPTER 11   LESSON 2

Objectives: Jingles, Vocabulary #1, Grammar (Practice Sentences), and Practice Exercise.

 JINGLE TIME

Have students turn to the Jingle Section of their books. The teacher will lead the students in reciting the previously-taught jingles.

 VOCABULARY TIME

Have students turn to page 6 in the Vocabulary Section of their books. Introduce the vocabulary words listed in the vocabulary box below by reciting them together with your students.

Chapter 11, Vocabulary Words #1
silly, around, beautiful, car

 GRAMMAR TIME

Put the Practice Sentences from the box below on the board or on notebook paper. Use these sentences as you practice the concepts that have been taught. For the greatest benefit, students must participate orally with the teacher.

Chapter 11, Practice Sentences for Lesson 2
1. The three silly clowns ran around happily.
2. A beautiful black car stopped suddenly.*
3. The cute little girls talked quietly.

TEACHING SCRIPT FOR PRACTICE SENTENCES

We will classify these three sentences to practice the Question and Answer Flows. We will classify the sentences together. Begin.

Question and Answer Flow for Sentence 1: The three silly clowns ran around happily.

1. Who ran around happily? clowns - SN (subject noun)
2. What is being said about clowns? clowns ran - V (verb)
3. Ran where? around - Adv (adverb)
4. Ran how? happily - Adv (adverb)

5. What kind of clowns? silly - Adj (adjective)
6. How many clowns? three - Adj (adjective)
7. The - A (*article adjective*)

Classified Sentence:

A	Adj	Adj	SN	V	Adv	Adv
The	three	silly	clowns	ran	around	happily.

CHAPTER 11 LESSON 2 CONTINUED

Question and Answer Flow for Sentence 2: A beautiful black car stopped suddenly.

1. What stopped suddenly? car - SN (subject noun)
2. What is being said about car? car stopped - V (verb)
3. Stopped how? suddenly - Adv (adverb)
4. What kind of car? black - Adj (adjective)
5. What kind of car? beautiful - Adj (adjective)
6. A - A (*article adjective*)

	A	Adj	Adj	SN	V	Adv
Classified Sentence:	A	beautiful	black	car	stopped	suddenly.

Question and Answer Flow for Sentence 3: The cute little girls talked quietly.

1. Who talked quietly? girls - SN (subject noun)
2. What is being said about girls? girls talked - V (verb)
3. Talked how? quietly - Adv (adverb)
4. What kind of girls? little - Adj (adjective)
5. What kind of girls? cute - Adj (adjective)
6. The - A (*article adjective*)

	A	Adj	Adj	SN	V	Adv
Classified Sentence:	The	cute	little	girls	talked	quietly.

 PRACTICE TIME

Have students turn to page 29 in the Practice Section of their books and find Chapter 11, Lesson 2, Practice *(1-2)*. Go over the directions to make sure they understand what to do. Check and discuss the Practices after students have finished. (*Chapter 11, Lesson 2, Practice keys are given below.*)

Chapter 11, Lesson 2, Practice 1: On notebook paper, write each sentence correctly. Capitalize the first word of each sentence and put a (**.**) or a (**?**) at the end.

1. an orange ball bounced slowly

   An orange ball bounced slowly**.**

2. was the sun shining brightly

   Was the sun shining brightly**?**

3. the bananas ripened quickly

   The bananas ripened quickly**.**

4. the bees buzzed wildly

   The bees buzzed wildly**.**

Chapter 11, Lesson 2, Practice 2: On notebook paper, write a sentence using the words in the Word Bank. Put the words you select in the same order as the Sentence Labels listed below. Write the correct label above each word in your sentence.

WORD BANK			
Nouns	**Verbs**	**Adjectives**	**Adverbs**
bats sparrows owls	dove, swooped, flew, landed	a, an, the, three, swift, hungry, old, young, brown, black	carelessly dangerously low, high, today

Sentence Labels: A   Adj   SN   V   Adv   (Bonus) A   Adj   Adj   SN   V   Adv   Adv

(End of lesson.)

CHAPTER 11   LESSON 3

Objectives: Jingles, Vocabulary #2, Grammar (Practice Sentences), Practice Exercise, and Activity.

 **JINGLE TIME**

Have students turn to the Jingle Section of their books. The teacher will lead the students in reciting the previously-taught jingles.

 VOCABULARY TIME

Have students turn to page 6 in the Vocabulary Section of their books. Introduce the vocabulary words listed in the vocabulary box below by reciting them together with your students.

Chapter 11, Vocabulary Words #2
weary, brothers, ants, crawled, noisily

 GRAMMAR TIME

Put the Practice Sentences from the box below on the board or on notebook paper. Use these sentences as you practice the concepts that have been taught. For the greatest benefit, students must participate orally with the teacher.

Chapter 11, Practice Sentences for Lesson 3
1. The weary brothers walked slowly home.
2. The three black ants crawled fast yesterday.
3. Five happy monkeys played noisily.

TEACHING SCRIPT FOR PRACTICE SENTENCES

We will classify these three sentences to practice what we have learned. We will classify the sentences together. Begin. (_You might have students write the labels above the sentences at this time._)

CHAPTER 11 LESSON 3 CONTINUED

Question and Answer Flow for Sentence 1: The weary brothers walked slowly home.

1. Who walked slowly home? brothers - SN (subject noun)
2. What is being said about brothers? brothers walked - V (verb)
3. Walked how? slowly - Adv (adverb)
4. Walked where? home - Adv (adverb)
5. What kind of brothers? weary - Adj (adjective)
6. The - A (*article adjective*)

Classified Sentence:

A	Adj	SN	V	Adv	Adv
The	weary	brothers	walked	slowly	home.

Question and Answer Flow for Sentence 2: The three black ants crawled fast yesterday.

1. What crawled fast yesterday? ants - SN (subject noun)
2. What is being said about ants? ants crawled - V (verb)
3. Crawled how? fast - Adv (adverb)
4. Crawled when? yesterday - Adv (adverb)
5. What kind of ants? black - Adj (adjective)
6. How many ants? three - Adj (adjective)
7. The - A (*article adjective*)

Classified Sentence:

A	Adj	Adj	SN	V	Adv	Adv
The	three	black	ants	crawled	fast	yesterday.

Question and Answer Flow for Sentence 3: Five happy monkeys played noisily.

1. What played noisily? monkeys - SN (subject noun)
2. What is being said about monkeys? monkeys played - V (verb)
3. Played how? noisily - Adv (adverb)
4. What kind of monkeys? happy - Adj (adjective)
5. How many monkeys? five - Adj (adjective)

Classified Sentence:

Adj	Adj	SN	V	Adv
Five	happy	monkeys	played	noisily.

TEACHER INSTRUCTIONS

Have students recite the Question and Answer Flows for the first two sentences with you again. This time, they should trace the labels on their desks with the first three fingers of their writing hand as they classify. Next, have students write the third sentence on a sheet of paper. Have them recite the Question and Answer Flow for the third sentence with you again, but this time they should write the labels above the words on their paper. This will give them practice writing the labels before they are tested.

CHAPTER 11 LESSON 4 CONTINUED

Question and Answer Flow for Sentence 2: The busy students worked hard.

1. Who worked hard? students - SN (subject noun)
2. What is being said about students?
   students worked - V (verb)
3. Worked how? hard - Adv (adverb)
4. What kind of students? busy - Adj (adjective)
5. The - A (article adjective)

Classified Sentence:	A	Adj	SN	V	Adv
	The	busy	students	worked	hard.

Question and Answer Flow for Sentence 3: The lazy green frog sat quietly.

1. What sat quietly? frog - SN (subject noun)
2. What is being said about frog? frog sat - V (verb)
3. Sat how? quietly - Adv (adverb)
4. What kind of frog? green - Adj (adjective)
5. What kind of frog? lazy - Adj (adjective)
6. The - A (article adjective)

Classified Sentence:	A	Adj	Adj	SN	V	Adv
	The	lazy	green	frog	sat	quietly.

ACTIVITY / ASSIGNMENT TIME

Have students turn to page 86 in the Activity Section of their books and find Chapter 11, Lesson 4, Activity. Go over the directions to make sure they understand what to do. Check and discuss the Activity after students have finished.

Chapter 11, Lesson 4, Activity: Using the scrambled letters below, circle every other letter, beginning with the first letter. Use the blank to write the new word created by writing each circled letter in order. (**s**p**a**t**i**k**d**=said) On the title lines, write the title that best describes the words in each column. Choose from these titles:　**Places**　　**People**　　**Airplanes**　　**Animals**

Title: People	Title: Places
c d h o i r l s d e r b e f n: **children**	p s a m r a k z: **park**
t h e u a n c y h u e w r h: **teacher**	f n a o r f m e: **farm**
s r i m n p g w e c r g: **singer**	l g i h b m r c a d r k y: **library**

WRITING TIME

Have students make an entry in their journals.

(End of lesson.)

CHAPTER 11   LESSON 5

Objectives: Jingles, Vocabulary #4, Grammar (Practice Sentences), Test, Check, and Writing (Journal).

 **JINGLE TIME**

Have students turn to the Jingle Section of their books. The teacher will lead the students in reciting the previously-taught jingles.

 VOCABULARY TIME

Have students turn to page 6 in the Vocabulary Section of their books. Introduce the vocabulary words listed in the vocabulary box below by reciting them together with your students.

Chapter 11, Vocabulary Words #4
funny, shy, fox, thin

 GRAMMAR TIME

Put the Practice Sentences from the box below on the board or on notebook paper. Use these sentences as you practice the concepts that have been taught. For the greatest benefit, students must participate orally with the teacher.

Chapter 11, Practice Sentences for Lesson 5
1. The two funny clowns laughed loudly.
2. The shy little fox ran slowly.
3. The three thin cats sat quietly.

TEACHING SCRIPT FOR PRACTICE SENTENCES

We will classify these three sentences to practice what we have learned. We will classify the sentences together. Begin.

Level 1 Homeschool Teacher's Manual

CHAPTER 11 LESSON 5 CONTINUED

Question and Answer Flow for Sentence 1: The two funny clowns laughed loudly.

1. Who laughed loudly? clowns - SN (subject noun)
2. What is being said about clowns?
   clowns laughed - V (verb)
3. Laughed how? loudly - Adv (adverb)
4. What kind of clowns? funny - Adj (adjective)
5. How many clowns? two - Adj (adjective)
6. The - A (article adjective)

Classified Sentence:	A	Adj	Adj	SN	V	Adv
	The	two	funny	clowns	laughed	loudly.

Question and Answer Flow for Sentence 2: The shy little fox ran slowly.

1. What ran slowly? fox - SN (subject noun)
2. What is being said about fox? fox ran - V (verb)
3. Ran how? slowly - Adv (adverb)
4. What kind of fox? little - Adj (adjective)
5. What kind of fox? shy - Adj (adjective)
6. The - A (article adjective)

Classified Sentence:	A	Adj	Adj	SN	V	Adv
	The	shy	little	fox	ran	slowly.

Question and Answer Flow for Sentence 3: The three thin cats sat quietly.

1. What sat quietly? cats - SN (subject noun)
2. What is being said about cats? cats sat - V (verb)
3. Sat how? quietly - Adv (adverb)
4. What kind of cats? thin – Adj (adjective)
5. How many cats? three – Adj (adjective)
6. The - A (article adjective)

Classified Sentence:	A	Adj	Adj	SN	V	Adv
	The	three	thin	cats	sat	quietly.

  TEST TIME

Have students turn to page 64 in the Test Section of their books and find Chapter 11 Test. Go over the directions to make sure they understand what to do. (*Chapter 11 Test key is on the next page.*)

Chapter 11 Test
(Student Page 64)

Exercise 1: Classify each sentence. Use **SN** for subject noun, **V** for verb, **Adv** for adverb, **Adj** for adjective, and **A** for article adjective. For Sentence 2, underline the complete subject <u>one</u> time and the complete predicate <u>two</u> times

	A	Adj	Adj	SN	V	Adv	Adv
1.	The	three	silly	clowns	ran	around	happily.

	A	Adj	Adj	SN	V	Adv
2.	A	beautiful	black	car	stopped	suddenly.

Exercise 2: Underline the **syn** if the words are synonyms. Underline the **ant** if the words are antonyms.

1. inside, outside	syn **ant**	2. form, shape	**syn** ant	3. end, finish	**syn** ant

---

Exercise 3: Name the four parts of speech that you have studied. (*You may use abbreviations.*)
(The order of the answers may vary.)

1. **noun (N)**   2. **verb (V)**   3. **adjective (Adj)**   4. **adverb (Adv)**

Exercise 4: On notebook paper, write each sentence correctly. Capitalize the first word of each sentence and put a (**.**) or a (**?**) at the end.

1. the yellow cab stopped suddenly   The yellow cab stopped suddenly**.**

2. did the home team win yesterday   **D**id the home team win yesterday**?**

Exercise 5: On notebook paper, write a sentence using the words in the Word Bank. Put the words you select in the same order as the Sentence Labels listed below. Write the correct label above each word in your sentence.

WORD BANK			
Nouns	**Verbs**	**Adjectives**	**Adverbs**
bird ant snake	scurried, climbed, crawled, flew, ate, slithered, hopped	a, an, the, two, busy, tiny, hungry, huge, green, pretty, yellow, black, funny, little, excited	hastily, slowly, quickly, suddenly, fast, today, silently, around, early, away
Sentence Labels: A Adj SN V Adv (Bonus) A Adj Adj SN V Adv Adv			

Exercise 6: In your journal, write a paragraph summarizing what you have learned this week.

CHECK TIME

After students have finished, check and discuss their test papers. Make sure they understand why their answers are right or wrong. Use the Question and Answer Flows on pages 115-116 in this chapter to check the sentences on the Chapter 11 Test. (*For total points, count each required answer as a point.*)

(End of lesson.)

CHAPTER 12   LESSON 1

Objectives: Jingles, Synonyms, Antonyms, Skill (A/An Choices), and Practice Exercise.

 **JINGLE TIME**

Have students turn to the Jingle Section in their books. The teacher will lead the students in reciting the previously-taught jingles.

 SYNONYM AND ANTONYM TIME

Have students turn to the Synonym and Antonym Section of their books. Introduce the new words listed for Chapter 12 in the box below. Make sure students know the meanings of the new synonyms and antonyms. Then, have students underline the correct answers in their books. They should study these words again before their test.

Chapter 12: Underline the **syn** if the words are synonyms. Underline the **ant** if the words are antonyms.

1. high, low	syn **ant**	2. open, close	syn **ant**	3. tiny, small	**syn** ant

 SKILL TIME

TEACHING SCRIPT FOR A / AN CHOICES

I am going to introduce how to use the words **a** and **an** correctly. This is an easy concept, but you need to practice in order to do it well. Look at Reference 7 on page 16 in your Reference Section. There are two rules at the top of the reference box. Follow along as I read these rules for choosing **a** or **an**. (*Read the information in the reference box below.*)

Reference 7: A and An Choices
Rule 1: Use the word **a** when the next word begins with a consonant sound. (*Example: a tree*) Rule 2: Use the word **an** when the next word begins with a vowel sound. (*Example: an orange*) **Sample Sentences:** Write **a** or **an** in the blanks. 1. David saw __**an**__ old eagle.   3. The chef baked __**a**__ pie. 2. David saw __**a**__ young eagle.   4. The chef baked __**an**__ apple pie.

CHAPTER 12 LESSON 1 CONTINUED

Now, we will discuss the sample sentences in the reference box. First, we should always read the directions very carefully before we start the exercise. The directions say to write *a* or *an* in the blanks.

Look at number 1. Before we can choose *a* or *an* to put in the blank, we have to look at the word that comes next. Does *eagle* start with a consonant or vowel sound? *(vowel sound)* The rule says to use the word *an* before words that begin with a vowel sound. We will write the word *an* in the blank before the word *eagle*.

Look at number 2. Does the word *bald* start with a consonant or vowel sound? *(consonant sound)* The rule says to use the word *a* before words that begin with a consonant sound. We will write the word *a* in the blank before the word *bald*.

Look at number 3. Does the word *pie* start with a consonant or a vowel sound? *(consonant sound)* The rule says to use the word *a* before words that begin with a consonant sound. We will write the word *a* in the blank before the word *pie*.

Look at number 4. Does the word *apple* start with a consonant or a vowel sound? *(vowel sound)* The rule says to use the word *an* before words that begin with a vowel sound. We will write the word *an* in the blank before the word *apple*.

 PRACTICE TIME

Have students turn to pages 30 and 31 in the Practice Section of their book and find Chapter 12, Lesson 1, Practice *(1-2)*. Go over the directions to make sure they understand what to do. Check and discuss the Practices after students have finished. *(Chapter 12, Lesson 1, Practice keys are given below.)*

Chapter 12, Lesson 1, Practice 1: Write *a* or *an* in the blanks.

1. __An__ awful storm frightened me.   3. The workers dug __a__ hole.   5. __an__ alarm   7. __a__ case

2. Columbus was __an__ explorer.   4. Jim found __an__ empty can.   6. __a__ scarf   8. __an__ acorn

Chapter 12, Lesson 1, Practice 2: On notebook paper, write a sentence using the words in the Word Bank. Put the words you select in the same order as the Sentence Labels listed below. Write the correct label above each word in your sentence.

WORD BANK			
Nouns	**Verbs**	**Adjectives**	**Adverbs**
birds rabbits grasshoppers	hopped, jumped, sat, nibbled, played, hid	a, an, the, cute, three, baby, brown, green, white, gentle, funny, small, shy	merrily, quietly, excitedly, noisily, yesterday, swiftly, slowly, rapidly
Sentence Labels: A Adj SN V Adv (Bonus) A Adj Adj SN V Adv Adv			

(End of lesson.)

CHAPTER 12   LESSON 2

Objectives: Jingles, Vocabulary #1, Grammar (Practice Sentences), Practice Exercise, and Activity.

 **JINGLE TIME**

Have students turn to the Jingle Section in their books. The teacher will lead the students in reciting the previously-taught jingles.

 VOCABULARY TIME

Have students turn to page 7 in the Vocabulary Section of their books. Introduce the vocabulary words listed in the vocabulary box below by reciting them together with your students.

Chapter 12, Vocabulary Words #1
tiger, seven, balloon, floated

 GRAMMAR TIME

Put the Practice Sentences from the box below on the board or on notebook paper. Use these sentences as you practice the concepts that have been taught. For the greatest benefit, students must participate orally with the teacher.

Chapter 12, Practice Sentences for Lesson 2
1. A large tiger jumped suddenly.
2. Seven happy students shouted loudly today.
3. The big yellow balloon floated away.

TEACHING SCRIPT FOR PRACTICE SENTENCES

We will classify these three sentences to practice what we have learned. We will classify the sentences together. Begin.

CHAPTER 12 LESSON 2 CONTINUED

Question and Answer Flow for Sentence 1: A large tiger jumped suddenly.

1. What jumped suddenly? tiger - SN (subject noun)
2. What is being said about tiger? tiger jumped - V (verb)
3. Jumped how? suddenly - Adv (adverb)

4. What kind of tiger? large - Adj (adjective)
5. A - A (article adjective)

Classified Sentence:

A	Adj	SN	V	Adv
A	large	tiger	jumped	suddenly.

Question and Answer Flow for Sentence 2: Seven happy students shouted loudly today.

1. Who shouted loudly today? students - SN (subject noun)
2. What is being said about students? students shouted - V (verb)
3. Shouted how? loudly - Adv (adverb)

4. Shouted when? today - Adv (adverb)
5. What kind of students? happy - Adj (adjective)
6. How many students? seven - Adj (adjective)

Classified Sentence:

Adj	Adj	SN	V	Adv	Adv
Seven	happy	students	shouted	loudly	today.

Question and Answer Flow for Sentence 3: The big yellow balloon floated away.

1. What floated away? balloon - SN (subject noun)
2. What is being said about balloon? balloon floated - V (verb)
3. Floated where? away - Adv (adverb)

4. What kind of balloon? yellow - Adj (adjective)
5. What kind of balloon? big - Adj (adjective)
6. The - A (article adjective)

Classified Sentence:

A	Adj	Adj	SN	V	Adv
The	big	yellow	balloon	floated	away.

 PRACTICE TIME

Have students turn to page 31 in the Practice Section of their book and find Chapter 12, Lesson 2, Practice *(1-2)*. Go over the directions to make sure they understand what to do. Check and discuss the Practices after students have finished. *(Chapter 12, Lesson 2, Practice keys are given below and on the next page.)*

Chapter 12, Lesson 2, Practice 1: Write *a* or *an* in the blanks.

1. The king built **a** castle.
2. She pointed to **an** exit.
3. Our group had **a** guide.
4. **An** elephant looked at me.
5. **an** inch
6. **a** hat
7. **a** hallway
8. **an** elk

CHAPTER 12 LESSON 2 CONTINUED

Chapter 12, Lesson 2, Practice 2: On notebook paper, write a sentence using the words in the Word Bank. Put the words you select in the same order as the Sentence Labels listed below. Write the correct label above each word in your sentence.

WORD BANK			
Nouns	**Verbs**	**Adjectives**	**Adverbs**
duck swan eagle	glided, flew, soared, landed, floated, swam, ran, ate	a, an, the, one, white, large, baby, beautiful, brown, strong, brave, loud, small	gracefully, quietly, rapidly, swiftly, high, far, away, gently, today, loudly, softly
Sentence Labels: A Adj SN V Adv (Bonus) A Adj Adj SN V Adv Adv			

ACTIVITY / ASSIGNMENT TIME

Have students turn to page 86 in the Activity Section of their books and find Chapter 12, Lesson 2, Activity. Go over the directions to make sure they understand what to do. Check and discuss the Activity after students have finished.

Chapter 12, Lesson 2, Activity: Follow the directions below to make "A – An" Fruit Trees. Use these fruits for the activity:

apple   apricot   cherry   coconut   lemon   orange   pear   plum

Take two large paper bags and draw a giant round (circle) tree with a trunk on each sack. Next, put a large "A" on the top of one tree and a large "An" on the top of the second tree. Then, draw a circle on the appropriate tree for each fruit listed above and write the name of each fruit inside the circle. Color the tree green, the trunk brown, and each circle of fruit a different color.

Finally, go through the house finding five items, that begin with a consonant sound, to put in the "A" sack and five items that begin with a vowel sound, to put in the "An" sack. Then, empty all the items into one big pile. The teacher will time you as you sort each item into the correct bags.

You can do this activity with others in the family. Have other family members put several different items in the sacks and empty the items into a big pile. You can time family and friends as they sort the items into the correct bags.

Key: an apple, **an** apricot, **a** cherry, **a** coconut, **a** lemon, **an** orange, **a** pear, **a** plum

---

(End of lesson.)

CHAPTER 12   LESSON 3

Objectives: Jingles, Vocabulary #2, Grammar (Practice Sentences), Practice Exercise, and Activity.

 **JINGLE TIME**

Have students turn to the Jingle Section in their books. The teacher will lead the students in reciting the previously-taught jingles.

 VOCABULARY TIME

Have students turn to page 7 in the Vocabulary Section of their books. Introduce the vocabulary words listed in the vocabulary box below by reciting them together with your students.

Chapter 12, Vocabulary Words #2
giant, slept, soundly, hopped

 GRAMMAR TIME

Put the Practice Sentences from the box below on the board or on notebook paper. Use these sentences as you practice the concepts that have been taught. For the greatest benefit, students must participate orally with the teacher.

Chapter 12, Practice Sentences for Lesson 3
1. A large horse ran swiftly.
2. The three giant bears slept soundly today.
3. The big green frog hopped away quickly.

TEACHING SCRIPT FOR PRACTICE SENTENCES

We will classify these three sentences to practice what we have learned. We will classify the sentences together. Begin.

Level 1 Homeschool Teacher's Manual

CHAPTER 12 LESSON 3 CONTINUED

Question and Answer Flow for Sentence 1: A large horse ran swiftly.

1. What ran swiftly? horse - SN (subject noun)
2. What is being said about horse? horse ran - V (verb)
3. Ran how? swiftly - Adv (adverb)

4. What kind of horse? large - Adj (adjective)
5. A - A *(article adjective)*

Classified Sentence:

A	Adj	SN	V	Adv
A	large	horse	ran	swiftly.

Question and Answer Flow for Sentence 2: The three giant bears slept soundly today.

1. What slept soundly today? bears - SN (subject noun)
2. What is being said about bears? bears slept - V (verb)
3. Slept how? soundly - Adv (adverb)
4. Slept when? today - Adv (adverb)

5. What kind of bears? giant - Adj (adjective)
6. How many bears? three - Adj (adjective)
7. The - A *(article adjective)*

Classified Sentence:

A	Adj	Adj	SN	V	Adv	Adv
The	three	giant	bears	slept	soundly	today.

Question and Answer Flow for Sentence 3: The big green frog hopped away quickly.

1. What hopped away quickly? frog - SN (subject noun)
2. What is being said about frog? frog hopped - V (verb)
3. Hopped where? away - Adv (adverb)
4. Hopped how? quickly - Adv (adverb)

5. What kind of frog? green - Adj (adjective)
6. What kind of frog? big - Adj (adjective)
7. The - A *(article adjective)*

Classified Sentence:

A	Adj	Adj	SN	V	Adv	Adv
The	big	green	frog	hopped	away	quickly.

TEACHER INSTRUCTIONS

Have students recite the Question and Answer Flows for the first <u>two</u> sentences with you again. This time, they should trace the labels on their desks with the first three fingers of their writing hand as they classify. Next, have students write the <u>third</u> sentence on a sheet of paper. Have them recite the Question and Answer Flow for the third sentence with you again, but this time they should write the labels above the words on their paper. This will give them practice writing the labels before they are tested.

CHAPTER 12 LESSON 3 CONTINUED

 PRACTICE TIME

Have students turn to page 32 in the Practice Section of their book and find Chapter 12, Lesson 3, Practice *(1-2)*. Go over the directions to make sure they understand what to do. Check and discuss the Practices after students have finished. (*Chapter 12, Lesson 3, Practice keys are given below.*)

Chapter 12, Lesson 3, Practice 1: Write *a* or *an* in the blanks.

1. A gorilla is __an__ animal.   3. Dad bought __a__ computer.   5. __an__ apron   7. __a__ ruler

2. The man carried __a__ package.   4. She bought __an__ extra suitcase.   6. __a__ lemon   8. __an__ office

Chapter 12, Lesson 3, Practice 2: On notebook paper, write a sentence using the words in the Word Bank. Put the words you select in the same order as the Sentence Labels listed below. Write the correct label above each word in your sentence.

WORD BANK			
Nouns	**Verbs**	**Adjectives**	**Adverbs**
cows horses goats	grazed, drank, walked, stood, ran, ate, worked, chewed, slept, kicked	a, an, the, two, black, lazy, old, brown, young, small, large, smart, frightened	calmly, excitedly, fast, happily, noisily, quietly, today, daily, soundly, hard
Sentence Labels: A Adj SN V Adv (Bonus) A Adj Adj SN V Adv Adv			

 ACTIVITY / ASSIGNMENT TIME

Give other family members the Word Bank and Sentence Labels above. Then, have students check the sentences other family members have written. Students may use the Sentence Checklist at the bottom of Reference 6 on page 15 in the Reference Section of their books to help them check family members' sentences.

Sentence Checklist

1. Did you follow the labels?
2. Did you use the words in the Word Bank?
3. Did you check for the five sentence parts?
   (*subject, verb, makes sense, starts with a capital letter, and ends with an end mark*)
4. Did you write neatly?

(End of lesson.)

Level 1 Homeschool Teacher's Manual

CHAPTER 12   LESSON 4

Objectives: Jingles, Vocabulary #3, Grammar (Practice Sentences), Activity, and Writing (Journal).

 **JINGLE TIME**

Have students turn to the Jingle Section in their books. The teacher will lead the students in reciting the previously-taught jingles.

 VOCABULARY TIME

Have students turn to page 7 in the Vocabulary Section of their books. Introduce the vocabulary words listed in the vocabulary box below by reciting them together with your students.

Chapter 12, Vocabulary Words #3
jets, landed, frightened, ate

 GRAMMAR TIME

Put the Practice Sentences from the box below on the board or on notebook paper. Use these sentences as you practice the concepts that have been taught. For the greatest benefit, students must participate orally with the teacher.

Chapter 12, Practice Sentences for Lesson 4
1. Two big jets landed today.
2. The frightened puppies ran home quickly.
3. Several hungry boys ate rapidly yesterday.

TEACHING SCRIPT FOR PRACTICE SENTENCES

We will classify these three sentences to practice what we have learned. We will classify the sentences together. Begin.

CHAPTER 12 LESSON 4 CONTINUED

Question and Answer Flow for Sentence 1: Two big jets landed today.

1. What landed today? jets - SN (subject noun)
2. What is being said about jets? jets landed - V (verb)
3. Landed when? today - Adv (adverb)
4. What kind of jets? big - Adj (adjective)
5. How many jets? two - Adj (adjective)

Classified Sentence:

Adj	Adj	SN	V	Adv
Two	big	jets	landed	today.

Question and Answer Flow for Sentence 2: The frightened puppies ran home quickly.

1. What ran home quickly? puppies - SN (subject noun)
2. What is being said about puppies? puppies ran - V (verb)
3. Ran where? home - Adv (adverb)
4. Ran how? quickly - Adv (adverb)
5. What kind of puppies? frightened - Adj (adjective)
6. The - A (*article adjective*)

Classified Sentence:

A	Adj	SN	V	Adv	Adv
The	frightened	puppies	ran	home	quickly.

Question and Answer Flow for Sentence 3: Several hungry boys ate rapidly yesterday.

1. Who ate rapidly yesterday? boys - SN (subject noun)
2. What is being said about boys? boys ate - V (verb)
3. Ate how? rapidly - Adv (adverb)
4. Ate when? yesterday - Adv (adverb)
5. What kind of boys? hungry - Adj (adjective)
6. How many boys? several - Adj (adjective)

Classified Sentence:

Adj	Adj	SN	V	Adv	Adv
Several	hungry	boys	ate	rapidly	yesterday.

ACTIVITY / ASSIGNMENT TIME

Have students write the three sentences they have just classified on a sheet of paper. Have them tape-record the Question and Answer Flows for all three sentences. Students should write labels above the sentences as they classify them. (*After the students have finished, check the tape and the sentence labels. Make sure students understand any mistakes they have made.*)

WRITING TIME

Have students make an entry in their journals.

(End of lesson.)

Level 1 Homeschool Teacher's Manual

CHAPTER 12   LESSON 5

Objectives: Jingles, Vocabulary #4, Grammar (Practice Sentences), Test, Check, and Writing (Journal).

 **JINGLE TIME**

Have students turn to the Jingle Section in their books. The teacher will lead the students in reciting the previously-taught jingles.

 VOCABULARY TIME

Have students turn to page 7 in the Vocabulary Section of their books. Introduce the vocabulary words listed in the vocabulary box below by reciting them together with your students.

Chapter 12, Vocabulary Words #4
red, flowers, grew, pretty

 GRAMMAR TIME

Put the Practice Sentences from the box below on the board or on notebook paper. Use these sentences as you practice the concepts that have been taught. For the greatest benefit, students must participate orally with the teacher.

Chapter 12, Practice Sentences for Lesson 5
1. The red flowers grew rapidly.
2. The seven pretty little kittens slept soundly.
3. Six large jets flew fast today.

TEACHING SCRIPT FOR PRACTICE SENTENCES

We will classify these three sentences to practice what we have learned. We will classify the sentences together. Begin.

CHAPTER 12 LESSON 5 CONTINUED

Question and Answer Flow for Sentence 1: The red flowers grew rapidly.

1. What grew rapidly? flowers - SN (subject noun)
2. What is being said about flowers?
   flowers grew - V (verb)
3. Grew how? rapidly - Adv (adverb)
4. What kind of flowers? red - Adj (adjective)
5. The - A *(article adjective)*

Classified Sentence:

A	Adj	SN	V	Adv
The	red	flowers	grew	rapidly.

Question and Answer Flow for Sentence 2: The seven pretty little kittens slept soundly.

1. What slept soundly? kittens - SN (subject noun)
2. What is being said about kittens? kittens slept - V (verb)
3. Slept how? soundly - Adv (adverb)
4. What kind of kittens? little - Adj (adjective)
5. What kind of kittens? pretty - Adj (adjective)
6. How many kittens? seven - Adj (adjective)
7. The - A *(article adjective)*

Classified Sentence:

A	Adj	Adj	Adj	SN	V	Adv
The	seven	pretty	little	kittens	slept	soundly.

Question and Answer Flow for Sentence 3: Six large jets flew fast today.

1. What flew fast today? jets - SN (subject noun)
2. What is being said about jets? jets flew - V (verb)
3. Flew how? fast - Adv (adverb)
4. Flew when? today - Adv (adverb)
5. What kind of jets? large - Adj (adjective)
6. How many jets? six - Adj (adjective)

Classified Sentence:

Adj	Adj	SN	V	Adv	Adv
Six	large	jets	flew	fast	today.

 **TEST TIME**

Have students turn to page 65 in the Test Section of their books and find Chapter 12 Test. Go over the directions to make sure they understand what to do. (*Chapter 12 Test key is on the next page.*)

Chapter 12 Test
(Student Page 65)

Exercise 1: Classify each sentence. Use **SN** for subject noun, **V** for verb, **Adv** for adverb, **Adj** for adjective, and **A** for article adjective. For Sentence 2, underline the complete subject <u>one</u> time and the complete predicate <u>two</u> times

```
    A    Adj   SN    V     Adv
1.  The  red  flowers grew  rapidly.
```

```
    Adj   Adj   SN    V     Adv   Adv
2.  Six   large jets  flew  fast  today.
```

Exercise 2: Underline the **syn** if the words are synonyms. Underline the **ant** if the words are antonyms.

1. open, close	syn **ant**	2. tiny, small	**syn** ant	3. high, low	syn **ant**

Exercise 3: Name the four parts of speech that you have studied. (*You may use abbreviations.*)
(The order of the answers may vary.)

1. **noun (N)**   2. **verb (V)**   3. **adjective (Adj)**   4. **adverb (Adv)**

Exercise 4: Write **a** or **an** in the blanks.

1. The cat chased **an** ant.   3. Pat carved **a** pumpkin.   5. **an** arm   7. **an** insect

2. We made **a** cake.   4. The house has **a** door.   6. **a** mat   8. **an** elevator

---

Exercise 5: On notebook paper, write a sentence using the words in the Word Bank. Put the words you select in the same order as the Sentence Labels listed below. Write the correct label above each word in your sentence.

WORD BANK

Nouns	Verbs	Adjectives	Adverbs
men women students	walked, laughed, ran, talked, fished, looked, shouted, stopped, worked, yawned, drove	a, an, the, several, young, friendly, big, happy, cheerful, busy, weary, tired, frightened, eager, excited	easily, happily, quietly, slowly, suddenly, today, rapidly, away, carefully, early, loudly

Sentence Labels: A Adj SN V Adv (Bonus) A Adj Adj SN V Adv Adv

---

Exercise 6: In your journal, write a paragraph summarizing what you have learned this week.

CHECK TIME

After students have finished, check and discuss their test papers. Make sure they understand why their answers are right or wrong. Use the Question and Answer Flows on page 136 in this chapter to check the sentences on the Chapter 12 Test. (*For total points, count each required answer as a point.*)

(End of lesson.)

CHAPTER 13   LESSON 1

Objectives: Jingles (Preposition, Object of the Preposition), Synonyms, and Antonyms.

 **JINGLE TIME**

Have students turn to the Jingle Section in their books and recite the previously-taught jingles. Then, lead students in reciting the new jingles (*Preposition and Object of the Prep*) below. Practice the new jingles several times until students can recite them smoothly. Emphasize reciting with a rhythm. (*Do not try to explain the new jingles at this time. Just have fun reciting them. Add motions for more fun and laughter.*)

Jingle 7: Preposition Jingle
A PREP PREP PREPOSITION Is a special group of words That connects a NOUN, NOUN, NOUN Or a PRO, PRO, PRONOUN To the rest of the sentence.

Jingle 8: Object of the Prep Jingle
Dum De Dum Dum! An O-P is a N-O-U-N or a P-R-O After the P-R-E-P In a S-E-N-T-E-N-C-E. Dum De Dum Dum - DONE!

Teacher's Note: Tell students that they will learn more about pronouns in Level 2.

 SYNONYM AND ANTONYM TIME

Have students turn to the Synonym and Antonym Section of their books. Introduce the new words listed for Chapter 13 in the box below. Make sure students know the meanings of the new synonyms and antonyms. Then, have students underline the correct answers in their books. They should study these words again before their test.

Chapter 13: Underline the **syn** if the words are synonyms. Underline the **ant** if the words are antonyms.

1. far, near syn **ant**	2. rush, hurry **syn** ant	3. part, piece **syn** ant

(End of lesson.)

CHAPTER 13   LESSON 2

Objectives: Jingles, Vocabulary #1, and Grammar (Introductory Sentences, Preposition, and Object of the Preposition), and Activity.

 **JINGLE TIME**

Have students turn to the Jingle Section in their books. The teacher will lead the students in reciting the previously-taught jingles.

 VOCABULARY TIME

Have students turn to page 7 in the Vocabulary Section of their books. Introduce the vocabulary words listed in the vocabulary box below by reciting them together with your students. Beginning with this lesson, new preposition words will have parentheses around them.

Chapter 13, Vocabulary Words #1
house, smoothly, runway, shade, (to, on, in)

 GRAMMAR TIME

Put the introductory sentences from the box below on the board. Use these sentences as you go through the new concepts covered in your teaching scripts. For the greatest benefit, students must participate orally with the teacher. (*You might put the introductory sentences on notebook paper if you are doing one-on-one instruction with your students.*)

Chapter 13, Introductory Sentences for Lesson 2
1. Five yellow cats raced to the house.
2. The two big jets landed smoothly on the runway.
3. A baby puppy sat in the shade.

TEACHING SCRIPT FOR PREPOSITION AND OBJECT OF THE PREPOSITION

Today, we will begin prepositions! Prepositions are really fun, and they help you write more interesting sentences. The Preposition Jingle has already told you a lot about prepositions, but now we are going to learn even more. A **preposition** is a joining word. It joins, or connects, a noun to the rest of the sentence. To know whether a word is a preposition, say the preposition, then ask the question *What* or *Whom*. If the answer is a noun, then the word is a preposition. **Prepositions** are labeled with a *P*.

CHAPTER 13 LESSON 2 CONTINUED

The noun that answers the question *What* or *Whom* after a preposition is called an **object of the preposition.** A noun that is an object of the preposition is labeled with an *OP*.

Look at Reference 8 on page 16 as I explain how to find a preposition and an object of the preposition in a sample sentence. (*Have students follow along as you read and discuss the information in the reference box below.*)

Reference 8: Preposition and Object of the Preposition

```
SN   V    P    A   OP
Sam fell down the hill.
```

In the sample sentence, *Sam fell **down the hill***, the word *down* is a preposition because it has the noun *hill* after it that answers the question **what**. To find the preposition and object of the preposition in the Question and Answer Flow, say:

down - Preposition
down what? hill - Object of the Preposition

Teacher's Note: At this time, your manual will no longer have the entire name written out for each part of speech used in the Question and Answer Flow. Instead of **adverb**, you will see **Adv**. You will continue to say **adverb** even though you see only the abbreviation **Adv**. You will say **subject noun** whenever you see the abbreviation **SN**. Always say **verb** whenever you see the abbreviation **V**. You will always say the word **preposition** every time you see the abbreviation **P**, and **object of the preposition** every time you see the abbreviation **OP**, etc. The **P** and **OP** will be written out for this lesson and the next one.

Now, I will show you how to classify a preposition and an object of the preposition by reciting the Question and Answer Flow for Sentence 1. Listen carefully. (*Classify Sentence 1.*)

Question and Answer Flow for Sentence 1: Five yellow cats raced to the house.

1. What raced to the house? cats - SN
2. What is being said about cats? cats raced - V
3. To - P (Say: to - preposition)
4. To what? house - OP (Say: house - object of the preposition)

5. The - A
6. What kind of cats? yellow - Adj
7. How many cats? five - Adj

Note: To check whether a word is a preposition, say the word and ask "what." If your answer is a noun, you will have a preposition. A preposition must have a noun after it.

Classified Sentence:	Adj	Adj	SN	V	P	A	OP
	Five	yellow	cats	raced	to	the	house.

I will now classify Sentence 1 again, but this time you classify it with me. I will lead you as we say the questions and answers together. Remember, it is very important that you say the questions with me as well as the answers. (*Classify Sentence 1 again with your students participating with you.*)

CHAPTER 13 LESSON 2 CONTINUED

Now, we will classify Sentences 2 and 3 together to practice classifying prepositions and objects of the prepositions. Begin.

Question and Answer Flow for Sentence 2: The two big jets landed smoothly on the runway.

1. What landed smoothly on the runway? jets - SN
2. What is being said about jets? jets landed - V
3. Landed how? smoothly - Adv
4. On - P (Say: on - preposition)
5. On what? runway - OP (Say: runway - object of the preposition)

6. The - A
7. What kind of jets? big - Adj
8. How many jets? two - Adj
9. The - A

Classified Sentence:

A	Adj	Adj	SN	V	Adv	P	A	OP
The	two	big	jets	landed	smoothly	on	the	runway.

Question and Answer Flow for Sentence 3: A baby puppy sat in the shade.

1. What sat in the shade? puppy - SN
2. What is being said about puppy? puppy sat - V
3. In - P (Say: in - preposition)
4. In what? shade - OP (Say: shade - object of the preposition)

5. The - A
6. What kind of puppy? baby - Adj
7. A - A

Classified Sentence:

A	Adj	SN	V	P	A	OP
A	baby	puppy	sat	in	the	shade.

TEACHER INSTRUCTIONS

Have students recite the Question and Answer Flows for the first <u>two</u> sentences with you again. This time, they should trace the labels on their desks with the first three fingers of their writing hand as they classify. Next, have students write the <u>third</u> sentence on a sheet of paper. Have them recite the Question and Answer Flow for the third sentence with you again, but this time they should write the labels above the words on their paper. This will give them practice writing the labels before they are tested.

ACTIVITY / ASSIGNMENT TIME

Have students turn to page 86 in the Activity Section of their books and find Chapter 13, Lesson 2, Activity. Go over the directions to make sure they understand what to do. Check and discuss the Activity after students have finished. *(The three preposition boxes that are shaded should be colored purple.)* *(Students could also play tic-tac-toe games with prepositions.)*

Chapter 13, Lesson 2, Activity: Find all the prepositions in the boxes below. Then, color each preposition box purple.

to	cats	in
jets	on	sat

(End of lesson.)

CHAPTER 13   LESSON 3
Objectives: Jingles, Vocabulary #2, and Grammar (Practice Sentences, Prepositional Phrases), and Activity.

 **JINGLE TIME**

Have students turn to the Jingle Section in their books. The teacher will lead the students in reciting the previously-taught jingles.

 VOCABULARY TIME

Have students turn to page 7 in the Vocabulary Section of their books. Introduce the vocabulary words listed in the vocabulary box below by reciting them together with your students.

Chapter 13, Vocabulary Words #2
bee, softly, poor, fell, mud, (by)

 GRAMMAR TIME

Put the Practice Sentences from the box below on the board or on notebook paper. Use these sentences as you practice the concepts that have been taught. For the greatest benefit, students must participate orally with the teacher.

Chapter 13, Practice Sentences for Lesson 3
1. The busy little bee landed softly on the flower.
2. The pretty red flowers grew by the house.
3. The poor girl fell in the mud.

TEACHING SCRIPT FOR PRACTICE SENTENCES

We will classify these three sentences to practice what we have learned. We will classify the sentences together. Begin. (*You might have students write the labels above the sentences at this time.*)

CHAPTER 13 LESSON 3 CONTINUED

Question and Answer Flow for Sentence 1: The busy little bee landed softly on the flower.

1. What landed softly on the flower? bee - SN
2. What is being said about bee? bee landed - V
3. Landed how? softly - Adv
4. On - P (Say: on - preposition)
5. On what? flower - OP (Say: flower - object of the preposition)

6. The - A
7. What kind of bee? little - Adj
8. What kind of bee? busy - Adj
9. The - A

Classified Sentence:

A	Adj	Adj	SN	V	Adv	P	A	OP
The	busy	little	bee	landed	softly	on	the	flower.

Question and Answer Flow for Sentence 2: The pretty red flowers grew by the house.

1. What grew by the house? flowers - SN
2. What is being said about flowers? flowers grew - V
3. By - P (Say: by - preposition)
4. By what? house - OP (Say: house - object of the preposition)

5. The - A
6. What kind flowers? red - Adj
7. What kind flowers? pretty - Adj
8. The - A

Classified Sentence:

A	Adj	Adj	SN	V	P	A	OP
The	pretty	red	flowers	grew	by	the	house.

Question and Answer Flow for Sentence 3: The poor girl fell in the mud.

1. Who fell in the mud? girl - SN
2. What is being said about girl? girl fell - V
3. In - P (Say: in - preposition)
4. In what? mud - OP (Say: mud - object of the preposition)

5. The - A
6. What kind of girl? poor - Adj
7. The - A

Classified Sentence:

A	Adj	SN	V	P	A	OP
The	poor	girl	fell	in	the	mud.

TEACHING SCRIPT FOR PREPOSITIONAL PHRASES

We have been classifying sentences with prepositions and objects of the prepositions. To make it easier to refer to the preposition and the object of the preposition together, we call them prepositional phrases. Let's say **prepositional phrase** three times. (*Have students repeat* **prepositional phrase** *three times.*)

Remember, a prepositional phrase means that we are talking about a preposition and the object of the preposition. A prepositional phrase tells more about the sentence and makes sense in the sentence. The prepositional phrase could have other words, like article adjectives, between the preposition and the object of the preposition. These extra words just become part of the prepositional phrase as long as they are between the preposition and the object of the preposition.

Now, we will list on the board the prepositional phrases in each sentence that we have classified.

Sentence 1: **on the flower**   Sentence 2: **by the house**   Sentence 3: **in the mud**

CHAPTER 13 LESSON 3 CONTINUED

ACTIVITY / ASSIGNMENT TIME

(There are several things that must be done before this activity begins. First, write each clue and put it in an envelope and seal it. Write Clue 1, Clue 2, Clue 3, etc. on the front of the envelopes. Next, you must put the envelopes in the designated places ahead of time. You must also have a prize hidden in the appropriate place.)

Tell students that they are going on a scavenger hunt. They will hunt for clues that will lead them to their prize. Each clue uses different verbs and prepositional phrases to help give directions. Tell them you will give them the first clue in a sealed envelope. Tell students that they have fifteen minutes to find the prize. *(Set the timer for an appropriate time for your child.)*

Clue 1: **Walk** slowly **to** the couch **in** the living room. For Clue 2, look **under** the left cushion.

Clue 2: **Run** quickly **to** the kitchen. For Clue 3, look **in** the cabinets **under** the kitchen sink.

Clue 3: **Skip to** your bedroom. For Clue 4, look **under** your mattress.

Clue 4: **Tip-toe to** the bathroom. For Clue 5, look **in** the tub.

Clue 5: **March to** the dining room. For Clue 6, look **in** your chair.

Clue 6: **Sing** the alphabet song. Then, turn around three times. For Clue 7, look **in a window**.
(You choose a window.)

Clue 7: This is the clue for which you have been hunting. This clue will tell you where to find your prize.
(Tell your child where to find the prize in this clue.)

(End of lesson.)

CHAPTER 13   LESSON 4

Objectives: Jingles, Vocabulary #3, Grammar (Practice Sentences, Adding Prepositions to Parts of Speech), and Writing (Journal)

 **JINGLE TIME**

Have students turn to the Jingle Section in their books. The teacher will lead the students in reciting the previously-taught jingles.

 VOCABULARY TIME

Have students turn to page 7 in the Vocabulary Section of their books. Introduce the vocabulary words listed in the vocabulary box below by reciting them together with your students.

Chapter 13, Vocabulary Words #3
huge, snake, road, tiny, (across, at)

 GRAMMAR TIME

Put the Practice Sentences from the box below on the board or on notebook paper. Use these sentences as you practice the concepts that have been taught. For the greatest benefit, students must participate orally with the teacher.

Chapter 13, Practice Sentences for Lesson 4
1. A huge snake crawled slowly across the road.
2. The excited children ran quickly to the puppies.
3. The tiny brown dog barked at the frog.

TEACHING SCRIPT FOR PRACTICE SENTENCES

We will classify these three sentences to practice what we have learned. We will classify the sentences together. Begin.

CHAPTER 13 LESSON 4 CONTINUED

Question and Answer Flow for Sentence 1: A huge snake crawled slowly across the road.

1. What crawled slowly across the road? snake - SN
2. What is being said about snake? snake crawled - V
3. Crawled how? slowly - Adv
4. Across - P

5. Across what? road - OP
6. The - A
7. What kind of snake? huge - Adj
8. A - A

Classified Sentence:

A	Adj	SN	V	Adv	P	A	OP
A	huge	snake	crawled	slowly	across	the	road.

Question and Answer Flow for Sentence 2: The excited children ran quickly to the puppies.

1. Who ran quickly to the puppies? children - SN
2. What is being said about children? children ran - V
3. Ran how? quickly - Adv
4. To - P

5. To what? puppies - OP
6. The - A
7. What kind of children? excited - Adj
8. The - A

Classified Sentence:

A	Adj	SN	V	Adv	P	A	OP
The	excited	children	ran	quickly	to	the	puppies.

Question and Answer Flow for Sentence 3: The tiny brown dog barked at the frog.

1. What barked at the frog? dog - SN
2. What is being said about dog? dog barked - V
3. At - P
4. At what? frog - OP

5. The - A
6. What kind of dog? brown - Adj
7. What kind of dog? tiny - Adj
8. The - A

Classified Sentence:

A	Adj	Adj	SN	V	P	A	OP
The	tiny	brown	dog	barked	at	the	frog.

TEACHING SCRIPT FOR ADDING THE PREPOSITION TO THE PARTS OF SPEECH

Until now, we have had only four parts of speech. Do you remember the names of the four parts of speech we have already learned? *(noun, verb, adjective, and adverb)* In this chapter, we have learned about prepositions. A preposition is also a part of speech; so, we will add it to our list. We do not add the object of the preposition because it is a noun, and nouns are already on our list. Now, you know five parts of speech. What are the five parts of speech we have studied? *(noun, verb, adjective, adverb, and preposition)* *(Recite the five parts of speech several times. Have students write the five parts of speech on notebook paper.)*

 WRITING TIME

Have students make an entry in their journals.

(End of lesson.)

CHAPTER 13   LESSON 5
Objectives: Jingles, Vocabulary #4, Grammar (Practice Sentences), Test, Check, and Writing (Journal).

 **JINGLE TIME**

Have students turn to the Jingle Section in their books. The teacher will lead the students in reciting the previously-taught jingles.

 VOCABULARY TIME

Have students turn to page 7 in the Vocabulary Section of their books. Introduce the vocabulary words listed in the vocabulary box below by reciting them together with your students.

Chapter 13, Vocabulary Words #4
friends, movies, dime, door

 GRAMMAR TIME

Put the Practice Sentences from the box below on the board or on notebook paper. Use these sentences as you practice the concepts that have been taught. For the greatest benefit, students must participate orally with the teacher.

Chapter 13, Practice Sentences for Lesson 5
1. Seven puppies ran to the children.
2. The three friends walked happily to the movies.
3. A dime fell by the door.

TEACHING SCRIPT FOR PRACTICE SENTENCES

We will classify these three sentences to practice the Question and Answer Flows. We will classify the sentences together. Begin.

CHAPTER 13 LESSON 5 CONTINUED

Question and Answer Flow for Sentence 1: Seven puppies ran to the children.

1. What ran to the children? puppies - SN
2. What is being said about puppies? puppies ran - V
3. To - P

4. To whom? children - OP
5. The - A
6. How many puppies? seven - Adj

Classified Sentence:

Adj	SN	V	P	A	OP
Seven	puppies	ran	to	the	children.

Question and Answer Flow for Sentence 2: The three friends walked happily to the movies.

1. Who walked happily to the movies? friends - SN
2. What is being said about friends? friends walked - V
3. Walked how? happily - Adv
4. To - P

5. To what? movies - OP
6. The - A
7. How many friends? three - Adj
8. The - A

Classified Sentence:

A	Adj	SN	V	Adv	P	A	OP
The	three	friends	walked	happily	to	the	movies.

Question and Answer Flow for Sentence 3: A dime fell by the door.

1. What fell by the door? dime - SN
2. What is being said about dime? dime fell - V
3. By - P

4. By what? door - OP
5. The - A
6. A - A

Classified Sentence:

A	SN	V	P	A	OP
A	dime	fell	by	the	door.

 TEST TIME

Have students turn to page 66 in the Test Section of their books and find Chapter 13 Test. Go over the directions to make sure they understand what to do. (*Chapter 13 Test key is on the next page.*)

Chapter 13 Test
(Student Page 66)

Exercise 1: Classify each sentence. Use **SN** for subject noun, **V** for verb, **Adv** for adverb, **Adj** for adjective, **A** for article adjective, **P** for preposition, and **OP** for object of the preposition. For Sentence 1, underline the complete subject <u>one</u> time and the complete predicate <u>two</u> times.

	A	Adj	Adj	SN	V	Adv	P	A	OP
1.	The	busy	little	bee	landed	softly	on	the	flower.

	A	Adj	SN	V	P	A	OP
2.	The	poor	girl	fell	in	the	mud.

Exercise 2: Underline the **syn** if the words are synonyms. Underline the **ant** if the words are antonyms.

1. part, piece	<u>**syn**</u> ant	2. far, near	syn <u>**ant**</u>	3. rush, hurry	<u>**syn**</u> ant

---

Exercise 3: Name the five parts of speech that you have studied. (*You may use abbreviations.*)
(The order of answers may vary.)

1. **Noun (N)**   2. **Verb (V)**   3. **Adjective (Adj)**   4. **Adverb (Adv)**   5. **Preposition (P)**

Exercise 4: Write *a* or *an* in the blanks.

1. He was stranded on __an__ island.   3. Pat planted __a__ garden.   5. __an__ odor   7. __an__ eel

2. I saw __a__ deer in the woods.   4. The birds built __a__ nest.   6. __a__ jar   8. __an__ album

---

Exercise 5: In your journal, write a paragraph summarizing what you have learned this week.

 **CHECK TIME**

After students have finished, check and discuss their test papers. Make sure they understand why their answers are right or wrong. Use the Question and Answer Flows on page 143 in this chapter to check the sentences on the Chapter 13 Test. (*For total points, count each required answer as a point.*)

(End of lesson.)

CHAPTER 14   LESSON 1
Objectives: Jingles, Synonyms, Antonyms, and Skill (Writing Sentences with Prepositional Phrases by Using Sentence Labels and the Parts-of-Speech Word Bank).

 **JINGLE TIME**

Have students turn to the Jingle Section in their books. The teacher will lead the students in reciting the previously-taught jingles.

 SYNONYM AND ANTONYM TIME

Have students turn to the Synonym and Antonym Section of their books. Introduce the new words listed for Chapter 14 in the box below. Make sure students know the meanings of the new synonyms and antonyms. Then, have students underline the correct answers in their books. They should study these words again before their test.

Chapter 14: Underline the **syn** if the words are synonyms. Underline the **ant** if the words are antonyms.

1. above, below	syn **ant**		2. old, new	syn **ant**		3. lean, thin	**syn** ant

 SKILL TIME

TEACHING SCRIPT FOR WRITING SENTENCES WITH PREPOSITIONAL PHRASES BY USING SENTENCE LABELS AND THE PARTS-OF-SPEECH WORD BANK

Today, we will write sentences that include a preposition and an object of the preposition. This activity is fun because we can easily make completely different sentences by simply choosing different parts of speech from our Word Bank. Look at Reference 9 on page 16 in your workbook.

(Use the reference box on the next page as you demonstrate how to do this activity. Students will write several sentences with you today. Make sure you go over the written directions given in the reference box so that your students will understand what to do when they see this activity again on a practice exercise or a test. Use the teaching script on the next page to walk students through how to write sentences using parts of speech from the Word Bank. Students can also make up their own words to use in writing their sentences. Read and discuss the sentence examples at the bottom of Reference 9. Explain to students that there are a number of different ways that the sentences can be written. The examples will give them a visual set of sentences to guide them as they make their own sentences.)

CHAPTER 14 LESSON 1 CONTINUED

Reference 9: Parts-of-Speech Word Bank With Prepositional Phrases				
On notebook paper, write a sentence using the words in the Word Bank. Put the words you select in the same order as the Sentence Labels listed below. Write the correct label above each word in your sentence.				
WORD BANK				
Nouns	**Verbs**	**Adjectives**	**Adverbs**	**Prepositional Phrases**
children dogs otters	swam splashed played	a, an, the, four, several, young, brown, happy, excited	gracefully, playfully, joyfully, happily, merrily, loudly	in the water on the beach by the trees
Sentence Labels: A Adj SN V Adv Prep Phrase or Adj SN V Adv Prep Phrase				

Examples:

1. Several children played merrily on the beach.
2. Four otters swam playfully in the water.
3. The young dogs splashed loudly in the water.
4. The brown dogs played happily by the trees.
5. The excited children splashed loudly in the water.
6. Several otters swam gracefully by the trees.

1. Go to the subject noun label (**SN**). You are looking for a word that tells who or what the sentence is about. Since the subject noun is a noun word, you must go to the noun Word Bank and choose a noun that you want to use for the subject noun. Remember, this noun tells *who* or *what* the sentence is about. After you have chosen a noun for the subject, put it **below** the label **SN**.

2. Next, go to the verb label (**V**). You are looking for a word that tells what the subject does. You must go to the verb Word Bank and choose a verb that tells what your subject does. Remember, the subject and verb must make sense and work together. After you have chosen a verb, put it **below** the label **V**.

3. After you have selected a verb, go to the adverb label (**Adv**). Since an adverb modifies the verb, you must go to the verb and ask an adverb question in order to select an adverb from the adverb Word Bank. Remember, the adverb questions are *how, when, or where*. After you have chosen an adverb, put it **below** the label **Adv**.

4. Now, you will select a preposition and an object of the preposition. Remember, a prepositional phrase means that we are talking about a preposition and an object of the preposition. A prepositional phrase tells more about the sentence and makes sense in the sentence. After you have chosen a prepositional phrase from the prepositional-phrase Word Bank, put it **below** the label **Prep Phrase**.

5. Now, we are ready to find adjectives. Since an adjective modifies a noun, you must go to a noun and ask an adjective question in order to select an adjective from the adjective Word Bank. Remember, the adjective questions are *what kind, which one, or how many*. After you have chosen an adjective, put it **below** the label **Adj**.

6. Our last label is for an article adjective. There are three article adjectives: **a, an**, and **the**. Remember, there are no questions for an article adjective, but you must make sure that the article adjective you choose makes sense in the sentence. Article adjectives are found in the adjective Word Bank because they are adjectives. After you have chosen an article adjective, put it **below** the label **A**.

7. The last step is to check your sentence for the five sentence parts. (*Subject, verb, makes sense, starts with a capital letter, and ends with an end mark.*) The best way to check for sentence sense is to read your sentence aloud. As you read your sentence, listen very carefully to what you have written.

(End of lesson.)

CHAPTER 14   LESSON 2

Objectives: Jingles, Vocabulary #1, Grammar (Practice Sentences, The Difference between Prepositions and Adverbs), Practice Exercise, and Activity.

 **JINGLE TIME**

Have students turn to the Jingle Section in their books. The teacher will lead the students in reciting the previously-taught jingles.

 VOCABULARY TIME

Have students turn to page 7 in the Vocabulary Section of their books. Introduce the vocabulary words listed in the vocabulary box below by reciting them together with your students.

Chapter 14, Vocabulary Words #1
jelly, jar, floor, lake

 GRAMMAR TIME

Put the Practice Sentences from the box below on the board or on notebook paper. Use these sentences as you practice the concepts that have been taught. For the greatest benefit, students must participate orally with the teacher.

Chapter 14, Practice Sentences for Lesson 2
1. The jelly jar fell on the floor.
2. The excited children swam noisily in the lake.
3. A huge black dog slept by the door.

TEACHING SCRIPT FOR PRACTICE SENTENCES

We will classify these three sentences to practice what we have learned. We will classify the sentences together. Begin.

Level 1 Homeschool Teacher's Manual

CHAPTER 14 LESSON 2 CONTINUED

Question and Answer Flow for Sentence 1: The jelly jar fell on the floor.

1. What fell on the floor? jar - SN
2. What is being said about jar? jar fell - V
3. On - P
4. On what? floor - OP

5. The - A
6. What kind of jar? jelly - Adj
7. The - A

Classified Sentence: A   Adj   SN   V   P   A   OP
                               The jelly jar fell on the floor.

Question and Answer Flow for Sentence 2: The excited children swam noisily in the lake.

1. Who swam noisily in the lake? children - SN
2. What is being said about children? children swam - V
3. Swam how? noisily - Adv
4. In - P

5. In what? lake - OP
6. The - A
7. What kind children? excited - Adj
8. The - A

Classified Sentence: A   Adj   SN   V   Adv   P   A   OP
                               The excited children swam noisily in the lake.

Question and Answer Flow for Sentence 3: A huge black dog slept by the door.

1. What slept by the door? dog - SN
2. What is being said about dog? dog slept - V
3. By - P
4. By what? door - OP

5. The - A
6. What kind of dog? black - Adj
7. What kind of dog? huge - Adj
8. A - A

Classified Sentence: A Adj   Adj   SN   V   P   A   OP
                               A huge black dog slept by the door.

TEACHING SCRIPT FOR LEARNING THE DIFFERENCE BETWEEN PREPOSITIONS AND ADVERBS

Now that you have classified several prepositions and objects of the prepositions, I will give you more information that will increase your understanding of prepositions. Today, we will learn the difference between prepositions and adverbs. Look at Reference 10 on page 17 as I explain the difference between prepositions and adverbs. (*Reference 10 is located on the next page.*)

Sometimes, a word can be either a <u>preposition</u> or an <u>adverb</u>, depending on how it is used in a sentence. For example, the word *down* can be an adverb or a preposition. How do you decide if the word *down* is an adverb or a preposition? If *down* is used alone, with no noun after it, it is an adverb. If *down* has a noun after it that answers the question *what* or *whom*, then *down* is a preposition, and the noun after *down* is an object of the preposition. (*Have students follow along as you read and discuss the information in the reference box on the next page.*)

CHAPTER 14 LESSON 2 CONTINUED

Reference 10: Knowing the Difference Between Prepositions and Adverbs

In the sample sentence, *Sam fell **down***, the word *down* is an adverb because it tells where and does not have a noun after it.
 	
In the sample sentence, *Sam fell **down the hill***, the word *down* is a preposition because it has the noun *hill* after it that answers the question **what**. To find the preposition and object of the preposition in the Question and Answer Flow, say:
 	
                        down - Preposition
            down what? hill - Object of the Preposition

Teacher's Note: *Extra information for the teacher:* A single word that modifies a verb is called an adverb. A prepositional phrase can also modify like adverbs and adjectives do. A prepositional phrase that modifies a verb is called an adverb, or adverbial, phrase. For example, the prepositional phrase (*down the hill*) tells *where* Sam fell. Prepositional phrases can also modify like adjectives. (*Students are not required to identify adjectival and adverbial phrases in sentences until seventh grade.*)

You will see the difference between adverbs and prepositions as we classify the first two sentences again. (*Follow the instructions given below. For reinforcement, explain the concept again, using the Practice Sentences that you are classifying for a second time.*)

TEACHER INSTRUCTIONS

Have students recite the Question and Answer Flows for the first <u>two</u> sentences with you again. This time, they should trace the labels on their desks with the first three fingers of their writing hand as they classify. The third sentence will not be classified again unless the students need the extra practice.

 PRACTICE TIME

Have students turn to pages 32 and 33 in the Practice Section of their book and find Chapter 14, Lesson 2, Practice (*1-2*). Go over the directions to make sure they understand what to do. Check and discuss the Practices after students have finished. (*Chapter 14, Lesson 2, Practice keys are given below and on the next page.*)

Chapter 14, Lesson 2, Practice 1: Write *a* or *an* in the blanks.

1. The farmer drove __a__ tractor.
2. Pat read __an__ adventure story.

3. He drove __a__ new car.
4. Sara picked __a__ red rose.

5. __an__ alligator
6. __an__ elbow

7. __a__ candle
8. __an__ orange

CHAPTER 14 LESSON 2 CONTINUED

Chapter 14, Lesson 2, Practice 2: On notebook paper, write a sentence using the words in the Word Bank. Put the words you select in the same order as the Sentence Labels listed below. Write the correct label above each word in your sentence.

WORD BANK

Nouns	Verbs	Adjectives	Adverbs	Prepositional Phrases
students children soldiers	talked, chatted, whispered, laughed	a, an, the, four, young, excited, busy, happy, lazy, little, silly, shy, tired	quietly cautiously secretly noisily	on the telephone across the table by the store in the restaurant

Sentence Labels: A Adj Adj SN V Adv Prep Phrase

ACTIVITY / ASSIGNMENT TIME

Have students turn to page 87 in the Activity Section of their book and find Chapter 14, Lesson 2, Activity. Go over the directions to make sure they understand what to do. Check and discuss the Activity after students have finished.

Chapter 14, Lesson 2, Activity: Write the correct prepositions in the blanks. Use these prepositions:

across   at   by   down   in   on   to

Jack was a little brown squirrel that lived **in** a big oak tree. Jack wanted a new adventure. He sat **in** his tree and looked directly **at** the road. That's it! He would go **on** a trip. He would go all the way **to** the road. Then, he would run back **to** his tree.

First, he looked around. The coast was clear. Jack scampered **down** the tree **to** the ground. Next, he ran **across** the yard **to** a big tree **by** the road. He looked around again. Nothing. He took a deep breath and darted **across** the road. There! He had done it! He had gone **across** the road! Wow!

Suddenly, Jack was worried. He heard a sound. Jack was frightened! He ran wildly **down** the road. Then, he dashed back **across** the road. His heart was pounding **in** his chest! He finally got back **to** his tree. He jumped **on** a limb. Then, he climbed rapidly **to** his house. Jack was finally **at** his house. Then, he heard the sound again. Jack took no more chances. He sat contentedly **by** the window and never wanted another adventure.

(End of lesson.)

CHAPTER 14   LESSON 3
Objectives: Jingles, Vocabulary #2, Grammar (Practice Sentences, The Complete Subject and the Complete Predicate with a Prepositional Phrase), and Practice Exercise.

 **JINGLE TIME**

Have students turn to the Jingle Section in their books. The teacher will lead the students in reciting the previously-taught jingles.

 VOCABULARY TIME

Have students turn to page 7 in the Vocabulary Section of their books. Introduce the vocabulary words listed in the vocabulary box below by reciting them together with your students.

Chapter 14, Vocabulary Words #2
music, store, camped, mountains

 GRAMMAR TIME

Put the Practice Sentences from the box below on the board or on notebook paper. Use these sentences as you practice the concepts that have been taught. For the greatest benefit, students must participate orally with the teacher.

Chapter 14, Practice Sentences for Lesson 3
1. The beautiful music played softly in the store.
2. Four happy friends camped in the mountains.
3. A frightened brown duck flew across the road today.

TEACHING SCRIPT FOR PRACTICE SENTENCES

We will classify these three sentences to practice what we have learned. We will classify the sentences together. Begin. (*You might have students write the labels above the sentences at this time.*)

CHAPTER 14 LESSON 3 CONTINUED

Question and Answer Flow for Sentence 1: The beautiful music played softly in the store.

1. What played softly in the store? music - SN
2. What is being said about music? music played - V
3. Played how? softly - Adv
4. In - P
5. In what? store - OP
6. The - A
7. What kind of music? beautiful - Adj
8. The - A

Classified Sentence:	A	Adj	SN	V	Adv	P	A	OP
	The	beautiful	music	played	softly	in	the	store.

Question and Answer Flow for Sentence 2: Four happy friends camped in the mountains.

1. Who camped in the mountains? friends - SN
2. What is being said about friends? friends camped - V
3. In - P
4. In what? mountains - OP
5. The - A
6. What kind of friends? happy - Adj
7. How many friends? four - Adj

Classified Sentence:	Adj	Adj	SN	V	P	A	OP
	Four	happy	friends	camped	in	the	mountains.

Question and Answer Flow for Sentence 3: A frightened brown duck flew across the road today.

1. What flew across the road today? duck - SN
2. What is being said about duck? duck flew - V
3. Across - P
4. Across what? road - OP
5. The - A
6. Flew when? today - Adv
7. What kind of duck? brown - Adj
8. What kind of duck? frightened - Adj
9. A - A

Classified Sentence:	A	Adj	Adj	SN	V	P	A	OP	Adv
	A	frightened	brown	duck	flew	across	the	road	today.

TEACHING SCRIPT FOR THE COMPLETE SUBJECT AND THE COMPLETE PREDICATE WITH A PREPOSITIONAL PHRASE

First, we will review prepositional phrases. When we refer to the preposition and the object of the preposition together, we call them a prepositional phrase. What is the prepositional phrase in Sentence 1? (*in the store*) Sentence 2? (*in the mountains*) Sentence 3? (*across the road*)

Now, we will learn how to find the **complete subject** and the **complete predicate** when we add a prepositional phrase to the sentence. Look at Sentence 1 that we just classified. Let's read Sentence 1 again. (*Read this sentence together: The beautiful music played softly in the store.*) Remember, the complete subject usually starts at the beginning of the sentence and includes every word up to the verb of the sentence.

Let's find the complete subject in Sentence 1. What is the complete subject? (*The beautiful music*) We will underline the complete subject one time to identify all the subject parts. (*The beautiful music*) Remember, you will never include the verb in the complete subject.

CHAPTER 14 LESSON 3 CONTINUED

The complete predicate usually starts with the verb and includes every word after the verb. What is the complete predicate in Sentence 1? (*played softly in the store*) We will underline the complete predicate two times to identify all the predicate parts. (*played softly in the store*) The prepositional phrase is part of the predicate because it comes after the verb. (*Mark the answers for the rest of the sentences in the same way.*)

 PRACTICE TIME

Have students turn to page 33 in the Practice Section of their book and find Chapter 14, Lesson 3, Practice (*1-2*). Go over the directions to make sure they understand what to do. Check and discuss the Practices after students have finished. (*Chapter 14, Lesson 3, Practice keys are given below.*)

Chapter 14, Lesson 3, Practice 1: On notebook paper, write a sentence using the words in the Word Bank. Put the words you select in the same order as the Sentence Labels listed below. Write the correct label above each word in your sentence.

WORD BANK

Nouns	Verbs	Adjectives	Adverbs	Prepositional Phrases
mouse squirrel raccoons	jumped moved ran	a, an, the, old, brown, young, three, eager,	loudly, quickly, noisily, silently, slowly, today	down the road across the yard on the porch

Sentence Labels: A Adj Adj SN V Adv Prep Phrase

Chapter 14, Lesson 3, Practice 2: Classify the sentence below. Use **SN** for subject noun, **V** for verb, **Adv** for adverb, **Adj** for adjective, **A** for article adjective, **P** for preposition, and **OP** for object of the preposition. Underline the complete subject <u>one</u> time and the complete predicate <u>two</u> times.

A	Adj	Adj	SN	V	Adv	P	A	OP
The	little	yellow	ducks	swam	happily	in	the	pond.

(End of lesson.)

Level 1 Homeschool Teacher's Manual

CHAPTER 14   LESSON 4

Objectives: Jingles, Vocabulary #3, Grammar (Practice Sentences), Activity, and Writing (Journal).

 **JINGLE TIME**

Have students turn to the Jingle Section of their books. The teacher will lead the students in reciting the previously-taught jingles.

 VOCABULARY TIME

Have students turn to page 7 in the Vocabulary Section of their books. Introduce the vocabulary words listed in the vocabulary box below by reciting them together with your students.

Chapter 14, Vocabulary Words #3
rabbit, rain, waited, bus

 GRAMMAR TIME

Put the Practice Sentences from the box below on the board or on notebook paper. Use these sentences as you practice the concepts that have been taught. For the greatest benefit, students must participate orally with the teacher.

Chapter 14, Practice Sentences for Lesson 4
1. The baby rabbit hopped quickly across the road.
2. The tiny green snake crawled slowly in the rain.
3. The excited children waited on the bus.

TEACHING SCRIPT FOR PRACTICE SENTENCES

We will classify these three sentences to practice what we have learned. We will classify the sentences together. Begin.

CHAPTER 14 LESSON 4 CONTINUED

Question and Answer Flow for Sentence 1: The baby rabbit hopped quickly across the road.

1. What hopped quickly across the road? rabbit - SN
2. What is being said about rabbit? rabbit hopped - V
3. Hopped how? quickly - Adv
4. Across - P
5. Across what? road - OP
6. The - A
7. What kind of rabbit? baby - Adj
8. The - A

Classified Sentence:

A	Adj	SN	V	Adv	P	A	OP
The	baby	rabbit	hopped	quickly	across	the	road.

Question and Answer Flow for Sentence 2: The tiny green snake crawled slowly in the rain.

1. What crawled slowly in the rain? snake - SN
2. What is being said about snake? snake crawled - V
3. Crawled how? slowly - Adv
4. In - P
5. In what? rain - OP
6. The - A
7. What kind of snake? green - Adj
8. What kind of snake? tiny - Adj
9. The - A

Classified Sentence:

A	Adj	Adj	SN	V	Adv	P	A	OP
The	tiny	green	snake	crawled	slowly	in	the	rain.

Question and Answer Flow for Sentence 3: The excited children waited on the bus.

1. Who waited on the bus? children - SN
2. What is being said about children? children waited - V
3. On - P
4. On what? bus - OP
5. The - A
6. What kind of children? excited - Adj
7. The - A

Classified Sentence:

A	Adj	SN	V	P	A	OP
The	excited	children	waited	on	the	bus.

ACTIVITY / ASSIGNMENT TIME

Have students write the three sentences from this lesson on a sheet of paper. Have them tape-record the Question and Answer Flows for all three sentences. Students should write labels above the sentences as they classify them. (*After the students have finished, check the tape and the sentence labels. Make sure students understand any mistakes they have made.*)

WRITING TIME

Have students make an entry in their journals.

(End of lesson.)

Level 1 Homeschool Teacher's Manual

CHAPTER 14   LESSON 5

Objectives: Jingles, Vocabulary #4, Grammar (Practice Sentences), Test, Check, and Writing (Journal).

 **JINGLE TIME**

Have students turn to the Jingle Section of their books. The teacher will lead the students in reciting the previously-taught jingles.

 VOCABULARY TIME

Have students turn to page 7 in the Vocabulary Section of their books. Introduce the vocabulary words listed in the vocabulary box below by reciting them together with your students.

Chapter 14, Vocabulary Words #4
window, waved, passengers, looked, bananas

 GRAMMAR TIME

Put the Practice Sentences from the box below on the board or on notebook paper. Use these sentences as you practice the concepts that have been taught. For the greatest benefit, students must participate orally with the teacher.

Chapter 14, Practice Sentences for Lesson 5
1. Two fat cats sat in the window.
2. The excited boys waved wildly at the passengers.
3. The little monkeys looked hungrily at the bananas.

TEACHING SCRIPT FOR PRACTICE SENTENCES

We will classify these three sentences to practice the Question and Answer Flows. We will classify the sentences together. Begin.

© SHURLEY INSTRUCTIONAL MATERIALS, INC.

CHAPTER 14 LESSON 5 CONTINUED

Question and Answer Flow for Sentence 1: Two fat cats sat in the window.

1. What sat in the window? cats - SN
2. What is being said about cats? cats sat - V
3. In - P
4. In what? window - OP

5. The - A
6. What kind of cats? fat - Adj
7. How many cats? two - Adj

Classified Sentence:

Adj	Adj	SN	V	P	A	OP
Two	fat	cats	sat	in	the	window.

Question and Answer Flow for Sentence 2: The excited boys waved wildly at the passengers.

1. Who waved wildly at the passengers? boys - SN
2. What is being said about boys? boys waved - V
3. Waved how? wildly - Adv
4. At - P

5. At whom? passengers - OP
6. The - A
7. What kind of boys? excited - Adj
8. The - A

Classified Sentence:

A	Adj	SN	V	Adv	P	A	OP
The	excited	boys	waved	wildly	at	the	passengers.

Question and Answer Flow for Sentence 3: The little monkeys looked hungrily at the bananas.

1. What looked hungrily at the bananas? monkeys - SN
2. What is being said about monkeys? monkeys looked - V
3. Looked how? hungrily - Adv
4. At - P

5. At what? bananas - OP
6. The - A
7. What kind of monkeys? little - Adj
8. The - A

Classified Sentence:

A	Adj	SN	V	Adv	P	A	OP
The	little	monkeys	looked	hungrily	at	the	bananas.

 **TEST TIME**

Have students turn to page 67 in the Test Section of their books and find Chapter 14 Test. Go over the directions to make sure they understand what to do. (*Chapter 14 Test key is on the next page.*)

Chapter 14 Test
(Student Page 67)

Exercise 1: Classify each sentence. Use **SN** for subject noun, **V** for verb, **Adv** for adverb, **Adj** for adjective, **A** for article adjective, **P** for preposition, and **OP** for object of the preposition. For Sentence 1, underline the complete subject <u>one</u> time and the complete predicate <u>two</u> times.

```
        A      Adj      SN        V       Adv      P     A      OP
1.     The   beautiful  music    played   softly   in   the    store.
```

```
       A      Adj      Adj     SN     V       P      A      OP     Adv
2.     A    frightened brown   duck   flew   across  the    road   today.
```

Exercise 2: Underline the **syn** if the words are synonyms. Underline the **ant** if the words are antonyms.

1. old, new	syn **ant**	2. lean, thin	**syn** ant	3. above, below	syn **ant**

Exercise 3: Name the five parts of speech that you have studied. (*You may use abbreviations.*)
(The order of answers may vary.)

1. **Noun (N)**   2. **Verb (V)**   3. **Adjective (Adj)**   4. **Adverb (Adv)**   5. **Preposition (P)**

Exercise 4: Write *a* or *an* in the blanks.

1. Jan boiled **an** egg.   3. The actor wore **a** mask.   5. **an** officer   7. **an** eye

2. He works in **a** factory.   4. Lisa ate **an** apple.   6. **a** fire   8. **a** napkin

---

Exercise 5: On notebook paper, write a sentence using the words in the Word Bank. Put the words you select in the same order as the Sentence Labels listed below. Write the correct label above each word in your sentence.

WORD BANK				
Nouns	**Verbs**	**Adjectives**	**Adverbs**	**Prepositional Phrases**
teacher coaches friend	waved smiled talked	a, an, the, friendly, busy, new, eager, several, enthusiastic	warmly, patiently, happily, today	at the children to the parents to the players
Sentence Labels: A Adj Adj SN V Adv Prep Phrase				

Exercise 6: In your journal, write a paragraph summarizing what you have learned this week.

 CHECK TIME

After students have finished, check and discuss their test papers. Make sure they understand why their answers are right or wrong. Use the Question and Answer Flows on page 157 in this chapter to check the sentences on the Chapter 14 Test. (*For total points, count each required answer as a point.*)

(End of lesson.)

CHAPTER 15   LESSON 1
Objectives: Jingles, Synonyms, Antonyms, Skill (Capitalization Rules), and Practice Exercise.

JINGLE TIME

Have students turn to the Jingle Section in their books. The teacher will lead the students in reciting the previously-taught jingles.

SYNONYM AND ANTONYM TIME

Have students turn to the Synonym and Antonym Section of their books. Introduce the new words listed for Chapter 15 in the box below. Make sure students know the meanings of the new synonyms and antonyms. Then, have students underline the correct answers in their books. They should study these words again before their test.

Chapter 15: Underline the **syn** if the words are synonyms. Underline the **ant** if the words are antonyms.
1. left, right syn **ant**   2. poor, rich syn **ant**   3. puzzle, riddle **syn** ant

SKILL TIME

TEACHING SCRIPT FOR CAPITALIZATION RULES

Today, we will look at several rules for capitalizing words. You have probably noticed that some words in sentences are capitalized and some are not. There are rules in our English language that tell us when to capitalize a word and when to leave the word alone. It is important for you to know how to capitalize sentences correctly. You are ready to learn how to use the rules for capitalization to correct capitalization mistakes in sentences.

Look on page 17 at Reference 11 for the capitalization rules that you will use. Let's read over the capitalization rules together. Begin. *(Go over the seven capitalization rules in Reference 11 on the next page.)*

CHAPTER 15 LESSON 1 CONTINUED

Reference 11: Capitalization Rules	
1. Capitalize the first word of a sentence.	5. Capitalize the months of the year. (*March, April*)
2. Capitalize the pronoun I.	6. Capitalize the names of cities. (*Dallas*)
3. Capitalize the names of people. (*Kelly, Billy*)	7. Capitalize the names of states. (*Missouri*)
4. Capitalize the days of the week. (*Monday, Tuesday*)	

Examples

Directions: Correct each capitalization mistake and write the rule number above the corrections. Put a (.) or a (**?**) at the end of each sentence.

<u> 1 </u> (capitalization rule numbers)
  T
1. the big dog barked loudly **.**   (**1 capital**)
	<u>1 (or 2) 4 5 </u> (capitalization rule numbers)
	  I F J
	4. i worked one friday in june **.** (**3 capitals**)

<u> 1   2 </u> (capitalization rule numbers)
  M   I
2. may i play here <u>**?**</u>   (**2 capitals**)
	<u> 1 3 6 7 </u> (capitalization rule numbers)
	  W J O F
	5. we talked to jim in orlando, florida **.** (**4 capitals**)

<u> 1 3 </u> (capitalization rule numbers) H T 3. he ran to tommy **.** (**2 capitals**)	

Now, I will show you how to use these seven rules to correct capitalization mistakes. Look at the examples at the bottom of Reference 11. At the end of each sentence, you will see the number of capitalization mistakes you must correct in bold print and in parentheses. (*Explain the word* ***parentheses*** *and show students the parentheses in Sentence 1.*) Sentence 1 has (**1 capital**) in parentheses and in bold print. This means you will correct one capital-letter mistake. For each correction, we must also select a rule number from the rule box. The rule number tells us why the correction was necessary. Let's go over the five examples so you can see how to make the corrections and how to write the rule numbers above the correction.

Let's read Example 1 together. (*the big dog barked loudly*) Now, let's go through the rules in the rule box. Is the first word of the sentence capitalized? (*No*) Since it is not capitalized, it is a capitalization mistake, and we must capitalize the first word. Do you see that a capital **T** has been written above the lowercase **t** in the first word? (*Have students point to the capital* ***T*** *correction above the lowercase* ***t.***) What rule number tells why we capitalized the first word? (*Rule 1*) Do you see that a number 1 has been written on the line above the capital **T** correction to show that Rule 1 explains this correction? (*Have students point to the rule number above the letter T.*)

Even though we have corrected the one mistake in the sentence, I want you to get in the habit of checking the rest of the sentence to make sure there are no more mistakes. We will continue using the rules to check for other mistakes. Do we have the pronoun **I** in the sentence? (*No*) Do we have any names of people? (*No*) Do we have any days of the week or months of the year? (*No*) Do we have the names of cities or states in our sentence? (*No*)

Since we have gone through all the capitalization rules, we have only one last thing to do. We must decide if the sentence is a statement or a question. Is this sentence a statement or a question? (*statement*) How do we end a statement? (*We put a period at the end.*)

Let's read Example 2 together. *(may i play here)* How many mistakes does it say we must correct? *(two)* Let's go through the rules in the rule box. Is the first word of the sentence capitalized? *(No)* Since it is not capitalized, it is a capitalization mistake, and we must capitalize the first word. A capital **M** has been written above the lowercase **m** in the first word. *(Have students point to the capital M correction above the lowercase m.)* What rule number tells why we capitalized the first word? *(Rule 1)* A number 1 has been written on the line above the capital **M** correction to show that Rule 1 explains this correction. *(Have students point to the rule number above the letter M.)*

We will continue using the rules to check for other mistakes. Do we have the pronoun **I** in the sentence? *(Yes)* In this sentence, the word **I** is a word that people use when they are talking about themselves. The word **I** must always be capitalized if it is not the alphabet letter *i*. The word **I** is a pronoun. A pronoun takes the place of a noun when naming a person. Instead of saying your own name when you talk about yourself, you can use the pronoun **I**. Whenever you see the word **I** in a sentence, you need to remember the rule that says the pronoun **I** should be capitalized. You are to capitalize the pronoun **I** no matter where it is used in a sentence.

A capital **I** has been written above the lowercase **i** in the example. *(Have students point to the capital I correction above the lowercase i.)* What rule number tells why we capitalized the pronoun **I**? *(Rule 2)* A number 2 has been written on the line above the capital **I** correction to show that Rule 2 explains this correction. *(Have students point to the rule number above the letter I.)*

Even though we have corrected the two mistakes in the sentence, we will continue using the rules to check for other mistakes. Do we have any names of people? *(No)* Do we have any days of the week or months of the year? *(No)* Do we have the names of cities or states in our sentence? *(No)*

Now that we have gone through all the capitalization rules, we have only one last thing to do. We must decide if the sentence is a statement or a question. Is this sentence a statement or a question? *(question)* How do we end a question? *(We put a question mark at the end.)*

Let's read Example 3 together. *(he ran to tommy)* How many mistakes does it say we must correct? *(two)* Let's go through the rules in the rule box. Is the first word of the sentence capitalized? *(No)* A capital **H** has been written above the lowercase **h** in the first word. *(Have students point to the capital H correction above the lowercase h.)* What rule number tells why we capitalized the first word? *(Rule 1)* A number 1 has been written on the line above the capital **H** correction to show that Rule 1 explains this correction. *(Have students point to the rule number above the letter H.)*

Do we have the pronoun **I** in this sentence? *(No)* Do we have any names of people? *(Yes)* Since the word *tommy* is the name of a person, it must be capitalized. A capital **T** has been written above the lowercase **t** in the example. *(Have students point to the capital T correction above the lowercase t.)* What rule number tells why we capitalized the name of a person? *(Rule 3)* A number 3 has been written on the line above the capital **T** correction to show that Rule 3 explains this correction. *(Have students point to the rule number above the letter T.)*

CHAPTER 15 LESSON 1 CONTINUED

Even though we have corrected the two mistakes in the sentence, we will continue using the rules to check for other mistakes. Do we have any days of the week or months of the year? *(No)* Do we have the names of cities or states in our sentence? *(No)*

Now that we have gone through all the capitalization rules, we have only one last thing to do. We must decide if the sentence is a statement or a question. Is this sentence a statement or a question? *(statement)* How do we end a statement? *(We put a period at the end.)*

Let's read Example 4 together. *(i worked one friday in june)* How many mistakes does it say we must correct? *(three)* Let's go through the rules in the rule box. Is the first word of the sentence capitalized? *(No)* A capital **I** has been written above the lowercase **i** for the first word. *(Have students point to the capital **I** correction above the lowercase **i**.)* Since the pronoun **I** happens to be the first word, we can use Rule 1 or Rule 2. What rule number tells why we capitalized the first word? *(Rule 1 or Rule 2)* A number 1 with a number 2 in parentheses has been written on the line above the capital **I** correction to show that Rule 1 or Rule 2 explains this correction. *(Have students point to the rule numbers above the letter **I**.)*

Do we have any names of people? *(No)* Do we have any days of the week? *(Yes)* Since the word *friday* is the name of a day of the week, it must be capitalized. A capital **F** has been written above the *lowercase* **f** in the example. *(Have students point to the capital **F** correction above the lowercase **f**.)* What rule number tells why we capitalized the name of a day of the week? *(Rule 4)* A number 4 has been written on the line above the capital **F** correction to show that Rule 4 explains this correction. *(Have students point to the rule number above the letter **F**.)*

Do we have any months of the year? *(Yes)* Since the word *june* is the name of a month of the year, it must be capitalized. A capital **J** has been written above the *lowercase* **j** in the example. *(Have students point to the capital **J** correction above the lowercase **j**.)* What rule number tells why we capitalized the name of a month of the year? *(Rule 5)* A number 5 has been written on the line above the capital **J** correction to show that Rule 5 explains this correction. *(Have students point to the rule number above the letter **J**.)*

Even though we have corrected the three mistakes in the sentence, we will continue using the rules to check for other mistakes. Do we have the names of cities or states in our sentence? *(No)*

Now that we have gone through all the capitalization rules, we have only one last thing to do. We must decide if the sentence is a statement or a question. Is this sentence a statement or a question? *(statement)* How do we end a statement? *(We put a period at the end.)*

Let's read Example 5 together. *(we talked to jim in orlando, florida)* How many mistakes does it say we must correct? *(four)* Let's go through the rules in the rule box. Is the first word of the sentence capitalized? *(No)* A capital **W** has been written above the *lowercase* **w** for the first word. *(Have students point to the capital **W** correction above the lowercase **w**.)* What rule number tells why we capitalized the first word? *(Rule 1)* A number 1 has been written on the line above the capital **W** correction to show that Rule 1 explains this correction. *(Have students point to the rule numbers above the letter **W**.)*

CHAPTER 15 LESSON 1 CONTINUED

Do we have any names of people? *(Yes)* Since the word *jim* is the name of a person, it must be capitalized. A capital **J** has been written above the *lowercase* **j** in the example. *(Have students point to the capital **J** correction above the lowercase **j**.)* What rule number tells why we capitalized the name of a person? *(Rule 3)* A number 3 has been written on the line above the capital **J** correction to show that Rule 3 explains this correction. *(Have students point to the rule number above the letter **J**.)*

Do we have any days of the week? *(No)* Do we have any months of the year? *(No)* Do we have any cities? *(Yes)* Since the word *orlando* is the name of a city, it must be capitalized. A capital **O** has been written above the *lowercase* **o** in the example. *(Have students point to the capital **O** correction above the lowercase **o**.)* What rule number tells why we capitalized the name of a city? *(Rule 6)* A number 6 has been written on the line above the capital **O** correction to show that Rule 6 explains this correction. *(Have students point to the rule number above the letter **O**.)*

Do we have any states? *(Yes)* Since the word *florida* is the name of a state, it must be capitalized. A capital **F** has been written above the *lowercase* **f** in the example. *(Have students point to the capital **F** correction above the lowercase **f**.)* What rule number tells why we capitalized the name of a state? *(Rule 7)* A number 7 has been written on the line above the capital **F** correction to show that Rule 7 explains this correction. *(Have students point to the rule number above the letter **F**.)*

We have corrected the four mistakes in the sentence. Now that we have gone through all the capitalization rules, we have only one last thing to do. We must decide if the sentence is a statement or a question. Is this sentence a statement or a question? *(statement)* How do we end a statement? *(We put a period at the end.)*

 PRACTICE TIME

Have students turn to page 34 in the Practice Section of their book and find Chapter 15, Lesson 1, Practice. Go over the directions to make sure they understand what to do. Check and discuss the Practice after students have finished. *(Chapter 15, Lesson 1, Practice key is given below.)*

Chapter 15, Lesson 1, Practice: Correct the capitalization mistakes and put the rule number above each correction. Use the rule numbers in Reference 11 on page 17 in the Reference Section of your book. Put a (**.**) or a (**?**) at the end of the sentence.

 1   3   4   (capitalization rule numbers)

 A   J   T

  alice   wrote   a   letter   to   julie   on   thursday _ **.** _ (3 capitals)

(End of lesson.)

CHAPTER 15   LESSON 2

Objectives: Jingles, Vocabulary #1, Grammar (Practice Sentences), and Practice Exercise.

 **JINGLE TIME**

Have students turn to the Jingle Section in their books. The teacher will lead the students in reciting the previously-taught jingles.

 VOCABULARY TIME

Have students turn to page 7 in the Vocabulary Section of their books. Introduce the vocabulary words listed in the vocabulary box below by reciting them together with your students.

Chapter 15, Vocabulary Words #1
grasshopper, garden, deer, swans

 GRAMMAR TIME

Put the Practice Sentences from the box below on the board or on notebook paper. Use these sentences as you practice the concepts that have been taught. For the greatest benefit, students must participate orally with the teacher.

Chapter 15, Practice Sentences for Lesson 2
1. The baby grasshopper hopped quickly to the garden.
2. Seven deer walked slowly away.
3. The beautiful swans flew across the lake.

TEACHING SCRIPT FOR PRACTICE SENTENCES

We will classify these three sentences to practice what we have learned. We will classify the sentences together. Begin.

CHAPTER 15 LESSON 2 CONTINUED

Question and Answer Flow for Sentence 1: The baby grasshopper hopped quickly to the garden.

1. What hopped quickly to the garden? grasshopper - SN
2. What is being said about grasshopper? grasshopper hopped - V
3. Hopped how? quickly - Adv
4. To - P

5. To what? garden - OP
6. The - A
7. What kind of grasshopper? baby - Adj
8. The - A

Classified Sentence:

A	Adj	SN	V	Adv	P	A	OP
The	baby	grasshopper	hopped	quickly	to	the	garden.

Question and Answer Flow for Sentence 2: Seven deer walked slowly away.

1. What walked slowly away? deer - SN
2. What is being said about deer? deer walked - V
3. Walked how? slowly - Adv

4. Walked where? away - Adv
5. How many deer? seven - Adj

Classified Sentence:

Adj	SN	V	Adv	Adv
Seven	deer	walked	slowly	away.

Question and Answer Flow for Sentence 3: The beautiful swans flew across the lake.

1. What flew across the lake? swans - SN
2. What is being said about swans? swans flew - V
3. Across - P
4. Across what? lake - OP

5. The - A
6. What kind of swans? beautiful - Adj
7. The - A

Classified Sentence:

A	Adj	SN	V	P	A	OP
The	beautiful	swans	flew	across	the	lake.

 PRACTICE TIME

Have students turn to page 34 in the Practice Section of their book and find Chapter 15, Lesson 2, Practice. Go over the directions to make sure they understand what to do. Check and discuss the Practice after students have finished. (*Chapter 15, Lesson 2, Practice key is given below.*)

Chapter 15, Lesson 2, Practice: Correct the capitalization mistakes and put the rule number above each correction. Use the rule numbers in Reference 11 on page 17 in the Reference Section of your book. Put a (**.**) or a (**?**) at the end of the sentence.

1		6	7		5	(capitalization rule numbers)
T		T	A		J	

timothy   moved   to   tuscon,   arizona,   last   july __ **.** **(4 capitals)**

(End of lesson.)

CHAPTER 15   LESSON 3

Objectives: Jingles, Vocabulary #2, Grammar (Practice Sentences), Practice Exercise, and Activity.

 **JINGLE TIME**

Have students turn to the Jingle Section in their books. The teacher will lead the students in reciting the previously-taught jingles.

 VOCABULARY TIME

Have students turn to page 7 in the Vocabulary Section of their books. Introduce the vocabulary words listed in the vocabulary box below by reciting them together with your students.

Chapter 15, Vocabulary Words #2
family, beach, crib, eight, small

 GRAMMAR TIME

Put the Practice Sentences from the box below on the board or on notebook paper. Use these sentences as you practice the concepts that have been taught. For the greatest benefit, students must participate orally with the teacher.

Chapter 15, Practice Sentences for Lesson 3
1. The excited family walked happily to the beach.
2. A tiny baby slept in the crib.
3. Eight small boys played in the garden.

TEACHING SCRIPT FOR PRACTICE SENTENCES

We will classify these three sentences to practice what we have learned. We will classify the sentences together. Begin.

CHAPTER 15 LESSON 3 CONTINUED

Question and Answer Flow for Sentence 1: The excited family walked happily to the beach.

1. Who walked happily to the beach? family - SN
2. What is being said about family? family walked - V
3. Walked how? happily - Adv
4. To - P

5. To what? beach - OP
6. The - A
7. What kind of family? excited - Adj
8. The - A

Classified Sentence:	A	Adj	SN	V	Adv	P	A	OP
	The	excited	family	walked	happily	to	the	beach.

Question and Answer Flow for Sentence 2: A tiny baby slept in the crib.

1. Who slept in the crib? baby - SN
2. What is being said about baby? baby slept - V
3. In - P
4. In what? crib - OP

5. The - A
6. What kind of baby? tiny - Adj
7. A - A

Classified Sentence:	A	Adj	SN	V	P	A	OP
	A	tiny	baby	slept	in	the	crib.

Question and Answer Flow for Sentence 3: Eight small boys played in the garden.

1. Who played in the garden? boys - SN
2. What is being said about boys? boys played - V
3. In - P
4. In what? garden - OP

5. The - A
6. What kind of boys? small - Adj
7. How many boys? eight - Adj

Classified Sentence:	Adj	Adj	SN	V	P	A	OP
	Eight	small	boys	played	in	the	garden.

 PRACTICE TIME

Have students turn to pages 34 and 35 in the Practice Section of their book and find Chapter 15, Lesson 3, Practice *(1-2)*. Go over the directions to make sure they understand what to do. Check and discuss the Practices after students have finished. (*Chapter 15, Lesson 3, Practice keys are given below and on the next page.*)

Chapter 15, Lesson 3, Practice 1: Correct the capitalization mistakes and put the rule number above each correction. Use the rule numbers in Reference 11 on page 17 in the Reference Section of your book. Put a (**.**) or a (**?**) at the end of the sentence.

   1   2   3   4   **(capitalization rule numbers)**

  M   I   M   W

1. may i visit mary on wednesday **?** **(4 capitals)**

Level 1 Homeschool Teacher's Manual

© SHURLEY INSTRUCTIONAL MATERIALS, INC.

CHAPTER 15 LESSON 3 CONTINUED

Chapter 15, Lesson 3, Practice 1 (continued):

1 (or 3)	6	7	(capitalization rule numbers)
C	S	W	

2. chris lives in seattle, washington __**.**__ **(3 capitals)**

Chapter 15, Lesson 3, Practice 2: On notebook paper, write a sentence using the words in the Word Bank. Put the words you select in the same order as the Sentence Labels listed below. Write the correct label above each word in your sentence.

WORD BANK

Nouns	Verbs	Adjectives	Adverbs	Prepositional Phrases
wind breeze storm	blew gusted howled	a, an, the, cold, refreshing, hot, severe, spring, soft, gentle, harsh, dark, summer, winter	loudly, strongly, suddenly, today, calmly, silently, yesterday	across the lake at night in the tunnel during the day in the mountains

Sentence Labels: A Adj SN V Adv Prep Phrase

Independent Exercise: Choose your own Sentence Labels.

 ## ACTIVITY / ASSIGNMENT TIME

Have students turn to page 87 in the Activity Section of their books and find Chapter 15, Lesson 3, Activity. Go over the directions to make sure they understand what to do. Check and discuss the Activity after students have finished.

Chapter 15, Lesson 3, Activity: Use the code in the box below to find <u>transportation</u> words. Using the code numbers, write the correct letters for each blank. Then, make up your own code for several words.

Code			Words						
1. g	7. o	13. l	s 3	h 10	i 9	p 11	b 15	i 9	c 6	y 16	c 6	l 13	e 5
2. t	8. r	14. d	t 2	a 4	x 12	i 9	t 2	r 8	a 4	c 6	t 2	o 7	r 8
3. s	9. i	15. b	s 3	l 13	e 5	d 14	t 2	u 18	g 1	b 15	o 7	a 4	t 2
4. a	10. h	16. y											
5. e	11. p	17. n	c 6	a 4	r 8	s 3	t 2	r 8	a 4	i 9	n 17	s 3		
6. c	12. x	18. u											

(End of lesson.)

CHAPTER 15   LESSON 4
Objectives: Jingles, Vocabulary #3, Grammar (Practice Sentences), Activity, and Writing (Journal)

 **JINGLE TIME**

Have students turn to the Jingle Section in their books. The teacher will lead the students in reciting the previously-taught jingles.

 VOCABULARY TIME

Have students turn to page 7 in the Vocabulary Section of their books. Introduce the vocabulary words listed in the vocabulary box below by reciting them together with your students.

Chapter 15, Vocabulary Words #3
church, old, gray, white, (down)

 GRAMMAR TIME

Put the Practice Sentences from the box below on the board or on notebook paper. Use these sentences as you practice the concepts that have been taught. For the greatest benefit, students must participate orally with the teacher.

Chapter 15, Practice Sentences for Lesson 4
1. Several friends walked happily to church.
2. The old gray horse walked slowly down the road.
3. Eight beautiful white swans landed on the lake.

TEACHING SCRIPT FOR PRACTICE SENTENCES

We will classify these three sentences to practice what we have learned. We will classify the sentences together. Begin.

Question and Answer Flow for Sentence 1: Several friends walked happily to church.
1. Who walked happily to church? friends - SN   4. To - P
2. What is being said about friends? friends walked - V   5. To what? church - OP
3. Walked how? happily - Adv   6. How many friends? several - Adj
Classified Sentence: Adj   SN   V   Adv   P   OP
Several   friends   walked   happily   to   church.

CHAPTER 15 LESSON 4 CONTINUED

Question and Answer Flow for Sentence 2: The old gray horse walked slowly down the road.

1. What walked slowly down the road? horse - SN
2. What is being said about horse? horse walked - V
3. Walked how? slowly - Adv
4. Down - P
5. Down what? road - OP

6. The - A
7. What kind of horse? gray - Adj
8. What kind of horse? old - Adj
9. The - A

Classified Sentence:

A	Adj	Adj	SN	V	Adv	P	A	OP
The	old	gray	horse	walked	slowly	down	the	road.

Question and Answer Flow for Sentence 3: Eight beautiful white swans landed on the lake.

1. What landed on the lake? swans - SN
2. What is being said about swans? swans landed - V
3. On - P
4. On what? lake - OP

5. The - A
6. What kind of swans? white - Adj
7. What kind of swans? beautiful - Adj
8. How many swans? eight - Adj

Classified Sentence:

Adj	Adj	Adj	SN	V	P	A	OP
Eight	beautiful	white	swans	landed	on	the	lake.

ACTIVITY / ASSIGNMENT TIME

Have students write the three sentences from this lesson on a sheet of paper. Have them tape-record the Question and Answer Flows for all three sentences. Students should write labels above the sentences as they classify them. (*After the students have finished, check the tape and the sentence labels. Make sure students understand any mistakes they have made.*)

WRITING TIME

Have students make an entry in their journals.

(End of lesson.)

CHAPTER 15   LESSON 5
Objectives: Jingles, Vocabulary #4, Grammar (Practice Sentences), Test, Check, and Writing (Journal).

 **JINGLE TIME**

Have students turn to the Jingle Section of their books. The teacher will lead the students in reciting the previously-taught jingles.

 VOCABULARY TIME

Have students turn to page 7 in the Vocabulary Section of their books. Introduce the vocabulary words listed in the vocabulary box below by reciting them together with your students.

Chapter 15, Vocabulary Words #4
shivering, whimpered, ocean, crashed, rocks

 GRAMMAR TIME

Put the Practice Sentences from the box below on the board or on notebook paper. Use these sentences as you practice the concepts that have been taught. For the greatest benefit, students must participate orally with the teacher.

Chapter 15, Practice Sentences for Lesson 5
1. The eight shivering puppies whimpered loudly.
2. The passengers slept on the bus.
3. The big ocean waves crashed loudly across the rocks.

TEACHING SCRIPT FOR PRACTICE SENTENCES

We will classify these three sentences to practice what we have learned. We will classify the sentences together. Begin.

CHAPTER 15 LESSON 5 CONTINUED

Question and Answer Flow for Sentence 1: The eight shivering puppies whimpered loudly.

1. What whimpered loudly? puppies - SN
2. What is being said about puppies? puppies whimpered - V
3. Whimpered how? loudly - Adv

4. What kind of puppies? shivering - Adj
5. How many puppies? eight - Adj
6. The - A

Classified Sentence:	A	Adj	Adj	SN	V	Adv
	The	eight	shivering	puppies	whimpered	loudly.

Question and Answer Flow for Sentence 2: The passengers slept on the bus.

1. Who slept on the bus? passengers - SN
2. What is being said about passengers? passengers slept - V
3. On - P

4. On what? bus - OP
5. The - A
6. The - A

Classified Sentence:	A	SN	V	P	A	OP
	The	passengers	slept	on	the	bus.

Question and Answer Flow for Sentence 3: The big ocean waves crashed loudly across the rocks.

1. What crashed loudly across the rocks? waves - SN
2. What is being said about waves? waves crashed - V
3. Crashed how? loudly - Adv
4. Across - P
5. Across what? rocks - OP

6. The - A
7. What kind of waves? ocean - Adj
8. What kind of waves? big - Adj
9. The - A

Classified Sentence:	A	Adj	Adj	SN	V	Adv	P	A	OP
	The	big	ocean	waves	crashed	loudly	across	the	rocks.

 **TEST TIME**

Have students turn to page 68 in the Test Section of their books and find Chapter 15 Test. Go over the directions to make sure they understand what to do. (*Chapter 15 Test key is on the next page.*)

Chapter 15 Test
(Student Page 68)

Exercise 1: Classify each sentence. Use **SN** for subject noun, **V** for verb, **Adv** for adverb, **Adj** for adjective, **A** for article adjective, **P** for preposition, and **OP** for object of the preposition. For Sentence 1, underline the complete subject <u>one</u> time and the complete predicate <u>two</u> times.

```
     A    Adj      Adj       SN        V        Adv
1.  The  eight  shivering  puppies  whimpered  loudly.
```

```
     A    Adj    Adj     SN      V       Adv      P     A    OP
2.  The  big   ocean   waves  crashed  loudly  across  the  rocks.
```

Exercise 2: Underline the **syn** if the words are synonyms. Underline the **ant** if the words are antonyms.

1. left, right syn **ant**	2. poor, rich syn **ant**	3. puzzle, riddle **syn** ant

Exercise 3: Name the five parts of speech that you have studied. (*You may use abbreviations.*) **(The order of answers may vary.)**

1. **Noun (N)**   2. **Verb (V)**   3. **Adjective (Adj)**   4. **Adverb (Adv)**   5. **Preposition (P)**

Exercise 4: Correct the capitalization mistakes and put the rule number above each correction. Use the rule numbers in Reference 11 on page 17 in the Reference Section of your book. Put a (**.**) or a (**?**) at the end of the sentence.

```
1 (or 2)                    3         4          (capitalization rule numbers)
I                           K         T
i  will  ride  to  school  with  katie  on  tuesday __.__ (3 capitals)
```

Exercise 5: On notebook paper, write a sentence using the words in the Word Bank. Put the words you select in the same order as the Sentence Labels listed below. Write the correct label above each word in your sentence.

WORD BANK				
Nouns	**Verbs**	**Adjectives**	**Adverbs**	**Prepositional Phrases**
fox squirrel raccoon	peeked stared glanced	a, an, the, baby, cute, tiny, tired, red, large, frisky, curious, hungry, playful	suddenly excitedly cautiously curiously	in the box at the boy at the house across the yard
Sentence Labels: A Adj Adj SN V Adv Prep Phrase				

Exercise 6: In your journal, write a paragraph summarizing what you have learned this week.

CHECK TIME

After students have finished, check and discuss their test papers. Make sure they understand why their answers are right or wrong. Use the Question and Answer Flows on page 177 in this chapter to check the sentences on the Chapter 15 Test. (*For total points, count each required answer as a point.*)

(End of lesson.)

CHAPTER 16   LESSON 1
Objectives: Jingles, Synonyms, Antonyms, Skill (Singular and Plural Nouns), Practice Exercise, and Activity.

 **JINGLE TIME**

Have students turn to the Jingle Section in their books. The teacher will lead the students in reciting the previously-taught jingles.

 SYNONYM AND ANTONYM TIME

Have students turn to the Synonym and Antonym Section of their books. Introduce the new words listed for Chapter 16 in the box below. Make sure students know the meanings of the new synonyms and antonyms. Then, have students underline the correct answers in their books. They should study these words again before their test.

Chapter 16: Underline the <u>**syn**</u> if the words are synonyms. Underline the <u>**ant**</u> if the words are antonyms.
1. on, off   syn   **ant**   2. tall, short   syn   **ant**   3. kind, good   **syn**   ant

 SKILL TIME

<u>*TEACHING SCRIPT FOR SINGULAR AND PLURAL NOUNS*</u>

Today, we will learn how to identify nouns as singular or plural. This is an easy skill, and you should not have any trouble learning it. We must first learn the general definitions for singular and plural. Look on page 17 at Reference 12 for the definitions of singular and plural nouns. Let's read over these definitions together. Begin. (*Go over the definitions for singular and plural nouns in Reference 12 on the next page.*)

A **singular noun** usually does not end in *s* or *es* and means only one. (*Discuss the examples in the reference box.*) There are a few exceptions which you may encounter occasionally. (*Read and discuss several exceptions.*)

Now, we will read the definition for a plural noun. A **plural noun** usually ends in *s* or *es* and means more than one. (*Discuss the examples in the reference box.*) Again, there are a few exceptions which I will explain. (*Read and discuss some exceptions. Have students name other plural nouns that do not end in **s**.*)

CHAPTER 16 LESSON 1 CONTINUED

Reference 12: Definitions for Singular and Plural Nouns
1. A **singular noun** usually does not end in *s* or *es* and means only one. (*ship, clown, cat*)   Underline: Exception: Some nouns that end in s are singular and mean only one. (*glass, mess, class*)
2. A **plural noun** usually ends in *s* or *es* and means more than one. (*ships, clowns, cats*)   Exception: Some nouns are made plural by changing their spelling. (*tooth - teeth, woman - women*)

Look on page 18 at Reference 13 for several examples of singular and plural nouns. Let's read and discuss these examples together. (*Go over the examples for singular and plural nouns in Reference 13 below.*)

Reference 13: Singular and Plural Nouns					
For each noun listed below, write **S** for singular or **P** for plural.					
Noun	**S or P**	**Noun**	**S or P**	**Noun**	**S or P**
1. trees	P	4. child	S	7. shoes	P
2. tooth	S	5. teeth	P	8. children	P
3. frog	S	6. bus	S	9. tiger	S

 PRACTICE TIME

Have students turn to page 35 in the Practice Section of their book and find Chapter 16, Lesson 1, Practice. Go over the directions to make sure they understand what to do. Check and discuss the Practice after students have finished. (*Chapter 16, Lesson 1, Practice key is given below.*)

Chapter 16, Lesson 1, Practice: For each noun listed below, write **S** for singular or **P** for plural.					
Noun	**S or P**	**Noun**	**S or P**	**Noun**	**S or P**
1. bears	P	5. ants	P	9. cars	P
2. goose	S	6. balloon	S	10. geese	P
3. babies	P	7. feet	P	11. church	S
4. dog	S	8. foot	S	12. windows	P

 ACTIVITY / ASSIGNMENT TIME

Walk through the house, identifying nouns as singular or plural. (*table, chairs, bed, books, pencils, couch, curtains, windows, doors, clothes, stove, etc.*) You could also have your child label each noun with an "S" for singular or a "P" for plural by placing on each noun a sticker or piece of paper with the "S" or "P" label on it.

(End of lesson.)

CHAPTER 16   LESSON 2

Objectives: Jingles, Vocabulary #1, Grammar (Practice Sentences), and Practice Exercise.

 **JINGLE TIME**

Have students turn to the Jingle Section in their books. The teacher will lead the students in reciting the previously-taught jingles.

 VOCABULARY TIME

Have students turn to page 7 in the Vocabulary Section of their books. Introduce the vocabulary words listed in the vocabulary box below by reciting them together with your students.

Chapter 16, Vocabulary Words #1
kites, high, sky

 GRAMMAR TIME

Put the Practice Sentences from the box below on the board or on notebook paper. Use these sentences as you practice the concepts that have been taught. For the greatest benefit, students must participate orally with the teacher.

Chapter 16, Practice Sentences for Lesson 2
1. Five large green kites flew high in the sky.
2. The family played happily in the ocean.
3. The hungry bird flew swiftly to the window.

TEACHING SCRIPT FOR PRACTICE SENTENCES

We will classify these three sentences to practice what we have learned. We will classify the sentences together. Begin.

CHAPTER 16 LESSON 2 CONTINUED

Question and Answer Flow for Sentence 1: Five large green kites flew high in the sky.

1. What flew high in the sky? kites - SN
2. What is being said about kites? kites flew - V
3. Flew how? high - Adv
4. In - P
5. In what? sky - OP

6. The - A
7. What kind of kites? green - Adj
8. What kind of kites? large - Adj
9. How many kites? five - Adj

Classified Sentence:

Adj	Adj	Adj	SN	V	Adv	P	A	OP
Five	large	green	kites	flew	high	in	the	sky.

Question and Answer Flow for Sentence 2: The family played happily in the ocean.

1. Who played happily in the ocean? family - SN
2. What is being said about family? family played - V
3. Played how? happily - Adv
4. In - P

5. In what? ocean - OP
6. The - A
7. The - A

Classified Sentence:

A	SN	V	Adv	P	A	OP
The	family	played	happily	in	the	ocean.

Question and Answer Flow for Sentence 3: The hungry bird flew swiftly to the window.

1. What flew swiftly to the window? bird - SN
2. What is being said about bird? bird flew - V
3. Flew how? swiftly - Adv
4. To - P

5. To what? window - OP
6. The - A
7. What kind of bird? hungry - Adj
8. The - A

Classified Sentence:

A	Adj	SN	V	Adv	P	A	OP
The	hungry	bird	flew	swiftly	to	the	window.

 PRACTICE TIME

Have students turn to page 35 in the Practice Section of their book and find Chapter 16, Lesson 2, Practice. Go over the directions to make sure they understand what to do. Check and discuss the Practice after students have finished. (*Chapter 16, Lesson 2, Practice key is given below.*)

Chapter 16, Lesson 2, Practice: For each noun listed below, write **S** for singular or **P** for plural.

Noun	S or P	Noun	S or P	Noun	S or P
1. sleds	P	5. women	P	9. turtles	P
2. flower	S	6. horse	S	10. mice	P
3. kittens	P	7. clowns	P	11. foxes	P
4. mouse	S	8. crib	S	12. pig	S

(End of lesson.)

Level 1 Homeschool Teacher's Manual

CHAPTER 16   LESSON 3
Objectives: Jingles, Vocabulary #2, Grammar (Practice Sentences), Practice Exercise, and Activity.

 **JINGLE TIME**

Have students turn to the Jingle Section in their books. The teacher will lead the students in reciting the previously-taught jingles.

 VOCABULARY TIME

Have students turn to page 7 in the Vocabulary Section of their books. Introduce the vocabulary words listed in the vocabulary box below by reciting them together with your students.

Chapter 16, Vocabulary Words #2
nine, silently, rolled

 GRAMMAR TIME

Put the Practice Sentences from the box below on the board or on notebook paper. Use these sentences as you practice the concepts that have been taught. For the greatest benefit, students must participate orally with the teacher.

Chapter 16, Practice Sentences for Lesson 3
1. Nine yellow kites flew silently across the lake.
2. The little girl sat quietly in church.
3. The huge rocks rolled suddenly down the mountain.

TEACHING SCRIPT FOR PRACTICE SENTENCES

We will classify these three sentences to practice what we have learned. We will classify the sentences together. Begin.

CHAPTER 16 LESSON 3 CONTINUED

Question and Answer Flow for Sentence 1: Nine yellow kites flew silently across the lake.

1. What flew silently across the lake? kites - SN
2. What is being said about kites? kites flew - V
3. Flew how? silently - Adv
4. Across - P
5. Across what? lake - OP
6. The - A
7. What kind of kites? yellow - Adj
8. How many kites? nine - Adj

Classified Sentence:

Adj	Adj	SN	V	Adv	P	A	OP
Nine	yellow	kites	flew	silently	across	the	lake.

Question and Answer Flow for Sentence 2: The little girl sat quietly in church.

1. Who sat quietly in church? girl - SN
2. What is being said about girl? girl sat - V
3. Sat how? quietly - Adv
4. In - P
5. In what? church - OP
6. What kind of girl? little - Adj
7. The - A

Classified Sentence:

A	Adj	SN	V	Adv	P	OP
The	little	girl	sat	quietly	in	church.

Question and Answer Flow for Sentence 3: The huge rocks rolled suddenly down the mountain.

1. What rolled suddenly down the mountain? rocks - SN
2. What is being said about rocks? rocks rolled - V
3. Rolled how? suddenly - Adv
4. Down - P
5. Down what? mountain - OP
6. The - A
7. What kind of rocks? huge - Adj
8. The - A

Classified Sentence:

A	Adj	SN	V	Adv	P	A	OP
The	huge	rocks	rolled	suddenly	down	the	mountain.

 PRACTICE TIME

Have students turn to page 36 in the Practice Section of their book and find Chapter 16, Lesson 3, Practice *(1-3)*. Go over the directions to make sure they understand what to do. Check and discuss the Practices after students have finished. (*Chapter 16, Lesson 3, Practice keys are given below and on the next page.*)

Chapter 16, Lesson 3, Practice 1: For each noun listed below, write **S** for singular or **P** for plural.

Noun	S or P	Noun	S or P	Noun	S or P
1. rabbits	P	5. families	P	9. ducks	P
2. airplane	S	6. kite	S	10. men	P
3. monkeys	P	7. trains	P	11. bird	S
4. man	S	8. butterfly	S	12. doll	S

CHAPTER 16 LESSON 3 CONTINUED

Chapter 16, Lesson 3, Practice 2: Correct the capitalization mistakes and put the rule number above each correction. Use the rule numbers in Reference 11 on page 17 in the Reference Section of your book. Put a (**.**) or a (**?**) at the end of the sentence.

1(or 2)	4	6	7	(capitalization rule numbers)
I	M	C	I	

i am leaving on monday for chicago, illinois __**.**__ **(4 capitals)**

Chapter 16, Lesson 3, Practice 3: On notebook paper, write a sentence using the words in the Word Bank. Put the words you select in the same order as the Sentence Labels listed below. Write the correct label above each word in your sentence.

WORD BANK

Nouns	Verbs	Adjectives	Adverbs	Prepositional Phrases
airplane helicopter jet	landed arrived flew	a, an, the, large, loud, new, swift, fast, big, blue, silver, army	promptly, carefully, safely, today, suddenly, around, rapidly,	on time at the airport on the runway to the ship

Sentence Labels: A Adj SN V Adv Prep Phrase

Independent Exercise: Choose your own Sentence Labels.

ACTIVITY / ASSIGNMENT TIME

Have students turn to page 88 and find Chapter 16, Lesson 3, Activity. Go over the directions to make sure they understand what to do. Check and discuss the Activity after students have finished.

Chapter 16, Lesson 3, Activity: In the Word Search Puzzle below, find the following adjective words. The words will appear "down" or "across" in the puzzle. Color the adjectives going down blue and the adjectives going across yellow.

BEAUTIFUL	*BOUNCY*	*CLEVER*	*CUTE*	*EARLY*	*GIANT*
HUGE	*ORANGE*	*STRONG*	*THICK*	*WEARY*	*YOUNG*

S	W	E	A	R	L	Y	H	T	C
T	E	A	U	T	I	F	U	H	U
R	A	Y	O	U	N	G	G	I	T
O	R	A	W	O	K	D	E	C	E
N	Y	O	U	N	G	E	Z	K	B
G	O	S	G	I	A	N	T	U	O
E	C	L	E	V	E	R	O	H	U
H	S	O	R	A	N	G	E	I	N
B	E	A	U	T	I	F	U	L	C
Z	D	U	H	T	E	W	D	K	Y

(End of lesson.)

CHAPTER 16   LESSON 4

Objectives: Jingles, Vocabulary #3, Grammar (Practice Sentences), Activity 1, Activity 2, and Writing (Journal).

 **JINGLE TIME**

Have students turn to the Jingle Section in their books. The teacher will lead the students in reciting the previously-taught jingles.

 VOCABULARY TIME

Have students turn to page 7 in the Vocabulary Section of their books. Introduce the vocabulary words listed in the vocabulary box below by reciting them together with your students.

Chapter 16, Vocabulary Words #3
pony, trotted, pink, pig

 GRAMMAR TIME

Put the Practice Sentences from the box below on the board or on notebook paper. Use these sentences as you practice the concepts that have been taught. For the greatest benefit, students must participate orally with the teacher.

Chapter 16, Practice Sentences for Lesson 4
1. The weary baby slept soundly in the car.
2. The small black pony trotted quickly down the road.
3. A pink pig rolled happily in the mud.

TEACHING SCRIPT FOR PRACTICE SENTENCES

We will classify these three sentences to practice what we have learned. We will classify the sentences together. Begin.

Question and Answer Flow for Sentence 1: The weary baby slept soundly in the car.

1. Who slept soundly in the car? baby - SN
2. What is being said about baby? baby slept - V
3. Slept how? soundly - Adv
4. In - P

5. In what? car - OP
6. The - A
7. What kind of baby? weary - Adj
8. The - A

Classified Sentence:

	A	Adj	SN	V	Adv	P	A	OP
	The	weary	baby	slept	soundly	in	the	car.

Level 1 Homeschool Teacher's Manual

CHAPTER 16 LESSON 4 CONTINUED

Question and Answer Flow for Sentence 2: The small black pony trotted quickly down the road.

1. What trotted quickly down the road? pony - SN
2. What is being said about pony? pony trotted - V
3. Trotted how? quickly - Adv
4. Down - P
5. Down what? road - OP

6. The - A
7. What kind of pony? black - Adj
8. What kind of pony? small - Adj
9. The - A

Classified Sentence:

A	Adj	Adj	SN	V	Adv	P	A	OP
The	small	black	pony	trotted	quickly	down	the	road.

Question and Answer Flow for Sentence 3: A pink pig rolled happily in the mud.

1. What rolled happily in the mud? pig - SN
2. What is being said about pig? pig rolled - V
3. Rolled how? happily - Adv
4. In - P

5. In what? mud - OP
6. The - A
7. What kind of pig? pink - Adj
8. A - A

Classified Sentence:

A	Adj	SN	V	Adv	P	A	OP
A	pink	pig	rolled	happily	in	the	mud.

ACTIVITY / ASSIGNMENT TIME

Activity 1:

Have students write the three sentences from this lesson on a sheet of paper. Have them tape-record the Question and Answer Flows for all three sentences. Students should write labels above the sentences as they classify them. (*After the students have finished, check the tape and the sentence labels. Make sure students understand any mistakes they have made.*)

Activity 2:

Have students turn to page 88 and find Chapter 16, Lesson 4, Activity. Go over the directions to make sure they understand what to do. Check and discuss the Activity after students have finished.

Chapter 16, Lesson 4, Activity: In the Word Search Puzzle below, find the following preposition words and color each one a different color. The words will appear "down" or "across" in the puzzle.

	ACROSS	*AT*	*BY*	*DOWN*	*IN*	*ON*	*TO*
A	T	A	B	I		N	E
Y	A	O	N	E		F	D
A	C	R	O	S		S	O
K	O	G	W	H		R	**W**
B	Y	M	N	T		O	N

WRITING TIME

Have students make an entry in their journals.

(End of lesson.)

CHAPTER 16   LESSON 5

Objectives: Jingles, Vocabulary #4, Grammar (Practice Sentences), Test, Check, and Writing (Journal).

 **JINGLE TIME**

Have students turn to the Jingle Section in their books. The teacher will lead the students in reciting the previously-taught jingles.

 VOCABULARY TIME

Have students turn to page 7 in the Vocabulary Section of their books. Introduce the vocabulary words listed in the vocabulary box below by reciting them together with your students.

Chapter 16, Vocabulary Words #4
bell, rang, valley, sailor, map

 GRAMMAR TIME

Put the Practice Sentences from the box below on the board or on notebook paper. Use these sentences as you practice the concepts that have been taught. For the greatest benefit, students must participate orally with the teacher.

Chapter 16, Practice Sentences for Lesson 5
1. The church bell rang loudly across the valley. 2. The fat frog sat on a rock. 3. The old sailor looked silently at the map.

TEACHING SCRIPT FOR PRACTICE SENTENCES

We will classify these three sentences to practice what we have learned. We will classify the sentences together. Begin.

CHAPTER 16 LESSON 5 CONTINUED

Question and Answer Flow for Sentence 1: The church bell rang loudly across the valley.

1. What rang loudly across the valley? bell - SN
2. What is being said about bell? bell rang - V
3. Rang how? loudly - Adv
4. Across - P

5. Across what? valley - OP
6. The - A
7. What kind of bell? church - Adj
8. The - A

Classified Sentence:

A	Adj	SN	V	Adv	P	A	OP
The	church	bell	rang	loudly	across	the	valley.

Question and Answer Flow for Sentence 2: The fat frog sat on a rock.

1. What sat on a rock? frog - SN
2. What is being said about frog? frog sat - V
3. On - P
4. On what? rock - OP

5. A - A
6. What kind of frog? fat - Adj
7. The - A

Classified Sentence:

A	Adj	SN	V	P	A	OP
The	fat	frog	sat	on	a	rock.

Question and Answer Flow for Sentence 3: The old sailor looked silently at the map.

1. Who looked silently at the map? sailor - SN
2. What is being said about sailor? sailor looked - V
3. Looked how? silently - Adv
4. At - P

5. At what? map - OP
6. The - A
7. What kind of sailor? old - Adj
8. The - A

Classified Sentence:

A	Adj	SN	V	Adv	P	A	OP
The	old	sailor	looked	silently	at	the	map.

 **TEST TIME**

Have students turn to page 69 in the Test Section of their books and find Chapter 16 Test. Go over the directions to make sure they understand what to do. (*Chapter 16 Test key is on the next page.*)

Chapter 16 Test
(Student Page 69)

Exercise 1: Classify each sentence. Use **SN** for subject noun, **V** for verb, **Adv** for adverb, **Adj** for adjective, **A** for article adjective, **P** for preposition, and **OP** for object of the preposition. For Sentence 1, underline the complete subject <u>one</u> time and the complete predicate <u>two</u> times.

```
       Adj    Adj      SN       V      Adv        P      A     OP
1.    Nine  yellow   kites    flew  silently  across   the   lake.
```

```
        A    Adj     SN       V      Adv       P      A      OP
2.     The  huge   rocks   rolled suddenly  down    the   mountain.
```

Exercise 2: Underline the **syn** if the words are synonyms. Underline the **ant** if the words are antonyms.

| 1. on, off | syn **ant** | 2. tall, short | syn **ant** | 3. kind, good | **syn** ant |

Exercise 3: Name the five parts of speech that you have studied. (*You may use abbreviations.*)
(The order of answers may vary.)

| 1. **Noun (N)** | 2. **Verb (V)** | 3. **Adjective (Adj)** | 4. **Adverb (Adv)** | 5. **Preposition (P)** |

Exercise 4: Correct the capitalization mistakes and put the rule number above each correction. Use the rule numbers in Reference 11 on page 17 in the Reference Section of your book. Put a (**.**) or a (**?**) at the end of the sentence.

```
   1     3              6      7_____(capitalization rule numbers)
   D     W              M      F
  does  walter  live  in  miami,  florida  ?    (4 capitals)
```

Exercise 5: For each noun listed below, write **S** for singular or **P** for plural.

Noun	S or P	Noun	S or P	Noun	S or P
1. bats	P	5. boys	P	9. parrot	S
2. woman	S	6. lady	S	10. children	P
3. nests	P	7. women	P	11. piano	S
4. apple	S	8. child	S	12. telephones	P

Exercise 6: In your journal, write a paragraph summarizing what you have learned this week.

 **CHECK TIME**

After students have finished, check and discuss their test papers. Make sure they understand why their answers are right or wrong. Use the Question and Answer Flows on page 184 in this chapter to check the sentences on the Chapter 16 Test. (*For total points, count each required answer as a point.*)

(End of lesson.)

CHAPTER 17   LESSON 1
Objectives: Jingles, Synonyms, Antonyms, Skill (Common and Proper Nouns), Practice Exercise, and Activity.

JINGLE TIME

Have students turn to the Jingle Section in their books. The teacher will lead the students in reciting the previously-taught jingles.

SYNONYM AND ANTONYM TIME

Have students turn to the Synonym and Antonym Section of their books. Introduce the new words listed for Chapter 17 in the box below. Make sure students know the meanings of the new synonyms and antonyms. Then, have students underline the correct answers in their books. They should study these words again before their test.

Chapter 17: Underline the <u>syn</u> if the words are synonyms. Underline the <u>ant</u> if the words are antonyms.
1. top, bottom   syn   **<u>ant</u>**   2. hard, firm   **<u>syn</u>**   ant   3. evil, bad   **<u>syn</u>**   ant

SKILL TIME

TEACHING SCRIPT FOR COMMON AND PROPER NOUNS

Today, we will learn how to identify nouns as common or proper. This is another easy skill, and you should not have any trouble learning it. However, we must first learn the general definitions for **common** and **proper**. Look on page 18 at Reference 14 for the definitions of common and proper nouns. Let's read over these definitions together. Begin. (_Go over the definitions for common and proper nouns in Reference 14 on the next page._)

A **common noun** names ANY person, place, or thing. A common noun is not capitalized because it does not name a specific person, place, or thing. (_Discuss the examples in the reference box._)

Now, we will read the definition for a proper noun. A **proper noun** is a noun that names a specific, or particular, person, place, or thing. Proper nouns are always capitalized no matter where they are located in the sentence. (_Discuss the examples in the reference box._)

CHAPTER 17 LESSON 1 CONTINUED

Reference 14: Definitions for Common and Proper Nouns
1. A **common noun** names ANY person, place, or thing. A common noun is not capitalized because it does not name a specific person, place, or thing. (*trees, lake*)
2. A **proper noun** is a noun that names a specific, or particular, person, place, or thing. Proper nouns are always capitalized no matter where they are located in the sentence. (*Matthew, Hawaii*)

Look on page 18 at Reference 15 for several examples of common and proper nouns. Let's read and discuss these examples together. (*Go over the examples for common and proper nouns in Reference 15 below.*)

Reference 15: Common and Proper Nouns					
For each noun listed below, write **C** for common or **P** for proper.					
Noun	**C or P**	**Noun**	**C or P**	**Noun**	**C or P**
1. Christmas	P	4. Texas	P	7. Denver	P
2. jar	C	5. Sam	P	8. coat	C
3. nurse	C	6. horse	C	9. girl	C

 PRACTICE TIME

Have students turn to page 37 in the Practice Section of their book and find Chapter 17, Lesson 1, Practice. Go over the directions to make sure they understand what to do. Check and discuss the Practice after students have finished. (*Chapter 17, Lesson 1, Practice key is given below.*)

Chapter 17, Lesson 1, Practice: For each noun listed below, write **C** for common or **P** for proper.					
Noun	**C or P**	**Noun**	**C or P**	**Noun**	**C or P**
1. student	C	5. Ted	P	9. Easter	P
2. Mr. Smith	P	6. England	P	10. cup	C
3. city	C	7. boy	C	11. clock	C
4. Kansas	P	8. Italy	P	12. map	C

 ACTIVITY / ASSIGNMENT TIME

Select a story book. Have students mark all proper nouns with a yellow marker. Discuss why the nouns are proper. Discuss whether the nouns are names of persons, places, or things. Explain that words that are capitalized at the beginning of sentences are not always proper nouns. They are capitalized because they are the first word of a sentence. Discuss the number of proper nouns in the story. Have students write a story using several proper nouns. Then, have them highlight the proper nouns in their story with their choice of colored markers.

(End of lesson.)

CHAPTER 17   LESSON 2

Objectives: Jingles, Vocabulary #1, Grammar (Practice Sentences, Practice and Improved Sentences), and Practice Exercise.

 **JINGLE TIME**

Have students turn to the Jingle Section in their books. The teacher will lead the students in reciting the previously-taught jingles.

 VOCABULARY TIME

Have students turn to page 7 in the Vocabulary Section of their books. Introduce the vocabulary words listed in the vocabulary box below by reciting them together with your students.

Chapter 17, Vocabulary Words #1
rode, train, went, zoo

 GRAMMAR TIME

Put the Practice Sentences from the box below on the board or on notebook paper. Use these sentences as you practice the concepts that have been taught. For the greatest benefit, students must participate orally with the teacher.

Chapter 17, Practice Sentences for Lesson 2
1. The happy girls rode on the train.
2. Several excited boys waved at the airplane.
3. The small children went to the zoo yesterday.

TEACHING SCRIPT FOR PRACTICE SENTENCES

We will classify these three sentences to practice what we have learned. We will classify the sentences together. Begin.

CHAPTER 17 LESSON 2 CONTINUED

Question and Answer Flow for Sentence 1: The happy girls rode on the train.

1. Who rode on the train? girls - SN
2. What is being said about girls? girls rode - V
3. On - P
4. On what? train - OP

5. The - A
6. What kind of girls? happy - Adj
7. The - A

Classified Sentence:

A	Adj	SN	V	P	A	OP
The	happy	girls	rode	on	the	train.

Question and Answer Flow for Sentence 2: Several excited boys waved at the airplane.

1. Who waved at the airplane? boys - SN
2. What is being said about boys? boys waved - V
3. At - P
4. At what? airplane - OP

5. The - A
6. What kind of boys? excited - Adj
7. How many boys? several - Adj

Classified Sentence:

Adj	Adj	SN	V	P	A	OP
Several	excited	boys	waved	at	the	airplane.

Question and Answer Flow for Sentence 3: The small children went to the zoo yesterday.

1. Who went to the zoo yesterday? children - SN
2. What is being said about children? children went - V
3. To - P
4. To what? zoo - OP

5. The - A
6. Went when? yesterday - Adv
7. What kind of children? small - Adj
8. The - A

Classified Sentence:

A	Adj	SN	V	P	A	OP	Adv
The	small	children	went	to	the	zoo	yesterday.

TEACHING SCRIPT FOR WRITING PRACTICE AND IMPROVED SENTENCES

I will now guide you through a Practice Sentence using prepositions; then, we will write an Improved Sentence. Get out a sheet of notebook paper and write the title **Practice Sentence** on the top line. I will write it on the board for you. Copy these labels across the page: **A Adj SN V Adv P A OP**. (*Write on the board the words Practice Sentence and the labels students will use so they can copy them correctly*.) Make sure you leave plenty of room for the words that you will write under the labels.

Before we begin, I want you to turn to page 18 in the Reference section of your book. Look at Reference 16. Remember, this is like a little dictionary of vocabulary words that you can use to help you write Practice and Improved Sentences. You will only use this list if you cannot think of a word by yourself. (*Reference 16 is provided on the next page. Read through the list of words for nouns, verbs, adjectives, adverbs, and prepositions if you think your students need a review.*)

CHAPTER 17 LESSON 2 CONTINUED

Reference 16: Sample Vocabulary Words for Practice and Improved Sentences				
Nouns	**Verbs**	**Adjectives**	**Adverbs**	**Prepositions**
boys girls	laughed	a, an, the	quietly	across
brother sailor	raced	hungry	quickly	at
cars ship	walked	red	happily	down
horse bears	sat	three	today	in
mother father	jumped	friendly	loudly	on
monkeys bees	sailed	angry	slowly	to
cats dogs	climbed	happy	noisily	by
students airplane	flew	sleepy	yesterday	

1. Go to the **SN** label for the subject noun. Think of a noun you want to use as your subject. Write the noun you have chosen on the line *under* the **SN** label.

2. Go to the **V** label for a verb. Think of a verb that tells what your subject does. Make sure that your verb makes sense with the subject noun. Write the verb you have chosen on the line *under* the **V** label.

3. Go to the **Adv** label for the adverb. Then, go to the verb in your sentence and ask an adverb question. What are the adverb questions? (*how, when, where*) Choose one adverb question to ask and write your adverb answer *under* the first **Adv** label.

4. Go to the **P** label for the preposition. Think of a preposition that tells something about your verb. You must be careful to choose a preposition that makes sense with the noun you will choose for the object of the preposition in your next step. If you want to check the preposition box to help you think of a preposition, do it now. Then, write the word you have chosen for a preposition *under* the **P** label.

5. Now, go to the **OP** label for object of the preposition. If you like the noun you thought of while thinking of a preposition, write it down under the **OP** label. You might want to think of another noun by asking *what* or *whom* after your preposition. Check to make sure the preposition and object of the preposition make sense together and also make sense with the rest of the sentence. Write the word you have chosen for the object of the preposition *under* the **OP** label. (*Give help as needed.*)

6. Go to the **A** label for the article adjective that is part of your prepositional phrase. What are the three article adjectives again? (*a, an,* and *the*). Now, you will choose one of these article adjectives that makes the best sense in your sentence. Write the article adjective you have chosen *under* the **A** label.

7. Go to the **Adj** label for the adjective. Then, go to the subject noun of your sentence and ask an adjective question. What are the adjective questions? (*what kind, which one, how many*) Choose one adjective question to ask and write your adjective answer *under* the **Adj** label next to the subject noun. Always check to make sure your answers are making sense in the sentence.

8. Go to the **A** label for article adjective. What are the three article adjectives again? (*a, an,* and *the*) Now, you will choose one of these article adjectives that makes the best sense in your sentence. Write the article adjective you have chosen *under* the **A** label.

9. Finally, check your Practice Sentence to make sure it has the necessary parts to be a complete sentence. What are the five parts of a complete sentence? (*subject, verb, complete sense, capital letter, and an end mark*) Does your Practice Sentence have the five parts of a complete sentence? (*Allow time for students to read over their sentences and to make any corrections they need to make.*)

10. Now, under your Practice Sentence, write the title **Improved Sentence** on another line. To improve your Practice Sentence, you will make one synonym change and one antonym change. Since it is harder to find words that can be changed to an antonym, it is usually wise to go through your sentence to find an antonym change first. Look through your sentence again to find words that can be improved with synonyms.

Now, I will give you time to write an Improved Sentence. If you need help, I will help you think of synonyms and antonyms for an Improved Sentence. (*Always encourage students to use a synonym-antonym book or a dictionary to help them develop an interesting and improved writing vocabulary.*)

 PRACTICE TIME

Have students turn to page 37 in the Practice Section of their book and find Chapter 17, Lesson 2, Practice. Go over the directions to make sure they understand what to do. Check and discuss the Practice after students have finished. (*Chapter 17, Lesson 2, Practice key is given below.*)

Chapter 17, Lesson 2, Practice: For each noun listed below, write **C** for common or **P** for proper.

Noun	C or P	Noun	C or P	Noun	C or P
1. Walker School	P	5. watch	C	9. Anna	P
2. Mandy	P	6. cloud	C	10. mail	C
3. milk	C	7. Mr. Jones	P	11. state	C
4. tiger	C	8. August	P	12. Thanksgiving	P

(End of lesson.)

Level 1 Homeschool Teacher's Manual

CHAPTER 17   LESSON 3

Objectives: Jingles, Vocabulary #2, Grammar (Practice Sentences, Practice and Improved Sentences), and Practice Exercise.

 **JINGLE TIME**

Have students turn to the Jingle Section in their books. The teacher will lead the students in reciting the previously-taught jingles.

 VOCABULARY TIME

Have students turn to page 7 in the Vocabulary Section of their books. Introduce the vocabulary words listed in the vocabulary box below by reciting them together with your students.

Chapter 17, Vocabulary Words #2
sun, city, opened, early, pond

 GRAMMAR TIME

Put the Practice Sentences from the box below on the board or on notebook paper. Use these sentences as you practice the concepts that have been taught. For the greatest benefit, students must participate orally with the teacher.

Chapter 17, Practice Sentences for Lesson 3
1. The cute little bears played happily in the sun.
2. The city zoo opened early.
3. A silly white duck waddled slowly to the pond.

TEACHING SCRIPT FOR PRACTICE SENTENCES

We will classify these three sentences to practice what we have learned. We will classify the sentences together. Begin. (*You might have students write the labels above the sentences at this time.*)

CHAPTER 17 LESSON 3 CONTINUED

Question and Answer Flow for Sentence 1: The cute little bears played happily in the sun.

1. What played happily in the sun? bears - SN
2. What is being said about bears? bears played - V
3. Played how? happily - Adv
4. In - P
5. In what? sun - OP
6. The - A
7. What kind of bears? little - Adj
8. What kind of bears? cute - Adj
9. The - A

Classified Sentence:

A	Adj	Adj	SN	V	Adv	P	A	OP
The	cute	little	bears	played	happily	in	the	sun.

Question and Answer Flow for Sentence 2: The city zoo opened early.

1. What opened early? zoo - SN
2. What is being said about zoo? zoo opened - V
3. Opened when? early - Adv
4. What kind of zoo? city - Adj
5. The - A

Classified Sentence:

A	Adj	SN	V	Adv
The	city	zoo	opened	early.

Question and Answer Flow for Sentence 3: A silly white duck waddled slowly to the pond.

1. What waddled slowly to the pond? duck - SN
2. What is being said about duck? duck waddled - V
3. Waddled how? slowly - Adv
4. To - P
5. To what? pond - OP
6. The - A
7. What kind of duck? white - Adj
8. What kind of duck? silly - Adj
9. A - A

Classified Sentence:

A	Adj	Adj	SN	V	Adv	P	A	OP
A	silly	white	duck	waddled	slowly	to	the	pond.

TEACHING SCRIPT FOR WRITING PRACTICE AND IMPROVED SENTENCES

I will guide you through a Practice Sentence; then, we will write an Improved Sentence. Get out a sheet of notebook paper and write the title **Practice Sentence** on the top line. I will write it on the board for you. Copy these labels across the page: **A Adj SN V Adv P A OP**. (*Write the words **Practice Sentence** and the labels students will use on the board so students can copy them correctly*.) Make sure you leave plenty of room for the words that you will write under the labels.

Before we begin, I want you to turn to page 18 in the Reference section of your book. Look at Reference 16. You can use these vocabulary words to help you write Practice and Improved Sentences if you need them. You should only use this list if you cannot think of a word by yourself. (*Guide students through their Practice and Improved Sentences by using the script on pages 194-195 in your teacher's manual. Read it word-for-word to your students. After they have finished, check and discuss their Practice and Improved sentences.*)

CHAPTER 17 LESSON 3 CONTINUED

 PRACTICE TIME

Have students turn to pages 37 and 38 in the Practice Section of their book and find Chapter 17, Lesson 3, Practice (1-3). Go over the directions to make sure they understand what to do. Check and discuss the Practices after students have finished. (*Chapter 17, Lesson 3, Practice keys are given below.*)

Chapter 17, Lesson 3, Practice 1: For each noun listed below, write **C** for common or **P** for proper.

Noun	C or P	Noun	C or P	Noun	C or P
1. cake	C	5. Monday	P	9. July	P
2. Mr. Brown	P	6. James	P	10. Africa	P
3. duck	C	7. key	C	11. Tuesday	P
4. January	P	8. barn	C	12. desk	C

Chapter 17, Lesson 3, Practice 2: For each noun listed below, write **S** for singular or **P** for plural.

Noun	S or P	Noun	S or P	Noun	S or P
1. friends	P	5. prunes	P	9. leg	S
2. bug	S	6. games	P	10. arm	S
3. stars	P	7. house	S	11. knee	S
4. bushes	P	8. street	S	12. letters	P

Chapter 17, Lesson 3, Practice 3: Correct the capitalization mistakes and put the rule number above each correction. Use the rule numbers in Reference 11 on page 17 in the Reference Section of your book. Put a (.) or a (**?**) at the end of the sentence.

1(or 3)   7   4   (capitalization rule numbers)

P   O   T

peter will arrive in oregon next tuesday ___ **.** ___ (3 capitals)

(End of lesson.)

CHAPTER 17   LESSON 4

Objectives: Jingles, Vocabulary #3, Grammar (Practice Sentences), Activity 1, and Activity 2.

 **JINGLE TIME**

Have students turn to the Jingle Section in their books. The teacher will lead the students in reciting the previously-taught jingles.

 VOCABULARY TIME

Have students turn to page 7 in the Vocabulary Section of their books. Introduce the vocabulary words listed in the vocabulary box below by reciting them together with your students.

Chapter 17, Vocabulary Words #3
library, book, carefully, ice

 GRAMMAR TIME

Put the Practice Sentences from the box below on the board or on notebook paper. Use these sentences as you practice the concepts that have been taught. For the greatest benefit, students must participate orally with the teacher.

Chapter 17, Practice Sentences for Lesson 4
1. The city library opened early today.
2. The library book fell on the floor.
3. The little girl walked carefully on the ice.

TEACHING SCRIPT FOR PRACTICE SENTENCES

We will classify these three sentences to practice what we have learned. We will classify the sentences together. Begin.

Question and Answer Flow for Sentence 1: The city library opened early today.

1. What opened early today? library - SN
2. What is being said about library? library opened - V
3. Opened when? early - Adv

4. Opened when? today - Adv
5. What kind of library? city - Adj
6. The - A

Classified Sentence:

	A	Adj	SN	V	Adv	Adv
	The	city	library	opened	early	today.

CHAPTER 17 LESSON 4 CONTINUED

Question and Answer Flow for Sentence 2: The library book fell on the floor.

1. What fell on the floor? book - SN
2. What is being said about book? book fell - V
3. On - P
4. On what? floor - OP
5. The - A
6. What kind of book? library - Adj
7. The - A

Classified Sentence:

A	Adj	SN	V	P	A	OP
The	library	book	fell	on	the	floor.

Question and Answer Flow for Sentence 3: The little girl walked carefully on the ice.

1. Who walked carefully on the ice? girl - SN
2. What is being said about girl? girl walked - V
3. Walked how? carefully - Adv
4. On - P
5. On what? ice - OP
6. The - A
7. What kind of girl? little - Adj
8. The - A

Classified Sentence:

A	Adj	SN	V	Adv	P	A	OP
The	little	girl	walked	carefully	on	the	ice.

ACTIVITY / ASSIGNMENT TIME

Activity 1:

Have students write the three sentences from this lesson on a sheet of paper. Have them tape-record the Question and Answer Flows for all three sentences. Students should write labels above the sentences as they classify them. (*After the students have finished, check the tape and the sentence labels. Make sure students understand any mistakes they have made.*)

Activity 2:

Have students turn to page 88 and find Chapter 17, Lesson 4, Activity. Go over the directions to make sure they understand what to do. Check and discuss the Activity after students have finished.

Chapter 17, Lesson 4, Activity: In the Word Search Puzzle below, find the following adverb words and color each one a different color. The words will appear "down" or "across" in the puzzle.

HAPPILY	*KINDLY*	*LOUDLY*	*RAPIDLY*	*SILENTLY*	*SLOWLY*	*TODAY*	*WARMLY*
S	K	W	A	R	M	L	Y
I	N	L	J	M	C	E	R
L	K	I	N	D	L	Y	A
E	L	O	U	D	L	Y	P
N	B	D	F	H	S	W	I
T		T	O	D	A	Y	D
L	S	L	O	W	L	Y	L
Y	Q	W	E	R	T	U	Y
S	H	A	P	P	I	L	Y

(End of lesson.)

CHAPTER 17   LESSON 5

Objectives: Jingles, Vocabulary #4, Grammar (Practice Sentences), Test, Check, and Writing (Journal).

 **JINGLE TIME**

Have students turn to the Jingle Section in their books. The teacher will lead the students in reciting the previously-taught jingles.

 VOCABULARY TIME

Have students turn to page 7 in the Vocabulary Section of their books. Introduce the vocabulary words listed in the vocabulary box below by reciting them together with your students.

Chapter 17, Vocabulary Words #4
volcano, erupted, ten, swam

 GRAMMAR TIME

Put the Practice Sentences from the box below on the board or on notebook paper. Use these sentences as you practice the concepts that have been taught. For the greatest benefit, students must participate orally with the teacher.

Chapter 17, Practice Sentences for Lesson 5
1. The big volcano erupted suddenly yesterday.
2. Several dogs barked loudly at the car.
3. Ten boys swam happily in the ocean.

TEACHING SCRIPT FOR PRACTICE SENTENCES

We will classify these three sentences to practice what we have learned. We will classify the sentences together. Begin.

CHAPTER 17 LESSON 5 CONTINUED

Question and Answer Flow for Sentence 1: The big volcano erupted suddenly yesterday.

1. What erupted suddenly yesterday? volcano - SN
2. What is being said about volcano? volcano erupted - V
3. Erupted how? suddenly - Adv

4. Erupted when? yesterday - Adv
5. What kind of volcano? big - Adj
6. The - A

Classified Sentence:

A	Adj	SN	V	Adv	Adv
The	big	volcano	erupted	suddenly	yesterday.

Question and Answer Flow for Sentence 2: Several dogs barked loudly at the car.

1. What barked loudly at the car? dogs - SN
2. What is being said about dogs? dogs barked - V
3. Barked how? loudly - Adv
4. At - P

5. At what? car - OP
6. The - A
7. How many dogs? several - Adj

Classified Sentence:

Adj	SN	V	Adv	P	A	OP
Several	dogs	barked	loudly	at	the	car.

Question and Answer Flow for Sentence 3: Ten boys swam happily in the ocean.

1. Who swam happily in the ocean? boys - SN
2. What is being said about boys? boys swam - V
3. Swam how? happily - Adv
4. In - P

5. In what? ocean - OP
6. The - A
7. How many boys? ten - Adj

Classified Sentence:

Adj	SN	V	Adv	P	A	OP
Ten	boys	swam	happily	in	the	ocean.

  TEST TIME

Have students turn to page 70 in the Test Section of their books and find Chapter 17 Test. Go over the directions to make sure they understand what to do. *(Chapter 17 Test key is on the next page.)*

Chapter 17 Test
(Student Page 70)

Exercise 1: Classify each sentence. Use **SN** for subject noun, **V** for verb, **Adv** for adverb, **Adj** for adjective, **A** for article adjective, **P** for preposition, and **OP** for object of the preposition. For Sentence 2, underline the complete subject <u>one</u> time and the complete predicate <u>two</u> times.

```
          A    Adj    SN       V       Adv       Adv
1.    The   big   volcano   erupted   suddenly   yesterday.

          Adj    SN     V      Adv     P     A     OP
2.    Several   dogs   barked   loudly   at   the   car.
```

Exercise 2: Underline the **syn** if the words are synonyms. Underline the **ant** if the words are antonyms.

| 1. top, bottom | syn **ant** | 2. evil, bad | **syn** ant | 3. hard, firm | **syn** ant |

Exercise 3: Name the five parts of speech that you have studied. (*You may use abbreviations.*)
(The order of answers may vary.)

1. **Noun (N)**   2. **Verb (V)**   3. **Adjective (Adj)**   4. **Adverb (Adv)**   5. **Preposition (P)**

Exercise 4: Correct the capitalization mistakes and put the rule number above each correction. Use the rule numbers in Reference 11 on page 17 in the Reference Section of your book. Put a (**.**) or a (**?**) at the end of the sentence.

```
 1(or 2)                   3         5        (capitalization rule numbers)

 I                         A         M

 i   would   like   to   visit   alex   in   march   __.   (3 capitals)
```

| **Exercise 5:** Write **S** for singular or **P** for plural. | |
Noun	S or P
1. jar	S
2. notebooks	P
3. computer	S
4. mice	P

| **Exercise 6:** Write **C** for Common or **P** for proper. | |
Noun	C or P
1. Mississippi	P
2. James	P
3. nephew	C
4. window	C

Exercise 7: In your journal, write a paragraph summarizing what you have learned this week.

 **CHECK TIME**

After students have finished, check and discuss their test papers. Make sure they understand why their answers are right or wrong. Use the Question and Answer Flows on page 203 in this chapter to check the sentences on the Chapter 17 Test. (*For total points, count each required answer as a point.*)

(End of lesson.)

CHAPTER 18   LESSON 1
Objectives: Jingles, Synonyms, Antonyms, Skills (Identifying Paragraphs and Topics, Supporting and Non-Supporting Ideas and Sentences), and Practice Exercise.

 **JINGLE TIME**

Have students turn to the Jingle Section in their books. The teacher will lead the students in reciting the previously-taught jingles.

 SYNONYM AND ANTONYM TIME

Have students turn to the Synonym and Antonym Section of their books. Introduce the new words listed for Chapter 18 in the box below. Make sure students know the meanings of the new synonyms and antonyms. Then, have students underline the correct answers in their books. They should study these words again before their test.

Chapter 18: Underline the <u>syn</u> if the words are synonyms. Underline the <u>ant</u> if the words are antonyms.
1. before, after   syn   **ant**   2. lost, found   syn   <u>**ant**</u>   3. sick, ill   <u>**syn**</u>   ant

 SKILL TIME

<u>*TEACHING SCRIPT FOR IDENTIFYING PARAGRAPHS AND TOPICS*</u>

You have been learning the parts of a sentence so you can write good sentences correctly. You will soon be using your sentence-writing skills in writing a paragraph. First, you must know the meaning of the word **paragraph** and the meaning of the word **topic**.

A paragraph is a group of sentences that tells about one topic. A topic tells what a paragraph is about, and the topic also tells what a group of words is about. That is why the topic is sometimes called the subject because it tells what things are about. The topic also tells the main way that things in a group are alike. We will find the topic for a group of words according to the ways they are alike.

Since it is very important to know what a paragraph is about before you begin writing, we will practice finding the topic first. We will find the topic of different sets of words. Turn to page 19 in the Reference Section and look at Reference 17. Follow along as I go over the directions with you. (*Read and discuss the directions in the reference box on the next page.*)

CHAPTER 18 LESSON 1 CONTINUED

Reference 17: The Topic		
Finding the topic: Write the name of the topic that best describes what each column of words is about. Choose from these topics: **Trees** **Colors** **Animals** **Books** **Holidays**		
(1) **Animals**	(2) **Holidays**	(3) **Colors**
squirrel raccoon rabbit	Thanksgiving Easter Christmas	purple black yellow

Let's read the words in the first column together. (*squirrel, raccoon, rabbit*) How are the words in the first column alike? (*They are all animals.*) Yes, they are all animals. The word **Animals** is a good topic for all the words in the first column because it best describes what all the words are about. Now, look at the topics listed in the directions at the top of the reference box. Do you see the word **Animals**? (*Have students respond.*) The topic **Animals** is written on the topic line above the first column because it best describes what all the words are about.

Look at the words in the middle column. How are the words **Thanksgiving, Easter**, and **Christmas** alike? (*They are all special days or holidays.*) Now, look at the topics listed in the directions at the top of the reference box. Which topic best names special days? (*Holidays*) Yes, the word **Holidays** is a good topic for all the words in the middle column because it best describes what all the words are about. The topic **Holidays** is written on the topic line above the middle column.

Look at the words in the last column. How are the words **purple, black**, and **yellow** alike? (*They are all colors.*) Look at the topics listed in the directions at the top of the reference box. Which topic best names different colors? (*Colors*) Yes, the word **Colors** is a good topic for all the words in the last column because it best describes what all the words are about. The topic **Colors** is written on the topic line above the last column.

TEACHING SCRIPT FOR IDENTIFYING SUPPORTING AND NON-SUPPORTING IDEAS

Now, we will learn to recognize words or ideas that tell about a topic. Whenever an idea tells about a topic, it is said to support the topic and is called a **supporting idea**. An idea that does not support the topic is called a **non-supporting idea** and cannot be used for that topic. Look at Reference 18 as I demonstrate supporting and non-supporting words and ideas. (*Read and discuss the directions in the reference box below.*)

Reference 18: Supporting and Non-Supporting Ideas		
Words and ideas that support the topic: In each column, cross out the one word or idea that does not support the underlined topic at the top.		
(1) **Zoo Animals**	(2) **Fruit**	(3) **Numbers**
monkey elephant tiger ~~umbrella~~	apple banana ~~wheat~~ peach	four ~~jelly~~ nine seven

What is the topic in the first column? (*Zoo Animals*) Which word in the list does not belong in the group called **Zoo Animals**? (*umbrella*) A line has been drawn through the word **umbrella** because it is not a zoo animal. (*Have students point to the non-supporting word.*)

What is the topic in the second column? (*Fruit*) Which word in the list does not belong in the group called **Fruit**? (*wheat*) A line has been drawn through the word **wheat** because it is not a fruit. (*Have students point to the non-supporting word.*)

What is the topic in the last column? (*Numbers*) Which word in the list does not belong in the group called **Numbers**? (*jelly*) A line has been drawn through the word **jelly** because it is not a number. (*Have students point to the non-supporting word.*)

TEACHING SCRIPT FOR IDENTIFYING SUPPORTING AND NON-SUPPORTING SENTENCES

As we learned earlier, whenever an idea or word tells about a topic, it is said to support the topic and is called a supporting idea. An idea that does not support the topic is called non-supporting and cannot be used for that topic.

Now, we will learn about **supporting** and **non-supporting** sentences. A supporting sentence only tells things about the topic. A non-supporting sentence does not tell things about the topic and cannot be used to support that topic. Earlier, we crossed out **words** that did not support the topic. Now, we will cross out **sentences** that do not support the topic. First, you have to think about the topic. Then, you read each sentence to see if the sentence supports the topic. When you read a sentence that does not support the topic, you are to draw a line through that whole sentence.

Look at Reference 19 on page 19 as I demonstrate supporting and non-supporting sentences. (*Read and discuss the directions in the reference box below.*)

Reference 19: Supporting and Non-Supporting Sentences

Sentences that support the topic: Read each topic. Then, cross out the one sentence that does not support the topic.

Topic: My New Tree House

1. My dad built a tree house for my birthday.
2. My tree house is way up in an oak tree.
3. ~~My dad gave me a bat for Christmas.~~
4. My friends come over, and we play in my new tree house.

What is the topic for the group of sentences in the reference box? (*My New Tree House*) Let's read the first sentence together. (*My dad built a tree house for my birthday.*) Does this sentence tell only things about the topic? (*Yes, it tells things about my new tree house.*)

We will read the second sentence together. (*My tree house is way up in an oak tree.*) Does this sentence tell only things about the topic? (*Yes, it tells things about my new tree house.*)

CHAPTER 18 LESSON 1 CONTINUED

We will now read the third sentence together. (*My dad gave me a bat for Christmas.*) Does this sentence tell only things about the topic? (*No, it tells things about my Christmas present.*) Since this sentence does not support the topic, a line has been drawn through it. (*My dad gave me a bat for Christmas.*)

We will read the last sentence together. (*My friends come over, and we play in my new tree house.*) Does this sentence tell only things about the topic? (*Yes, it tells things about my new tree house.*)

 PRACTICE TIME

Have students turn to pages 38 and 39 in the Practice Section of their book and find Chapter 18, Lesson 1, Practice (*1-3*). Go over the directions to make sure they understand what to do. Check and discuss the Practices after students have finished. (*Chapter 18, Lesson 1, Practice keys are given below.*)

Chapter 18, Lesson 1, Practice 1: Write the name of the topic that best describes what each column of words is about. Choose from these topics: **Colors   City Things   Animals   Country Things   Shapes**.

(1) City Things	(2) Country Things	(3) Shapes
skyscraper	tractor	triangle
taxi	farm	square
subway	barn	circle

Chapter 18, Lesson 1, Practice 2: In each column, cross out the one idea that does not support the underlined topic at the top.

(1) Kitchen Things	(2) Breakfast	(3) Birds
skillet	cereal	hawk
~~umpire~~	toast	eagle
oven	eggs	~~rat~~
spoon	~~automobile~~	robin

Chapter 18, Lesson 1, Practice 3: Read each topic. Then, cross out the one sentence that does not support the topic.

A. Topic: My Dog Buddy

1. My dog's name is Buddy.
2. Buddy likes to play fetch.
3. Buddy sleeps beside my bed at night.
4. ~~My horse's name is Flash.~~

B. Topic: Summer Vacation

1. My family takes a vacation every summer.
2. This summer we are going to Hawaii.
3. ~~We visited Grandmother on Thanksgiving.~~
4. Last summer, we went to Florida.

(End of lesson.)

CHAPTER 18   LESSON 2

Objectives: Jingles, Vocabulary #1, Grammar (Practice Sentences), Practice Exercise, and Activity.

 **JINGLE TIME**

Have students turn to the Jingle Section in their books. The teacher will lead the students in reciting the previously-taught jingles.

 VOCABULARY TIME

Have students turn to page 7 in the Vocabulary Section in their books. Introduce the vocabulary words listed in the vocabulary box below by reciting them together with your students.

Chapter 18, Vocabulary Words #1
Tim, street, otters, water, salty, popcorn

 GRAMMAR TIME

Put the Practice Sentences from the box below on the board or on notebook paper. Use these sentences as you practice the concepts that have been taught. For the greatest benefit, students must participate orally with the teacher.

Chapter 18, Practice Sentences for Lesson 2
1. Tim raced across the street.
2. The brown otters played happily in the water.
3. The salty popcorn fell on the floor.

TEACHING SCRIPT FOR PRACTICE SENTENCES

We will classify these three sentences to practice what we have learned. We will classify the sentences together. Begin.

CHAPTER 18 LESSON 2 CONTINUED

Question and Answer Flow for Sentence 1: Tim raced across the street.

1. Who raced across the street? Tim - SN
2. What is being said about Tim? Tim raced - V
3. Across - P
4. Across what? street - OP
5. The - A

Classified Sentence:

SN	V	P	A	OP
Tim	raced	across	the	street.

Question and Answer Flow for Sentence 2: The brown otters played happily in the water.

1. What played happily in the water? otters - SN
2. What is being said about otters? otters played - V
3. Played how? happily - Adv
4. In - P
5. In what? water - OP
6. The - A
7. What kind of otters? brown - Adj
8. The - A

Classified Sentence:

A	Adj	SN	V	Adv	P	A	OP
The	brown	otters	played	happily	in	the	water.

Question and Answer Flow for Sentence 3: The salty popcorn fell on the floor.

1. What fell on the floor? popcorn - SN
2. What is being said about popcorn? popcorn fell - V
3. On - P
4. On what? floor - OP
5. The - A
6. What kind of popcorn? salty - Adj
7. The - A

Classified Sentence:

A	Adj	SN	V	P	A	OP
The	salty	popcorn	fell	on	the	floor.

 PRACTICE TIME

Have students turn to pages 39 and 40 in the Practice Section of their book and find Chapter 18, Lesson 2, Practice *(1-4)*. Go over the directions to make sure they understand what to do. Check and discuss the Practices after students have finished. (*Chapter 18, Lesson 2, Practice keys are given below and on the next page.*)

Chapter 18, Lesson 2, Practice 1: Correct the capitalization mistakes and put the rule number above each correction. Use the rule numbers in Reference 11 on page 17 in the Reference Section of your book. Put a (.) or a (?) at the end of the sentence.

1 (or 3)	3	6	5	(capitalization rule numbers)
S	B	A	F	

stephen and billy will travel to atlanta in february ___**.** (4 capitals)

Level 1 Homeschool Teacher's Manual

CHAPTER 18 LESSON 2 CONTINUED

Chapter 18, Lesson 2, Practice 2: Write the name of the topic that best describes what each column of words is about. Choose from these topics: **Colors** **Transportation** **Farm Animals** **Kitchen Things** **Green Things**.

(1) Green Things	(2) Transportation	(3) Farm Animals
leaf	car	goat
grasshopper	truck	pig
grass	van	cow

Chapter 18, Lesson 2, Practice 3: In each column, cross out the one idea that does not support the underlined topic at the top.

(1) Flowers	(2) Clothing	(3) Yellow Things
rose	socks	banana
~~ocean~~	pants	school bus
daisy	skirt	~~lake~~
tulip	~~lamp~~	lemon

Chapter 18, Lesson 2, Practice 4: Read each topic. Then, cross out the one sentence that does not support the topic.

A. Topic: The Library

1. The library is full of wonderful books.
2. The library is open six days a week.
3. I like to borrow many books from the library.
4. ~~I need to go grocery shopping today.~~

B. Topic: A Day at the Lake

1. Every summer, we spend a day at the lake.
2. We rent a boat early in the morning.
3. ~~My brother got a new computer.~~
4. My dad and I ski behind the boat.

ACTIVITY / ASSIGNMENT TIME

Have students write the three sentences from this lesson on a sheet of paper. Have them tape-record the Question and Answer Flows for all three sentences. Students should write labels above the sentences as they classify them. They especially need the second practice during the first year in the program. (*After the students have finished, check the tape and the sentence labels. Make sure students understand any mistakes they have made.*)

(End of lesson.)

CHAPTER 18   LESSON 3

Objectives: Jingles, Vocabulary #2, Grammar (Practice Sentences), and Practice Exercise.

JINGLE TIME

Have students turn to the Jingle Section in their books. The teacher will lead the students in reciting the previously-taught jingles.

VOCABULARY TIME

Have students turn to page 7 in the Vocabulary Section in their books. Introduce the vocabulary words listed in the vocabulary box below by reciting them together with your students.

Chapter 18, Vocabulary Words #2
clever, field, new, sleds, hill

GRAMMAR TIME

Put the Practice Sentences from the box below on the board or on notebook paper. Use these sentences as you practice the concepts that have been taught. For the greatest benefit, students must participate orally with the teacher.

Chapter 18, Practice Sentences for Lesson 3
1. The students walked happily to the library.
2. A clever red fox ran swiftly across the field.
3. Three new sleds raced rapidly down the hill.

TEACHING SCRIPT FOR PRACTICE SENTENCES

We will classify these three sentences to practice what we have learned. We will classify the sentences together. Begin. (*You might have students write the labels above the sentences at this time.*)

CHAPTER 18 LESSON 3 CONTINUED

Question and Answer Flow for Sentence 1: **The students walked happily to the library.**

1. Who walked happily to the library? students - SN
2. What is being said about students? students walked - V
3. Walked how? happily - Adv
4. To - P

5. To what? library - OP
6. The - A
7. The - A

Classified Sentence:

A	SN	V	Adv	P	A	OP
The	students	walked	happily	to	the	library.

Question and Answer Flow for Sentence 2: **A clever red fox ran swiftly across the field.**

1. What ran swiftly across the field? fox - SN
2. What is being said about fox? fox ran - V
3. Ran how? swiftly - Adv
4. Across - P
5. Across what? field - OP

6. The - A
7. What kind of fox? red - Adj
8. What kind of fox? clever - Adj
9. A - A

Classified Sentence:

A	Adj	Adj	SN	V	Adv	P	A	OP
A	clever	red	fox	ran	swiftly	across	the	field.

Question and Answer Flow for Sentence 3: **Three new sleds raced rapidly down the hill.**

1. What raced rapidly down the hill? sleds - SN
2. What is being said about sleds? sleds raced - V
3. Raced how? rapidly - Adv
4. Down - P

5. Down what? hill - OP
6. The - A
7. What kind of sleds? new - Adj
8. How many sleds? three - Adj

Classified Sentence:

Adj	Adj	SN	V	Adv	P	A	OP
Three	new	sleds	raced	rapidly	down	the	hill.

 PRACTICE TIME

Have students turn to pages 41 and 42 in the Practice Section and find Chapter 18, Lesson 3, Practice *(1-5)*. Go over the directions to make sure they understand what to do. Check and discuss the Practices after students have finished. *(Chapter 18, Lesson 3, Practice keys are given below and on the next page.)*

Chapter 18, Lesson 3, Practice 1: Write the name of the topic that best describes what each column of words is about. Choose from these topics: **Colors   Winter Things   Ocean Animals   Yellow Things   Summer Things**.

(1)	(2)	(3)
Winter Things	**Ocean Animals**	**Yellow Things**
gloves	dolphin	sun
coat	whale	butter
snow	shark	corn

CHAPTER 18 LESSON 3 CONTINUED

Chapter 18, Lesson 3, Practice 2: In each column, cross out the one idea that does not support the underlined topic at the top.

(1) People	(2) States	(3) Farm Words
police officer	Nevada	tractor
~~hippopotamus~~	Louisiana	plow
teacher	Vermont	~~plastic~~
mother	~~cheese~~	barn

Chapter 18, Lesson 3, Practice 3: Read each topic. Then, cross out the one sentence that does not support the topic.

A. Topic: Uncle David

1. Uncle David works on a farm.
2. Uncle David lives in Oklahoma.
3. Uncle David is my favorite uncle.
4. ~~Aunt Rita works in a clothing factory.~~

B. Topic: Our House

1. We live in a small white house.
2. Our house is on Elm Street.
3. ~~Joey lives in Dallas.~~
4. We have lived in our house for ten years.

Chapter 18, Lesson 3, Practice 4: Correct the capitalization mistakes and put the rule number above each correction. Use the rule numbers in Reference 11 on page 17 in the Reference Section of your book. Put a (.) or a (?) at the end of the sentence.

  1(or 3) _____ 4 _____ (capitalization rule numbers)

  J   W

jack will bring punch and cookies on wednesday night __·__ **(2 capitals)**

Chapter 18, Lesson 3, Practice 5: On notebook paper, write a sentence using the words in the Word Bank. Put the words you select in the same order as the Sentence Labels listed below. Write the correct label above each word in your sentence.

WORD BANK				
Nouns	**Verbs**	**Adjectives**	**Adverbs**	**Prepositional Phrases**
clown kite balloon friend	waved, shouted, soared, talked, floated, walked	a, an, the, silly, large, funny, best, old, new, giant, happy, green, silly	eagerly, high, excitedly, often, silently, loudly, today	to the children in the sky to the mall to the crowd

Sentence Labels: A Adj Adj SN V Adv Prep Phrase

Independent Exercise: Choose your own Sentence Labels and Words.

(End of lesson.)

CHAPTER 18   LESSON 4

Objectives: Jingles, Vocabulary #3, Grammar (Practice Sentences, Practice and Improved Sentences), and Practice Exercise.

 **JINGLE TIME**

Have students turn to the Jingle Section in their books. The teacher will lead the students in reciting the previously-taught jingles.

 VOCABULARY TIME

Have students turn to page 7 in the Vocabulary Section in their books. Introduce the vocabulary words listed in the vocabulary box below by reciting them together with your students.

Chapter 18, Vocabulary Words #3
snow, shines, brightly, gate

 GRAMMAR TIME

Put the Practice Sentences from the box below on the board or on notebook paper. Use these sentences as you practice the concepts that have been taught. For the greatest benefit, students must participate orally with the teacher.

Chapter 18, Practice Sentences for Lesson 4
1. The excited children played in the snow today. 2. The sun shines brightly in the sky. 3. Pink flowers grew by the gate.

TEACHING SCRIPT FOR PRACTICE SENTENCES

We will classify these three sentences to practice what we have learned. We will classify the sentences together. Begin.

Question and Answer Flow for Sentence 1: The excited children played in the snow today.

1. Who played in the snow today? children - SN
2. What is being said about children? children played - V
3. In - P
4. In what? snow - OP

5. The - A
6. Played when? today - Adv
7. What kind of children? excited - Adj
8. The - A

Classified Sentence:	A	Adj	SN	V	P	A	OP	Adv
	The	excited	children	played	in	the	snow	today.

CHAPTER 18 LESSON 4 CONTINUED

Question and Answer Flow for Sentence 2: The sun shines brightly in the sky.

1. What shines brightly in the sky? sun - SN
2. What is being said about sun? sun shines - V
3. Shines how? brightly - Adv
4. In - P

5. In what? sky - OP
6. The - A
7. The - A

Classified Sentence:

A	SN	V	Adv	P	A	OP
The	sun	shines	brightly	in	the	sky.

Question and Answer Flow for Sentence 3: Pink flowers grew by the gate.

1. What grew by the gate? flowers - SN
2. What is being said about flowers? flowers grew - V
3. By - P

4. By what? gate - OP
5. The - A
6. What kind of flowers? pink - Adj

Classified Sentence:

Adj	SN	V	P	A	OP
Pink	flowers	grew	by	the	gate.

TEACHING SCRIPT FOR WRITING PRACTICE AND IMPROVED SENTENCES

I will now guide you through a Practice Sentence; then, we will write an Improved Sentence. Get out a sheet of notebook paper and write the title *Practice Sentence* on the top line. I will write it on the board for you. Copy these labels across the page: **A Adj Adj SN V Adv P A OP**. (*Write the words Practice Sentence and the labels students will use on the board so students can copy them correctly*.) Make sure you leave plenty of room for the words that you will write under the labels.

Before we begin, I want you to turn to page 18 in the Reference Section of your book. Look at Reference 16. You can use these vocabulary words to help you write Practice and Improved Sentences if you need them. You should only use this list if you cannot think of a word by yourself. (*Guide students through their Practice and Improved Sentences by using the script on pages 194-195 in your teacher's manual. Read it word-for-word to your students. After they have finished, check and discuss their Practice and Improved Sentences.*)

 PRACTICE TIME

Have students turn to pages 42 and 43 in the Practice Section of their books and find Chapter 18, Lesson 4, Practice *(1-4)*. Go over the directions to make sure they understand what to do. Check and discuss the Practices after students have finished. (*Chapter 18, Lesson 4, Practice keys are given on the next page.*)

CHAPTER 18 LESSON 4 CONTINUED

Chapter 18, Lesson 4, Practice 1: Write the name of the topic that best describes what each column of words is about. Choose from these topics: **Numbers** **Table Things** **Animals** **Weather Words** **Drinks**.

(1) Weather Words	(2) Numbers	(3) Drinks
cloudy	eight	punch
rainy	two	soda
windy	three	juice

Chapter 18, Lesson 4, Practice 2: In each column, cross out the one idea that does not support the underlined topic at the top.

(1) Brown Things	(2) Beans	(3) Vegetables
dirt	refried	carrots
~~sky~~	green	squash
chocolate	pinto	~~gravy~~
otter	~~mail~~	broccoli

Chapter 18, Lesson 4, Practice 3: Read each topic. Then, cross out the one sentence that does not support the topic.

A. Topic: Happiness

1. Happiness is being with my mom.
2. Happiness is a warm hug.
3. Happiness is a beautiful rainbow.
4. ~~Scary movies frighten me.~~

B. Topic: My New Shoes

1. My new shoes are white.
2. My new shoes feel comfortable on my feet.
3. ~~My old shoes were black.~~
4. My new shoes have purple laces.

Chapter 18, Lesson 4, Practice 4: Correct the capitalization mistakes and put the rule number above each correction. Use the rule numbers in Reference 11 on page 17 in the Reference Section of your book. Put a (.) or a (?) at the end of the sentence.

1	2	3	(capitalization rule numbers)
M	I	J	

may i have another piece of janet's pie _?_ **(3 capitals)**

(End of lesson.)

CHAPTER 18   LESSON 5

Objectives: Jingles, Vocabulary #4, Grammar (Practice Sentences), Test, Check, Writing (Journal), and Activity.

 **JINGLE TIME**

Have students turn to the Jingle Section in their books. The teacher will lead the students in reciting the previously-taught jingles.

 VOCABULARY TIME

Have students turn to page 7 in the Vocabulary Section in their books. Introduce the vocabulary words listed in the vocabulary box below by reciting them together with your students.

Chapter 18, Vocabulary Words #4
barn, mouse, James

 GRAMMAR TIME

Put the Practice Sentences from the box below on the board or on notebook paper. Use these sentences as you practice the concepts that have been taught. For the greatest benefit, students must participate orally with the teacher.

Chapter 18, Practice Sentences for Lesson 5
1. The frightened horses ran to the barn.
2. The frightened mouse ran across the floor.
3. James laughed loudly at the clowns today.

TEACHING SCRIPT FOR PRACTICE SENTENCES

We will classify these three sentences to practice what we have learned. We will classify the sentences together. Begin.

CHAPTER 18 LESSON 5 CONTINUED

Question and Answer Flow for Sentence 1: The frightened horses ran to the barn.

1. What ran to the barn? horses - SN
2. What is being said about horses? horses ran - V
3. To - P
4. To what? barn - OP

5. The - A
6. What kind of horses? frightened - Adj
7. The - A

Classified Sentence:

A	Adj	SN	V	P	A	OP
The	frightened	horses	ran	to	the	barn.

Question and Answer Flow for Sentence 2: The frightened mouse ran across the floor.

1. What ran across the floor? mouse - SN
2. What is being said about mouse? mouse ran - V
3. Across - P
4. Across what? floor - OP

5. The - A
6. What kind of mouse? frightened - Adj
7. The - A

Classified Sentence:

A	Adj	SN	V	P	A	OP
The	frightened	mouse	ran	across	the	floor.

Question and Answer Flow for Sentence 3: James laughed loudly at the clowns today.

1. Who laughed loudly at the clowns today? James - SN
2. What is being said about James? James laughed - V
3. Laughed how? loudly - Adv
4. At - P

5. At whom? clowns - OP
6. The - A
7. Laughed when? today - Adv

Classified Sentence:

SN	V	Adv	P	A	OP	Adv
James	laughed	loudly	at	the	clowns	today.

 TEST TIME

Have students turn to page 71 in the Test Section in their books and find Chapter 18 Test. Go over the directions to make sure they understand what to do. (*Chapter 18 Test key is on the next page.*)

Chapter 18 Test
(Student Page 71)

Exercise 1: Classify each sentence. Use **SN** for subject noun, **V** for verb, **Adv** for adverb, **Adj** for adjective, **A** for article adjective, **P** for preposition, and **OP** for object of the preposition. For Sentence 1, underline the complete subject <u>one</u> time and the complete predicate <u>two</u> times.

       A   Adj   SN   V   P   A   OP   Adv

1. The excited children played in the snow today.

      Adj   SN   V   P   A   OP

2. Pink flowers grew by the gate.

Exercise 2: Underline the **syn** if the words are synonyms. Underline the **ant** if the words are antonyms.

1. sick, ill	**syn** ant	2. before, after	syn **ant**	3. lost, found	syn **ant**

Exercise 3: Name the five parts of speech that you have studied. (*You may use abbreviations.*)
(The order of answers may vary.)

1. **Noun (N)**   2. **Verb (V)**   3. **Adjective (Adj)**   4. **Adverb (Adv)**   5. **Preposition (P)**

Exercise 4: Write the name of the topic that best describes what each column of words is about. Choose from these topics: **Colors   Family   Animals   Bathroom Things   Food**

(1) **Food**	(2) **Family**	(3) **Bathroom Things**
bread	uncle	shower
meat	cousin	shampoo
pasta	sister	towel

Exercise 5: In each column, cross out the one idea that does not support the underlined topic at the top.

(1) **Months**	(2) **Desserts**	(3) **Days**
July	pie	Saturday
~~jail~~	cake	Wednesday
January	cookie	~~France~~
June	~~playground~~	Thursday

Exercise 6: Read each topic. Then, cross out the one sentence that does not support the topic.

A. Topic: My Favorite Color

1. My favorite color is yellow.
2. Yellow reminds me of sunshine.
3. I painted my room yellow.
4. ~~Red and blue make purple.~~

B. Topic: In the City

1. I take a taxi to work every day in the city.
2. My apartment in the city is on the fifth floor.
3. ~~I grew up in the country.~~
4. I have lived in the city for three years.

Exercise 7: In your journal, write a paragraph summarizing what you have learned this week.

CHAPTER 18 LESSON 5 CONTINUED

CHECK TIME

After students have finished, check and discuss their test papers. Make sure they understand why their answers are right or wrong. Use the Question and Answer Flows on pages 215 and 216 in this chapter to check the sentences on the Chapter 18 Test. *(For total points, count each required answer as a point.)*

ACTIVITY / ASSIGNMENT TIME

This is a great listening exercise for students. Before you read the lists below to your students, tell them that they are to raise their hands whenever they hear a word that **does not** match the topic given. You will tell them the topic just before you recite the list of items. When you have finished with the sample topics listed below, have students help you create a new list. *(The words in bold indicate when students should raise their hands.)*

<u>**Colors:**</u> pink, navy, blue, **leaves**, orange, teal, yellow, **car**, green, **grass**, **flowers**, purple, **bracelet**

<u>**Parts of the Body:**</u> head, toe, **gloves**, shoulder, wrist, eye, **engine**, ear, stomach, **hat**, **shoes**

<u>**Fruits:**</u> grape, peach, **beans**, **eggs**, pineapple, banana, **milk**, strawberry, **pecan**, cherry, **crackers**

<u>**People:**</u> artist, athlete, **grasshopper**, baby, **circle**, farmer, doctor, **pumpkin**, grandmother, **gloves**, neighbor

<u>**Months of the Year:**</u> February, December, **Saturday**, June, **Sunday**, March, May, **green**, July, **rain**, April

<u>**Grammar Words:**</u> noun, verb, **mop**, adjective, **sky**, adverb, article, **square**, preposition, **pizza**, pronoun

(End of lesson.)

CHAPTER 19   LESSON 1
Objectives: Jingles, Synonyms, Antonyms, Skill (Two-Point Paragraph), and Writing Assignment #1.

 **JINGLE TIME**

Have students turn to the Jingle Section of their books. The teacher will lead the students in reciting the previously-taught jingles.

 SYNONYM AND ANTONYM TIME

Have students turn to the Synonym and Antonym Section of their books. Introduce the new words listed for Chapter 19 in the box below. Make sure students know the meanings of the new synonyms and antonyms. Then, have students underline the correct answers in their books. They should study these words again before their test.

Chapter 19: Underline the **syn** if the words are synonyms. Underline the **ant** if the words are antonyms.

1. front, back	syn **ant**	2. early, late	syn **ant**	3. simple, easy	**syn** ant

 SKILL TIME

TEACHING SCRIPT FOR THE TWO-POINT PARAGRAPH

Teacher's Note:
As students write their two-point paragraphs, it is very important that they follow the exact writing pattern that this lesson teaches. If this is done consistently, the students will learn to organize their writing by learning how to do these things: write a topic sentence from any given topic, write sentences that support the topic, and write a concluding sentence that summarizes their paragraph.

Teaching students how to write a two-point paragraph gives students several advantages:

1. It gives students a definite, concrete pattern to follow when asked to write a paragraph.
2. It gives students the practice they need in organizing their writing. They can also work in cooperative-learning groups to write, check, and discuss their paragraphs.
3. It gives students a chance to greatly improve their self-confidence because, as they advance in the program, they become stronger and more independent in all areas of their grammar and writing skills.

Level 1 Homeschool Teacher's Manual

CHAPTER 19 LESSON 1 CONTINUED

Teacher's Note: Put the following writing definitions on the board.

---

1. **Paragraph** - a group of sentences that is written about one particular subject, or topic.
2. **Topic** - the subject of the paragraph; the topic tells what the paragraph is about.
3. **Expository writing** - the discussion or telling of ideas by giving facts, directions, explanations, definitions, and examples.

As a student, you want to be prepared to be a good writer. As a part of that preparation, today, we will learn about expository writing and how to organize your writing by writing a two-point paragraph. First, let's look at some key definitions to be sure that we know what we are talking about.

Look at the first two definitions. A **paragraph** is a group of sentences that is written about one particular subject, or topic. A **topic** is the subject of the paragraph; the topic tells what the paragraph is about.

Now, let's look at the last definition. It is **expository writing**. Everyone say "expository writing" together so we can feel this type of writing on our tongues: **Expository writing**! Expository writing is the discussion or telling of ideas by giving facts or directions or by explaining something to others. So, the purpose of expository writing is to give information by giving facts or directions or by explaining something.   As you can see from the definition, expository writing is informational because it gives some type of information. Since expository writing deals with information of some kind, it is very important to focus on making the meaning clear and understandable. The reader must be able to understand exactly what the writer means.

Now that we know what expository writing is, we must learn more about it because the first type of paragraph that we learn to write is an EXPOSITORY paragraph. What makes any type of writing easy is knowing exactly what to do when you are given a writing assignment.

The first thing you learn to do is organize your writing. Expository writing may be organized in different ways. One of the most common ways to write an expository paragraph is by using a **two-point paragraph format.** The two-point paragraph format is a way of organizing the sentences in your expository paragraph that will help make your meaning clear and understandable.

Now, you will learn how to write a two-point expository paragraph. I am going to give you a topic about which you are to write your paragraph. Remember, a topic tells what the paragraph is about because it is the subject of the paragraph. In order to make sure you understand, we are going to write a two-point expository paragraph together following these specific steps.

TEACHING SCRIPT FOR SELECTING THE TWO-POINTS OF THE PARAGRAPH

The first thing we learn is how to select and list the points that we are going to write about. Let's begin with our topic. Remember that a topic is a subject. The topic about which we are going to write our paragraph is "Favorite Colors." I will write this on the board under "Topic." (_Demonstrate by writing on the board._)

CHAPTER 19 LESSON 1 CONTINUED

Topic
My Favorite Colors

Do you have some favorite colors about which you could write? Yes! So do I. Now, let's see how we are going to write this paragraph. Remember that I told you this paragraph is called a two-point paragraph. First, we are going to look at our topic, "Favorite colors," and see if we can list two favorite colors about which we can write.

Teacher's Note:
You may want students to name their favorite colors, but the teaching example will use the colors **orange** and **green**.

Orange and green: these are two good favorite colors. I will list these two colors on the board under "2 points about the topic." They will be the two points for our two-point expository paragraph. (*Demonstrate by writing on the board.*)

2 points about the topic

1. _____orange_____   2. _____green_____

Now, let's set them aside for a minute and begin our paragraph. We are going to use these two items shortly.

Teacher's Note: The simplified outline below will give you a quick view of what you will be covering with your students in your discussion of the two-point expository paragraph. Write each part on the board only as it is being discussed so that your students will not be overwhelmed by the amount of written work that they see on the board.

The Two-Point Expository Paragraph Outline	
	Topic
	2 points about the topic
Introduction	Sentence #1: **Topic** sentence
	Sentence #2: A **two-point** sentence
Body	Sentence #3: A **first-point** sentence
	Sentence #4: A **supporting** sentence for the first point
	Sentence #5: A **second-point** sentence
	Sentence #6: A **supporting** sentence for the second point
Conclusion	Sentence #7: A **concluding** sentence

Teacher's Note: As you work through the steps, be sure to show students how the paragraph's sentences are divided into three parts: the introduction (*topic and two-point sentence*), the body (*the two main points and their supporting sentences*), and the conclusion (*the concluding sentence*).

CHAPTER 19 LESSON 1 CONTINUED

TEACHING SCRIPT FOR WRITING THE TOPIC SENTENCE

First, we must write what is called a topic sentence. A topic sentence is very important because it tells the main idea of our paragraph. We are going to let the topic sentence be the first sentence in our paragraph because it tells everyone what our paragraph is going to be about. In many paragraphs, it is not the first sentence. Later, we can learn to put the topic sentence in other places in the paragraph. For now, it is important that we make it the first sentence in our two-point paragraph.

The topic sentence for a two-point paragraph needs three things:

1. It needs to tell the main idea of a paragraph.
2. It needs to be general because the other sentences in the paragraph must tell about the topic sentence.
3. It needs to tell the number of points that will be discussed in the paragraph.

When you write a topic sentence for a two-point paragraph, follow these two easy steps:

1. You will use all or some of the words in the topic.
2. You will tell the number of points or ideas you will discuss in your paragraph.

Now, we are going to write a topic sentence by following the two easy steps we have just discussed. Look at our topic, "My Favorite Colors." Without actually listing the two specific points, orange and green, let's write a sentence that makes a general statement about the main idea of our topic and tells the number of points we will list later.

How about using "I have two favorite colors" as our topic sentence? I will write this on the board under "Sentence #1: Topic sentence." (*Demonstrate by writing on the board. Read the sentence to your students.*)

Sentence #1: Topic sentence
I have two favorite colors.

Look at the topic sentence on the board. Notice that in this sentence, we have mentioned our topic, "My Favorite Colors," and we have stated that there are two of these colors; we will tell what the two points are in the next sentence.

Also, notice that we did not say, "I am going to tell you about my two favorite colors." We do not need to tell the reader we are going to tell him something. We simply do it. To say "I am going to tell you" is called "writing about your writing," and it is not effective writing. Do not "write about your writing."

TEACHING SCRIPT FOR WRITING THE TWO-POINT SENTENCE

Now that we have our topic sentence, our next sentence will list the two specific points our paragraph will discuss. Our next sentence could be, "These colors are orange and green." I will write this on the board under "Sentence #2: A two-point sentence." (*Demonstrate by writing the information below on the board. Read the sentence to your students.*)

Sentence #2: A two-point sentence
These colors are orange and green.

CHAPTER 19 LESSON 1 CONTINUED

Look at the order in which I have listed the two colors. You must always be aware of the order in which you list your two points because it will be the same order in which you discuss these points later in your paragraph. Depending on your two points as well as your purpose in writing, you will select the order of your two points. I have chosen to place these in this order: first, orange and then, green.

Notice three things we have done here:

1. We have put our two items in the order we have chosen, remembering that we will be discussing these points in this order later in our paragraph. (*orange and green*)
2. We have written our first sentence, and our first sentence tells us the number of points that will be discussed in the rest of the paragraph. (*I have two favorite colors.*)
3. We have started our two-point sentence with words that helped us connect it to our first sentence. (*These colors are orange and green.*)

Notice how we have used repetition to link our two sentences. Our first sentence mentions **"favorite colors"** by stating **"I have two favorite colors."** Sentence number two, **"These colors are orange and green,"** refers to sentence number one by stating **"These colors,"** meaning the favorite colors just mentioned in sentence number one. Although you will not want to use repetition in every sentence to link sentences, repetition is a good device for making your paragraph flow smoothly.

TEACHING SCRIPT FOR DEVELOPING AND SUPPORTING THE POINTS OF THE PARAGRAPH

After you have stated the general topic sentence and then followed it by the more specific two-point sentence, you will begin to discuss each of the two points, one at a time. DO NOT FORGET: You are going to discuss them in the order in which you listed them in sentence number two. You will begin your third sentence by stating, **"My first favorite color is orange."** This is your first point. I will write this on the board under "Sentence #3: A first-point sentence." (*Demonstrate by writing the information below on the board. Read the sentence to your students.*)

Sentence #3: A first-point sentence
My first favorite color is orange.

Next, you will write one sentence about orange. It can be a descriptive sentence about orange. It can be a reason why you like orange, but it must be about orange being your favorite color. This is called a supporting sentence. I will now write a supporting sentence on the board under "Sentence #4: A supporting sentence for the first point." You can use this sentence or make up your own: **"I like orange because my pet goldfish is a bright shade of orange."** (*Demonstrate by writing the information below on the board. Read the sentence to your students.*)

Sentence #4: A supporting sentence for the first point
I like orange because my pet goldfish is a bright shade of orange.

When you keep your writing focused on the topic you are assigned, your paragraph will have what we call "unity," or it will be a "unified" paragraph. In a unified paragraph, all sentences work together to form one idea about the subject or topic.

CHAPTER 19 LESSON 1 CONTINUED

As you get more skilled at two-point writing, you may write two or more sentences about each of your points, but for now stay with one sentence for each point. Each of the sentences that you write following your listed points should support what you have stated in that point. Use only ideas that support. Discard non-supporting ideas.

So far, we have introduced our topic and listed our two specific points. We have begun to discuss our two points and have completed the first point along with a sentence that supports the first point. So far, we have four sentences.

The fifth sentence will introduce the second point of our two-point paragraph. Your second point is "green." Since "green" is the second item you listed, your fifth sentence should state, **"My second favorite color is green."** I will write this on the board under "Sentence #5: A second-point sentence." (*Demonstrate by writing the information below on the board. Read the sentence to your students.*)

Sentence #5: A second-point sentence
My second favorite color is green.

Just as you wrote the sentence supporting the statement of your first point, so now you must write a sentence supporting your statement about green being your second favorite color. I will write the next supporting sentence on the board under "Sentence #6: A supporting sentence for the second point." (*Demonstrate by writing the information below on the board. Read the sentence to your students.*)

Sentence #6: A supporting sentence for the second point
Green makes me think of grass, leaves, and going outside to play in the summertime.

By now, you can begin to see a pattern to your paragraph. So far, you have written six sentences in your paragraph. Your seventh sentence will be your last, or final, sentence.

TEACHING SCRIPT FOR WRITING THE CONCLUSION OF THE PARAGRAPH

We have now introduced our topic, or subject, listed each of our two points, and made one supporting statement about each point. Now, we need to complete our paragraph, leaving the reader with the impression that he has read a finished product. In order to complete our paragraph, we need a conclusion, or final sentence.

There are different ways to write a concluding sentence, but one of the best and simplest is the summary statement. This means that the main points of the paragraph are stated again briefly in one sentence.

When you write a concluding sentence, follow these two easy steps:
1. You will use some of the words in your topic sentence.
2. You will add an extra, or concluding, thought about your paragraph.

Your final sentence could be, **"My two favorite colors make me happy because they remind me of fun things."** I will write this on the board under "Sentence #7: A concluding sentence." (*Demonstrate by writing the information below on the board. Read the sentence again to your students.*)

Sentence #7: A concluding sentence
My two favorite colors make me happy because they remind me of fun things.

CHAPTER 19 LESSON 1 CONTINUED

TEACHING SCRIPT FOR CHECKING THE FINISHED PARAGRAPH

It is good to get in the habit of checking over your writing after you have finished. Just reading your finished paragraph several times slowly will help you see and hear things that you may want to correct. It also helps to have a checklist that tells specific areas to check to make sure you do not lose points for careless mistakes. A general checklist is provided at the bottom of the two-point paragraph example in Reference 20 on page 20 in the Reference section of your book.

Look at your reference page as I read what it tells you to do as you write each sentence of your two-point paragraph. (*Read and discuss each section of the two-point paragraph example in Reference 20. Tell students to use this reference page if they need it when they write a two-point paragraph. It will help them organize their writing, and it will help them see the pattern of a two-point expository paragraph. The two-point paragraph example is located at the end of this lesson on page 229.*)

Teacher's Note: There was no discussion or guidelines for writing a title for the paragraph. Single paragraphs are often written without titles - the decision is left to the teacher or writer. Remind students that this is an expository paragraph, which means that its purpose is to inform or explain. The two-point format is a way of organizing an expository paragraph.

TEACHER INSTRUCTIONS FOR WRITING ASSIGNMENT #1

For Writing Assignment #1, have students turn to page 44 and look at Writing Outline 1 in the Practice Section of their books. (*A Writing Outline sample is reproduced for you at the end of this lesson on page 230.*) Students will begin to copy the two-point paragraph that you have on the board. In this lesson, students will write the topic, list the two points about the topic, and write the first two sentences. Students will finish copying the rest of the two-point paragraph in the next lesson. Remind students to edit each sentence for capital letters and end-mark punctuation.

Writing Assignment Box

Writing Assignment #1: Copy the sample Two-Point Expository Paragraph on the Writing Outline.
(For this lesson, students will write the topic, list the two points, and write the first two sentences.)

Writing topic: My Favorite Colors

Take up the writing outlines at the end of the writing period. You will hand them back to be finished during the next lesson.

Teacher's Note:
It is important for students to copy the same paragraph that was just demonstrated in class. As students progress to writing the two-point paragraph on their writing paper, they will begin to understand what a paragraph is and how it is constructed.

(End of lesson.)

CHAPTER 19 LESSON 1 CONTINUED

Reference 20: Two-Point Expository Paragraph Example

List of colors: red, blue, green, yellow, white, orange, brown, black, pink, gray, and purple.

Topic: **My Favorite colors**
Two main points: 1. **orange** 2. **green**

Sentence #1 – <u>Topic Sentence</u> (*Use words in the topic and tell how many points will be used.*)
I have two favorite colors.

Sentence #2 – <u>Two-Point Sentence</u> (*List the 2 points in the order you will present them.*)
These colors are orange and green.

Sentence #3 – <u>First Point</u>
My first favorite color is orange.

Sentence #4 – <u>Supporting Sentence</u> for the first point.
I like orange because my pet goldfish is a bright shade of orange.

Sentence #5 – <u>Second Point</u>
My second favorite color is green.

Sentence #6 – <u>Supporting Sentence</u> for the second point.
Green makes me think of grass, leaves, and going outside to play in the summertime.

Sentence #7 – <u>Concluding (final) Sentence</u>. (*Restate the topic sentence and add an extra thought.*)
My two favorite colors make me happy because they remind me of fun things.

SAMPLE PARAGRAPH   **My Favorite Colors**

    I have two favorite colors. These colors are orange and green. My first favorite color is orange. I like orange because my pet goldfish is a bright shade of orange. My second favorite color is green. Green makes me think of grass, leaves, and going outside to play in the summertime. My two favorite colors make me happy because they remind me of fun things.

General Checklist: Check the Finished Paragraph	The Two-Point Expository Paragraph Outline
(1) Have you followed the pattern for a two-point paragraph? (*Indent, topic sentence, 2-point sentence, 2 main points, 2 supporting sentences, and a concluding sentence.*) (2) Do you have complete sentences? (3) Have you capitalized the first word and put an end mark at the end of every sentence? (4) Have you checked your sentences for capitalization and end-mark mistakes?	Topic 2 points about the topic Sentence #1: **Topic** sentence Sentence #2: A **two-point** sentence Sentence #3: A **first-point** sentence Sentence #4: A **supporting** sentence for the first point Sentence #5: A **second-point** sentence Sentence #6: A **supporting** sentence for the second point Sentence #7: A **concluding** sentence

CHAPTER 19 LESSON 1 CONTINUED

Chapter 19, Lesson 1, Practice: Use Writing Outline 1 for Writing Assignment #1. Use this two-point outline form to guide you as you write a two-point expository paragraph.

Writing Outline 1

Write a topic: _____

Write 2 points to list about the topic.

1. _____   2. _____

Sentence #1   Topic sentence (*Use words in the topic and tell how many points will be used.*)

_____

_____

Sentence #2   2-point sentence (*List your 2 points in the order that you will present them.*)

_____

_____

Sentence #3   State your first point in a complete sentence.

_____

_____

Sentence #4   Write a supporting sentence for the first point.

_____

_____

Sentence #5   State your second point in a complete sentence.

_____

_____

Sentence #6   Write a supporting sentence for the second point.

_____

_____

Sentence #7   Concluding sentence (*Restate the topic sentence and add an extra thought.*)

_____

_____

Level 1 Homeschool Teacher's Manual

CHAPTER 19 LESSON 2

Objectives: Jingles, Vocabulary #1, Grammar (Practice Sentences), Skill (Two-Point Paragraph, continued), and Writing Assignment #1, continued.

JINGLE TIME

Have students turn to the Jingle Section of their books. The teacher will lead the students in reciting the previously-taught jingles.

VOCABULARY TIME

Have students turn to page 8 in the Vocabulary Section of their books. Introduce the vocabulary words listed in the vocabulary box below by reciting them together with your students.

Chapter 19, Vocabulary Words #1
log, wagon, scampered

GRAMMAR TIME

Put the Practice Sentences from the box below on the board or on notebook paper. Use these sentences as you practice the concepts that have been taught. For the greatest benefit, students must participate orally with the teacher.

Chapter 19, Practice Sentences for Lesson 2
1. A green frog jumped on the log.
2. The large red wagon rolled smoothly down the street.
3. A tiny gray mouse scampered quickly home.

TEACHING SCRIPT FOR PRACTICE SENTENCES

We will classify these three sentences to practice what we have learned. We will classify the sentences together. Begin.

Question and Answer Flow for Sentence 1: A green frog jumped on the log.

1. What jumped on the log? frog - SN
2. What is being said about frog? frog jumped - V
3. On - P
4. On what? log - OP

5. The - A
6. What kind of frog? green - Adj
7. A - A

Classified Sentence:

	A	Adj	SN	V	P	A	OP
	A	green	frog	jumped	on	the	log.

CHAPTER 19 LESSON 2 CONTINUED

Question and Answer Flow for Sentence 2: The large red wagon rolled smoothly down the street.

1. What rolled smoothly down the street? wagon - SN
2. What is being said about wagon? wagon rolled - V
3. Rolled how? smoothly - Adv
4. Down - P
5. Down what? street - OP
6. The - A
7. What kind of wagon? red - Adj
8. What kind of wagon? large - Adj
9. The - A

Classified Sentence:

A	Adj	Adj	SN	V	Adv	P	A	OP
The	large	red	wagon	rolled	smoothly	down	the	street.

Question and Answer Flow for Sentence 3: A tiny gray mouse scampered quickly home.

1. What scampered quickly home? mouse - SN
2. What is being said about mouse? mouse scampered - V
3. Scampered how? quickly - Adv
4. Scampered where? home - Adv
5. What kind of mouse? gray - Adj
6. What kind of mouse? tiny - Adj
7. A - A

Classified Sentence:

A	Adj	Adj	SN	V	Adv	Adv
A	tiny	gray	mouse	scampered	quickly	home.

SKILL TIME

TEACHER INSTRUCTIONS FOR WRITING ASSIGNMENT #1 (CONTINUED)

Today, students will finish copying Writing Assignment #1 on their outline forms. *(Put the sentences in bold type from Reference 20 on the board to make it easier for students to copy the assignment. You could also choose to make an extra copy of Reference 20 for students to use.)* Have students go to Writing Outline 1 on page 44 in the Practice Section of their books. Go through the two-point example and show them how to check what they have already written.

Writing Assignment Box

Writing Assignment #1 (continued): Two-Point Expository Paragraph on Writing Outline 1.
(For this lesson, students will begin writing with Sentence #3 and complete the paragraph.)

Writing topic: My Favorite Colors

Show students how to begin with Sentence #3 and copy the first point on their outline papers. Students will finish copying the sentences of the two-point paragraph. Remind students to edit each sentence for capital letters and end-mark punctuation after they write each sentence. Students will use their outline forms to copy their sentences onto writing paper in paragraph form in the next lesson.

(End of lesson.)

CHAPTER 19   LESSON 3

Objectives: Jingles, Vocabulary #2, Grammar (Practice Sentences), Skill (Two-Point Paragraph, continued), Writing Assignment #1 (continued), and Activity.

 **JINGLE TIME**

Have students turn to the Jingle Section of their books. The teacher will lead the students in reciting the previously-taught jingles.

 VOCABULARY TIME

Have students turn to page 8 in the Vocabulary Section of their books. Introduce the vocabulary words listed in the vocabulary box below by reciting them together with your students.

Chapter 19, Vocabulary Words #2
Anna, fog, tall, Sam

 GRAMMAR TIME

Put the Practice Sentences from the box below on the board or on notebook paper. Use these sentences as you practice the concepts that have been taught. For the greatest benefit, students must participate orally with the teacher.

Chapter 19, Practice Sentences for Lesson 3
1. Anna drove carefully in the fog.
2. Two tall boys walked slowly across the yard.
3. Sam played in the mud.

TEACHING SCRIPT FOR PRACTICE SENTENCES

We will classify these three sentences to practice what we have learned. We will classify the sentences together. Begin.

CHAPTER 19 LESSON 3 CONTINUED

Question and Answer Flow for Sentence 1: Anna drove carefully in the fog.

1. Who drove carefully in the fog? Anna - SN
2. What is being said about Anna? Anna drove - V
3. Drove how? carefully - Adv

4. In - P
5. In what? fog - OP
6. The - A

Classified Sentence:

SN	V	Adv	P	A	OP
Anna	drove	carefully	in	the	fog.

Question and Answer Flow for Sentence 2: Two tall boys walked slowly across the yard.

1. Who walked slowly across the yard? boys - SN
2. What is being said about boys? boys walked - V
3. Walked how? slowly - Adv
4. Across - P

5. Across what? yard - OP
6. The - A
7. What kind of boys? tall - Adj
8. How many boys? two - Adj

Classified Sentence:

Adj	Adj	SN	V	Adv	P	A	OP
Two	tall	boys	walked	slowly	across	the	yard.

Question and Answer Flow for Sentence 3: Sam played in the mud.

1. Who played in the mud? Sam - SN
2. What is being said about Sam? Sam played - V
3. In - P

4. In what? mud - OP
5. The - A

Classified Sentence:

SN	V	P	A	OP
Sam	played	in	the	mud.

SKILL TIME

TEACHER INSTRUCTIONS FOR WRITING ASSIGNMENT #1 (CONTINUED)

Today, students will transfer the sentences they have written on the outline sheet to writing paper in a paragraph format. Have students go to Writing Outline 1 on page 44 in the Practice Section of their books.

Explain to students that they will copy the sentences from their outline onto their writing paper in paragraph form. Remind them that a paragraph is a group of sentences that is written about one topic. Tell students they must remember to indent a paragraph before they begin writing. (_Show students how to indent a paragraph on their writing paper._)

CHAPTER 19 LESSON 3 CONTINUED

Guide your students as they learn how to place the sentences on their paper. Make sure they understand that in a paragraph each sentence should be written immediately after the previous one instead of beginning each sentence to the left of the page. Remind them to edit each sentence for capital letters and end-mark punctuation after they have written it. Take up the writing papers at the end of the writing period to check.

Writing Assignment Box

Writing Assignment #1 (continued): Two-Point Expository Paragraph.
(For this lesson, students will rewrite their paragraph from the outline onto notebook paper or in a writing booklet.)

Writing topic: My Favorite Colors

At the beginning, you must check students' papers carefully for form mistakes. This will ensure that students are learning the two-point format correctly. These are some of the things necessary to check at the beginning:

1. Did students indent the paragraph?
2. Did students capitalize the first word and put an end mark at the end of every sentence?
3. Did students follow the two-point paragraph pattern?

 ACTIVITY / ASSIGNMENT TIME

Have students turn to page 89 in the Activity Section of their books and find Chapter 19, Lesson 3, Activity. Go over the directions to make sure they understand what to do. Check and discuss the Activity after students have finished.

Chapter 19, Lesson 3, Activity: Use the code in the box below to find <u>animal</u> words. Using the code numbers, write the correct letters for each blank. Then, make up your own code for several words.

Code			Words						
1. w	8. t	15. c	w o l f				c a m e l s		
			1 4 7 12				15 17 11 3 7 9		
2. b	9. s	16. u							
3. e	10. r	17. a	g o a t				t u r t l e s		
4. o	11. m	18. h	14 4 17 8				8 16 10 8 7 3 9		
5. i	12. f	19. k							
6. n	13. d		b i r d				c h i c k e n		
			2 5 10 13				15 18 5 15 19 3 6		
7. l	14. g								

(End of lesson.)

CHAPTER 19   LESSON 4
Objectives: Jingles, Vocabulary #3, Grammar (Practice Sentences), and Writing Assignment #2.

 **JINGLE TIME**

Have students turn to the Jingle Section of their books. The teacher will lead the students in reciting the previously-taught jingles.

 VOCABULARY TIME

Have students turn to page 8 in the Vocabulary Section of their books. Introduce the vocabulary words listed in the vocabulary box below by reciting them together with your students.

Chapter 19, Vocabulary Words #3
gathered, roses, circus, pranced, proudly

 GRAMMAR TIME

Put the Practice Sentences from the box below on the board or on notebook paper. Use these sentences as you practice the concepts that have been taught. For the greatest benefit, students must participate orally with the teacher.

Chapter 19, Practice Sentences for Lesson 4
1. The students gathered in the library.
2. The red roses grew by the road.
3. The big circus horses pranced proudly around.

TEACHING SCRIPT FOR PRACTICE SENTENCES

We will classify these three sentences to practice what we have learned. We will classify the sentences together. Begin.

Question and Answer Flow for Sentence 1: The students gathered in the library.
1. Who gathered in the library? students - SN   4. In what? library - OP
2. What is being said about students? students gathered - V   5. The - A
3. In - P   6. The - A
Classified Sentence: A   SN   V   P   A   OP
The students gathered in the library.

CHAPTER 19 LESSON 4 CONTINUED

Question and Answer Flow for Sentence 2: The red roses grew by the road.

1. What grew by the road? roses - SN
2. What is being said about roses? roses grew - V
3. By - P
4. By what? road - OP

5. The - A
6. What kind of roses? red - Adj
7. The - A

Classified Sentence:	A	Adj	SN	V	P	A	OP
	The	red	roses	grew	by	the	road.

Question and Answer Flow for Sentence 3: The big circus horses pranced proudly around.

1. What pranced proudly around? horses - SN
2. What is being said about horses? horses pranced - V
3. Pranced how? proudly - Adv
4. Pranced where? around - Adv

5. What kind of horses? circus - Adj
6. What kind of horses? big - Adj
7. The - A

Classified Sentence:	A	Adj	Adj	SN	V	Adv	Adv
	The	big	circus	horses	pranced	proudly	around.

 ## WRITING TIME

TEACHER INSTRUCTIONS FOR WRITING ASSIGNMENT #2

Give Writing Assignment #2 from the box below. (_Students will now write their own paragraph about their favorite colors._) Students will use a new writing outline, Writing Outline 2, so they can do Writing Assignment #2 on the outline form. This outline is located on page 45 in the Practice Section of their student books.

Have students turn to Reference 20 on page 20 in the Reference section of their books. Tell students to choose two favorite colors from the list of colors at the top of the reference box. Go through the two-point example again and show them how to begin their paragraph. Also, show them how they will use some of the words on the outline to write their own sentences. (_Students should finish writing these sentences on their outlines during this lesson._) Remind students to edit each sentence for capital letters and end-mark punctuation after they have written it.

Writing Assignment Box

Writing Assignment #2: Two-Point Expository Paragraph
Writing topic choices: My Favorite Colors

Students will use their outline forms to copy their sentences onto writing paper in paragraph form in the next lesson.

(End of lesson.)

CHAPTER 19   LESSON 5

Objectives: Jingles, Vocabulary #4, Grammar (Practice Sentences), Test, Check, Writing (Journal), and Writing Assignment #2, continued.

JINGLE TIME

Have students turn to the Jingle Section of their books. The teacher will lead the students in reciting the previously-taught jingles.

VOCABULARY TIME

Have students turn to page 8 in the Vocabulary Section of their books. Introduce the vocabulary words listed in the vocabulary box below by reciting them together with your students.

Chapter 19, Vocabulary Words #4
kind, nurse, patient

GRAMMAR TIME

Put the Practice Sentences from the box below on the board or on notebook paper. Use these sentences as you practice the concepts that have been taught. For the greatest benefit, students must participate orally with the teacher.

Chapter 19, Practice Sentences for Lesson 5
1. The kind nurse talked quietly to the patient.
2. The big black car raced away.
3. The three busy brothers worked hard.

TEACHING SCRIPT FOR PRACTICE SENTENCES

We will classify these three sentences to practice what we have learned. We will classify the sentences together. Begin.

CHAPTER 19 LESSON 5 CONTINUED

Question and Answer Flow for Sentence 1: The kind nurse talked quietly to the patient.

1. Who talked quietly to the patient? nurse - SN
2. What is being said about nurse? nurse talked - V
3. Talked how? quietly - Adv
4. To - P

5. To whom? patient - OP
6. The - A
7. What kind of nurse? kind - Adj
8. The - A

	Adj	SN	V	Adv	P	A	OP
Classified Sentence: A							
The	kind	nurse	talked	quietly	to	the	patient.

Question and Answer Flow for Sentence 2: The big black car raced away.

1. What raced away? car - SN
2. What is being said about car? car raced - V
3. Raced where? away - Adv

4. What kind of car? black - Adj
5. What kind of car? big - Adj
6. The - A

	Adj	Adj	SN	V	Adv
Classified Sentence: A					
The	big	black	car	raced	away.

Question and Answer Flow for Sentence 3: The three busy brothers worked hard.

1. Who worked hard? brothers - SN
2. What is being said about brothers? brothers worked - V
3. Worked how? hard - Adv

4. What kind of brothers? busy - Adj
5. How many brothers? three - Adj
6. The - A

	Adj	Adj	SN	V	Adv
Classified Sentence: A					
The	three	busy	brothers	worked	hard.

TEST TIME

Have students turn to page 72 in the Test Section of their books and find Chapter 19 Test. Go over the directions to make sure they understand what to do. (*Chapter 19 Test key is on the next page.*)

Chapter 19 Test
(Student Page 72)

Exercise 1: Classify each sentence. Use **SN** for subject noun, **V** for verb, **Adv** for adverb, **Adj** for adjective, **A** for article adjective, **P** for preposition, and **OP** for object of the preposition. For Sentence 1, underline the complete subject <u>one</u> time and the complete predicate <u>two</u> times.

```
      A    Adj   SN     V     Adv    P   A    OP
1.   The   kind nurse talked quietly to the patient.
```

```
      A   Adj  Adj   SN     V    Adv
2.   The three busy brothers worked hard.
```

Exercise 2: Underline the **syn** if the words are synonyms. Underline the **ant** if the words are antonyms.

1. front, back   syn **ant**   2. simple, easy   **syn** ant   3. early, late   syn **ant**

Exercise 3: Name the five parts of speech that you have studied. (*You may use abbreviations.*)
(The order of answers may vary.)

1. **Noun (N)**   2. **Verb (V)**   3. **Adjective (Adj)**   4. **Adverb (Adv)**   5. **Preposition (P)**

Exercise 4: Correct the capitalization mistakes and put the rule number above each correction. Use the rule numbers in Reference 11 on page 17 in the Reference Section of your book. Put a (.) or a (?) at the end of the sentence.

```
  1    3                          6    6    7    (capitalization rule numbers)
  D    B                          J    C    M
 does bob work at a factory in jefferson city, missouri ?  (5 capitals)
```

Exercise 5: Write the name of the topic that best describes what each column of words is about. Choose from these topics: **Colors   Clothing   Animals   Kitchen Things   Plants**

(1) Animals	(2) Clothing	(3) Plants
deer	sweater	tree
swan	shorts	grass
bear	shirts	flowers

Exercise 6: In each column, cross out the one idea that does not support the underlined topic at the top.

(1) School Supplies	(2) Winter Weather	(3) People
paper	snow	customer
~~turkey~~	sleet	teenager
pencil	ice	~~pickle~~
ruler	~~chicken~~	sister

Exercise 7: In your journal, write a paragraph summarizing what you have learned this week.

CHAPTER 19 LESSON 5 CONTINUED

 **CHECK TIME**

After students have finished, check and discuss their test papers. Make sure they understand why their answers are right or wrong. Use the Question and Answer Flows on page 239 in this chapter to check the sentences on the Chapter 19 Test. (*For total points, count each required answer as a point.*)

 **WRITING TIME**

TEACHER INSTRUCTIONS FOR WRITING ASSIGNMENT #2 (CONTINUED)

Students will now transfer the sentences they have written on the outline sheet to writing paper in a paragraph format. Have students go to Writing Outline 2 on page 45 in the Practice Section of their books.

Tell students that they will copy the sentences from their outline onto their writing paper in paragraph form. Tell students they must remember to indent a paragraph before they begin writing. (*Show students again how to indent a paragraph on their writing paper.*) Guide your students as they learn how to place the sentences on their paper. Make sure they understand that in a paragraph, each sentence is to follow immediately after the previous one instead of beginning each sentence to the left of the page. Remind them to edit each sentence for capital letters and end-mark punctuation after they have written it.

After students have finished, check and discuss their writing assignments. At the beginning, you must check students' papers carefully for form mistakes. This will ensure that students are learning the two-point format correctly. These are some of the things necessary to check at the beginning:

1. Did students indent the paragraph?
2. Did students capitalize the first word and put an end mark at the end of every sentence?
3. Did students follow the two-point paragraph pattern?

(End of lesson.)

CHAPTER 20   LESSON 1

Objectives: Jingles, Synonyms, Antonyms, Skill (Changing Plural Categories to Singular Points), Writing Assignment #3, and Activity.

 **JINGLE TIME**

Have students turn to the Jingle Section of their books. The teacher will lead the students in reciting the previously-taught jingles.

 SYNONYM AND ANTONYM TIME

Have students turn to the Synonym and Antonym Section of their books. Introduce the new words listed for Chapter 20 in the box below. Make sure students know the meanings of the new synonyms and antonyms. Then, have students underline the correct answers in their books. They should study these words again before their test.

Chapter 20: Underline the **syn** if the words are synonyms. Underline the **ant** if the words are antonyms.		
1. first, last syn **ant**	2. slow, quick syn **ant**	3. raise, lift **syn** ant

 SKILL TIME

TEACHING SCRIPT FOR CHANGING PLURAL CATEGORIES TO SINGULAR POINTS

When you have a topic such as *My favorite animals*, you will usually name your favorite animals by groups, like beavers and otters. When this happens, you need to change some plural points to singular points. I am going to use a sample paragraph to show you some things you need to do.

First, I will read the paragraph to you. Then, I will go through each of the two points in the paragraph and show you how to write it correctly.

(*Have students look at Reference 21 on page 21 in the Reference Section. Read the paragraph from beginning to end to your class. Then, read the teaching script given for each sentence in the paragraph. You may also want to put each sentence on the board as you demonstrate it to your students. Your students will not copy this teaching example as they did the first teaching example. Today, students will write about their favorite animal directly on their writing paper.*)

CHAPTER 20 LESSON 1 CONTINUED

Reference 21: Paragraph for Singular and Plural Points

Two-Point Expository Paragraph

Topic: My favorite animals
2-points: 1. beavers 2. otters

      I have two favorite animals. These animals are beavers and otters. My first favorite animal is a beaver. I think watching beavers build a dam across a river is very fascinating. My second favorite animal is an otter. I like otters because they are so funny when they play in the water. My two favorite animals are fun to watch at work and at play.

Notice that I have written the **topic** first because it is the subject of the paragraph. Writing the topic first helps me to focus on what the paragraph is about. Next, I have listed the two points that I am going to discuss. Again, having the two points written down before I begin helps me focus on what I will say in the paragraph.

I am now ready to begin my paragraph because I am clear about my topic and about the points I will cover as I write. I start with a **topic sentence** because it tells the reader what the paragraph is about: *I have two favorite animals.* Knowing what the paragraph is about helps the reader focus on the main points as the reader progresses through the paragraph.

My next sentence is the **two-point sentence**: *These animals are beavers and otters.* The two-point sentence lists the two main points that will be discussed in the paragraph: *beavers* and *otters.* I want you to notice that each of the two points listed is plural (*beavers* and *otters*). These main points are actually groups of animals, and that is why they are listed as plural words.

Now, let's look at the sentence I have written for the first point. The sentence for the first point starts out like this: *My first favorite animal is.* Since this phrase is singular, I must change my plural listing to a singular listing to agree with the type of sentence I am writing. To do this, I will change *beavers* from plural to singular: *My first favorite animal is a beaver.* Usually, an article adjective is needed to make the sentence sound better. What is the article adjective that I used? (a)

Just remember: If your two points are plural, you usually make them singular as you name them for your first point and second point. Use an article adjective with your singular form to make it sound better. Notice that the second point is done in the same way. Look at its form as I read it to you. (**2nd point:** *My second favorite animal is an otter.*)

After each main point, I have a **supporting sentence**. Supporting sentences make each point clearer by telling extra information about each main point. Remember, I have stated in my main points that beavers and otters are two of my favorite animals. Each supporting sentence should state some kind of information that proves each of the main points. (**1st Supporting sentence:** *I think watching beavers build a dam across a river is very fascinating.* **2nd Supporting sentence:** *I like otters because they are so funny when they play in the water.*) Notice that I also used the plural forms again in the supporting sentences.

My last sentence is a **concluding sentence**. It summarizes my two points by restating some of the words in the topic sentence and by adding an extra thought that finalizes the paragraph. (**Concluding sentence:** *My two favorite animals are fun to watch at work and at play.*)

CHAPTER 20 LESSON 1 CONTINUED

TEACHER INSTRUCTIONS FOR WRITING ASSIGNMENT #3

Give Writing Assignment #3 from the box below. Remind students to use Reference 20 on page 20 to help them write their two-point paragraph. Today, students may write their paragraph directly onto their writing paper instead of using the outline sheet. *(If students need to write their paragraphs on an outline sheet, make a copy of the Writing Outline 1 sample on page 230 and allow them to do so.)*

Writing Assignment Box

Writing Assignment #3: Two-Point Expository Paragraph
Writing topic: My Favorite Animals

After students have finished, check and discuss their writing assignment. Remember, at the beginning, you must check students' papers carefully for form mistakes. This will ensure that students are learning the two-point format correctly. These are some of the things necessary to check at the beginning:

1. Did students indent the paragraph?
2. Did students capitalize the first word and put an end mark at the end of every sentence?
3. Did students follow the two-point paragraph pattern?

 ACTIVITY / ASSIGNMENT TIME

Students will decorate a folder to collect and store all of their writing assignments. Give each student a folder with brads and have them label the outside with the title "My Writing Folder for 20__," indicating the current year. Have them decorate the outside of the folder with markers and glitter. After the glue on the folder has dried, they should put their writing papers in the brads of the folder. This is a great way to keep important writing papers together. Students may want to illustrate some of the stories or paragraphs. Any new writing assignments that they complete during the remainder of the year should also be added to their folder.

(End of lesson.)

CHAPTER 20   LESSON 2

Objectives: Jingles, Vocabulary #1, Grammar (Practice Sentences), and Writing Assignment #4.

 **JINGLE TIME**

Have students turn to the Jingle Section of their books. The teacher will lead the students in reciting the previously-taught jingles.

 VOCABULARY TIME

Have students turn to page 8 in the Vocabulary Section of their books. Introduce the vocabulary words listed in the vocabulary box below by reciting them together with your students.

Chapter 20, Vocabulary Words #1
excitedly, boat, fireflies, glowed, dark

 GRAMMAR TIME

Put the Practice Sentences from the box below on the board or on notebook paper. Use these sentences as you practice the concepts that have been taught. For the greatest benefit, students must participate orally with the teacher.

Chapter 20, Practice Sentences for Lesson 2
1. The three friends raced excitedly to the boat.
2. The cute little fireflies glowed brightly in the dark.
3. The two clever boys looked quietly at the map.

TEACHING SCRIPT FOR PRACTICE SENTENCES

We will classify these three sentences to practice what we have learned. We will classify the sentences together. Begin.

CHAPTER 20 LESSON 2 CONTINUED

Question and Answer Flow for Sentence 1: The three friends raced excitedly to the boat.

1. Who raced excitedly to the boat? friends - SN
2. What is being said about friends? friends raced - V
3. Raced how? excitedly - Adv
4. To - P

5. To what? boat - OP
6. The - A
7. How many friends? three - Adj
8. The - A

Classified Sentence:

A	Adj	SN	V	Adv	P	A	OP
The	three	friends	raced	excitedly	to	the	boat.

Question and Answer Flow for Sentence 2: The cute little fireflies glowed brightly in the dark.

1. What glowed brightly in the dark? fireflies - SN
2. What is being said about fireflies? fireflies glowed - V
3. Glowed how? brightly - Adv
4. In - P
5. In what? dark - OP

6. The - A
7. What kind of fireflies? little - Adj
8. What kind of fireflies? cute - Adj
9. The - A

Classified Sentence:

A	Adj	Adj	SN	V	Adv	P	A	OP
The	cute	little	fireflies	glowed	brightly	in	the	dark.

Question and Answer Flow for Sentence 3: The two clever boys looked quietly at the map.

1. Who looked quietly at the map? boys - SN
2. What is being said about boys? boys looked - V
3. Looked how? quietly - Adv
4. At - P
5. At what? map - OP

6. The - A
7. What kind of boys? clever - Adj
8. How many boys? two - Adj
9. The - A

Classified Sentence:

A	Adj	Adj	SN	V	Adv	P	A	OP
The	two	clever	boys	looked	quietly	at	the	map.

 WRITING TIME

Give Writing Assignment #4 from the box below. Remind students to use Reference 20 on page 20 to help them write their two-point paragraph. Today, students may write their paragraph directly onto their writing paper instead of using the outline sheet. After students have finished, check and discuss their writing assignment. *(Have each student add this assignment to his/her writing folder.)*

Writing Assignment Box

Writing Assignment #4: Two-Point Expository Paragraph
Writing topic: My Favorite Holidays

(End of lesson.)

Level 1 Homeschool Teacher's Manual

CHAPTER 20   LESSON 3

Objectives: Jingles, Vocabulary #2, Grammar (Practice Sentences), and Writing Assignment #5.

 **JINGLE TIME**

Have students turn to the Jingle Section of their books. The teacher will lead the students in reciting the previously-taught jingles.

 VOCABULARY TIME

Have students turn to page 8 in the Vocabulary Section of their books. Introduce the vocabulary words listed in the vocabulary box below by reciting them together with your students.

Chapter 20, Vocabulary Words #2
animals, tree, mall

 GRAMMAR TIME

Put the Practice Sentences from the box below on the board or on notebook paper. Use these sentences as you practice the concepts that have been taught. For the greatest benefit, students must participate orally with the teacher.

Chapter 20, Practice Sentences for Lesson 3
1. The frightened animals ran quickly away.
2. A big tree fell across the road.
3. Sam walked to the mall yesterday.

TEACHING SCRIPT FOR PRACTICE SENTENCES

We will classify these three sentences to practice what we have learned. We will classify the sentences together. Begin. (*You might have students write the labels above the sentences at this time.*)

CHAPTER 20 LESSON 3 CONTINUED

Question and Answer Flow for Sentence 1: The frightened animals ran quickly away.

1. What ran quickly away? animals - SN
2. What is being said about animals? animals ran - V
3. Ran how? quickly - Adv
4. Ran where? away - Adv
5. What kind of animals? frightened - Adj
6. The - A

Classified Sentence:
    A   Adj   SN   V   Adv   Adv
    The frightened animals ran quickly away.

Question and Answer Flow for Sentence 2: A big tree fell across the road.

1. What fell across the road? tree - SN
2. What is being said about tree? tree fell - V
3. Across - P
4. Across what? road - OP
5. The - A
6. What kind of tree? big - Adj
7. A - A

Classified Sentence:
    A Adj SN V P   A   OP
    A big tree fell across the road.

Question and Answer Flow for Sentence 3: Sam walked to the mall yesterday.

1. Who walked to the mall yesterday? Sam - SN
2. What is being said about Sam? Sam walked - V
3. To - P
4. To what? mall - OP
5. The - A
6. Walked when? yesterday - Adv

Classified Sentence:
    SN   V   P   A   OP   Adv
    Sam walked to the mall yesterday.

 WRITING TIME

Give Writing Assignment #5 from the box below. Remind students to use Reference 20 on page 20 to help them write their two-point paragraph. Today, students may write their paragraph directly onto their writing paper instead of using the outline sheet. After students have finished, check and discuss their writing assignment. *(Have each student add this assignment to his/her writing folder.)*

Writing Assignment Box

Writing Assignment #5: Two-Point Expository Paragraph

Writing topic: My Favorite Summer Activities

(End of lesson.)

CHAPTER 20   LESSON 4

Objectives: Jingles, Vocabulary #3, Grammar (Practice Sentences), and Writing Assignment #6.

 JINGLE TIME

Have students turn to the Jingle Section of their books. The teacher will lead the students in reciting the previously-taught jingles.

 VOCABULARY TIME

Have students turn to page 8 in the Vocabulary Section of their books. Introduce the vocabulary words listed in the vocabulary box below by reciting them together with your students.

Chapter 20, Vocabulary Words #3
neighborhood, airport, strong, fished, stream

 GRAMMAR TIME

Put the Practice Sentences from the box below on the board or on notebook paper. Use these sentences as you practice the concepts that have been taught. For the greatest benefit, students must participate orally with the teacher.

Chapter 20, Practice Sentences for Lesson 4
1. The neighborhood children played happily in the sun.
2. The big jet landed smoothly at the airport.
3. The strong brown bear fished in the stream.

TEACHING SCRIPT FOR PRACTICE SENTENCES

We will classify these three sentences to practice what we have learned. We will classify the sentences together. Begin.

Question and Answer Flow for Sentence 1: The neighborhood children played happily in the sun.

1. Who played happily in the sun? children - SN
2. What is being said about children? children played - V
3. Played how? happily - Adv
4. In - P

5. In what? sun - OP
6. The - A
7. What kind of children? neighborhood - Adj
8. The - A

Classified Sentence:

A	Adj	SN	V	Adv	P	A	OP
The	neighborhood	children	played	happily	in	the	sun.

CHAPTER 20 LESSON 4 CONTINUED

Question and Answer Flow for Sentence 2: The big jet landed smoothly at the airport.

1. What landed smoothly at the airport? jet - SN
2. What is being said about jet? jet landed - V
3. Landed how? smoothly - Adv
4. At - P
5. At what? airport - OP
6. The - A
7. What kind of jet? big - Adj
8. The - A

Classified Sentence:

A	Adj	SN	V	Adv	P	A	OP
The	big	jet	landed	smoothly	at	the	airport.

Question and Answer Flow for Sentence 3: The strong brown bear fished in the stream.

1. What fished in the stream? bear - SN
2. What is being said about bear? bear fished - V
3. In - P
4. In what? stream - OP
5. The - A
6. What kind of bear? brown - Adj
7. What kind of bear? strong - Adj
8. The - A

Classified Sentence:

A	Adj	Adj	SN	V	P	A	OP
The	strong	brown	bear	fished	in	the	stream.

 WRITING TIME

Give Writing Assignment #6 from the box below. Remind students to use Reference 20 on page 20 to help them write their two-point paragraph. After students have finished, check and discuss their writing assignment. *(Have each student add this assignment to his/her writing folder.)*

Writing Assignment Box

Writing Assignment #6: Two-Point Expository Paragraph

Writing topic: My Favorite Toys or Games

(End of lesson.)

CHAPTER 20   LESSON 5

Objectives: Jingles, Vocabulary #4, Grammar (Practice Sentences), Test, Check, Writing (Journal, Writing Assignment #7), and Activity.

 **JINGLE TIME**

Have students turn to the Jingle Section of their books. The teacher will lead the students in reciting the previously-taught jingles.

 VOCABULARY TIME

Have students turn to page 8 in the Vocabulary Section of their books. Introduce the vocabulary words listed in the vocabulary box below by reciting them together with your students.

Chapter 20, Vocabulary Words #4
purple, summer, blue, blew

 GRAMMAR TIME

Put the Practice Sentences from the box below on the board or on notebook paper. Use these sentences as you practice the concepts that have been taught. For the greatest benefit, students must participate orally with the teacher.

Chapter 20, Practice Sentences for Lesson 5
1. The tiny purple flowers grew quickly in the summer.
2. The blue car stopped at the store.
3. A cold wind blew across the lake yesterday.

TEACHING SCRIPT FOR PRACTICE SENTENCES

We will classify these three sentences to practice what we have learned. We will classify the sentences together. Begin.

CHAPTER 20 LESSON 5 CONTINUED

Question and Answer Flow for Sentence 1: The tiny purple flowers grew quickly in the summer.

1. What grew quickly in the summer? flowers - SN
2. What is being said about flowers? flowers grew - V
3. Grew how? quickly - Adv
4. In - P
5. In what? summer - OP
6. The - A
7. What kind of flowers? purple - Adj
8. What kind of flowers? tiny - Adj
9. The - A

Classified Sentence:

A	Adj	Adj	SN	V	Adv	P	A	OP
The	tiny	purple	flowers	grew	quickly	in	the	summer.

Question and Answer Flow for Sentence 2: The blue car stopped at the store.

1. What stopped at the store? car - SN
2. What is being said about car? car stopped - V
3. At - P
4. At what? store - OP
5. The - A
6. What kind of car? blue - Adj
7. The - A

Classified Sentence:

A	Adj	SN	V	P	A	OP
The	blue	car	stopped	at	the	store.

Question and Answer Flow for Sentence 3: A cold wind blew across the lake yesterday.

1. What blew across the lake yesterday? wind - SN
2. What is being said about wind? wind blew - V
3. Across - P
4. Across what? lake - OP
5. The - A
6. Blew when? yesterday - Adv
7. What kind of wind? cold - Adj
8. A - A

Classified Sentence:

A	Adj	SN	V	P	A	OP	Adv
A	cold	wind	blew	across	the	lake	yesterday.

TEST TIME

Have students turn to page 73 in the Test Section of their books and find Chapter 20 Test. Go over the directions to make sure they understand what to do. (*Chapter 20 Test key is on the next page.*)

Chapter 20 Test
(Student Page 73)

Exercise 1: Classify each sentence. Use **SN** for subject noun, **V** for verb, **Adv** for adverb, **Adj** for adjective, **A** for article adjective, **P** for preposition, and **OP** for object of the preposition. For Sentence 2, underline the complete subject <u>one</u> time and the complete predicate <u>two</u> times.

```
      A    Adj   SN     V      Adv     P    A    OP
1.   The  three friends raced excitedly to  the  boat.

      A    Adj   Adj    SN      V      Adv    P   A    OP
2.   The  cute  little fireflies glowed brightly in  the  dark.
```

Exercise 2: Underline the **syn** if the words are synonyms. Underline the **ant** if the words are antonyms.

1. slow, quick	syn **ant**	2. first, last	syn **ant**	3. raise, lift	**syn** ant

---

Exercise 3: Name the five parts of speech that you have studied. (*You may use abbreviations.*)
(The order of answers may vary.)

1. **Noun (N)**   2. **Verb (V)**   3. **Adjective (Adj)**   4. **Adverb (Adv)**   5. **Preposition (P)**

Exercise 4: Correct the capitalization mistakes and put the rule number above each correction. Use the rule numbers in Reference 11 on page 17 in the Reference Section of your book. Put a (**.**) or a (**?**) at the end of the sentence.

```
  1                    6                   4         5       (capitalization rule numbers)
  O                    T                   F         J
 our company meets in tulsa on the second friday in july _._  (4 capitals)
```

Exercise 5: Write the name of the topic that best describes what each column of words is about. Choose from these topics: **Colors**   **People**   **Ocean Animals**   **Shapes**   **Sports**

(1) Ocean Animals	(2) Sports	(3) People
whale	baseball	pilot
shrimp	football	niece
shark	tennis	pastor

Exercise 6: In each column, cross out the one idea that does not support the underlined topic.

(1) Vegetables	(2) Months	(3) Insects
beans	December	wasp
~~finger~~	April	mosquito
corn	October	~~butter~~
potato	~~Jacob~~	ant

Exercise 7: In your journal, write a paragraph summarizing what you have learned this week.

CHAPTER 20 LESSON 5 CONTINUED

CHECK TIME

After students have finished, check and discuss their test papers. Make sure they understand why their answers are right or wrong. Use the Question and Answer Flows on page 246 in this chapter to check the sentences on the Chapter 20 Test. (*For total points, count each required answer as a point.*)

WRITING TIME

Give Writing Assignment #7 from the box below. Remind students to use Reference 20 on page 20 to help them write their two-point paragraph. After students have finished, check and discuss their writing assignment. (*Have each student add this assignment to his/her writing folder.*)

Writing Assignment Box
Writing Assignment #7: Two-Point Expository Paragraph
Writing topic: My Favorite Friends

ACTIVITY / ASSIGNMENT TIME

Have students turn to page 89 and find Chapter 20, Lesson 5, Activity. Go over the directions to make sure they understand what to do. Check and discuss the Activity after students have finished.

Chapter 20, Lesson 5, Activity: In the Word Search Puzzle below, find the following vocabulary words and color each word a color of your choice. All the words begin with the letter *P*. The words will appear "down" or "across."

PARADE	PARK	PASSENGER	PATH	PIG	PINK	PLAYED	PONY	POOL
POOR	POPCORN	PORCH	PRETTY	PROUDLY	PUMPKINS	PUPPIES	PURPLE	

P	U	R	P	L	E	P	I	N	K
P	P	X	P	L	P	P	O	N	Y
A	A	P	R	U	O	P	O	O	L
R	S	U	E	M	R	X	P	Z	X
K	S	M	T	Q	C	S	R	P	P
P	E	P	T	A	H	Z	O	A	O
L	N	K	Y	P	I	G	U	R	P
A	G	I	X	C	X	A	D	A	C
Y	E	N	P	A	T	H	L	D	O
E	R	S	P	O	O	R	Y	E	R
D	P	U	P	P	I	E	S	C	N

(End of lesson.)

CHAPTER 21   LESSON 1

Objectives: Jingles, Synonyms, Antonyms, Skill (Identifying Complete Sentences and Sentence Fragments), and Practice Exercise.

JINGLE TIME

Have students turn to the Jingle Section of their books. The teacher will lead the students in reciting the previously-taught jingles.

SYNONYM AND ANTONYM TIME

Have students turn to the Synonym and Antonym Section of their books. Introduce the new words listed for Chapter 21 in the box below. Make sure students know the meanings of the new synonyms and antonyms. Then, have students underline the correct answers in their books. They should study these words again before their test.

Chapter 21: Underline the <u>**syn**</u> if the words are synonyms. Underline the <u>**ant**</u> if the words are antonyms.		
1. sweet, sour syn **<u>ant</u>**	2. below, beneath **<u>syn</u>** ant	3. aid, help **<u>syn</u>** ant

SKILL TIME

TEACHING SCRIPT FOR IDENTIFYING COMPLETE SENTENCES AND SENTENCE FRAGMENTS

Today, we are going to learn the difference between a complete sentence and a fragment. Most of the time you will have no trouble writing a complete sentence because you know the five rules to make a complete sentence. Let's repeat the sentence jingle again to make sure we are all focused on the same thing. (_Recite the Sentence Jingle._)

When you are writing, sometimes you will put a thought down without checking the five parts. If you do not have a subject, verb, and a complete thought, you could have a sentence fragment. This lesson will teach you how to recognize and prevent sentence fragments so all your sentences will be correct.

Prepositional phrases are sentence fragments if they are used as sentences because they do not have subjects or verbs and do not make complete sense. Turn to page 21 in your Reference section. Look at Reference 22 as I go over it with you. (_Read and discuss the information in the reference box on the next page._)

CHAPTER 21 LESSON 1 CONTINUED

Reference 22: Complete Sentences and Sentence Fragments

Identifying complete sentences and sentence fragments: Write **S** for a complete sentence and **F** for a sentence fragment on the line beside each group of words below.

S	1.	The fish were swimming around in the aquarium.
F	2.	For a few dollars.
S	3.	The replacement part arrived yesterday.
S	4.	George laughed.
F	5.	Played during the recital.
F	6.	The peaches on the trees.

 PRACTICE TIME

Have students turn to page 46 in the Practice Section of their book and find Chapter 21, Lesson 1, Practice. Go over the directions to make sure they understand what to do. Check and discuss the Practice after students have finished. (*Chapter 21, Lesson 1, Practice key is given below.*)

Chapter 21, Lesson 1, Practice: Write **S** for a complete sentence and **F** for a sentence fragment on the line beside each group of words below.

S	1.	The cookies baked in the oven.
S	2.	Bells rang.
F	3.	A brown camel.
F	4.	That new book.
F	5.	Watches baseball.
F	6.	Across the street.
S	7.	Every soldier waited for orders.
S	8.	Tray rode his new bicycle.
F	9.	Circled the tall tower.
F	10.	A painted pony.
S	11.	The driver stopped quickly.
F	12.	At the park.
S	13.	The children played in the yard.
F	14.	In the end.
F	15.	Flowers in the garden.

(End of lesson.)

Level 1 Homeschool Teacher's Manual

CHAPTER 21   LESSON 2

Objectives: Jingles, Vocabulary #1, Grammar (Practice Sentences), Skill (Matching Subject Parts and Predicate Parts), Practice Exercise, and Activity.

 **JINGLE TIME**

Have students turn to the Jingle Section of their books. The teacher will lead the students in reciting the previously-taught jingles.

 VOCABULARY TIME

Have students turn to page 8 in the Vocabulary Section of their books. Introduce the vocabulary words listed in the vocabulary box below by reciting them together with your students.

Chapter 21, Vocabulary Words #1
orange, socks

 GRAMMAR TIME

Put the Practice Sentences from the box below on the board or on notebook paper. Use these sentences as you practice the concepts that have been taught. For the greatest benefit, students must participate orally with the teacher.

Chapter 21, Practice Sentences for Lesson 2
1. The pretty orange socks glowed in the dark.
2. Three pretty yellow birds jumped around in the snow.
3. The excited dogs barked loudly today.

TEACHING SCRIPT FOR PRACTICE SENTENCES

We will classify these three sentences to practice what we have learned. We will classify the sentences together. Begin.

CHAPTER 21 LESSON 2 CONTINUED

Question and Answer Flow for Sentence 1: The pretty orange socks glowed in the dark.

1. What glowed in the dark? socks - SN
2. What is being said about socks? socks glowed - V
3. In - P
4. In what? dark - OP

5. The - A
6. What kind of socks? orange - Adj
7. What kind of socks? pretty - Adj
8. The - A

Classified Sentence:

A	Adj	Adj	SN	V	P	A	OP
The	pretty	orange	socks	glowed	in	the	dark.

Question and Answer Flow for Sentence 2: Three pretty yellow birds jumped around in the snow.

1. What jumped around in the snow? birds - SN
2. What is being said about birds? birds jumped - V
3. Jumped where? around - Adv
4. In - P
5. In what? snow - OP

6. The - A
7. What kind of birds? yellow - Adj
8. What kind of birds? pretty - Adj
9. How many birds? three - Adj

Classified Sentence:

Adj	Adj	Adj	SN	V	Adv	P	A	OP
Three	pretty	yellow	birds	jumped	around	in	the	snow.

Question and Answer Flow for Sentence 3: The excited dogs barked loudly today.

1. What barked loudly today? dogs - SN
2. What is being said about dogs? dogs barked - V
3. Barked how? loudly - Adv

4. Barked when? today - Adv
5. What kind of dogs? excited - Adj
6. The - A

Classified Sentence:

A	Adj	SN	V	Adv	Adv
The	excited	dogs	barked	loudly	today.

SKILL TIME

TEACHING SCRIPT FOR MATCHING SUBJECT PARTS AND PREDICATE PARTS

Today, we will learn to match subject parts and predicate parts that make sense in a sentence. This type of exercise will help strengthen your ability to recognize a complete sentence. Look at Reference 23 on page 21 as I go over it with you. (*Read and discuss the information in the reference box below.*)

Reference 23: Matching Subject Parts and Predicate Parts

Match each subject part with the correct predicate part by writing the correct sentence number in the blank.

1.	The purple crayon	**3**	climbed to the top of the tree.
2.	A white truck	**1**	broke in half.
3.	Two black cats	**4**	hurt my eyes.
4.	The bright light	**2**	parked in front of the store.

CHAPTER 21 LESSON 2 CONTINUED

 PRACTICE TIME

Have students turn to pages 46 and 47 in the Practice Section of their books and find Chapter 21, Lesson 2, Practice *(1-2)*. Go over the directions to make sure they understand what to do. Check and discuss the Practices after students have finished. *(Chapter 21, Lesson 2, Practice keys are given below.)*

Chapter 21, Lesson 2, Practice 1: Match each subject part with the correct predicate part by writing the correct sentence number in the blank.

1.	A horse	**4**	was in a new movie.
2.	The wildflowers	**3**	was printed yesterday.
3.	The newspaper	**1**	galloped through the pasture.
4.	That actor	**5**	appeared above the trees.
5.	The beautiful rainbow	**2**	bloomed in the field.

Chapter 21, Lesson 2, Practice 2: Write **S** for a complete sentence and **F** for a sentence fragment on the line beside each group of words below.

F	1.	A curious raccoon.
S	2.	Travis walked to the store.
F	3.	Lives in the alley.
F	4.	This broken toy.
S	5.	The soup cooked.
F	6.	People in the stands.
S	7.	The couple sat on the couch.
S	8.	Jamie parked her car in the garage.
F	9.	Five new kittens.
S	10.	I did well on the test.

 ACTIVITY / ASSIGNMENT TIME

Have students write the three sentences from this lesson on a sheet of paper. Have them tape-record the Question and Answer Flows for all three sentences. Students should write labels above the words in the sentences as they classify them. They especially need the second practice if this is their first year in the program. *(After the students have finished, check the tape and the sentence labels. Make sure students understand any mistakes they have made.)*

(End of lesson.)

CHAPTER 21   LESSON 3

Objectives: Jingles, Vocabulary #2, Grammar (Practice Sentences, Practice and Improved Sentence), and Practice Exercise.

 **JINGLE TIME**

Have students turn to the Jingle Section of their books. The teacher will lead the students in reciting the previously-taught jingles.

 VOCABULARY TIME

Have students turn to page 8 in the Vocabulary Section of their books. Introduce the vocabulary words listed in the vocabulary box below by reciting them together with your students.

Chapter 21, Vocabulary Words #2
fireman, climbed, roof, butterfly, Dan

 GRAMMAR TIME

Put the Practice Sentences from the box below on the board or on notebook paper. Use these sentences as you practice the concepts that have been taught. For the greatest benefit, students must participate orally with the teacher.

Chapter 21, Practice Sentences for Lesson 3
1. The fireman climbed carefully to the roof.
2. The beautiful butterfly flew quickly away.
3. Dan walked slowly by the water.

TEACHING SCRIPT FOR PRACTICE SENTENCES

We will classify these three sentences to practice what we have learned. We will classify the sentences together. Begin. (_You might have students write the labels above the sentences at this time._)

CHAPTER 21 LESSON 3 CONTINUED

Question and Answer Flow for Sentence 1: The fireman climbed carefully to the roof.

1. Who climbed carefully to the roof? fireman - SN
2. What is being said about fireman? fireman climbed - V
3. Climbed how? carefully - Adv
4. To - P

5. To what? roof - OP
6. The - A
7. The - A

Classified Sentence:	A	SN	V	Adv	P	A	OP
	The	fireman	climbed	carefully	to	the	roof.

Question and Answer Flow for Sentence 2: The beautiful butterfly flew quickly away.

1. What flew quickly away? butterfly - SN
2. What is being said about butterfly? butterfly flew - V
3. Flew how? quickly - Adv

4. Flew where? away - Adv
5. What kind of butterfly? beautiful - Adj
6. The - A

Classified Sentence:	A	Adj	SN	V	Adv	Adv
	The	beautiful	butterfly	flew	quickly	away.

Question and Answer Flow for Sentence 3: Dan walked slowly by the water.

1. Who walked slowly by the water? Dan - SN
2. What is being said about Dan? Dan walked - V
3. Walked how? slowly - Adv

4. By - P
5. By what? water - OP
6. The - A

Classified Sentence:	SN	V	Adv	P	A	OP
	Dan	walked	slowly	by	the	water.

TEACHING SCRIPT FOR WRITING PRACTICE AND IMPROVED SENTENCES

I will now guide you through a Practice Sentence; then, we will write an Improved Sentence. Get out a sheet of notebook paper and write the title **Practice Sentence** on the top line. I will write it on the board for you. Copy these labels across the page: **A Adj SN V Adv P A OP**. Make sure you leave plenty of room for the words that you will write under the labels. (*Write the words Practice Sentence and the labels students will use on the board so students can copy them correctly.*)

Before we begin, I want you to turn to page 18 in the Reference Section of your book. Look at Reference 16. You can use these vocabulary words to help you write Practice and Improved Sentences if you need them. You should only use this list if you cannot think of a word by yourself. (*Guide students through their Practice and Improved Sentences by using the script on pages 194-195 in your teacher's manual. Read it word-for-word to your students. After they have finished, check and discuss their Practice and Improved Sentences.*)

CHAPTER 21 LESSON 3 CONTINUED

 PRACTICE TIME

Have students turn to pages 47 and 48 in the Practice Section of their books and find Chapter 21, Lesson 3, Practice *(1-2)*. Go over the directions to make sure they understand what to do. Check and discuss the Practices after students have finished. (*Chapter 21, Lesson 3, Practice keys are given below.*)

Chapter 21, Lesson 3, Practice 1: Match each subject part with the correct predicate part by writing the correct sentence number in the blank.

1. The glass vase	4	fit nicely.
2. The dentist	3	chased the robber.
3. Five police officers	1	shattered on the floor.
4. My Easter dress	5	squeezed under the fence.
5. A bunny	2	cleaned my teeth.

Chapter 21, Lesson 3, Practice 2: Write **S** for a complete sentence and **F** for a sentence fragment on the line beside each group of words below.

F	1.	An empty box.
S	2.	We swam across the pool.
F	3.	Flies a plane.
S	4.	I talked with Susan.
F	5.	Near the end of the road.
F	6.	Trapped in the cave.
S	7.	Ball rolled.
S	8.	The rain fell hard.
F	9.	The two churches.
S	10.	The children ran fast.

(End of lesson.)

CHAPTER 21   LESSON 4

Objectives: Jingles, Vocabulary #3, Grammar (Practice Sentences), and Writing Assignment #8.

 **JINGLE TIME**

Have students turn to the Jingle Section of their books. The teacher will lead the students in reciting the previously-taught jingles.

 VOCABULARY TIME

Have students turn to page 8 in the Vocabulary Section of their books. Introduce the vocabulary words listed in the vocabulary box below by reciting them together with your students.

Chapter 21, Vocabulary Words #3
candles, burned, lost

 GRAMMAR TIME

Put the Practice Sentences from the box below on the board or on notebook paper. Use these sentences as you practice the concepts that have been taught. For the greatest benefit, students must participate orally with the teacher.

Chapter 21, Practice Sentences for Lesson 4
1. Several tiny butterflies flew to the flowers.
2. The huge candles burned brightly in the window.
3. The little lost puppy whimpered loudly.

TEACHING SCRIPT FOR PRACTICE SENTENCES

We will classify these three sentences to practice what we have learned. We will classify the sentences together. Begin.

Question and Answer Flow for Sentence 1: Several tiny butterflies flew to the flowers.

1. What flew to the flowers? butterflies - SN
2. What is being said about butterflies? butterflies flew - V
3. To - P
4. To what? flowers - OP
5. The - A
6. What kind of butterflies? tiny - Adj
7. How many butterflies? several - Adj

Classified Sentence:

Adj	Adj	SN	V	P	A	OP
Several	tiny	butterflies	flew	to	the	flowers.

CHAPTER 21 LESSON 4 CONTINUED

Question and Answer Flow for Sentence 2: The huge candles burned brightly in the window.

1. What burned brightly in the window? candles - SN
2. What is being said about candles? candles burned - V
3. Burned how? brightly - Adv
4. In - P

5. In what? window - OP
6. The - A
7. What kind of candles? huge - Adj
8. The - A

Classified Sentence:

A	Adj	SN	V	Adv	P	A	OP
The	huge	candles	burned	brightly	in	the	window.

Question and Answer Flow for Sentence 3: The little lost puppy whimpered loudly.

1. What whimpered loudly? puppy - SN
2. What is being said about puppy? puppy whimpered - V
3. Whimpered how? loudly - Adv

4. What kind of puppy? lost - Adj
5. What kind of puppy? little - Adj
6. The - A

Classified Sentence:

A	Adj	Adj	SN	V	Adv
The	little	lost	puppy	whimpered	loudly.

 WRITING TIME

Give Writing Assignment #8 from the box below. Remind students to use Reference 20 on page 20 to help them write their two-point paragraph. After students have finished, check and discuss their writing assignments. *(Have each student add this assignment to his/her writing folder.)*

Writing Assignment Box

Writing Assignment #8: Two-Point Expository Paragraph

Writing topic: My Favorite Foods

(End of lesson.)

CHAPTER 21   LESSON 5

Objectives: Jingles, Vocabulary #4, Grammar (Practice Sentences), Test, Check, Writing (Journal), and Activity.

 **JINGLE TIME**

Have students turn to the Jingle Section of their books. The teacher will lead the students in reciting the previously-taught jingles.

 VOCABULARY TIME

Have students turn to page 8 in the Vocabulary Section of their books. Introduce the vocabulary words listed in the vocabulary box below by reciting them together with your students.

Chapter 21, Vocabulary Words #4
Sarah, dressed, warmly, winter

 GRAMMAR TIME

Put the Practice Sentences from the box below on the board or on notebook paper. Use these sentences as you practice the concepts that have been taught. For the greatest benefit, students must participate orally with the teacher.

Chapter 21, Practice Sentences for Lesson 5
1. Sarah went to the lake yesterday.
2. The wild tiger jumped across the road today.
3. The little children dressed warmly in the winter.

TEACHING SCRIPT FOR PRACTICE SENTENCES

We will classify these three sentences to practice what we have learned. We will classify the sentences together. Begin.

CHAPTER 21 LESSON 5 CONTINUED

Question and Answer Flow for Sentence 1: Sarah went to the lake yesterday.

1. Who went to the lake yesterday? Sarah - SN
2. What is being said about Sarah? Sarah went - V
3. To - P

4. To what? lake - OP
5. The - A
6. Went when? yesterday - Adv

Classified Sentence:

SN	V	P	A	OP	Adv
Sarah	went	to	the	lake	yesterday.

Question and Answer Flow for Sentence 2: The wild tiger jumped across the road today.

1. What jumped across the road today? tiger - SN
2. What is being said about tiger? tiger jumped - V
3. Across - P
4. Across what? road - OP

5. The - A
6. Jumped when? today - Adv
7. What kind of tiger? wild - Adj
8. The - A

Classified Sentence:

A	Adj	SN	V	P	A	OP	Adv
The	wild	tiger	jumped	across	the	road	today.

Question and Answer Flow for Sentence 3: The little children dressed warmly in the winter.

1. Who dressed warmly in the winter? children - SN
2. What is being said about children? children dressed - V
3. Dressed how? warmly - Adv
4. In - P

5. In what? winter - OP
6. The - A
7. What kind of children? little - Adj
8. The - A

Classified Sentence:

A	Adj	SN	V	Adv	P	A	OP
The	little	children	dressed	warmly	in	the	winter.

TEST TIME

Have students turn to page 74 in the Test Section of their books and find Chapter 21 Test. Go over the directions to make sure they understand what to do. (*Chapter 21 Test key is on the next page.*)

Chapter 21 Test
(Student Page 74)

Exercise 1: Classify each sentence. Use **SN** for subject noun, **V** for verb, **Adv** for adverb, **Adj** for adjective, **A** for article adjective, **P** for preposition, and **OP** for object of the preposition. For Sentence 2, underline the complete subject <u>one</u> time and the complete predicate <u>two</u> times.

```
       A      Adj       SN        V       Adv      Adv
1.    The   beautiful  butterfly  flew   quickly   away.

       A      SN        V        Adv      P     A     OP
2.    The    fireman   climbed  carefully  to   the   roof.
```

Exercise 2: Underline the **syn** if the words are synonyms. Underline the **ant** if the words are antonyms.

1. below, beneath	**<u>syn</u>** ant	2. sweet, sour	syn **<u>ant</u>**	3. aid, help	**<u>syn</u>** ant

---

Exercise 3: Name the five parts of speech that you have studied. (*You may use abbreviations.*)
(The order of answers may vary.)

1. **Noun (N)**   2. **Verb (V)**   3. **Adjective (Adj)**   4. **Adverb (Adv)**   5. **Preposition (P)**

Exercise 4: Match each subject part with the correct predicate part by writing the correct sentence number in the blank.

1.	The player	4	climbed in the trees.
2.	The fire	3	hatched today.
3.	The tiny egg	1	threw the ball.
4.	Three monkeys	5	baked in the oven.
5.	An apple pie	2	burned brightly.

Exercise 5: Write **S** for a complete sentence and **F** for a sentence fragment on the line beside each group of words below.

S   1. The ants marched across the ground.   F   6. The pain in his right hand.

F   2. To the man in the car.   F   7. Paid for the ticket with cash.

S   3. Many workers ride the subway.   F   8. At the bottom of the closet.

F   4. That new building.   S   9. Telephone rang.

S   5. Walter made several friends on the bus.

Exercise 6: In your journal, write a paragraph summarizing what you have learned this week.

CHAPTER 21 LESSON 5 CONTINUED

CHECK TIME

After students have finished, check and discuss their test papers. Make sure they understand why their answers are right or wrong. Use the Question and Answer Flows on page 261 in this chapter to check the sentences on the Chapter 21 Test. *(For total points, count each required answer as a point.)*

ACTIVITY / ASSIGNMENT TIME

(You will need 10 balloons, a basket, a piece of paper, masking tape, and a magic marker for this activity.)

Find a basket from around the house. (A laundry basket, trash can, or an empty bucket will do fine for this activity.) You will label the basket with a piece of paper that has the words "complete sentence" on it. Tape the label to the basket. Then, blow up the 10 balloons. Write one of the 10 sample groups of words below on each balloon with a magic marker. *(Another option: Write the groups of words on strips of paper and tie each strip to a balloon.)*

1. Children laughed.
2. May I help you?
3. On the left side.
4. A talented artist.
5. The red lobster.

6. Tiptoed quietly through the hall.
7. She closed the door.
8. Can you pass the butter?
9. Behind the bookshelf.
10. Hiding in the bushes.

Place the basket anywhere on the floor. Have students grab a balloon and read the words on the balloon. If the words make a complete sentence, students are to place the balloon in the basket. If the words do not form a complete sentence, students should identify them as a fragment and pop the balloon. *(There are 4 complete sentences and 6 fragments.)*

(End of lesson.)

CHAPTER 22   LESSON 1

Objectives: Jingles, Synonyms, Antonyms, Skill (Contractions), and Practice Exercise.

 **JINGLE TIME**

Have students turn to the Jingle Section of their books. The teacher will lead the students in reciting the previously-taught jingles.

 SYNONYM AND ANTONYM TIME

Have students turn to the Synonym and Antonym Section of their books. Introduce the new words listed for Chapter 22 in the box below. Make sure students know the meanings of the new synonyms and antonyms. Then, have students underline the correct answers in their books. They should study these words again before their test.

Chapter 22: Underline the **syn** if the words are synonyms. Underline the **ant** if the words are antonyms.

| 1. night, day | syn | **ant** | | 2. shout, whisper | syn | **ant** | | 3. bashful, shy | **syn** | ant |

 SKILL TIME

*TEACHING SCRIPT FOR THE CONTRACTIONS **ISN'T, AREN'T, WASN'T, AND WEREN'T***

You will learn about contractions in this chapter. Contractions are not hard, but you need a lot of practice in writing and in using them correctly. A **contraction** is two words shortened into one word, and the new word always has an apostrophe. The apostrophe takes the place of the letters that have been left out.

Look at Reference 24 on page 21 in the Reference section of your book. In this lesson, we will study the four contractions listed in this reference box. We will learn about the contractions *isn't aren't, wasn't,* and *weren't. (Reference 24 is located on the next page.)*

CHAPTER 22 LESSON 1 CONTINUED

Reference 24: Contractions			
isn't **is not**	**aren't** **are not**	**wasn't** **was not**	**weren't** **were not**
The pen **is not** here.	The books **are not** new.	The cat **was not** outside.	The boys **were not** early.
The pen **isn't** here.	The books **aren't** new.	The cat **wasn't** outside.	The boys **weren't** early.

Look at the contraction *isn't*. When *is* and *not* are put together, the letter *o* is left out. We must use an apostrophe in place of the missing *o*. When you write a sentence, you can use the contraction *isn't* or the two words *is not* without changing the meaning of the sentence. Let's read the sentences under the contraction *isn't*. *(Read and discuss the sentences and make sure students see that the meanings do not change.)*

Look at the contraction *aren't*. When *are* and *not* are put together, the letter *o* is left out. We must use an apostrophe in place of the missing *o*. When you write a sentence, you can use the contraction *aren't* or the two words *are not* without changing the meaning of the sentence. Let's read the sentences under the contraction *aren't*. *(Read and discuss the sentences and make sure students see that the meanings do not change.)*

Look at the contractions *wasn't* and *weren't*. When *was* and *not* were put together, the letter *o* was left out. The letter *o* was also left out when *were* and *not* were put together. We use an apostrophe in place of the missing *o* in each word. When you write a sentence, you can use the contraction *wasn't* or the two words *was not* without changing the meaning of the sentence. You can also write *were not* as *weren't* without changing the meaning of the sentence.

Let's read the sentences under the contraction *wasn't*. *(Read and discuss the sentences and make sure students see that the meanings do not change.)* Let's read the sentences under the contraction *weren't*. *(Read and discuss the sentences and make sure students see that the meanings do not change. Have students recite all four contractions with you several times.)*

 PRACTICE TIME

Have students turn to pages 48 and 49 in the Practice Section of their books and find Chapter 22, Lesson 1, Practices *(1-4)*. Go over the directions to make sure they understand what to do. Check and discuss the Practice after students have finished. *(Chapter 22, Lesson 1, Practice keys are given below and on the next page.)*

Chapter 22, Lesson 1, Practice 1: Write the correct contraction in each blank.

1. are not	**aren't**		5. is not	**isn't**	
2. is not	**isn't**		6. are not	**aren't**	
3. was not	**wasn't**		7. were not	**weren't**	
4. were not	**weren't**		8. was not	**wasn't**	

CHAPTER 22 LESSON 1 CONTINUED

Chapter 22, Lesson 1, Practice 2: Write the correct words beside each contraction.

1. aren't	are not		5. isn't	is not
2. isn't	is not		6. aren't	are not
3. wasn't	was not		7. weren't	were not
4. weren't	were not		8. wasn't	was not

Chapter 22, Lesson 1, Practice 3: Underline the correct contraction at the right for the words that are underlined in each sentence.

1. My crayons <u>are not</u> missing.	isn't	**<u>aren't</u>**
2. His pencil <u>is not</u> sharp.	**<u>isn't</u>**	aren't
3. The books <u>are not</u> expensive.	isn't	**<u>aren't</u>**
4. The officer <u>was not</u> here.	**<u>wasn't</u>**	weren't
5. My brother <u>was not</u> ill.	**<u>wasn't</u>**	weren't
6. My notes <u>were not</u> in order.	wasn't	**<u>weren't</u>**

Chapter 22, Lesson 1, Practice 4: Write the correct contraction in the blank for the words that are underlined in each sentence. Use Reference 24 on page 21 to help you.

1. The bread <u>was not</u> fresh.   **wasn't**

2. My clothes <u>are not</u> packed.   **aren't**

3. The students <u>were not</u> on time.   **weren't**

4. The baby <u>is not</u> happy.   **isn't**

(End of lesson.)

CHAPTER 22   LESSON 2

Objectives: Jingles, Vocabulary #1, Grammar (Practice Sentences), Skill (Contractions), Practice Exercise, and Activity.

JINGLE TIME

Have students turn to the Jingle Section of their books. The teacher will lead the students in reciting the previously-taught jingles.

VOCABULARY TIME

Have students turn to page 8 in the Vocabulary Section of their books. Introduce the vocabulary words listed in the vocabulary box below by reciting them together with your students.

Chapter 22, Vocabulary Words #1
ground, melted, goats, stood, porch

GRAMMAR TIME

Put the Practice Sentences from the box below on the board or on notebook paper. Use these sentences as you practice the concepts that have been taught. For the greatest benefit, students must participate orally with the teacher.

Chapter 22, Practice Sentences for Lesson 2
1. The beautiful house burned slowly to the ground.
2. The cold snow melted quickly in the sun.
3. Two silly goats stood on the porch.

TEACHING SCRIPT FOR PRACTICE SENTENCES

We will classify these three sentences to practice what we have learned. We will classify the sentences together. Begin.

Level 1 Homeschool Teacher's Manual

CHAPTER 22 LESSON 2 CONTINUED

Question and Answer Flow for Sentence 1: The beautiful house burned slowly to the ground.

1. What burned slowly to the ground? house - SN
2. What is being said about house? house burned - V
3. Burned how? slowly - Adv
4. To - P

5. To what? ground - OP
6. The - A
7. What kind of house? beautiful - Adj
8. The - A

Classified Sentence:	A	Adj	SN	V	Adv	P	A	OP
	The	beautiful	house	burned	slowly	to	the	ground.

Question and Answer Flow for Sentence 2: The cold snow melted quickly in the sun.

1. What melted quickly in the sun? snow - SN
2. What is being said about snow? snow melted - V
3. Melted how? quickly - Adv
4. In - P

5. In what? sun - OP
6. The - A
7. What kind of snow? cold - Adj
8. The - A

Classified Sentence:	A	Adj	SN	V	Adv	P	A	OP
	The	cold	snow	melted	quickly	in	the	sun.

Question and Answer Flow for Sentence 3: Two silly goats stood on the porch.

1. What stood on the porch? goats - SN
2. What is being said about goats? goats stood - V
3. On - P
4. On what? porch - OP

5. The - A
6. What kind of goats? silly - Adj
7. How many goats? two - Adj

Classified Sentence:	Adj	Adj	SN	V	P	A	OP
	Two	silly	goats	stood	on	the	porch.

TEACHING SCRIPT FOR THE CONTRACTIONS *I'M, CAN'T, DON'T, DOESN'T, AND DIDN'T*

Remember, a **contraction** is two words shortened into one word, and the new word always has an apostrophe. The apostrophe takes the place of the letter or letters that have been left out.

We have a new contraction chart to study. It contains five new contractions. Look at Reference 25 on page 22 in the Reference section of your book. This reference box will show you how these contractions are made.

Reference 25: More Contractions				
I'm I am	**can't cannot**	**don't do not**	**doesn't does not**	**didn't did not**
I **am** not home.	You **cannot** go.	We **do not** see you.	The man **does not** hear.	I **did not** know.
I'm not home.	You **can't** go.	We **don't** see you.	The man **doesn't** hear.	I **didn't** know.

CHAPTER 22 LESSON 2 CONTINUED

First, we will recite the contractions and the words used to make the contractions. *(Recite these words together: I'm – I am, can't – cannot, don't – do not, doesn't – does not, didn't – did not.)*

Point to the contraction *I'm.* When *I* and *am* are put together, the letter *a* is left out and an apostrophe is used in place of the missing *a.* Point to the contraction *can't.* When *can* and *not* are put together, the letters *n* and *o* are left out. An apostrophe is used in place of the two missing letters.

Look at the contraction *don't.* When *do* and *not* are put together, what letter is left out? *(o)* What do we use in place of the missing *o*? *(an apostrophe)* Look at the contraction *doesn't.* When *does* and *not* are put together, what letter is left out? *(o)* What do we use in place of the missing *o*? *(an apostrophe)* Now, look at the contraction *didn't.* When *did* and *not* are put together, what letter is left out? *(o)* What do we use in place of the missing *o*? *(an apostrophe)*

When you write a sentence, you can use a contraction or the two words from which a contraction is made without changing the meaning of the sentence. Let's read the sentences under each contraction. *(Read and discuss the sentences and make sure students see that the meanings do not change.)*

 PRACTICE TIME

Have students turn to pages 49 and 50 in the Practice Section of their books and find Chapter 22, Lesson 2, Practice *(1-3).* Go over the directions to make sure they understand what to do. Check and discuss the Practices after students have finished. *(Chapter 22, Lesson 2, Practice keys are given below and on the next page.)*

Chapter 22, Lesson 2, Practice 1: Write the correct contraction in each blank. Use Reference 25 on page 22 to help you.

1. I am   **I'm**

2. cannot   **can't**

3. do not   **don't**

4. does not   **doesn't**

5. did not   **didn't**

Chapter 22, Lesson 2, Practice 2: Write the correct words beside each contraction. Use Reference 25 on page 22 to help you.

1. didn't   **did not**

2. can't   **cannot**

3. doesn't   **does not**

4. I'm   **I am**

5. don't   **do not**

CHAPTER 22 LESSON 2 CONTINUED

Chapter 22, Lesson 2, Practice 3: Write the correct contraction in the blank for the words that are underlined in each sentence. Use Reference 25 on page 22 to help you.

1. My mother knows that <u>I am</u> responsible.   **I'm** _____

2. Those boys <u>cannot</u> play.   **can't** _____

3. The rain <u>did not</u> stop for days.   **didn't** _____

4. His room <u>does not</u> need to be cleaned.   **doesn't** _____

5. The stores <u>do not</u> open today.   **don't** _____

ACTIVITY / ASSIGNMENT TIME

Contraction Memory

To play contraction memory, follow the directions below:

1. Using five sheets of construction paper, cut each sheet into four pieces. *(You will use eighteen pieces.)*

2. Using the words below, copy each one on a piece of construction paper. *(There is a total of 18 words below.)*

> **I'm, I am, can't, cannot, don't, do not, doesn't, does not, didn't, did not, isn't, is not, aren't, are not, wasn't, was not, weren't, were not**

3. Spread the eighteen cards face down on the floor in front of students.

4. Have students take turns choosing 2 cards and turning them face up.

   a. If the cards match (contraction and word), the student may keep the cards and choose 2 more.
   b. If the cards do not match, the cards must be turned face down on the playing surface, and the next player begins his turn.

5. Repeat step #4 until all cards have been matched and put aside.

6. The player with the most matches at the end of the game wins.

Key			
I'm, I am	didn't, did not	don't, do not	doesn't, does not
can't, cannot	isn't, is not	aren't, are not	wasn't, was not
			weren't, were not

(End of lesson.)

CHAPTER 22   LESSON 3

Objectives: Jingles, Vocabulary #2, Grammar (Practice Sentences), and Practice Exercise.

 **JINGLE TIME**

Have students turn to the Jingle Section of their books. The teacher will lead the students in reciting the previously-taught jingles.

 VOCABULARY TIME

Have students turn to page 8 in the Vocabulary Section of their books. Introduce the vocabulary words listed in the vocabulary box below by reciting them together with your students.

Chapter 22, Vocabulary Words #2
birthday, cake, pool

 GRAMMAR TIME

Put the Practice Sentences from the box below on the board or on notebook paper. Use these sentences as you practice the concepts that have been taught. For the greatest benefit, students must participate orally with the teacher.

Chapter 22, Practice Sentences for Lesson 3
1. The pretty birthday candles melted slowly on the cake.
2. The excited children ran to the pool.
3. A tiny brown mouse ran suddenly across the floor.

TEACHING SCRIPT FOR PRACTICE SENTENCES

We will classify these three sentences to practice what we have learned. We will classify the sentences together. Begin. (*You might have students write the labels above the sentences at this time.*)

CHAPTER 22 LESSON 3 CONTINUED

Question and Answer Flow for Sentence 1: The pretty birthday candles melted slowly on the cake.

1. What melted slowly on the cake? candles - SN
2. What is being said about candles? candles melted - V
3. Melted how? slowly - Adv
4. On - P
5. On what? cake - OP

6. The - A
7. What kind of candles? birthday - Adj
8. What kind of candles? pretty - Adj
9. The - A

Classified Sentence:

A	Adj	Adj	SN	V	Adv	P	A	OP
The	pretty	birthday	candles	melted	slowly	on	the	cake.

Question and Answer Flow for Sentence 2: The excited children ran to the pool.

1. Who ran to the pool? children - SN
2. What is being said about children? children ran - V
3. To - P
4. To what? pool - OP

5. The - A
6. What kind of children? excited - Adj
7. The - A

Classified Sentence:

A	Adj	SN	V	P	A	OP
The	excited	children	ran	to	the	pool.

Question and Answer Flow for Sentence 3: A tiny brown mouse ran suddenly across the floor.

1. What ran suddenly across the floor? mouse - SN
2. What is being said about mouse? mouse ran - V
3. Ran how? suddenly - Adv
4. Across - P
5. Across what? floor - OP

6. The - A
7. What kind of mouse? brown - Adj
8. What kind of mouse? tiny - Adj
9. A - A

Classified Sentence:

A	Adj	Adj	SN	V	Adv	P	A	OP
A	tiny	brown	mouse	ran	suddenly	across	the	floor.

 PRACTICE TIME

Have students turn to pages 50 and 51 in the Practice Section of their books and find Chapter 22, Lesson 3, Practice *(1-3)*. Go over the directions to make sure they understand what to do. Check and discuss the Practices after students have finished. *(Chapter 22, Lesson 3, Practice keys are given on the next page.)*

CHAPTER 22 LESSON 3 CONTINUED

Chapter 22, Lesson 3, Practice 1: Write the correct contraction in each blank. Use the contraction references to help you.

1. do not	don't		5. are not	aren't	
2. cannot	can't		6. is not	isn't	
3. were not	weren't		7. did not	didn't	
4. I am	I'm		8. does not	doesn't	

Chapter 22, Lesson 3, Practice 2: Write the correct words beside each contraction. Use the contraction references to help you.

1. I'm	I am		5. weren't	were not	
2. isn't	is not		6. can't	cannot	
3. doesn't	does not		7. didn't	did not	
4. wasn't	was not		8. aren't	are not	

Chapter 22, Lesson 3, Practice 3: Write the correct contraction in the blank for the words that are underlined in each sentence. Use the contraction references to help you.

1. The machines <u>are not</u> broken.   aren't

2. I <u>cannot</u> play the tuba.   can't

3. The students <u>did not</u> read the directions.   didn't

4. Harry <u>does not</u> play basketball.   doesn't

5. The numbers <u>do not</u> make sense.   don't

6. Jill knows that <u>I am</u> busy.   I'm

7. Kathy <u>is not</u> coming to my party.   isn't

8. Patrick <u>was not</u> paying attention.   wasn't

9. The fans <u>were not</u> allowed on the field.   weren't

(End of lesson.)

Level 1 Homeschool Teacher's Manual

CHAPTER 22   LESSON 4

Objectives: Jingles, Vocabulary #3, Grammar (Practice Sentences), and Writing Assignment #9.

 **JINGLE TIME**

Have students turn to the Jingle Section of their books. The teacher will lead the students in reciting the previously-taught jingles.

 VOCABULARY TIME

Have students turn to page 8 in the Vocabulary Section of their books. Introduce the vocabulary words listed in the vocabulary box below by reciting them together with your students.

Chapter 22, Vocabulary Words #3
best, coins, path

 GRAMMAR TIME

Put the Practice Sentences from the box below on the board or on notebook paper. Use these sentences as you practice the concepts that have been taught. For the greatest benefit, students must participate orally with the teacher.

Chapter 22, Practice Sentences for Lesson 4
1. Two best friends played happily in the yard today.
2. The six coins fell on the floor.
3. The pretty pink flowers grew by the path.

TEACHING SCRIPT FOR PRACTICE SENTENCES

We will classify these three sentences to practice what we have learned. We will classify the sentences together. Begin.

Question and Answer Flow for Sentence 1: Two best friends played happily in the yard today.

1. Who played happily in the yard today? friends - SN
2. What is being said about friends? friends played - V
3. Played how? happily - Adv
4. In - P
5. In what? yard - OP

6. The - A
7. Played when? today - Adv
8. What kind of friends? best - Adj
9. How many friends? two - Adj

Classified Sentence:

Adj	Adj	SN	V	Adv	P	A	OP	Adv
Two	best	friends	played	happily	in	the	yard	today.

CHAPTER 22 LESSON 4 CONTINUED

Question and Answer Flow for Sentence 2: The six coins fell on the floor.

1. What fell on the floor? coins - SN
2. What is being said about coins? coins fell - V
3. On - P
4. On what? floor - OP
5. The - A
6. How many coins? six - Adj
7. The - A

Classified Sentence:

A	Adj	SN	V	P	A	OP
The	six	coins	fell	on	the	floor.

Question and Answer Flow for Sentence 3: The pretty pink flowers grew by the path.

1. What grew by the path? flowers - SN
2. What is being said about flowers? flowers grew - V
3. By - P
4. By what? path - OP
5. The - A
6. What kind of flowers? pink - Adj
7. What kind of flowers? pretty - Adj
8. The - A

Classified Sentence:

A	Adj	Adj	SN	V	P	A	OP
The	pretty	pink	flowers	grew	by	the	path.

 WRITING TIME

Give Writing Assignment #9 from the box below. Remind students to use Reference 20 on page 20 to help them write their two-point paragraph. After students have finished, check and discuss their writing assignment. *(Have each student add this assignment to his/her writing folder.)*

Writing Assignment Box

Writing Assignment #9: Two-Point Expository Paragraph

Writing topic: Things That Make Me Happy

(End of lesson.)

CHAPTER 22   LESSON 5
Objectives: Jingles, Vocabulary #4, Grammar (Practice Sentences), Test, Check, and Writing (Journal).

 **JINGLE TIME**

Have students turn to the Jingle Section of their books. The teacher will lead the students in reciting the previously-taught jingles.

 VOCABULARY TIME

Have students turn to page 8 in the Vocabulary Section of their books. Introduce the vocabulary words listed in the vocabulary box below by reciting them together with your students.

Chapter 22, Vocabulary Words #4
hall, Mom, shopped, park

 GRAMMAR TIME

Put the Practice Sentences from the box below on the board or on notebook paper. Use these sentences as you practice the concepts that have been taught. For the greatest benefit, students must participate orally with the teacher.

Chapter 22, Practice Sentences for Lesson 5
1. The students walked noisily down the hall.
2. Mom shopped at the mall today.
3. Several families ate in the park yesterday.

TEACHING SCRIPT FOR PRACTICE SENTENCES

We will classify these three sentences to practice what we have learned. We will classify the sentences together. Begin.

CHAPTER 22 LESSON 5 CONTINUED

Question and Answer Flow for Sentence 1: The students walked noisily down the hall.

1. Who walked noisily down the hall? students - SN
2. What is being said about students? students walked - V
3. Walked how? noisily - Adv
4. Down - P
5. Down what? hall - OP
6. The - A
7. The - A

Classified Sentence:

A	SN	V	Adv	P	A	OP
The	students	walked	noisily	down	the	hall.

Question and Answer Flow for Sentence 2: Mom shopped at the mall today.

1. Who shopped at the mall today? Mom - SN
2. What is being said about Mom? Mom shopped - V
3. At - P
4. At what? mall - OP
5. The - A
6. Shopped when? today - Adv

Classified Sentence:

SN	V	P	A	OP	Adv
Mom	shopped	at	the	mall	today.

Question and Answer Flow for Sentence 3: Several families ate in the park yesterday.

1. Who ate in the park yesterday? families - SN
2. What is being said about families? families ate - V
3. In - P
4. In what? park - OP
5. The - A
6. Ate when? yesterday - Adv
7. How many families? several - Adj

Classified Sentence:

Adj	SN	V	P	A	OP	Adv
Several	families	ate	in	the	park	yesterday.

 **TEST TIME**

Have students turn to page 75 in the Test Section of their books and find Chapter 22 Test. Go over the directions to make sure they understand what to do. (*Chapter 22 Test key is on the next page.*)

Chapter 22 Test
(Student Page 75)

Exercise 1: Classify each sentence. Use **SN** for subject noun, **V** for verb, **Adv** for adverb, **Adj** for adjective, **A** for article adjective, **P** for preposition, and **OP** for object of the preposition. For Sentence 1, underline the complete subject <u>one</u> time and the complete predicate <u>two</u> times.

       A   Adj   Adj   SN   V   Adv   P   A   OP
1.   <u>The   pretty   birthday   candles</u>   <u>melted   slowly   on   the   cake</u>.

       A   Adj   SN   V   P   A   OP
2.   The   excited   children   ran   to   the   pool.

Exercise 2: Underline the **syn** if the words are synonyms. Underline the **ant** if the words are antonyms.

| 1. night, day | syn **ant** | 2. bashful, shy | **syn** ant | 3. shout, whisper | syn **ant** |

Exercise 3: Name the five parts of speech that you have studied. (*You may use abbreviations.*)
(The order of answers may vary.)

1. **Noun (N)**   2. **Verb (V)**   3. **Adjective (Adj)**   4. **Adverb (Adv)**   5. **Preposition (P)**

Exercise 4: Correct the capitalization mistakes and put the rule number above each correction. Use the rule numbers in Reference 11 on page 17 in the Reference Section of your book. Put a (**.**) or a (**?**) at the end of the sentence.

1   4   5   (capitalization rule numbers)

O   S   S

our   church   meets   every   sunday   night   in   september **_.__** **(3 capitals)**

Exercise 5: Write the correct contraction in each blank. Use the contraction references to help you.

1. do not	**don't**
2. cannot	**can't**
3. I am	**I'm**
4. are not	**aren't**
5. were not	**weren't**

Exercise 6: Write the correct words beside each contraction. Use the contraction references to help you.

1. didn't	**did not**
2. wasn't	**was not**
3. doesn't	**does not**
4. isn't	**is not**
5. I'm	**I am**

Exercise 7: In your journal, write a paragraph summarizing what you have learned this week.

 **CHECK TIME**

After students have finished, check and discuss their test papers. Make sure they understand why their answers are right or wrong. Use the Question and Answer Flows on page 277 in this chapter to check the sentences on the Chapter 22 Test. (*For total points, count each required answer as a point.*)

(End of lesson.)

CHAPTER 23   LESSON 1

Objectives: Jingles, Synonyms, Antonyms, Skill (Identifying Present, Past, and Future Tenses), Practice Exercise, and Activity.

 **JINGLE TIME**

Have students turn to the Jingle Section of their books. The teacher will lead the students in reciting the previously-taught jingles.

 SYNONYM AND ANTONYM TIME

Have students turn to the Synonym and Antonym Section of their books. Introduce the new words listed for Chapter 23 in the box below. Make sure students know the meanings of the new synonyms and antonyms. Then, have students underline the correct answers in their books. They should study these words again before their test.

Chapter 23: Underline the **syn** if the words are synonyms. Underline the **ant** if the words are antonyms.		
1. sell, buy syn **ant**	2. ask, tell syn **ant**	3. calm, quiet **syn** ant

 SKILL TIME

TEACHING SCRIPT FOR IDENTIFYING PRESENT, PAST, AND FUTURE TENSES

Now, you are going to learn three very interesting things about verbs that will help you make correct verb choices when you speak and write. Look at Reference 26 on page 22 while I go over this important information with you. (_Read and discuss the information in Reference 26 on the next page._)

CHAPTER 23 LESSON 1 CONTINUED

Reference 26: Present, Past, and Future Verb Tenses

When you are writing paragraphs, you must use verbs that are in the same tense. **Tense** means time. The tense of a verb shows the time of the action. There are three basic tenses that show when an action takes place. They are **past tense, present tense,** and **future tense**. Now, you will learn to recognize each kind of tense.

1. The **past tense** shows that something has happened sometime in the past. Most past tense verbs are made past tense by adding an **-ed** to the end of the word. If a verb uses **-ed** to make the past tense form, it is called a **regular** past tense verb: listen-**listened**, talk-**talked**, play-**played**, jump-**jumped**.

    Other past tense verbs are made past tense by changing their **spelling form** and not by adding **-ed**. If a verb uses a spelling change to make the past tense form, it is called an **irregular** past tense verb: give-**gave**, take-**took**, sell-**sold**, buy-**bought**. *(The verbs are listed as regular or irregular for you.)*

2. The **present tense** shows that something is happening now, in the present. Present tense verbs can end with an **-s** for singular subjects or without an **-s** for plural subjects: **listens-listen, talks-talk, plays-play, jumps-jump, gives-give, takes-take, sells-sell, buys-buy.** *(The verbs are listed as regular or irregular for you.)*

3. The **future tense** shows that something will happen at some time in the future. The future tense form always has the helping verb *will* before the main verb. Future tense verb examples: **will talk, will listen, will play, will jump, will see, will give, will take, will sell, will buy.**

Example: Identify the tense of each underlined verb by writing a number **1** for past tense, a number **2** for present tense, or a number **3** for future tense.

Verb Tense	Regular Verbs	Verb Tense	Irregular Verbs
1	1. She <u>listened</u> to the radio.	2	4. Larry <u>sells</u> used cars.
2	2. She <u>listens</u> to the radio.	1	5. Larry <u>sold</u> used cars.
3	3. She <u>will listen</u> to the radio.	3	6. Larry <u>will sell</u> used cars.

TEACHING SCRIPT FOR INTRODUCING NEW VERBS AND THEIR TENSES

We will learn some new verbs and their tenses. *(Put the new verbs below on the board and go through each one to make sure your students understand them. Have your students chant the verbs with you as you go through the different tenses.)*

Regular Verb List			Irregular Verb List		
Past tense	**Present tense**	**Future tense**	**Past tense**	**Present tense**	**Future tense**
1. talked	2. talk	3. will talk	7. took	8. take	9. will take
4. yelled	5. yell	6. will yell	10. drove	11. drive	12. will drive

CHAPTER 23 LESSON 1 CONTINUED

 PRACTICE TIME

Have students turn to pages 51 and 52 in the Practice Section of their books and find Chapter 23, Lesson 1, Practice *(1-2)*. Go over the directions to make sure they understand what to do. Check and discuss the Practices after students have finished. (*Chapter 23, Lesson 1, Practice keys are given below.*)

Chapter 23, Lesson 1, Practice 1: Identify the tense of each underlined verb by writing a number **1** for past tense, a number **2** for present tense, or a number **3** for future tense.

Verb Tense	Regular Verbs	Verb Tense	Irregular Verbs
3	1. Kelly <u>will play</u> with her dolls.	2	7. The sisters <u>take</u> piano lessons.
1	2. Kelly <u>played</u> with her dolls.	3	8. The sisters <u>will take</u> piano lessons.
2	3. Kelly <u>plays</u> with her dolls.	1	9. The sisters <u>took</u> piano lessons.
2	4. The hockey players <u>skate</u>.	2	10. Mary <u>buys</u> a blue dress.
3	5. The hockey players <u>will skate</u>.	3	11. Mary <u>will buy</u> a blue dress.
1	6. The hockey players <u>skated</u>.	1	12. Mary <u>bought</u> a blue dress.

Chapter 23, Lesson 1, Practice 2: Chant the following verbs to hear the different tenses.

Regular Verbs			Irregular Verbs		
listened	listen	will listen	bought	buy	will buy
talked	talk	will talk	took	take	will take
skated	skate	will skate	drove	drive	will drive
played	play	will play	sold	sell	will sell

 ACTIVITY / ASSIGNMENT TIME

Tell students they will now use some of the verbs they chanted during Practice Time to help them learn more about verb tenses. Explain that the words *today*, *yesterday*, and *tomorrow* help indicate time. **Yesterday** shows *past* time, **today** shows *present* time, and **tomorrow** shows *future* time. Using the three verbs below, have students recite the correct verb tenses for the words **yesterday**, **today**, and **tomorrow**.

Talk	Play	Drive
1. I talked yesterday.	4. I played yesterday.	7. I drove yesterday.
2. I talk today.	5. I play today.	8. I drive today.
3. I will talk tomorrow.	6. I will play tomorrow.	9. I will drive tomorrow.

(End of lesson.)

CHAPTER 23   LESSON 2

Objectives: Jingles, Vocabulary #1, Grammar (Practice Sentences), and Practice Exercise.

 **JINGLE TIME**

Have students turn to the Jingle Section of their books. The teacher will lead the students in reciting the previously-taught jingles.

 VOCABULARY TIME

Have students turn to page 8 in the Vocabulary Section of their books. Introduce the vocabulary words listed in the vocabulary box below by reciting them together with your students.

Chapter 23, Vocabulary Words #1
donkeys, geese

 GRAMMAR TIME

Put the Practice Sentences from the box below on the board or on notebook paper. Use these sentences as you practice the concepts that have been taught. For the greatest benefit, students must participate orally with the teacher.

Chapter 23, Practice Sentences for Lesson 2
1. Several little donkeys trotted quickly to the barn.
2. Ten geese flew high in the sky.
3. The tired geese landed silently in the water.

TEACHING SCRIPT FOR PRACTICE SENTENCES

We will classify these three sentences to practice what we have learned. We will classify the sentences together. Begin.

CHAPTER 23 LESSON 2 CONTINUED

Question and Answer Flow for Sentence 1: Several little donkeys trotted quickly to the barn.

1. What trotted quickly to the barn? donkeys - SN
2. What is being said about donkeys? donkeys trotted - V
3. Trotted how? quickly - Adv
4. To - P

5. To what? barn - OP
6. The - A
7. What kind of donkeys? little - Adj
8. How many donkeys? several - Adj

Classified Sentence:

Adj	Adj	SN	V	Adv	P	A	OP
Several	little	donkeys	trotted	quickly	to	the	barn.

Question and Answer Flow for Sentence 2: Ten geese flew high in the sky.

1. What flew high in the sky? geese - SN
2. What is being said about geese? geese flew - V
3. Flew where? high - Adv
4. In - P

5. In what? sky - OP
6. The - A
7. How many geese? ten - Adj

Classified Sentence:

Adj	SN	V	Adv	P	A	OP
Ten	geese	flew	high	in	the	sky.

Question and Answer Flow for Sentence 3: The tired geese landed silently in the water.

1. What landed silently in the water? geese - SN
2. What is being said about geese? geese landed - V
3. Landed how? silently - Adv
4. In - P

5. In what? water - OP
6. The - A
7. What kind of geese? tired - Adj
8. The - A

Classified Sentence:

A	Adj	SN	V	Adv	P	A	OP
The	tired	geese	landed	silently	in	the	water.

 PRACTICE TIME

Have students turn to page 52 in the Practice Section of their books and find Chapter 23, Lesson 2, Practice. Go over the directions to make sure they understand what to do. Check and discuss the Practice after students have finished. (*Chapter 23, Lesson 2, Practice key is given below.*)

Chapter 23, Lesson 2, Practice: Identify the tense of each underlined verb by writing a number **1** for past tense, a number **2** for present tense, or a number **3** for future tense.

Verb Tense		Regular Verbs	Verb Tense		Irregular Verbs
3	1.	Tim <u>will jump</u> into the pool.	2	6.	Jim <u>drives</u> to church.
1	2.	Tim <u>jumped</u> into the pool.	3	7.	Jim <u>will drive</u> to church.
2	3.	Tim <u>jumps</u> into the pool.	1	8.	Jim <u>drove</u> to church.
2	4.	Mom <u>yells</u> loudly for our team.	3	9.	She <u>will sing</u> for a large audience.
3	5.	Mom <u>will yell</u> loudly for our team.	2	10.	She <u>sings</u> for a large audience.

(End of lesson.)

CHAPTER 23   LESSON 3

Objectives: Jingles, Vocabulary #2, Grammar (Practice Sentences), and Practice Exercise.

 **JINGLE TIME**

Have students turn to the Jingle Section of their books. The teacher will lead the students in reciting the previously-taught jingles.

 VOCABULARY TIME

Have students turn to page 8 in the Vocabulary Section of their books. Introduce the vocabulary words listed in the vocabulary box below by reciting them together with your students.

Chapter 23, Vocabulary Words #2
sand, truck, turned, pumpkins

 GRAMMAR TIME

Put the Practice Sentences from the box below on the board or on notebook paper. Use these sentences as you practice the concepts that have been taught. For the greatest benefit, students must participate orally with the teacher.

Chapter 23, Practice Sentences for Lesson 3
1. The small boys played happily in the sand yesterday.
2. The old truck turned around slowly in the road.
3. Six orange pumpkins grew in the garden.

TEACHING SCRIPT FOR PRACTICE SENTENCES

We will classify these three sentences to practice what we have learned. We will classify the sentences together. Begin. (*You might have students write the labels above the sentences at this time.*)

CHAPTER 23 LESSON 3 CONTINUED

Question and Answer Flow for Sentence 1: The small boys played happily in the sand yesterday.

1. Who played happily in the sand yesterday? boys - SN
2. What is being said about boys? boys played - V
3. Played how? happily - Adv
4. In - P
5. In what? sand - OP
6. The - A
7. Played when? yesterday - Adv
8. What kind of boys? small - Adj
9. The - A

Classified Sentence:

A	Adj	SN	V	Adv	P	A	OP	Adv
The	small	boys	played	happily	in	the	sand	yesterday.

Question and Answer Flow for Sentence 2: The old truck turned around slowly in the road.

1. What turned around slowly in the road? truck - SN
2. What is being said about truck? truck turned - V
3. Turned where? around - Adv
4. Turned how? slowly - Adv
5. In - P
6. In what? road - OP
7. The - A
8. What kind of truck? old - Adj
9. The - A

Classified Sentence:

A	Adj	SN	V	Adv	Adv	P	A	OP
The	old	truck	turned	around	slowly	in	the	road.

Question and Answer Flow for Sentence 3: Six orange pumpkins grew in the garden.

1. What grew in the garden? pumpkins - SN
2. What is being said about pumpkins? pumpkins grew - V
3. In - P
4. In what? garden - OP
5. The - A
6. What kind of pumpkins? orange - Adj
7. How many pumpkins? six - Adj

Classified Sentence:

Adj	Adj	SN	V	P	A	OP
Six	orange	pumpkins	grew	in	the	garden.

 PRACTICE TIME

Have students turn to page 52 in the Practice Section of their books and find Chapter 23, Lesson 3, Practice. Go over the directions to make sure they understand what to do. Check and discuss the Practice after students have finished. (*Chapter 23, Lesson 3, Practice key is given below.*)

Chapter 23, Lesson 3, Practice: Identify the tense of each underlined verb by writing a number **1** for past tense, a number **2** for present tense, or a number **3** for future tense.

Verb Tense		Regular Verbs	Verb Tense		Irregular Verbs
3	1.	The truck <u>will back</u> into the ditch.	2	6.	Grandma <u>speaks</u> softly.
1	2.	The truck <u>backed</u> into the ditch.	3	7.	Grandma <u>will speak</u> softly.
2	3.	The truck <u>backs</u> into the ditch.	1	8.	Grandma <u>spoke</u> softly.
2	4.	The planes <u>circle</u> the runway.	2	9.	The workers <u>dig</u> a deep hole.
3	5.	The planes <u>will circle</u> the runway.	1	10.	The workers <u>dug</u> a deep hole.

(End of lesson.)

CHAPTER 23   LESSON 4

Objectives: Jingles, Vocabulary #3, Grammar (Practice Sentences), and Writing Assignment #10.

 **JINGLE TIME**

Have students turn to the Jingle Section of their books. The teacher will lead the students in reciting the previously-taught jingles.

 VOCABULARY TIME

Have students turn to page 8 in the Vocabulary Section of their books. Introduce the vocabulary words listed in the vocabulary box below by reciting them together with your students.

Chapter 23, Vocabulary Words #3
young, smiled, spider

 GRAMMAR TIME

Put the Practice Sentences from the box below on the board or on notebook paper. Use these sentences as you practice the concepts that have been taught. For the greatest benefit, students must participate orally with the teacher.

Chapter 23, Practice Sentences for Lesson 4
1. The three friends worked at the mall.
2. The young nurse smiled at the children.
3. The huge spider crawled quickly across the road.

TEACHING SCRIPT FOR PRACTICE SENTENCES

We will classify these three sentences to practice what we have learned. We will classify the sentences together. Begin.

Question and Answer Flow for Sentence 1: The three friends worked at the mall.

1. Who worked at the mall? friends - SN
2. What is being said about friends? friends worked - V
3. At - P
4. At what? mall - OP

5. The - A
6. How many friends? three - Adj
7. The - A

Classified Sentence:

A	Adj	SN	V	P	A	OP
The	three	friends	worked	at	the	mall.

CHAPTER 23 LESSON 4 CONTINUED

Question and Answer Flow for Sentence 2: The young nurse smiled at the children.

1. Who smiled at the children? nurse - SN
2. What is being said about nurse? nurse smiled - V
3. At - P
4. At whom? children - OP

5. The - A
6. What kind of nurse? young - Adj
7. The - A

Classified Sentence:

A	Adj	SN	V	P	A	OP
The	young	nurse	smiled	at	the	children.

Question and Answer Flow for Sentence 3: The huge spider crawled quickly across the road.

1. What crawled quickly across the road? spider - SN
2. What is being said about spider? spider crawled - V
3. Crawled how? quickly - Adv
4. Across - P

5. Across what? road - OP
6. The - A
7. What kind of spider? huge - Adj
8. The - A

Classified Sentence:

A	Adj	SN	V	Adv	P	A	OP
The	huge	spider	crawled	quickly	across	the	road.

 WRITING TIME

Give Writing Assignment #10 from the box below. Remind students to use Reference 20 on page 20 to help them write their two-point paragraph. After students have finished, check and discuss their writing assignment. *(Have each student add this assignment to his/her writing folder.)*

Writing Assignment Box

Writing Assignment #10: Two-Point Expository Paragraph

Writing topic: My Favorite Shows or TV Programs

(End of lesson.)

CHAPTER 23   LESSON 5
Objectives: Jingles, Vocabulary #4, Grammar (Practice Sentences), Test, Check, Writing (Journal), Activity 1, and Activity 2.

 **JINGLE TIME**

Have students turn to the Jingle Section of their books. The teacher will lead the students in reciting the previously-taught jingles.

 VOCABULARY TIME

Have students turn to page 8 in the Vocabulary Section of their books. Introduce the vocabulary words listed in the vocabulary box below by reciting them together with your students.

Chapter 23, Vocabulary Words #4
eggs, hatched, cheerfully, school

 GRAMMAR TIME

Put the Practice Sentences from the box below on the board or on notebook paper. Use these sentences as you practice the concepts that have been taught. For the greatest benefit, students must participate orally with the teacher.

Chapter 23, Practice Sentences for Lesson 5
1. The small brown eggs hatched yesterday.
2. The family ate cheerfully in the kitchen tonight.
3. Tim drove quickly to school.

TEACHING SCRIPT FOR PRACTICE SENTENCES

We will classify these three sentences to practice what we have learned. We will classify the sentences together. Begin.

CHAPTER 23 LESSON 5 CONTINUED

Question and Answer Flow for Sentence 1: The small brown eggs hatched yesterday.

1. What hatched yesterday? eggs - SN
2. What is being said about eggs? eggs hatched - V
3. Hatched when? yesterday - Adv

4. What kind of eggs? brown - Adj
5. What kind of eggs? small - Adj
6. The - A

Classified Sentence:

A	Adj	Adj	SN	V	Adv
The	small	brown	eggs	hatched	yesterday.

Question and Answer Flow for Sentence 2: The family ate cheerfully in the kitchen tonight.

1. Who ate cheerfully in the kitchen tonight? family - SN
2. What is being said about family? family ate - V
3. Ate how? cheerfully - Adv
4. In - P

5. In what? kitchen - OP
6. The - A
7. Ate when? tonight - Adv
8. The - A

Classified Sentence:

A	SN	V	Adv	P	A	OP	Adv
The	family	ate	cheerfully	in	the	kitchen	tonight.

Question and Answer Flow for Sentence 3: Tim drove quickly to school.

1. Who drove quickly to school? Tim - SN
2. What is being said about Tim? Tim drove - V
3. Drove how? quickly - Adv

4. To - P
5. To what? school - OP

Classified Sentence:

SN	V	Adv	P	OP
Tim	drove	quickly	to	school.

 **TEST TIME**

Have students turn to page 76 in the Test Section of their books and find Chapter 23 Test. Go over the directions to make sure they understand what to do. (*Chapter 23 Test key is on the next page.*)

Chapter 23 Test
(Student Page 76)

Exercise 1: Classify each sentence. Use **SN** for subject noun, **V** for verb, **Adv** for adverb, **Adj** for adjective, **A** for article adjective, **P** for preposition, and **OP** for object of the preposition. For Sentence 2, underline the complete subject <u>one</u> time and the complete predicate <u>two</u> times.

```
      A      SN     V      Adv       P    A      OP      Adv
1.   The   family  ate  cheerfully  in  the   kitchen  tonight.
```

```
     SN     V      Adv    P     OP
2.   Tim   drove  quickly  to  school.
```

Exercise 2: Underline the <u>syn</u> if the words are synonyms. Underline the <u>ant</u> if the words are antonyms.

| 1. calm, quiet | <u>**syn**</u> ant | | 2. ask, tell | syn <u>**ant**</u> | | 3. sell, buy | syn <u>**ant**</u> |

Exercise 3: Name the five parts of speech that you have studied. (*You may use abbreviations.*)
(The order of answers may vary.)

| 1. **Noun (N)** | 2. **Verb (V)** | 3. **Adjective (Adj)** | 4. **Adverb (Adv)** | 5. **Preposition (P)** |

Exercise 4: Identify the tense of each underlined verb by writing a number **1** for past tense, a number **2** for present tense, or a number **3** for future tense.

Verb Tense	Regular Verbs	Verb Tense	Irregular Verbs
1	1. The girls <u>skipped</u> down the street.	2	7. Mom <u>gives</u> me a big hug.
3	2. The girls <u>will skip</u> down the street.	3	8. Mom <u>will give</u> me a big hug.
2	3. The girls <u>skip</u> down the street.	1	9. Mom <u>gave</u> me a big hug.
2	4. Janet <u>works</u> at the bank.	1	10. The wind <u>blew</u> against the window.
3	5. Janet <u>will work</u> at the bank.	3	11. The wind <u>will blow</u> against the window.
1	6. Janet <u>worked</u> at the bank.	2	12. The wind <u>blows</u> against the window.

Exercise 5: Write the correct contraction in each blank. Use the contraction references to help you.

1. do not	**don't**
2. cannot	**can't**
3. I am	**I'm**
4. are not	**aren't**
5. were not	**weren't**

Exercise 6: Write the correct words beside each contraction. Use the contraction references to help you.

1. didn't	**did not**
2. wasn't	**was not**
3. doesn't	**does not**
4. isn't	**is not**
5. I'm	**I am**

Exercise 7: In your journal, write a paragraph summarizing what you have learned this week.

CHAPTER 23 LESSON 5 CONTINUED

CHECK TIME

After students have finished, check and discuss their test papers. Make sure they understand why their answers are right or wrong. Use the Question and Answer Flows on page 294 in this chapter to check the sentences on the Chapter 23 Test. (*For total points, count each required answer as a point.*)

ACTIVITY / ASSIGNMENT TIME

<u>Activity 1:</u>

This activity will expose students to a variety of descriptive words and increase their vocabulary. First, you should pick a familiar object to describe to the students. Ask students to close their eyes or use a blindfold for more fun. Without using the name of the object, give hints about the object. Use one descriptive word at a time. Students must keep their eyes closed the entire time the object is being described. Keep score by adding up the number of hints you have to give before the students could guess the object.

Then, give the students a turn to pick out an object and give descriptive hints to you. Again, keep up with the number of hints given before the object is guessed. Play this guessing game for several rounds. The player with the lowest score at the end of the game wins. This game can also be played with family members and friends.

<u>Activity 2:</u>

Have students turn to page 90 in the Activity Section of their books and find Chapter 23, Lesson 5, Activity. Go over the directions to make sure they understand what to do. Check and discuss the Activity after students have finished.

Chapter 23, Lesson 5, Activity: Using the scrambled letters below, circle every other letter, beginning with the first letter. Use the blank to write the new word created by writing each circled letter in order. (**wpicnkd=wind**) On the title lines, write the title that best describes the words in each column. Choose from these titles: **Science** **Clothes** **Animals** **Verbs**	
Title: Clothes	**Title: Verbs**
r o a y i u n x c t o r a h t: **raincoat**	w s a m l a k b e r d: **walked**
j h a u c n k y e u t w: **jacket**	s n h o o f u e t w: **shout**
s r o m c p k w s c: **socks**	s g m h i m l c e d d: **smiled**

(End of lesson.)

CHAPTER 24   LESSON 1
Objectives: Jingles, Synonyms, Antonyms, Skill (Five Parts of a Friendly Letter), and Practice Exercise.

JINGLE TIME

Have students turn to the Jingle Section of their books. The teacher will lead the students in reciting the previously-taught jingles.

SYNONYM AND ANTONYM TIME

Have students turn to the Synonym and Antonym Section of their books. Introduce the new words listed for Chapter 24 in the box below. Make sure students know the meanings of the new synonyms and antonyms. Then, have students underline the correct answers in their books. They should study these words again before their test.

Chapter 24: Underline the **syn** if the words are synonyms. Underline the **ant** if the words are antonyms.

1. wild, tame	syn **ant**		2. add, subtract	syn **ant**		3. push, shove	**syn** ant

SKILL TIME

TEACHING SCRIPT FOR THE FIVE PARTS OF A FRIENDLY LETTER

Close your eyes. Now, picture a good friend or favorite relative that you really like but don't get to see very often. Open your eyes. The memory of that favorite person in your life brought a smile to your face, didn't it? Remember, keeping in touch with favorite people brings smiles to their faces. Writing a letter is a great way to stay in touch with people you care about and who care about you.

A letter written to or received from friends or relatives is called a **friendly letter**. Turn to page 23 and look at Reference 27. Follow along as I read some tips that will make your friendly letter interesting and enjoyable to read. (*Read the tips on the next page to your students.*)

CHAPTER 24 LESSON 1 CONTINUED

Reference 27: Tips for Writing Friendly Letters

Tip #1: Write as if you were talking to the person face-to-face. Share information about yourself and mutual friends. Tell stories, conversations, or jokes. Share pictures, articles, drawings, poems, etc. Avoid saying something about someone else that you'll be sorry for later.

Tip #2: If you are writing a return letter, be sure to answer any questions that were asked. Repeat the question so that your reader will know what you are writing about. (You asked about . . .)

Tip #3: End your letter in a positive way so that your reader will want to write a return letter.

Now that you know what things to write about, you must learn to put your friendly letter in correct friendly-letter form. The friendly letter has five parts: the heading, the friendly greeting, the body, the closing, and the signature.

Each of the parts of a friendly letter has a specific place where it should be written in order for your letter to have correct friendly-letter form. Look at the friendly-letter example in Reference 28 on page 23 in your book. We will now go over each of the five parts as we discuss the type of information in each part. You will also see where each part is placed in a friendly letter as we study it. (*Go over the example reproduced below with your students.*)

Reference 28: Friendly Letter Example

1. Heading
Write your address.
Write the date.

23 Circle Drive
Dallas, TX 93312
April 3, 20_____

2. Friendly Greeting
Name the person receiving the letter.
Use a comma.

Dear Jonathan,

3. Body (Indent Paragraphs)
Write what you want to say. Indent.

    Are you playing baseball again this year? I would really like to come to watch one of your games. Please let me know when your season begins.

4. Closing
Capitalize the first word.
Use a comma.

Your cousin,

5. Signature
Sign your name.

Timothy

CHAPTER 24 LESSON 1 CONTINUED

Now, we will go over the friendly-letter example again. This time you will repeat all the parts with me. Put your finger on each part as we say it. (*Recite all the friendly-letter parts with your students.*)

 PRACTICE TIME

Have students turn to page 53 in the Practice Section of their book and find Chapter 24, Lesson 1, Practice. Go over the directions to make sure they understand what to do. Check and discuss the Practice after students have finished. (*Chapter 24, Lesson 1, Practice key is given below.*)

Chapter 24, Lesson 1, Practice: Write the parts of a friendly letter in the correct places in the friendly letter below.

1. **Heading**   2. **Greeting**   3. **Closing**   4. **Signature**

19 Dogwood Lane   Dear Samuel,   Your friend,   Ruth
Benton, KS 24550
July 23, 20_____

5. **Body**

We just got back from our trip to Alaska. It was so much fun. I have so much to tell you!

Friendly Letter

Heading
19 Dogwood Lane
Benton, KS 24550
July 23, 20_____

Greeting
Dear Samuel,

Body

We jut got back from our trip to Alaska. It was so much fun. I have so much to tell you!

Closing
Your friend,

Signature
Ruth

(End of lesson.)

CHAPTER 24   LESSON 2

Objectives: Jingles, Vocabulary #1, Grammar (Practice Sentences), and Practice Exercise.

 **JINGLE TIME**

Have students turn to the Jingle Section of their books. The teacher will lead the students in reciting the previously-taught jingles.

 VOCABULARY TIME

Have students turn to page 8 in the Vocabulary Section of their books. Introduce the vocabulary words listed in the vocabulary box below by reciting them together with your students.

Chapter 24, Vocabulary Words #1
Grandmother, mailbox, together

 GRAMMAR TIME

Put the Practice Sentences from the box below on the board or on notebook paper. Use these sentences as you practice the concepts that have been taught. For the greatest benefit, students must participate orally with the teacher.

Chapter 24, Practice Sentences for Lesson 2
1. Grandmother walked to the mailbox.
2. The sleepy baby cried loudly.
3. Two yellow kites crashed together in the air.

TEACHING SCRIPT FOR PRACTICE SENTENCES

We will classify these three sentences to practice what we have learned. We will classify the sentences together. Begin.

CHAPTER 24 LESSON 2 CONTINUED

Question and Answer Flow for Sentence 1: Grandmother walked to the mailbox.

1. Who walked to the mailbox? Grandmother - SN
2. What is being said about Grandmother? Grandmother walked - V
3. To - P

4. To what? mailbox - OP
5. The - A

Classified Sentence:

SN	V	P	A	OP
Grandmother	walked	to	the	mailbox.

Question and Answer Flow for Sentence 2: The sleepy baby cried loudly.

1. Who cried loudly? baby - SN
2. What is being said about baby? baby cried - V
3. Cried how? loudly - Adv

4. What kind of baby? sleepy - Adj
5. The - A

Classified Sentence:

A	Adj	SN	V	Adv
The	sleepy	baby	cried	loudly.

Question and Answer Flow for Sentence 3: Two yellow kites crashed together in the air.

1. What crashed together in the air? kites - SN
2. What is being said about kites? kites crashed - V
3. Crashed how? together - Adv
4. In - P

5. In what? air - OP
6. The - A
7. What kind of kites? yellow - Adj
8. How many kites? two - Adj

Classified Sentence:

Adj	Adj	SN	V	Adv	P	A	OP
Two	yellow	kites	crashed	together	in	the	air.

 PRACTICE TIME

Have students turn to pages 53 and 54 in the Practice Section of their books and find Chapter 24, Lesson 2, Practice *(1-2)*. Go over the directions to make sure they understand what to do. Check and discuss the Practices after students have finished. (*Chapter 24, Lesson 2, Practice key and instructions are given below.*)

Chapter 24, Lesson 2, Practice 1: Identify the tense of each underlined verb by writing a number **1** for past tense, a number **2** for present tense, or a number **3** for future tense.

Verb Tense	Regular Verbs		Verb Tense	Irregular Verbs	
3	1.	The band <u>will march</u> in the parade.	2	4.	The ship <u>sinks</u> quickly.
1	2.	The band <u>marched</u> in the parade.	3	5.	The ship <u>will sink</u> quickly.
2	3.	The band <u>marches</u> in the parade.	1	6.	The ship <u>sank</u> quickly.

Chapter 24, Lesson 2, Practice 2: On notebook paper, write a friendly letter to a friend or relative. Use References 27 and 28 as a guide to make sure your letter is in the correct friendly-letter format. Have your parents help you address an envelope. Mail your letter and wait for a response.

(End of lesson.)

CHAPTER 24   LESSON 3

Objectives: Jingles, Vocabulary #2, Grammar (Practice Sentences), and Practice Exercise.

 **JINGLE TIME**

Have students turn to the Jingle Section of their books. The teacher will lead the students in reciting the previously-taught jingles.

 VOCABULARY TIME

Have students turn to page 8 in the Vocabulary Section of their books. Introduce the vocabulary words listed in the vocabulary box below by reciting them together with your students.

Chapter 24, Vocabulary Words #2
bloomed, trail, camel, desert

 GRAMMAR TIME

Put the Practice Sentences from the box below on the board or on notebook paper. Use these sentences as you practice the concepts that have been taught. For the greatest benefit, students must participate orally with the teacher.

Chapter 24, Practice Sentences for Lesson 3
1. A frightened bird flew quickly to the tree.
2. Huge pink flowers bloomed by the trail.
3. The tall camel raced across the desert.

TEACHING SCRIPT FOR PRACTICE SENTENCES

We will classify these three sentences to practice what we have learned. We will classify the sentences together. Begin. (*You might have students write the labels above the sentences at this time.*)

CHAPTER 24 LESSON 3 CONTINUED

Question and Answer Flow for Sentence 1: A frightened bird flew quickly to the tree.

1. What flew quickly to the tree? bird - SN
2. What is being said about bird? bird flew - V
3. Flew how? quickly - Adv
4. To - P

5. To what? tree - OP
6. The - A
7. What kind of bird? frightened - Adj
8. A - A

Classified Sentence:

A	Adj	SN	V	Adv	P	A	OP
A	frightened	bird	flew	quickly	to	the	tree.

Question and Answer Flow for Sentence 2: Huge pink flowers bloomed by the trail.

1. What bloomed by the trail? flowers - SN
2. What is being said about flowers? flowers bloomed - V
3. By - P
4. By what? trail - OP

5. The - A
6. What kind of flowers? pink - Adj
7. What kind of flowers? huge - Adj

Classified Sentence:

Adj	Adj	SN	V	P	A	OP
Huge	pink	flowers	bloomed	by	the	trail.

Question and Answer Flow for Sentence 3: The tall camel raced across the desert.

1. What raced across the desert? camel - SN
2. What is being said about camel? camel raced - V
3. Across - P
4. Across what? desert - OP

5. The - A
6. What kind of camel? tall - Adj
7. The - A

Classified Sentence:

A	Adj	SN	V	P	A	OP
The	tall	camel	raced	across	the	desert.

 ## PRACTICE TIME

Have students turn to page 54 in the Practice Section of their books and find Chapter 24, Lesson 3, Practice *(1-2)*. Go over the directions to make sure they understand what to do. Check and discuss the Practices after students have finished. (*Chapter 24, Lesson 3, Practice key and instructions are given below.*)

Chapter 24, Lesson 3, Practice 1: Identify the tense of each underlined verb by writing a number **1** for past tense, a number **2** for present tense, or a number **3** for future tense.

Verb Tense	Regular Verbs	Verb Tense	Irregular Verbs
3	1. The cookies <u>will bake</u> in the oven.	3	4. The choir <u>will sing</u> in the early service.
2	2. The cookies <u>bake</u> in the oven.	1	5. The choir <u>sang</u> in the early service.
1	3. The cookies <u>baked</u> in the oven.	2	6. The choir <u>sings</u> in the early service.

Chapter 24, Lesson 3, Practice 2: On notebook paper, write a friendly letter to a friend or relative. Use References 27 and 28 as a guide to make sure your letter is in the correct friendly-letter format. Have your parents help you address an envelope. Mail your letter and wait for a response.

(End of lesson.)

CHAPTER 24   LESSON 4

Objectives: Jingles, Vocabulary #3, Grammar (Practice Sentences), and Writing Assignment #11.

 **JINGLE TIME**

Have students turn to the Jingle Section of their books. The teacher will lead the students in reciting the previously-taught jingles.

 VOCABULARY TIME

Have students turn to page 8 in the Vocabulary Section of their books. Introduce the vocabulary words listed in the vocabulary box below by reciting them together with your students.

Chapter 24, Vocabulary Words #3
eagle, gracefully, bouncy, grandchildren

 GRAMMAR TIME

Put the Practice Sentences from the box below on the board or on notebook paper. Use these sentences as you practice the concepts that have been taught. For the greatest benefit, students must participate orally with the teacher.

Chapter 24, Practice Sentences for Lesson 4
1. The large eagle flew gracefully across the valley.
2. The bouncy little puppies barked loudly in the store.
3. Grandmother laughed at the grandchildren.

TEACHING SCRIPT FOR PRACTICE SENTENCES

We will classify these three sentences to practice what we have learned. We will classify the sentences together. Begin.

Question and Answer Flow for Sentence 1: The large eagle flew gracefully across the valley.

1. What flew gracefully across the valley? eagle - SN
2. What is being said about eagle? eagle flew - V
3. Flew how? gracefully - Adv
4. Across - P
5. Across what? valley - OP
6. The - A
7. What kind of eagle? large - Adj
8. The - A

Classified Sentence:

A	Adj	SN	V	Adv	P	A	OP
The	large	eagle	flew	gracefully	across	the	valley.

CHAPTER 24 LESSON 4 CONTINUED

Question and Answer Flow for Sentence 2: The bouncy little puppies barked loudly in the store.

1. What barked loudly in the store? puppies - SN
2. What is being said about puppies? puppies barked - V
3. Barked how? loudly - Adv
4. In - P
5. In what? store - OP

6. The - A
7. What kind of puppies? little - Adj
8. What kind of puppies? bouncy - Adj
9. The - A

Classified Sentence:	A	Adj	Adj	SN	V	Adv	P	A	OP
	The	bouncy	little	puppies	barked	loudly	in	the	store.

Question and Answer Flow for Sentence 3: Grandmother laughed at the grandchildren.

1. Who laughed at the grandchildren? Grandmother - SN
2. What is being said about Grandmother? Grandmother laughed - V
3. At - P

4. At whom? grandchildren - OP
5. The - A

Classified Sentence:	SN	V	P	A	OP
	Grandmother	laughed	at	the	grandchildren.

 WRITING TIME

Give Writing Assignment #11 from the box below. Remind students to use Reference 20 on page 20 to help them write their two-point paragraph. After students have finished, check and discuss their writing assignment. *(Have each student add this assignment to his/her writing folder.)*

Writing Assignment Box

Writing Assignment #11: Two-Point Expository Paragraph

Writing topic: Things Firemen Do

(End of lesson.)

CHAPTER 24   LESSON 5

Objectives: Jingles, Vocabulary #4, Grammar (Practice Sentences), Test, Check, Writing (Journal), and Activity.

 **JINGLE TIME**

Have students turn to the Jingle Section of their books. The teacher will lead the students in reciting the previously-taught jingles.

 VOCABULARY TIME

Have students turn to page 8 in the Vocabulary Section of their books. Introduce the vocabulary words listed in the vocabulary box below by reciting them together with your students.

Chapter 24, Vocabulary Words #4
raccoons, soldiers, marched, parade

 GRAMMAR TIME

Put the Practice Sentences from the box below on the board or on notebook paper. Use these sentences as you practice the concepts that have been taught. For the greatest benefit, students must participate orally with the teacher.

Chapter 24, Practice Sentences for Lesson 5
1. The six baby raccoons walked slowly across the ice.
2. The young students ate early today.
3. The young soldiers marched proudly in the parade.

TEACHING SCRIPT FOR PRACTICE SENTENCES

We will classify these three sentences to practice what we have learned. We will classify the sentences together. Begin.

CHAPTER 24 LESSON 5 CONTINUED

Question and Answer Flow for Sentence 1: The six baby raccoons walked slowly across the ice.

1. What walked slowly across the ice? raccoons - SN
2. What is being said about raccoons? raccoons walked - V
3. Walked how? slowly - Adv
4. Across - P
5. Across what? ice - OP
6. The - A
7. What kind of raccoons? baby - Adj
8. How many raccoons? six - Adj
9. The - A

Classified Sentence:

A	Adj	Adj	SN	V	Adv	P	A	OP
The	six	baby	raccoons	walked	slowly	across	the	ice.

Question and Answer Flow for Sentence 2: The young students ate early today.

1. Who ate early today? students - SN
2. What is being said about students? students ate - V
3. Ate when? early - Adv
4. Ate when? today - Adv
5. What kind of students? young - Adj
6. The - A

Classified Sentence:

A	Adj	SN	V	Adv	Adv
The	young	students	ate	early	today.

Question and Answer Flow for Sentence 3: The young soldiers marched proudly in the parade.

1. Who marched proudly in the parade? soldiers - SN
2. What is being said about soldiers? soldiers marched - V
3. Marched how? proudly - Adv
4. In - P
5. In what? parade - OP
6. The - A
7. What kind of soldiers? young - Adj
8. The - A

Classified Sentence:

A	Adj	SN	V	Adv	P	A	OP
The	young	soldiers	marched	proudly	in	the	parade.

TEST TIME

Have students turn to page 77 in the Test Section of their books and find Chapter 24 Test. Go over the directions to make sure they understand what to do. (*Chapter 24 Test key is on the next page.*)

Chapter 24 Test
(Student Page 77)

Exercise 1: Classify each sentence. Use **SN** for subject noun, **V** for verb, **Adv** for adverb, **Adj** for adjective, **A** for article adjective, **P** for preposition, and **OP** for object of the preposition. For Sentence 2, underline the complete subject <u>one</u> time and the complete predicate <u>two</u> times.

```
        A    Adj   Adj    SN       V      Adv    P    A     OP
1.     The  bouncy little puppies barked loudly  in  the   store.

              SN        V       P    A       OP
2.     Grandmother   laughed   at  the   grandchildren.
```

Exercise 2: Underline the **syn** if the words are synonyms. Underline the **ant** if the words are antonyms.

1. wild, tame	syn **ant**	2. push, shove	**syn** ant	3. add, subtract	syn **ant**

Exercise 3: Name the five parts of speech that you have studied. (*You may use abbreviations.*)
(The order of answers may vary.)

1. **Noun (N)** 2. **Verb (V)** 3. **Adjective (Adj)** 4. **Adverb (Adv)** 5. **Preposition (P)**

Exercise 4: Identify the tense of each underlined verb by writing a number **1** for past tense, a number **2** for present tense, or a number **3** for future tense.

Verb Tense	Regular Verbs
3	1. The cars <u>will race</u> around the track.
1	2. The cars <u>raced</u> around the track.
2	3. The cars <u>race</u> around the track.

Verb Tense	Irregular Verbs
2	4. My flowers <u>grow</u> in the spring.
3	5. My flowers <u>will grow</u> in the spring.
1	6. My flowers <u>grew</u> in the spring.

Exercise 5: Write the correct contraction in each blank. Use the contraction references to help you.

1. do not — **don't**
2. cannot — **can't**
3. I am — **I'm**
4. are not — **aren't**
5. were not — **weren't**

Exercise 6: Write the correct words beside each contraction. Use the contraction references to help you.

1. didn't — **did not**
2. wasn't — **was not**
3. doesn't — **does not**
4. isn't — **is not**
5. I'm — **I am**

Exercise 7: On notebook paper, write a friendly letter to a friend or relative. Use References 27 and 28 as a guide to make sure your letter is in the correct friendly-letter format. Have your parents help you address an envelope. Mail your letter and wait for a response.

Exercise 8: In your journal, write a paragraph summarizing what you have learned this week.

CHAPTER 24 LESSON 5 CONTINUED

CHECK TIME

After students have finished, check and discuss their test papers. Make sure they understand why their answers are right or wrong. Use the Question and Answer Flows on page 305 in this chapter to check the sentences on the Chapter 24 Test. (*For total points, count each required answer as a point.*)

ACTIVITY / ASSIGNMENT TIME

Capitalization Rules Booklet

Materials Needed: 7 sheets of hole-punched paper (*plain white, colored, or notebook paper*), a folder with brads; colors; stickers or cutouts (*for decoration*); a story book that can be cut up.

Have students write one capitalization rule on each sheet of paper. (*Optional: They could type and print a label for each rule and stick or glue the label to the top of each sheet.*)

Next, give students a story book and have them find and cut out examples of as many capitalization rules as they can find. Examples can be sentences or words.

Then, have students glue their cut-out examples under the correct capitalization rule. Finally, have students insert the capitalization-rule pages into the brads of their folder and decorate the folder. Have students share their folders with friends and family members.

(End of lesson.)

CHAPTER 25   LESSON 1
Objectives: Jingles, Synonyms, Antonyms, Skill (Thank-You Notes), Practice Exercise, and Activity.

 **JINGLE TIME**

Have students turn to the Jingle Section of their books. The teacher will lead the students in reciting the previously-taught jingles.

 SYNONYM AND ANTONYM TIME

Have students turn to the Synonym and Antonym Section of their books. Introduce the new words listed for Chapter 25 in the box below. Make sure students know the meanings of the new synonyms and antonyms. Then, have students underline the correct answers in their books. They should study these words again before their test.

Chapter 25: Underline the **syn** if the words are synonyms. Underline the **ant** if the words are antonyms.

| 1. bright, dim | syn **ant** | | 2. round, square | syn **ant** | | 3. pull, tug | **syn** ant |

 SKILL TIME

TEACHING SCRIPT FOR THANK-YOU NOTES

Close your eyes again. Relax and clear your mind of extra thoughts. Now, think of a person who has done something nice for you or has given you a gift. If you absolutely cannot think of anyone, make up someone. Open your eyes. After such a nice gesture, that person deserves a thank-you note from you. So, it is time we learn about thank-you notes.

You usually write thank-you notes to thank someone for a gift or for doing something nice for you. In either case, a thank-you note should include at least three statements.

1. You should tell the person <u>what</u> you are thanking him/her for.

2. You should tell the person <u>how the gift was used</u> or <u>how it helped</u>.

3. You should tell the person <u>how much you appreciated the gift or action</u>.

CHAPTER 25 LESSON 1 CONTINUED

A thank-you note should follow the same form as a friendly letter: heading, greeting, body, closing, and signature. Look at References 29 and 30 on page 24. Follow along as I read the information about thank-you notes. (*Go over the information and examples reproduced below with your students.*)

Reference 29: Thank-You Note for a Gift

What -   Thank you for...
             (tell color, kind, and item)
Use -   Tell how the gift is used.
Thanks - I appreciate your thinking of me at this time.

Example 1: Gift

Heading
3132 Apple Street
Greenwood, KS 15023
June 3, 20____

Greeting
Dear Mrs. Smith,

Body
    Thank you for the book about sea animals. It has been a wonderful research tool for my science project. Thank you for your kindness.

Closing
Sincerely,
Signature
Elizabeth

Reference 30: Thank-You Note for an Action

What -   Thank you for...
             (tell action)
Use -   Tell how the action helped.
Thanks - I appreciate your remembering me.

Example 2: Action

Heading
239 Bluebird Lane
Charleston, SC 99173
August 1, 20____

Greeting
Dear Linda,

Body
    Thank you for visiting me in the hospital. I was so thrilled to see a familiar face. I appreciate your kindness.

Closing
Your friend,
Signature
Kathleen

CHAPTER 25 LESSON 1 CONTINUED

Now, we will go over the thank-you notes again. This time, you will recite all the parts with me. Put your finger on each part as we say it. (*Recite all the thank-you note parts with your students.*)

PRACTICE TIME

Have students turn to page 54 in the Practice Section of their books and find Chapter 25, Lesson 1, Practice. Go over the directions to make sure they understand what to do. Check and discuss the Practice after students have finished. (*Chapter 25, Lesson 1, Practice instructions are given below.*)

Chapter 25, Lesson 1, Practice: First, think of a person who has done something nice for you or has given you a gift (even the gift of time). On notebook paper, write a thank-you note to that person. Use the information in Reference 29 or 30 as a guide. Have your parents help you address an envelope. Mail your thank-you note.

ACTIVITY / ASSIGNMENT TIME

Today, students will make a noun collage. Explain that a collage, as an art piece, is a free form that is the result of pasting different sizes, shapes, and colors on a single sheet of posterboard. The result is a kaleidoscope which draws the viewers' eyes in many directions. The effect is one in which the artist takes the viewer on a journey.

First, have students divide a large piece of posterboard into three sections. These sections can be drawn in any direction that is pleasing to the students. As the posterboard is sectioned into thirds for a study of nouns, designate one third for people, another third for places, and the other third for things.

Have students clip noun pictures from storybooks, magazines, advertising circulars, discarded catalogs, and the Yellow Pages of old telephone directories. Have them glue the noun pictures in the appropriate section. They could also write a title for each section (Person, Place, or Thing).

(End of lesson.)

CHAPTER 25   LESSON 2
Objectives: Jingles, Vocabulary #1, Grammar (Practice Sentences), and Practice Exercise.

 JINGLE TIME

Have students turn to the Jingle Section of their books. The teacher will lead the students in reciting the previously-taught jingles.

 VOCABULARY TIME

Have students turn to page 8 in the Vocabulary Section of their books. Introduce the vocabulary words listed in the vocabulary box below by reciting them together with your students.

Chapter 25, Vocabulary Words #1
stray, teacher, kindly

GRAMMAR TIME

Put the Practice Sentences from the box below on the board or on notebook paper. Use these sentences as you practice the concepts that have been taught. For the greatest benefit, students must participate orally with the teacher.

Chapter 25, Practice Sentences for Lesson 2
1. A stray dog ran swiftly away.
2. The young teacher spoke kindly to the student.
3. The children waved at the soldiers.

TEACHING SCRIPT FOR PRACTICE SENTENCES

We will classify these three sentences to practice what we have learned. We will classify the sentences together. Begin.

CHAPTER 25 LESSON 2 CONTINUED

Question and Answer Flow for Sentence 1: A stray dog ran swiftly away.

1. What ran swiftly away? dog - SN
2. What is being said about dog? dog ran - V
3. Ran how? swiftly - Adv
4. Ran where? away - Adv
5. What kind of dog? stray - Adj
6. A - A

Classified Sentence:

A	Adj	SN	V	Adv	Adv
A	stray	dog	ran	swiftly	away.

Question and Answer Flow for Sentence 2: The young teacher spoke kindly to the student.

1. Who spoke kindly to the student? teacher - SN
2. What is being said about teacher? teacher spoke - V
3. Spoke how? kindly - Adv
4. To - P
5. To whom? student - OP
6. The - A
7. What kind of teacher? young - Adj
8. The - A

Classified Sentence:

A	Adj	SN	V	Adv	P	A	OP
The	young	teacher	spoke	kindly	to	the	student.

Question and Answer Flow for Sentence 3: The children waved at the soldiers.

1. Who waved at the soldiers? children - SN
2. What is being said about children? children waved - V
3. At - P
4. At whom? soldiers - OP
5. The - A
6. The - A

Classified Sentence:

A	SN	V	P	A	OP
The	children	waved	at	the	soldiers.

 PRACTICE TIME

Have students turn to pages 54 and 55 in the Practice Section of their books and find Chapter 25, Lesson 2, Practice (1-2). Go over the directions to make sure they understand what to do. Check and discuss the Practices after students have finished. (*Chapter 25, Lesson 2, Practice key and instructions are given below.*)

Chapter 25, Lesson 2, Practice 1: Identify the tense of each underlined verb by writing a number **1** for past tense, a number **2** for present tense, or a number **3** for future tense.

Verb Tense	Regular Verbs	Verb Tense	Irregular Verbs
3	1. The road <u>will curve</u> around the lake.	1	4. The author <u>wrote</u> a new play.
1	2. The road <u>curved</u> around the lake.	2	5. The author <u>writes</u> a new play.
2	3. The road <u>curves</u> around the lake.	3	6. The author <u>will write</u> a new play.

Chapter 25, Lesson 2, Practice 2: First, think of a person who has done something nice for you or has given you a gift (even the gift of time). On notebook paper, write a thank-you note to that person. Use the information in Reference 29 or 30 as a guide. Have your parents help you address an envelope. Mail your thank-you note.

(End of lesson.)

CHAPTER 25   LESSON 3

Objectives: Jingles, Vocabulary #2, Grammar (Practice Sentences), and Practice Exercise.

 **JINGLE TIME**

Have students turn to the Jingle Section of their books. The teacher will lead the students in reciting the previously-taught jingles.

 VOCABULARY TIME

Have students turn to page 8 in the Vocabulary Section of their books. Introduce the vocabulary words listed in the vocabulary box below by reciting them together with your students.

Chapter 25, Vocabulary Words #2
sisters, smoke, drifted, stared, hungrily, honey

 GRAMMAR TIME

Put the Practice Sentences from the box below on the board or on notebook paper. Use these sentences as you practice the concepts that have been taught. For the greatest benefit, students must participate orally with the teacher.

Chapter 25, Practice Sentences for Lesson 3
1. Two sisters worked together at the library.
2. The dark smoke drifted across the road.
3. A big bear stared hungrily at the honey.

TEACHING SCRIPT FOR PRACTICE SENTENCES

We will classify these three sentences to practice what we have learned. We will classify the sentences together. Begin. (*You might have students write the labels above the sentences at this time.*)

CHAPTER 25 LESSON 3 CONTINUED

Question and Answer Flow for Sentence 1: Two sisters worked together at the library.

1. Who worked together at the library? sisters - SN
2. What is being said about sisters? sisters worked - V
3. Worked how? together - Adv
4. At - P

5. At what? library - OP
6. The - A
7. How many sisters? two - Adj

Classified Sentence:

Adj	SN	V	Adv	P	A	OP
Two	sisters	worked	together	at	the	library.

Question and Answer Flow for Sentence 2: The dark smoke drifted across the road.

1. What drifted across the road? smoke - SN
2. What is being said about smoke? smoke drifted - V
3. Across - P
4. Across what? road - OP

5. The - A
6. What kind of smoke? dark - Adj
7. The - A

Classified Sentence:

A	Adj	SN	V	P	A	OP
The	dark	smoke	drifted	across	the	road.

Question and Answer Flow for Sentence 3: A big bear stared hungrily at the honey.

1. What stared hungrily at the honey? bear - SN
2. What is being said about bear? bear stared - V
3. Stared how? hungrily - Adv
4. At - P

5. At what? honey - OP
6. The - A
7. What kind of bear? big - Adj
8. A - A

Classified Sentence:

A	Adj	SN	V	Adv	P	A	OP
A	big	bear	stared	hungrily	at	the	honey.

 PRACTICE TIME

Have students turn to page 55 in the Practice Section of their books and find Chapter 25, Lesson 3, Practice (1-2). Go over the directions to make sure they understand what to do. Check and discuss the Practices after students have finished. (*Chapter 25, Lesson 3, Practice key and instructions are given below.*)

Chapter 25, Lesson 3, Practice 1: Identify the tense of each underlined verb by writing a number **1** for past tense, a number **2** for present tense, or a number **3** for future tense.

Verb Tense	Regular Verbs	Verb Tense	Irregular Verbs
3	1. Billy <u>will wash</u> the dishes.	2	4. The players <u>shake</u> hands.
1	2. Billy <u>washed</u> the dishes.	3	5. The players <u>will shake</u> hands.
2	3. Billy <u>washes</u> the dishes.	1	6. The players <u>shook</u> hands.

Chapter 25, Lesson 3, Practice 2: Think of a person who has done something nice for you or has given you a gift (even the gift of time). On notebook paper, write a thank-you note to that person. Use the information in Reference 29 or 30 as a guide. Have your parents help you address an envelope. Mail your thank-you note.

(End of lesson.)

Level 1 Homeschool Teacher's Manual

CHAPTER 25   LESSON 4

Objectives: Jingles, Vocabulary #3, Grammar (Practice Sentences), and Writing Assignment #12.

 **JINGLE TIME**

Have students turn to the Jingle Section of their books. The teacher will lead the students in reciting the previously-taught jingles.

 VOCABULARY TIME

Have students turn to page 8 in the Vocabulary Section of their books. Introduce the vocabulary words listed in the vocabulary box below by reciting them together with your students.

Chapter 25, Vocabulary Words #3
bubbles, distant, twinkled, thick

 GRAMMAR TIME

Put the Practice Sentences from the box below on the board or on notebook paper. Use these sentences as you practice the concepts that have been taught. For the greatest benefit, students must participate orally with the teacher.

Chapter 25, Practice Sentences for Lesson 4
1. The pretty pink bubbles floated away.
2. The distant stars twinkled brightly in the sky.
3. The thick winter ice melted slowly in the heat.

TEACHING SCRIPT FOR PRACTICE SENTENCES

We will classify these three sentences to practice what we have learned. We will classify the sentences together. Begin.

Question and Answer Flow for Sentence 1: The pretty pink bubbles floated away.	
1. What floated away? bubbles - SN	4. What kind of bubbles? pink - Adj
2. What is being said about bubbles? bubbles floated - V	5. What kind of bubbles? pretty - Adj
3. Floated where? away - Adv	6. The - A

Classified Sentence: A   Adj   Adj   SN   V   Adv
                         The   pretty   pink   bubbles   floated   away.

CHAPTER 25 LESSON 4 CONTINUED

Question and Answer Flow for Sentence 2: The distant stars twinkled brightly in the sky.

1. What twinkled brightly in the sky? stars - SN
2. What is being said about stars? stars twinkled - V
3. Twinkled how? brightly - Adv
4. In - P

5. In what? sky - OP
6. The - A
7. What kind of stars? distant - Adj
8. The - A

Classified Sentence:

A	Adj	SN	V	Adv	P	A	OP
The	distant	stars	twinkled	brightly	in	the	sky.

Question and Answer Flow for Sentence 3: The thick winter ice melted slowly in the heat.

1. What melted slowly in the heat? ice - SN
2. What is being said about ice? ice melted - V
3. Melted how? slowly - Adv
4. In - P
5. In what? heat - OP

6. The - A
7. What kind of ice? winter - Adj
8. What kind of ice? thick - Adj
9. The - A

Classified Sentence:

A	Adj	Adj	SN	V	Adv	P	A	OP
The	thick	winter	ice	melted	slowly	in	the	heat.

 WRITING TIME

Give Writing Assignment #12 from the box below. Remind students to use Reference 20 on page 20 to help them write their two-point paragraph. After students have finished, check and discuss their writing assignment. *(Have each student add this assignment to his/her writing folder.)*

Writing Assignment Box

Writing Assignment #12: Two-Point Expository Paragraph

Writing topic: Things I Like About My Family

(End of lesson.)

CHAPTER 25   LESSON 5

Objectives: Jingles, Vocabulary #4, Grammar (Practice Sentences), Test, Check, and Writing (Journal).

 **JINGLE TIME**

Have students turn to the Jingle Section of their books. The teacher will lead the students in reciting the previously-taught jingles.

 VOCABULARY TIME

Have students turn to page 8 in the Vocabulary Section of their books. Introduce the vocabulary words listed in the vocabulary box below by reciting them together with your students.

Chapter 25, Vocabulary Words #4
angry, buzzed, overhead, beetle

 GRAMMAR TIME

Put the Practice Sentences from the box below on the board or on notebook paper. Use these sentences as you practice the concepts that have been taught. For the greatest benefit, students must participate orally with the teacher.

Chapter 25, Practice Sentences for Lesson 5
1. The angry bees buzzed overhead.
2. The tiny beetle crawled carefully across the rocks.
3. The white snow melted quickly.

TEACHING SCRIPT FOR PRACTICE SENTENCES

We will classify these three sentences to practice what we have learned. We will classify the sentences together. Begin.

CHAPTER 25 LESSON 5 CONTINUED

Question and Answer Flow for Sentence 1: The angry bees buzzed overhead.

1. What buzzed overhead? bees - SN
2. What is being said about bees? bees buzzed - V
3. Buzzed where? overhead - Adv

4. What kind of bees? angry - Adj
5. The - A

Classified Sentence:	A	Adj	SN	V	Adv
	The	angry	bees	buzzed	overhead.

Question and Answer Flow for Sentence 2: The tiny beetle crawled carefully across the rocks.

1. What crawled carefully across the rocks? beetle - SN
2. What is being said about beetle? beetle crawled - V
3. Crawled how? carefully - Adv
4. Across - P

5. Across what? rocks - OP
6. The - A
7. What kind of beetle? tiny - Adj
8. The - A

Classified Sentence:	A	Adj	SN	V	Adv	P	A	OP
	The	tiny	beetle	crawled	carefully	across	the	rocks.

Question and Answer Flow for Sentence 3: The white snow melted quickly.

1. What melted quickly? snow - SN
2. What is being said about snow? snow melted - V
3. Melted how? quickly - Adv

4. What kind of snow? white - Adj
5. The - A

Classified Sentence:	A	Adj	SN	V	Adv
	The	white	snow	melted	quickly.

 TEST TIME

Have students turn to page 78 in the Test Section of their books and find Chapter 25 Test. Go over the directions to make sure they understand what to do. (*Chapter 25 Test key is on the next page.*)

Chapter 25 Test
(Student Page 78)

Exercise 1: Classify each sentence. Use **SN** for subject noun, **V** for verb, **Adv** for adverb, **Adj** for adjective, **A** for article adjective, **P** for preposition, and **OP** for object of the preposition. For Sentence 1, underline the complete subject <u>one</u> time and the complete predicate <u>two</u> times.

```
      A     Adj    SN       V       Adv       P     A     OP
1.   The    tiny  beetle  crawled  carefully  across  the  rocks.
```

```
      A     Adj    SN       V       Adv
2.   The   white  snow   melted   quickly.
```

Exercise 2: Underline the <u>**syn**</u> if the words are synonyms. Underline the <u>**ant**</u> if the words are antonyms.

1. round, square	syn **ant**	2. pull, tug	**syn** ant	3. bright, dim	syn **ant**

Exercise 3: Name the five parts of speech that you have studied. (*You may use abbreviations.*)
(The order of answers may vary.)

1. **Noun (N)**   2. **Verb (V)**   3. **Adjective (Adj)**   4. **Adverb (Adv)**   5. **Preposition (P)**

Exercise 4: Write the correct contraction in each blank. Use the contraction references to help you.

1. do not   **don't**
2. cannot   **can't**
3. I am   **I'm**
4. are not   **aren't**
5. were not **weren't**

Exercise 5: Write the correct words beside each contraction. Use the contraction references to help you.

1. didn't   **did not**
2. wasn't   **was not**
3. doesn't   **does not**
4. isn't   **is not**
5. I'm   **I am**

Exercise 6: First, think of a person who has done something nice for you or has given you a gift (even the gift of time). On notebook paper, write a thank-you note to that person. Use the information in Reference 29 or 30 as a guide. Have your parents help you address an envelope. Mail your thank-you note.

Exercise 7: In your journal, write a paragraph summarizing what you have learned this week.

 **CHECK TIME**

After students have finished, check and discuss their test papers. Make sure they understand why their answers are right or wrong. Use the Question and Answer Flows on page 320 in this chapter to check the sentences on the Chapter 25 Test. (*For total points, count each required answer as a point.*)

(End of lesson.)

CHAPTER 26 LESSON 1

Objectives: Skill (Introduce Alphabetizing), Practice Exercise, and Activity.

SKILL TIME

TEACHING SCRIPT FOR INTRODUCING ALPHABETIZING

Today, we are going to review the alphabet by reciting all the letters in order. (*Recite the letters of the alphabet with your students.*) When we talk about alphabetical order, we are talking about arranging words in the same sequence as the alphabet. This is called alphabetizing, or putting things in ABC order.

There are several reasons for learning to alphabetize words. Alphabetical order is often used to arrange words or facts so that they can be easily found. How are words in a dictionary arranged? (*in alphabetical order*) How are names in a phone book listed? (*in alphabetical order*) How are the names of students enrolled in a school listed? (*in alphabetical order*) How are the names of students in a Sunday school class listed? (*in alphabetical order*) As you can see, learning about alphabetical order is very important because it makes things in our lives so much easier.

First, we will learn to put letters in alphabetical order. I will write a group of letters on the board, and I want you to tell me how the letters should be arranged alphabetically. (*Write the following letters on the board and discuss the correct alphabetical order.*)

1. k e p v (**e, k, p, v**)

2. d z n y g j (**d, g, j, n, y, z**)

3. u c l t a s f (**a, c, f, l, s, t, u**)

You have just practiced alphabetizing letters of the alphabet. Next, you will practice alphabetizing words. Sometimes, studying involves looking up <u>words</u> in a dictionary. You may need to see if you have spelled a word correctly, or you may want to check a word's meaning. A dictionary gives you the correct spelling, pronunciation, meanings, and usage of words. We learn to alphabetize words because words are arranged in alphabetical order in a dictionary. The best way to learn alphabetizing is to alphabetize letters and words for practice. Look at Reference 31 on page 25 in your Reference section.

Reference 31: Alphabetical Order									
Directions: Put each group of words in alphabetical order. Use numbers to show the order in each column.									
Animal Words		**"G" Words**		**Farm Words**		**Color Words**		**"L" Words**	
2	1. rabbit	**2**	3. garden	**1**	5. barn	**1**	7. black	**2**	9. light
1	2. donkey	**1**	4. game	**2**	6. tractor	**2**	8. blue	**1**	10. leg

CHAPTER 26 LESSON 1 CONTINUED

There is a simple way to put words in alphabetical order. When the first letters of the words to be alphabetized are different, you only have to look at the first letter to put words in alphabetical order. Let's read the directions for the sample. (*Read the directions.*) Look at the two words under the title "Animal Words." In the words *rabbit* and *donkey*, the first letters, *r* and *d,* are different. Since *d* comes before *r* in the alphabet, *donkey* comes before *rabbit*. A number *1* has been written in the blank in front of *donkey* and a number *2* has been written in the blank in front of *rabbit*, as demonstrated in the example.

When the first letters of words to be alphabetized are the same, you should look at the second or third letters to put them in alphabetical order. Now, look at the two words *garden* and *game* under "G Words." In the words *garden* and *game*, the first two letters are the same. Go to the third letter in each word. Since *m* comes before *r* in the alphabet, *game* comes before *garden*. A number *1* has been written in the blank in front of *game* and a number *2* has been written in the blank in front of *garden*, as demonstrated in the example. (*Have students demonstrate this process orally with the rest of the sample words.*)

 PRACTICE TIME

Have students turn to page 55 in the Practice Section of their books and find Chapter 26, Lesson 1, Practice. Go over the directions to make sure they understand what to do. If students need a review, have them study the information and examples in the Reference Section of their books. Check and discuss the Practice after students have finished. (*Chapter 26, Lesson 1, Practice key is given below.*)

Chapter 26, Lesson 1, Practice: Put each group of words in alphabetical order. Write numbers in the blanks to show the order in each column.

Winter Words		Family Words		"S" Words		Fruit Words	
3	1. snow	3	4. sister	2	7. ship	2	10. banana
2	2. ice	2	5. father	3	8. sun	1	11. apple
1	3. coat	1	6. aunt	1	9. seven	3	12. orange

 ACTIVITY / ASSIGNMENT TIME

Have students make up different lists to be alphabetized correctly. These lists might include the following: toys, sports, animals, colors, food, etc. Students could recruit family members to help them make the lists. Family members could also alphabetize students' lists. Students should make a key to check each list. There should only be three or four words to alphabetize in each list.

(End of lesson.)

CHAPTER 26   LESSON 2

Objectives: Skill (Practice Alphabetizing), and Practice Exercise.

SKILL TIME

TEACHING SCRIPT FOR REVIEWING ALPHABETIZING

Today, we are going to review the alphabet by reciting all the letters in order. (*Recite the letters of the alphabet with your students.*) Remember, when we talk about alphabetical order, we are talking about putting words in the same sequence as the alphabet. We will practice alphabetizing during Practice Time.

PRACTICE TIME

Have students turn to pages 55 and 56 in the Practice Section of their books and find Chapter 26, Lesson 2, Practice (*1-3*). Go over the directions to make sure they understand what to do. If students need a review, have them study the information and examples in the Reference Section of their books. Check and discuss the Practices after students have finished. (*Chapter 26, Lesson 2, Practice keys are given below.*)

Chapter 26, Lesson 2, Practice 1: Write the letters in each group below in alphabetical order.

1. g o c w _____**(c, g, o, w)**_____

2. x f n k a t _____**(a, f, k, n, t, x)**_____

Chapter 26, Lesson 2, Practice 2: Put each group of words in alphabetical order. Write numbers in the blanks to show the order in each column.

Space Words		City Words		"R" Words	
2	1. stars	**1**	3. park	**1**	5. rabbit
1	2. moon	**2**	4. skyscraper	**2**	6. road

Chapter 26, Lesson 2, Practice 3: Put each group of words in alphabetical order. Write numbers in the blanks to show the order in each column.

Summer Words		"T" Words		Vegetable Words	
1	1. sunscreen	**1**	4. tank	**2**	7. corn
2	2. swimsuit	**2**	5. toy	**3**	8. potato
3	3. vacation	**3**	6. two	**1**	9. carrot

(End of lesson.)

Level 1 Homeschool Teacher's Manual

CHAPTER 26   LESSON 3

Objectives: Skill (Practice Alphabetizing), and Practice Exercise.

SKILL TIME

TEACHING SCRIPT FOR REVIEWING ALPHABETIZING

Today, we are going to review the alphabet by repeating all the letters in order. (*Repeat the letters of the alphabet with your students.*) Remember, when we talk about alphabetical order, we are talking about arranging words in the same sequence as the alphabet. We will practice alphabetizing during Practice Time.

PRACTICE TIME

Have students turn to pages 56 and 57 in the Practice Section of their books and find Chapter 26, Lesson 3, Practice *(1-3)*. Go over the directions to make sure they understand what to do. If students need a review, have them study the information and examples in the Reference Section of their books. Check and discuss the Practices after students have finished. (*Chapter 26, Lesson 3, Practice keys are given below.*)

Chapter 26, Lesson 3, Practice 1: Write the letters in each group below in alphabetical order.

1. b w j m _____**(b, j, m, w)**_____

2. z p a u o e _____**(a, e, o, p, u, z)**_____

Chapter 26, Lesson 3, Practice 2: Put each group of words in alphabetical order. Write numbers in the blanks to show the order in each column.

State Words		Ocean Words		"O" Words	
1	1. Alaska	**1**	3. waves	**2**	5. otter
2	2. Arizona	**2**	4. whale	**1**	6. old

Chapter 26, Lesson 3, Practice 3: Put each group of words in alphabetical order. Write numbers in the blanks to show the order in each column.

Breakfast Words		"D" Words		Movie Words	
3	1. toast	**3**	4. duck	**2**	7. popcorn
1	2. eggs	**2**	5. donkey	**3**	8. soda
2	3. milk	**1**	6. dog	**1**	9. candy

(End of lesson.)

CHAPTER 26   LESSON 4

Objectives: Skill (Review Alphabetizing), Practice Exercise, Writing Assignment #13, and Activity.

SKILL TIME

TEACHING SCRIPT FOR REVIEWING ALPHABETIZING

Today, we are going to review the alphabet by repeating all the letters in order. (*Repeat the letters of the alphabet with your students.*) Remember, when we talk about alphabetical order, we are talking about arranging words in the same sequence as the alphabet. We will practice alphabetizing during Practice Time.

PRACTICE TIME

Have students turn to page 57 in the Practice Section of their books and find Chapter 26, Lesson 4, Practice *(1-3)*. Go over the directions to make sure they understand what to do. If students need a review, have them study the information and examples in the Reference Section of their books. Check and discuss the Practices after students have finished. (*Chapter 26, Lesson 4, Practice keys are given below.*)

Chapter 26, Lesson 4, Practice 1: Write the letters in each group below in alphabetical order.

1. l h r c   **(c, h, l, r)**

2. f i k o w r   **(f, i, k, o, r, w)**

Chapter 26, Lesson 4, Practice 2: Put each group of words in alphabetical order. Write numbers in the blanks to show the order in each column.

Transportation Words		Tool Words		"J" Words	
2	1. bus	**1**	3. drill	**2**	5. jet
1	2. boat	**2**	4. hammer	**1**	6. jelly

Chapter 26, Lesson 4, Practice 3: Put each group of words in alphabetical order. Write numbers in the blanks to show the order in each column.

Hospital Words		"D" Words		Clothing Words	
2	1. nurse	**1**	4. deer	**1**	7. shirt
3	2. patient	**3**	5. duck	**2**	8. skirt
1	3. doctor	**2**	6. dog	**3**	9. sweater

Level 1 Homeschool Teacher's Manual

CHAPTER 26 LESSON 4 CONTINUED

 **WRITING TIME**

Give Writing Assignment #13 from the box below. Remind students to use Reference 20 on page 20 to help them write their two-point paragraph. After students have finished, check and discuss their writing assignment.

Writing Assignment Box

Writing Assignment #13: Two-Point Expository Paragraph

Writing topic: My Favorite Places To Eat

 ACTIVITY / ASSIGNMENT TIME

Have students turn to page 90 in the Activity Section of their books and find Chapter 26, Lesson 4, Activity. Go over the directions to make sure they understand what to do. Check and discuss the Activity after students have finished.

Chapter 26, Lesson 4, Activity: Using the scrambled letters below, circle every other letter, beginning with the first letter. Use the blank to write the new word created by writing each circled letter in order. (**npicnke**=nine) On the title lines, write the title that best describes the words in each column. Choose from these titles: **Colors** **Weather** **Shapes** **Animals**

Title: **Shapes**

t m r y i u a x n o g r l h e: **triangle**

r n e u c g t y a d n w g p l c e h: **rectangle**

s a q m u p a w r c e w: **square**

Title: **Weather**

w s i m n a d b y r: **windy**

c n l k o a u e d w y: **cloudy**

s g u h n m n c y d: **sunny**

(End of lesson.)

CHAPTER 26   LESSON 5

Objectives: Test, Check, and Writing (Journal).

TEST TIME

Have students turn to page 79 in the Test Section of their books and find Chapter 26 Test. Go over the directions to make sure they understand what to do. (*Chapter 26 Test key is on the next page.*)

CHECK TIME

After students have finished, check and discuss their test papers. Make sure they understand why their answers are right or wrong. Use the Question and Answer Flows below to check the sentences on Chapter 26 Test. (*Students will classify sentences independently. Give extra help as needed. For total points, count each required answer as a point.*)

Question and Answer Flow for Sentence 1: The cute little rabbits hopped quickly away.

1. What hopped quickly away? rabbits - SN
2. What is being said about rabbits? rabbits hopped - V
3. Hopped how? quickly - Adv
4. Hopped where? away - Adv
5. What kind of rabbits? little - Adj
6. What kind of rabbits? cute - Adj
7. The - A

Classified Sentence:

A	Adj	Adj	SN	V	Adv	Adv
The	cute	little	rabbits	hopped	quickly	away.

Question and Answer Flow for Sentence 2: Several young children played happily in the park.

1. Who played happily in the park? children - SN
2. What is being said about children? children played - V
3. Played how? happily - Adv
4. In - P
5. In what? park - OP
6. The - A
7. What kind of children? young - Adj
8. How many children? several - Adj

Classified Sentence:

Adj	Adj	SN	V	Adv	P	A	OP
Several	young	children	played	happily	in	the	park.

(End of lesson.)

Chapter 26 Test
(Student Page 79)

Exercise 1: Classify each sentence. Use **SN** for subject noun, **V** for verb, **Adv** for adverb, **Adj** for adjective, **A** for article adjective, **P** for preposition, and **OP** for object of the preposition. For Sentence 1, underline the complete subject <u>one</u> time and the complete predicate <u>two</u> times.

	A	Adj	Adj	SN	V	Adv	Adv		
1.	<u>The</u>	<u>cute</u>	<u>little</u>	<u>rabbits</u>	<u>hopped</u>	<u>quickly</u>	<u>away</u>.		

	Adj	Adj	SN	V	Adv	P	A	OP
2.	Several	young	children	played	happily	in	the	park.

Exercise 2: Write the letters in each group below in alphabetical order.

1. k d r n   **(d, k, n, r)**

2. h a s m o u   **(a, h, m, o, s, u)**

Exercise 3: Put each group of words in alphabetical order. Use numbers to show the order in each column.

	Zoo Words		Color Words		"B" Words
2	1. giraffe	4	5. yellow	3	9. brothers
3	2. monkey	1	6. green	4	10. buzzed
1	3. elephant	2	7. pink	2	11. beavers
4	4. tiger	3	8. red	1	12. balloon

Exercise 4: Put each group of words in alphabetical order. Use numbers to show the order in each column.

	Food Words		"C" Words		Tree Words
5	1. taco	3	6. clowns	3	11. oak
1	2. hamburger	4	7. crib	2	12. maple
3	3. pizza	5	8. cute	5	13. walnut
2	4. hotdogs	2	9. church	1	14. cedar
4	5. steak	1	10. cats	4	15. pine

Exercise 5: In your journal, write a paragraph summarizing what you have learned this week.

CHAPTER 27   LESSON 1

Objectives: Skill (Three Main Parts of the Library) and Activity.

SKILL TIME

TEACHING SCRIPT FOR INTRODUCING THE THREE MAIN PARTS OF THE LIBRARY

Whenever you go to the library to look up information, it should be a fun and easy experience. In order for you to enjoy the library and to utilize it to its full potential, you will need to know about some of the major sections of the library and the most common materials found in the library. We are going to discuss three of the major sections of the library. Look at Reference 32 on page 25. (*Discuss the three main parts of the library listed below with your students.*)

Reference 32: Three Main Parts of the Library
Fiction Section Fiction books contain stories about people, places, or things that are not true. **Nonfiction Section** Nonfiction books contain information and stories that are true. **Reference Section** The Reference Section is designed to help you find information on many topics. The most common reference books are the dictionary and the encyclopedia.

ACTIVITY / ASSIGNMENT TIME

Make cards from large sheets of different-colored construction paper and have students print these titles on them: *Fiction Section, Nonfiction Section,* and *Reference Section.* Have students print the correct information from Reference 32 on the back of each corresponding card. Spread the cards out with only the section names showing. Call out the name of each section, one at a time. As you name each section, have a student select the correct card and read the information printed there. (*Extension: Have students repeat this activity with several members of the family.*)

Next, gather several of your students' books that they have at home and put them in a book pile. Be sure to include books from each main section of the library: *Fiction Section, Nonfiction Section, and Reference Section.* Have students place each book in the appropriate category. Have students point to each book and tell why that book was placed in a specific category. Finally, have students select a book from the Fiction Section to read aloud.

(End of lesson.)

CHAPTER 27   LESSON 2

Objectives: Skill (Sequencing, Using a Fairy Tale—*The Little Red Hen*) and Activity.

SKILL TIME

TEACHER INSTRUCTIONS FOR SEQUENCING, USING A FAIRY TALE—THE LITTLE RED HEN

Sequencing is important to know the order of things. We will use fairy tales to teach and practice this concept. This early exposure to classic storytelling at its best is an experience you do not want your children to miss. You may use the fairy tale listed in this chapter, or you may choose another fairy tale or story. Buy two copies of the fairy-tale version that you like best. You will use one copy to read and the other copy to tear apart and laminate for sequencing activities. *(Have the fairy tale torn apart and laminated before starting this lesson. You could use a clear roll of contact paper to cover both sides of the story pieces. This is a quick, easy way to laminate things at home. You might also use clear protective sheets that could be put in a notebook. Later, you will use these laminated story pieces as an independent sequencing activity.)*

Read *The Little Red Hen* fairy tale to your students. Have students listen for pleasure as well as for comprehension of the overall story line. Read the fairy tale with a high level of expression because your students will imitate you. Show your students by example how much fun fairy tales can be. On the first day, it is usually best to read the fairy tale at least two times to give students a feel for the tone of the story. *(You could have an older student read the fairy tale the second time.)*

After you have read the story, ask your students some basic comprehension questions. Check to make sure they know the characters, the main character, the role each character plays in the story, the problem presented in the story, and how the problem was solved. Discuss the setting *(when/where)* of the story and whether it was important to the overall story plan. Then, discuss the ending. Did the story end like they expected it to end? Could they think of another ending? What part did they like best? Also, make sure students know that fairy tales are not real. They are "pretend" stories.

This sequencing time should be completed with the teacher's help. Mix up the pictures on the floor or table. Lead the students through what happened first, second, and third, until the story has been retold. As you discuss what happens first, have a student find the picture for the first part. Next, discuss what happens second as the student finds the picture for the second part. Continue this process until all the pictures are in order.

Arrange the pictures with one or two of them out of order. Show students how important it is to keep the correct sequence in a story. If they get any of the pictures out of order, it will change the story. *(You might try arranging the cards in a different order to see if another story order would make better sense.)*

ACTIVITY / ASSIGNMENT TIME

To review the three main parts of a library, spread the title cards from the previous activity with only the Titles showing. Call out the name of each section, one at a time. As you name each section, have a student select the correct card and read the information printed on the back.

(End of lesson.)

CHAPTER 27   LESSON 3
Objectives: Practice Exercises and Activity.

 PRACTICE TIME

Have students turn to page 58 in the Practice Section of their books and find Chapter 27, Lesson 3, Practice *(1-2)*. Go over the directions to make sure they understand what to do. Check and discuss the Practices after students have finished. *(Chapter 27, Lesson 3, Practice keys are given below.)*

Chapter 27, Lesson 3, Practice 1: Underline the correct answer in each sentence.

1. Nonfiction books contain information and stories that are **(true, not true)**.

2. Fiction books contain information and stories that are **(true, not true)**.

3. The most common reference books are the dictionary and the encyclopedia. **(true, not true)**

Chapter 27, Lesson 3, Practice 2: Put each group of words in alphabetical order. Write numbers in the blanks to show the order in each column.

Adjective Words		"G" Words		Cleaning Words	
2	1. squirmy	**3**	4. grasshopper	**3**	7. rags
3	2. strong	**2**	5. goats	**1**	8. broom
1	3. silly	**1**	6. giant	**2**	9. mop

 ACTIVITY / ASSIGNMENT TIME

Discuss students' favorite fiction books and nonfiction books. Discuss how they use the two main reference books in the Reference section (dictionary and encyclopedia). Discuss the parts of the library that they like best. Discuss why libraries are important. Find out how much each student really knows about the library. Then, tell them they are going to learn much more about a library by visiting their local library.

Take students on a field trip to visit their local library. Have each of them take a pencil and a notebook to take notes and draw a picture of the library. After they return home, have students make a book about the library. First, they could write about the different areas of the library and their library experience. Then, they could draw pictures or cut and paste library pictures to go along with their stories. Finally, have students put the pages in a notebook. Have them take a picture of the library they visited and paste the picture on the front of the book. After they write a title for their book, they can share it with others. *(The library may have brochures that can be picked up and included in students' notebooks.)*

(End of lesson.)

CHAPTER 27 LESSON 4

Objectives: Skill (Sequencing, Using a Fairy Tale—*The Little Red Hen*), Practice Exercise, Writing Assignment #14, and Activity.

SKILL TIME

TEACHER INSTRUCTIONS FOR MORE SEQUENCING, USING THE LITTLE RED HEN

This sequencing time should be completed without the teacher's help. Mix-up the pictures of *The Little Red Hen* and have each student put the pictures in order as he/she tells the story from beginning to end without stopping. (*If you do not already have a gifted storyteller, you soon will have one.*) Give students several opportunities to sequence the story cards. Put the laminated story cards into a Practice Center so students can sequence or read their favorite fairy tales.

PRACTICE TIME

Have students turn to page 58 in the Practice Section of their books and find Chapter 27, Lesson 4, Practice *(1-2)*. Go over the directions to make sure they understand what to do. Check and discuss the Practices after students have finished. (*Chapter 27, Lesson 4, Practice keys are given below.*)

Chapter 27, Lesson 4, Practice 1: Underline the correct answer in each sentence.

1. Nonfiction books contain information and stories that are (**true, not true**).

2. Fiction books contain information and stories that are (**true, <u>not true</u>**).

3. The most common reference books are the dictionary and the encyclopedia. (**<u>true</u>, not true**)

Chapter 27, Lesson 4, Practice 2: Put each group of words in alphabetical order. Write numbers in the blanks to show the order in each column.

Preposition Words		Verb Words		Pet Words	
__1__	1. in	__2__	4. erupted	__3__	7. pony
__3__	2. to	__1__	5. camped	__1__	8. cat
__2__	3. on	__3__	6. yawned	__2__	9. dog

CHAPTER 27 LESSON 4 CONTINUED

WRITING TIME

Give Writing Assignment #14 from the box below. Remind students to use Reference 20 on page 20 to help them write their two-point paragraph. After students have finished, check and discuss their writing assignments.

Writing Assignment Box

Writing Assignment #14: **Two-Point Expository Paragraph**

Writing topic: My Favorite Books

ACTIVITY / ASSIGNMENT TIME

Make bread for your students to eat. (*Bread ideas: bread machine, frozen bread, homemade bread*) Have them gather around as you tell them the steps you are taking to make the bread. Tell them cooking is a form of sequencing, too. Each time you go to the next step, ask them what they think you would do next. As you walk your students through the cooking steps, give them the extra vocabulary they will need to relate to the cooking project. Give students a piece of bread to eat when it is ready. Discuss the role bread played in the fairy tale, *The Little Red Hen*.

(End of lesson.)

<table>
<tr><td colspan="2">CHAPTER 27   LESSON 5</td></tr>
<tr><td colspan="2">Objectives: Test, Check, Writing (Journal), Activity 1, and Activity 2.</td></tr>
</table>

TEST TIME

Have students turn to page 80 in the Test Section of their books and find Chapter 27 Test. Go over the directions to make sure they understand what to do. (*Chapter 27 Test key is on the next page.*)

CHECK TIME

After students have finished, check and discuss their test papers. Use the Question and Answer Flows below to check the sentences on Chapter 27 Test. (*For total points, count each required answer as a point.*)

Question and Answer Flow for Sentence 1: The funny frog hopped in the water.

1. What hopped in the water? frog - SN
2. What is being said about frog? frog hopped - V
3. In - P
4. In what? water - OP
5. The - A
6. What kind of frog? funny - Adj
7. The - A

Classified Sentence:

A	Adj	SN	V	P	A	OP
The	funny	frog	hopped	in	the	water.

Question and Answer Flow for Sentence 2: The three pretty lamps burned brightly today.

1. What burned brightly today? lamps - SN
2. What is being said about lamps? lamps burned - V
3. Burned how? brightly - Adv
4. Burned when? today - Adv
5. What kind of lamps? pretty - Adj
6. How many lamps? three - Adj
7. The - A

Classified Sentence:

A	Adj	Adj	SN	V	Adv	Adv
The	three	pretty	lamps	burned	brightly	today.

ACTIVITY / ASSIGNMENT TIME

Activity 1:
Dramatize *The Little Red Hen* fairy tale. If you have only one student, have that student play multiple parts. Tell students where they need to stand and where they need to move for the action parts. When you get to the part of the story that has repeated lines, you say the lines first, then have students repeat them.

Activity 2:
Have students cut out patterns of the characters, decorate them, and glue them onto craft sticks to make puppets. Dramatize the fairy tale using the stick puppets. Hang the puppets on a clothesline across the corner of the child's room.

Chapter 27 Test
(Student Page 80)

Exercise 1: Classify each sentence. Use **SN** for subject noun, **V** for verb, **Adv** for adverb, **Adj** for adjective, **A** for article adjective, **P** for preposition, and **OP** for object of the preposition. For Sentence 1, underline the complete subject <u>one</u> time and the complete predicate <u>two</u> times.

```
         A     Adj    SN      V     P    A     OP
1.      The   funny  frog  hopped  in  the   water.
```

```
         A     Adj    Adj    SN      V      Adv     Adv
2.      The   three  pretty lamps  burned  brightly today.
```

Exercise 2: Name the five parts of speech that you have studied. (*You may use abbreviations.*)
(The order of answers may vary.)

| 1. **Noun (N)** | 2. **Verb (V)** | 3. **Adjective (Adj)** | 4. **Adverb (Adv)** | 5. **Preposition (P)** |

Exercise 3: Write the correct contraction in each blank. Use the contraction references to help you.

1. do not	**don't**
2. cannot	**can't**
3. I am	**I'm**
4. are not	**aren't**
5. were not	**weren't**

Exercise 4: Write the correct words beside each contraction. Use the contraction references to help you.

1. didn't	**did not**
2. wasn't	**was not**
3. doesn't	**does not**
4. isn't	**is not**
5. I'm	**I am**

Exercise 5: Underline the correct answer in each sentence.
1. Fiction books contain information and stories that are (**true**, **not true**).
2. Nonfiction books contain information and stories that are (**true**, **not true**).
3. The most common reference books are the dictionary and the encyclopedia. (**true**, **not true**)

Exercise 6: Put each group of words in alphabetical order. Use numbers to show the order in each column.

Number Words		**Adverb Words**		**Proper Noun Words**	
4	1. two	2	5. carefully	2	9. Dan
3	2. three	1	6. away	1	10. Anna
2	3. four	4	7. today	4	11. Tim
1	4. five	3	8. suddenly	3	12. Sam

Exercise 7: In your journal, write a paragraph summarizing what you have learned this week.

(End of lesson.)

CHAPTER 28   LESSON 1
Objectives: Skill (Sequencing, Using a Fairy Tale—*Cinderella*) and Activity.

SKILL TIME

TEACHER INSTRUCTIONS FOR SEQUENCING, USING A FAIRY TALE—CINDERELLA

You may use the fairy tale listed in this chapter, or you may choose another fairy tale or story. Buy two copies of the fairy-tale version that you like best. You will use one copy to read and the other copy to tear apart and laminate for sequencing activities. (*Have the fairy tale torn apart and laminated before starting this lesson. You could use a clear roll of contact paper to cover both sides of the story pieces. This is a quick, easy way to laminate things at home. You might also use clear protective sheets that could be put in a notebook. Later, you will use these laminated story pieces as an independent sequencing activity.*)

Read the *Cinderella* fairy tale to your students. Have students listen for pleasure as well as for comprehension of the overall story line. Read the fairy tale with a high level of expression because your students will imitate you. Show your students by example how much fun fairy tales can be. On the first day, it is usually best to read the fairy tale at least two times to give students a feel for the tone of the story. (*You could have an older student read the fairy tale the second time.*)

After you have read the story, ask your students some basic comprehension questions. Check to make sure they know the characters, the main character, the role each character plays in the story, the problem presented in the story, and how the problem was solved. Discuss the setting (*when/where*) of the story and whether it was important to the overall story plan. Then, discuss the ending. Did the story end like they expected it to end? Could they think of another ending? What part did they like best? Also, make sure students know that fairy tales are not real. They are "pretend" stories.

This sequencing time should be completed with the teacher's help. Mix up the pictures on the floor or table. Lead the students through what happened first, second, and third, until the story has been retold. As you discuss what happens first, have students find the picture for the first part. Next, discuss what happens second as students find the picture for the second part. Continue this process until all the pictures are in order.

Arrange the pictures with one or two pictures out of order. Show students how important it is to keep the correct sequence in a story. If they get any of the pictures out of order, it will change the story. (*You might try arranging the cards in a different order to see if another story order would make better sense.*)

ACTIVITY / ASSIGNMENT TIME

Make several patterns in the shape of a glass slipper. Have students trace two glass slippers on white paper. They should cut out and glue the slippers on construction paper. Let students use iridescent glitter paint to make their glass slippers shiny.

(End of lesson.)

CHAPTER 28   LESSON 2

Objectives: Big Book Time (Making a Big Book, *Piggy Under the Fence*, Reading, Questions, Information About Big Books), and Activity.

BIG BOOK TIME

TEACHING SCRIPT FOR MAKING A BIG BOOK

Preparations before beginning this lesson: Write the sample story below on a big chart or on large sheets of construction paper. Illustrate the story by pasting pictures beside each paragraph to help students recognize what the paragraphs are saying. You might also write the story in different colored markers.

Today, we will learn about Big Books. A Big Book is a story written on large sheets of paper or on a big chart. Everything is enlarged so that we can see and read the story together. We can make up stories for Big Books, or we can copy stories from our favorite books.

We can also make smaller books from the Big Book stories for you to keep. For our first big book, we will use a story called "Piggy Under the Fence." *(Follow the procedure for Big Book Time on the next page: Reading, Questions, and Activity.)*

Reference 33: "Piggy Under the Fence"

In the barnyard lived a cute little pig named Piggy. Piggy loved to crawl under the fence. Piggy said, "Under, under, under. Under the fence. My! My! My! I LOVE to crawl under the fence!"

First, the farmer caught Piggy crawling under the fence. The farmer said, "Under, under, under. Under the fence. My! My! My! Piggy LOVES to crawl under the fence! I do not know what to do."

Next, the farmer's wife caught Piggy crawling under the fence. The farmer's wife said, "Under, under, under. Under the fence. My! My! My! Piggy LOVES to crawl under the fence! I do not know what to do."

Then, the farmer's children caught Piggy crawling under the fence. The farmer's children said, "Under, under, under. Under the fence. My! My! My! Piggy LOVES to crawl under the fence! We do not know what to do."

But Piggy's mother did not smile. Piggy's mother said, "Under, under, under. Under the fence. My! My! My! I know what to do. If Piggy crawls under the fence again, Piggy will go over my knee!"

Piggy looked at the fence. Piggy looked at his mother. Then, Piggy said, "Under, under, under. Under the fence. My! My! My! I do NOT like to crawl under the fence anymore!"

CHAPTER 28 LESSON 2 CONTINUED

Reading Time

1. Gather your students in your story area.

2. Read the story aloud to your children. As you read, run your finger or a pointer along under the phrases, pausing only when your voice pauses.

3. After you have read the story once, stop to ask a few questions. Ask questions to check comprehension of story details and story order. Then, ask questions about how characters felt and why things happened in the story. *(You may use some of the sample questions below to get you started.)*

4. Next, read the story again and invite your students to read along with you. Read a little slower this time. Again, as you read, run your finger or a pointer under the phrases. Make sure you are expressive during any dialogue. If you model this, your children will imitate you.

5. Now, have students read the story with you in their book. It is located on page 25 in Reference 33.

Questions for the story, "Piggy Under the Fence."

1. Where did Piggy live? *(In the barnyard)*

2. What did Piggy love to do? *(Crawl under the fence)*

3. What did Piggy say at the beginning of the story? *("Under, under, under. Under the fence. My! My! My! I LOVE to crawl under the fence!")*

4. Who caught Piggy crawling under the fence the first time? *(The farmer)*

5. Who caught Piggy crawling under the fence the second time? *(The farmer's wife)*

6. Who caught Piggy crawling under the fence the third time? *(The farmer's children)*

7. What did the farmer, the farmer's wife, and the farmer's children do when they caught Piggy crawling under the fence? *(They did not know what to do. Each one said, "I do not know what to do.")*

8. Did Piggy's mother know what to do? *(Yes, Piggy's mother knew what to do.)*

9. What did Piggy's mother say would happen if Piggy crawled under the fence again? *(Piggy would go over her knee.)*

10. How do you think Piggy's mother felt about Piggy crawling under the fence? *(She did not like Piggy crawling under the fence because Piggy might get hurt or lost. Other reasonable answers should also be accepted.)*

11. What did Piggy say at the end of the story? *("Under, under, under. Under the fence. My! My! My! I do NOT like to crawl under the fence anymore!")*

12. Why do you think Piggy decided not to crawl under the fence anymore? *(He did not want to take the consequences for disobeying his mother.)*

ACTIVITY / ASSIGNMENT TIME

Select some kind of activity for students, such as a craft, a chalk picture, cooking, or dramatization, etc. Dramatization: Read the story again and let the children act it out. Some students may play several parts. *(Use the information on the next page to give you more details about Big Book Time.)*

CHAPTER 28 LESSON 2 CONTINUED

What children can learn from Big Book time:

1. Reading is fun!

2. Reading is done from top to bottom and left to right.

3. Reading is done in phrases and rhythms instead of word-by-word.

4. Reading is done with expression of feeling, like conversation.

5. Written language is really our thoughts and ideas expressed on paper. Being able to read and write unlocks a whole new world of exchanging ideas.

6. Written language has rules, like letter sounds, simple capitalization and punctuation, singular and plural nouns, sentence sense, verb usage, and paragraphing. These concepts are not drilled during Big Book reading, but are simply pointed out after the story is read.

Guidelines for selecting a book:

1. Choose books that contain the 3 R's: Rhythm, Rhyme, and Repetition. Children LOVE catchy verses, rocking rhythms, and phrases and sounds that repeat over and over! Why? They can join in because it's fun, and because they get caught up in the joy of learning about new things. At this age, children <u>want</u> to learn more about written language (reading and writing). When they are involved in reading with rhythm, rhyme, and repetition, they can enjoy language experiences <u>while</u> they are learning the rules of language (letter sounds, syntax, spelling, and punctuation).

2. Choose books that contain humor. Whether it comes in large doses or small sprinklings done tongue-in-cheek, children are drawn to books that tell a funny story, gently poke fun, or contain silly rhymes.

3. Choose books or poems with a simple topic or story line.

4. Choose books or poems that are fairly short in length.

5. If the book you like isn't big, convert it to a Big Book by putting it on a big chart and adding simple illustrations. You can draw them yourself or use pictures from computer clip art or pattern books. It is important that the story or poem is large enough for your students to gather around and see the printed words as well as the pictures. They love the pictures, and they enjoy the story; but they also enjoy learning about written language.

More about Big Books:

1. The complete Big Book reading and book-making project should take no more than three to four days for a book.

2. Remember, you are reading the story together every day, and you do not want your students to get tired of it. It is best to end while they are still excited.

3. Children can read from their student books to parents, grandparents, brothers, sisters, and other relatives or friends.

4. The entire Big Book experience can be a joyful and esteem-building adventure for both student <u>and</u> teacher. It is a great memory builder! What better place to help kids fall in love with language than at home!

(End of lesson.)

CHAPTER 28   LESSON 3

Objectives: Big Book Time (Reading, Language Study, Questions, and Book-Making).

BIG BOOK TIME

Preparations before beginning this lesson: Have "Piggy Under the Fence" on a big chart or large book, duplicate text pages for student books, and have various materials available for book covers.

Reading Time

1. Gather students in the story area.
2. Continue to invite children to read the story with you every day during Big Book Time.
3. Make this a fun time!

Language Study Time

*After reading the story, point out capitalization/punctuation rules, plurals, spellings of words that rhyme, etc. You can also build word-recognition and vocabulary skills by highlighting several letters or certain words in a story. (Example: Identify the letters **a, i,** and **m** by marking them with a marker. Identify the words **loves**, **crawl**, and **knee** by marking them with a marker.) You can also look for subject nouns, verbs, or describing words. Pick out only a few things to do. Make this part of the lesson <u>brief</u>. Do not bog down students here. Remember, the primary objective is to create a love for reading and language.*

Questions for "Piggy Under the Fence."

1. What are the words that are repeated? *(Under, under, under) (My! My! My!)*
2. Can you find the words "Under the Fence"? *(Hold up a card with the words "Under the Fence" printed on it. Have the children find "Under the Fence" in the story.)*
3. How many times does "Under the Fence" appear in the story? *(sixteen)*
4. Can you find the words "But Piggy's mother did not smile"? *(Hold up a card with the words "But Piggy's mother did not smile" on it. Have the children find "But Piggy's mother did not smile" in the story.)*
5. Can you find the word "fence"? *(Hold up a card with the word "fence" printed on it. Have the children find "fence" in the story.)*

Book-Making Time

(1.) **Printing the story.** There are several options for printing the story. **Option 1:** Put the text directly on full or half sheets. *(This is easier.)* **Option 2:** Put the text all on one sheet and have students cut it apart and glue it on each page. **Option 3:** Have students write each paragraph on one sheet of paper. Be sure to put numerals on the pages to help children sequence the text pages.

(2.) **Sequencing the story.** Help students put their text pages in the proper sequence. Use the numerals on the page for sequencing. Check to make sure the pages are in order.

(3.) **Making book covers.** A variety of cover material is available, such as construction paper, file folders, poster board, and wallpaper samples, which can be cut into shapes to go with the book content, and so on. Use your creativity! Students need to make and decorate the front and back covers of their books.

(4.) **Binding the books.** Put the front cover on top and the back cover on the bottom. With the text in story order, have students bind the pages, using staples, hole punch, tabs, yarn, or plastic spirals on the left side. Have each child write the title on the front cover and his/her name on the back cover.

(End of lesson.)

CHAPTER 28   LESSON 4

Objectives: Big Book Time (Reading, Language Study, Questions, and Book-Making).

BIG BOOK TIME

Preparations before beginning this lesson: Gather the following supplies for students to illustrate their books: Stencils cut from craft sponge, dye-cut figures, scissors, glue *(preferably glue sticks)*, paint *(tempera or water color)*, paint brushes, and crayons.

Reading Time

1. Gather students in the story area.
2. Continue to invite children to read the story with you every day during Big Book Time.
3. Make this a fun time!

Language Study Time

*After reading the story, point out capitalization/punctuation rules, plurals, spellings of words that rhyme, etc. You can also build word-recognition and vocabulary skills by highlighting several letters or certain words in a story. (Example: Identify the letters **s, t,** and **r** by marking them with a marker. Identify the words **the**, **caught**, and **looked** by marking them with a marker.) You can also look for subject nouns, verbs, or describing words. Pick out only a few things to do. Make this part of the lesson <u>brief</u>. Do not bog down students here. Remember, the primary objective is to create a love for reading and language.*

Questions for "Piggy Under the Fence."

1. Can you find the word "mother"? *(Hold up a card with the word "mother" printed on it. Have the students identify the word "mother" in the story.)*
2. Can you find the word "said"? *(Hold up a card with the word "said" printed on it. Have the students identify the word "said" in the story.)*

Book-Making Time

(1.) After books are bound and covered, they can be illustrated in a variety of ways. Stencils of characters can be traced, cut, and glued at appropriate places in the story. Character-and-object stencils can be cut from craft sponge for sponge-stencil painting. Dye-cut figures can be glued. Figures can be duplicated, colored, cut out and glued, or painted with tempera or water color.

(2.) If students use glue, caution them that too much glue will ruin their books. Glue sticks work best. If students use tempera paint or water colors, a paper towel placed between wet pages will allow them to paint several pages in one day.

(3.) The biggest challenge is to make sure that the text on each page matches the illustration. Give advice and extra help while students are illustrating their books.

(End of lesson.)

CHAPTER 28   LESSON 5

Objectives: Big Book Time (Reading, Language Study, and Story Expansion), Writing Assignment #15, and Activity.

BIG BOOK TIME

Preparations before beginning this lesson: As students create their own stories, you will need to write them on a big chart. You will also need to gather supplies for students to illustrate their new stories.

Reading Time

1. Gather students in the story area.
2. Have children read the story from their "books" while you read from the Big Book.
3. Make this a fun time!

Language Study Time

After reading the story, point out capitalization/punctuation rules, plurals, spellings of words that rhyme, etc. You can also build word-recognition and vocabulary skills by highlighting several letters or certain words in a story. (Example: Mark all the words that begin with a capital letter. Identify the ones that are proper nouns. Circle words that are plural.) You can also look for subject nouns, verbs, or describing words. Pick out only a few things to do. Make this part of the lesson <u>brief</u>. Do not bog down students here. Remember, the primary objective is to create a love for reading and language.

Story Expansion: Rewriting the story

You can extend a book experience by following a favorite Big Book with an activity in which the class "rewrites" the story using a different topic but the same rhythm. Students especially love to do this because it is THEIR story and they become AUTHORS.

1. Tell students that they are going to rewrite this story. Help them decide the parts they like the best about the story.
2. Help students decide on a new topic and a new repeated phrase.
3. Guide the students in thinking of situations for each paragraph that would require a response for the repeated phrase they have chosen.
4. As your students think of sentences, write them on a big chart. Leave room after each paragraph for an illustration.
5. When the new story is written, tear it off the big chart and let students illustrate the paragraphs. Laminate it and hang it low enough in the room for the children to "read" by themselves.
   (**Note:** *If your children are still excited, you can do another Big Book.*)

WRITING TIME

On a sheet of paper, write a paragraph or a page summarizing what you have enjoyed most about this year in Shurley English. You could choose an activity that you did, a specific skill that you learned, or maybe your favorite jingle. *(See Writing Assignment box on the next page.)* Once you have finished your assignment, place it in the brads of your writing folder. Make sure you write today's date and the grade level you have just finished.

CHAPTER 28 LESSON 5 CONTINUED

Writing Assignment Box

Writing Assignment #15: Two-Point Expository Paragraph

Writing topic: What I Enjoyed Most About Shurley English

ACTIVITY / ASSIGNMENT TIME

Have students close their eyes and picture a family member, close friend, or relative. After a few moments, ask students to write a detailed description of that person. Tell them they should start from the person's head and finish at his/her feet. Tell students to have fun and be creative. Remind them to include hair, eyes, color, size, shape, arms, hands, legs, feet, nose, ears, voice, etc. Let students finish their written descriptions. Then, have them take out a sheet of plain white paper. Using only their written description, students must draw the person they described. Tell students that if they did not mention eyes, they cannot include eyes in their drawing. If they did not include color in their description, then their drawing must be black and white. If they mentioned feet, but not legs, then their person must have only feet.

Next, have students write a story about the person they described. After they have finished, have them put the story, the description, and the drawing into their writing folder. Students could have other people guess who the person is that they described before the story is read. Other family members could also do descriptions, drawings, and stories of different people and have others guess who they represent.

(End of lesson.)

TEACHER INDEX

Due to the tremendous amount of review of concepts provided, this index lists only the page numbers on which the topic is introduced.

Level 1
Jingles & Introductory Sentences

Track	Description
1	Introduction
2	Noun Jingle
3	Verb Jingle
4	Sentence Jingle
5	Adverb Jingle
6	Adjective Jingle
7	Article Adjective Jingle
8	The Preposition Jingle
9	Object of the Preposition Jingle
10	Chapter 6, Lesson 2 Introductory Sentences
11	Chapter 7, Lesson 2 Introductory Sentences
12	Chapter 8, Lesson 2 Introductory Sentences
13	Chapter 9, Lesson 2 Introductory Sentences
14	Chapter 13, Lesson 2 Introductory Sentences

Shurley Instructional Materials, Inc.
366 SIM Drive
Cabot, AR 72023

ISBN 1-58561-050-X